CONVERGENCE AND DIVERGENCE OF NATIONAL FINANCIAL SYSTEMS: EVIDENCE FROM THE GOLD STANDARDS, 1871–1971

FINANCIAL HISTORY

Series Editor: Robert E. Wright

Titles in this Series

1 Slave Agriculture and Financial Markets in Antebellum America: The Bank of the United States in Mississippi, 1831–1852
Richard Holcombe Kilbourne, Jr

2 The Political Economy of Sentiment: Paper Credit and the Scottish Enlightenment in Early Republic Boston, 1780–1820
Jose R. Torre

3 Baring Brothers and the Birth of Modern Finance
Peter E. Austin

4 Gambling on the American Dream: Atlantic City and the Casino Era
James R. Karmel

5 Government Debts and Financial Markets in Europe
Fausto Piola Caselli (ed.)

6 Virginia and the Panic of 1819: The First Great Depression and the Commonwealth
Clyde A. Haulman

7 Towards Modern Public Finance: The American War with Mexico, 1846–1848
James W. Cummings

8 The Revenue Imperative: The Union's Financial Policies during the American Civil War
Jane Flaherty

9 Guilty Money: The City of London in Victorian and Edwardian Culture, 1815–1914
Ranald C. Michie

10 Financial Markets and the Banking Sector: Roles and Responsibilities in a Global World
Elisabeth Paulet (ed.)

11 Argentina's Parallel Currency: The Economy of the Poor
Georgina M. Gómez

12 The Rise and Fall of the American System: Nationalism and the Development of the American Economy, 1790–1837
Songho Ha

FORTHCOMING TITLES

Benjamin Franklin and the Invention of Microfinance
Bruce Yenawine, ed. Michele Costello

Federal Banking in Brazil: Policies and Competitive Advantages
Kurt E. von Mettenheim

The Development of International Insurance
Robin Pearson (ed.)

The Development of the Art Market in England: Money as Muse, 1730–1900
Thomas M. Bayer and John R. Page

Camille Gutt and Postwar International Finance
Jean F. Crombois

CONVERGENCE AND DIVERGENCE OF NATIONAL FINANCIAL SYSTEMS: EVIDENCE FROM THE GOLD STANDARDS, 1871–1971

EDITED BY

Patrice Baubeau and Anders Ögren

LONDON AND NEW YORK

First published 2010 by Pickering & Chatto (Publishers) Limited

Published 2016 by Routledge
2 Park Square, Milton Park, Abingdon, Oxfordshire OX14 4RN
711 Third Avenue, New York, NY 10017, USA

First issued in paperback 2015

Routledge is an imprint of the Taylor & Francis Group, an informa business

British Library Cataloguing in Publication Data

Convergence and divergence of national financial systems: evidence from the gold standards, 1871–1971. – (Financial history)
1. Finance. 2. Gold standard – History. 3. Convergence (Economics)
I. Series II. Baubeau, Patrice. III. Ogren, Anders, 1967–
332-dc22

ISBN-13: 978-1-138-66331-2 (pbk)
ISBN-13: 978-1-8519-6648-6 (hbk)

Typeset by Pickering & Chatto (Publishers) Limited

CONTENTS

ACKNOWLEDGEMENTS

This project was made possible by a 'Young Researchers' research grant from the French *Agence Nationale de la Recherche* – ANR contract nbr ANR-05-JCJC-0238-01, which helped fund a series of workshops and conferences in France and abroad through which our 'history matters in convergence' theme took shape, and allowed for the translations and publication of the present volume. What was not funded by the ANR was supported by IDHE-Nanterre directed by Prof. Michel Lescure.

It is always difficult to pay tribute to all the people that lent a hand in a collective research, because one hesitates between a research directory and the highlighting of the closest and most inspiring colleagues. In this respect, nothing would have been possible without the special dedication of a few – namely Angelo Riva – and the constant scientific support of Michel Boutillier, Hubert Bonin, Youssef Cassis, Pierre Gervais, Pierre-Cyrille Hautcœur, Akinobu Kuroda, Paul Lagneau-Ymonet, Michel Lescure, Amir Rezaee, Bruno Théret. And special thanks to Fabienne Le Pendeven, CNRS, whose professionalism compensated for the University chaos and Mark Pollard, Daire Carr and Paul Lee at Pickering & Chatto, who made this book possible.

LIST OF FIGURES AND TABLES

INTRODUCTION: THE CONVERGENCE OF NATIONAL FINANCIAL SYSTEMS: WISHFUL THINKING OR IRRESISTIBLE TREND?

Patrice Baubeau

Finance and the Economy

Although they have a very long history, academic studies of financial structures have developed in three general steps apparently sound assumptions during the last fifty years or so.

The first step came after World War I and in the wake of the Great Depression, as a sustained effort to establish reliable data series, while new theories were being put forward, to explain the collapse of the gold standard, as well as the economic gyrations that followed World War I. Thus motivated, states and central banks tried to institute new institutional designs, as during the so-called great conferences of Genoa (1922), London (1933) or Bretton Woods (1944). This set the stage for an international drive towards more comprehensive, reliable and comparable statistics covering monetary and financial matters. At the same time, central banks all over the developed world engaged into more academic-like research, leading to a serious upheaval of both the quantity and quality of their published material, even on a retrospective basis. But whether the institutions were ill-designed or the goal of a Gold-standard built-in balancing mechanism was an illusion, these conferences were mostly in vain, failing to design stable and enduring international monetary and financial systems. At best they ended up with a temporary alleviation of the main problems but succeeded in creating multilateral institutions whose usefulness would prove to be well beyond the scope of their original charters, such as the BIS, the World Bank or the IMF.

Building upon this new ideas and data, a general reappraisal of past monetary and financial history marked the 1960s. Milton Friedman, Anna Schwartz and Philip Cagan[1] at the NBER were among the main contributors to this second step, but they were joined by many, most notably John Gurley and Edward Shaw,[2] Alexander Gerschenkron and Raymond Goldsmith. Economic history started then to accumulate many documented cases and new pools of data related to financial issues, banks and crises. But the last two authors provided economist historians with two key elements.

First, Alexander Gerschenkron[3] built an ambiguous but durable analytical framework. Indeed, acknowledging the wide variety in national experiences, he escaped the trap of a 'one size fits all' framework of economic development and replaced it by an agonistic drive to modernization, explaining both complementarity among nation-state economies and non-market solutions to relative backwardness, i.e. banks and state planning and finance (Table I.1).

Table I.1. Stages of financial development according to A. Gerschekron.[4]

Development Stages	Forerunning Area	Mild Relative Backwardness Area	Severe Relative Backwardness Area
Stage 1	Market Finance	Bank Finance	State Finance
Stage 2		Market Finance	Bank Finance
Stage 3			Market Finance

Raymond Goldsmith,[5] bridging the gap of the promised second volume from Gurley and Shaw, followed a very different path, that of 'financial deepening': using several ratios, he showed an empirically strong relationship between financial and economic development. This occurred more or less at the time when the basic monetary and economic assumptions upon which rested budgetary and monetary policies in OECD countries started to stumble and shatter. A solution to the problems encountered in most developed countries and in the international financial system at large could be found at the crossroads of Gerschenkron's and Goldsmith's views – whatever they intended. Indeed, a common interpretation of the 1950s and 1960s growth in Europe and Japan rested upon the catching up of the United States that nonetheless provided capitals after the Second World War, but also methods and a stable international environment of gradual commercial opening. In two decades time, Western Europe and Japan had progressed from severe to mild relative backwardness and, most logically, their financial systems should have adapted to this transition, while in fact most states retained the financial power gained during the Great Depression and the War. Another approach to the problem was to pinpoint the limits of an essentially debt-driven growth financed through monetary expansion that did not allow enough financial deepening from the point of view of savers, investors and companies.

The final collapse of Bretton Woods, in 1976, was soon followed by an extraordinary market rally. By rally, we mean that market did not only bully during the 1980s and 1990s as never before in the twentieth century, but also that political and business executives, backed by academics, declared market mechanisms to be superior to any centralized allocation of capital, leading to a third step in financial structures studies. Building on new methodologies, such as panel and OLS regressions, time-series analysis, and Granger-causality, papers started to study in a systematic way the relationship between finance and growth.[6] As soon as 1993 and 1996, Robert King and Ross Levine[7] and John Boyd and Bruce Smith [8] transformed the correlation established by Goldsmith between financial and economic development into a causality, running from financial development and institutions to economic growth, along theoretical paths formerly developed by Joseph Schumpeter. A few years later, Gerschenkron's intuitions were developed and tested in a more thorough manner by several scholars, notably Richard Sylla, Richard Tilly and Gabriel Tortella[9] Douglas J. Forsyth and Daniel Verdier,[10] or Carolin Fohlin.[11]

Consequently, it is not possible anymore to try to understand economic development without paying tribute to financial structures, institutions and incentives. From the bottom – Grameen banks – to the top – deep, large and effective markets – of the ladder, financial issues have been playing a key role in the Washington consensus as well as in the domestic developments in most OECD countries since the 'Volker's revolution'.

But there are still issues to be settled. One cannot really doubt the fact that financial innovation has been paving the way for the renewed growth of the 1980s and 90s, but does that mean that finance is a permanent feature of economic development, i.e. that it is a 'prerequisite' to growth? Or does that relationship stand the trial only during specific periods of time? Recent studies seem indeed to cast some doubts,[12] at least acknowledging the existence of different periods where causalities can have different directions, i.e. to the right Joan Robinson,[13] at least sometimes.

Finance and History

Accordingly, the issue of 'history matters' is our main drive in this volume. But we intend to push the matter a bit further. Indeed, behind the stories of 'relative backwardness' and 'financial deepening', lies a convergence[14] theory. Lets state it this way: everything being equal, if an economic system develops it will tend to reduce its relative backwardness towards the leader(s) and so to diminish the role devoted to special-purpose financial institutions, i.e. state finance and banks. Or: everything being equal, financial deepening will allow for a more efficient allocation of capital, which, in turn, will provide for a more effective selection of the innovations and economic opportunities, and more productivity growth. So, everything being equal, countries should tend to converge towards some form of market-based financial system. The problem, of course, is that financial structures still differ a lot from country to country, even between those of comparable wealth.

Theoretical and empirical inquiries on such issues have been developing for over twenty years, as several review papers testify,[15] fuelled by the apparent bank-to-market shift ignited in OECD countries at the end of the 1970s and the return of financial crises, almost nonexistent in developed countries during the Bretton Woods era. Academic issues also help explain this interest, with the impact of informational economics, either in the form of information asymmetry studies, or in the form of game-theory or institutional economics. This literature is dominated by the assumption that markets are more efficient in relatively developed economies,[16] whatever the broader context, and has been concerned with discovering the main factor behind the different types of financial systems one can observe today. Indeed, such a factor may help explain why a country would rather rely on information-gathering and processing organizations or on individual agents meeting on a market, leaning, for example, towards a 'bank-based' or a 'market-based' system, or a centralized/decentralized process.

Nevertheless one can still roughly divide the explanations for why a country would adhere to the one type or the other in two categories: 1) Structural explanations or 2) Developmental (or evolutionary) explanations.

The first category of explanations relies on almost permanent factors such as the legal basis, the distribution of political power, the existence of entrenched social or economic powers and so on which exert a constant and long-term influence on the institutional development and the economic rules of the game that play a key role in regard to the financial structures.[17] The second category is more concerned with the pattern of economic and financial development over time, and relies on the link between specific difficulties or challenges (regional imbalances, information asymmetry, relative backwardness...) and the build-up of institutional solutions to these difficulties.[18]

Academic historians tend to rely more on the second approach, which lets them expand historical explanations and careful contextual analysis.[19] Nevertheless, these distinctly different types of explanations share two common conclusions in most academic works, that convergence among financial systems is not only possible, it is more or less bound to take place given an open international capital market and, second, that path dependency is a very strong feature of financial systems.

But as this volume demonstrates, history is not a quiet river: here and again, crises, upheavals, innovations, revolutions, wars and so on shatter the orderly manner of the world, which is rather the orderly view of it we tend to develop when time passes, taking for granted what does seem rooted. Indeed, if financial structures are dependent on specific historical events, convergence among national financial systems will only be a theoretical construction since any historical event at any time may disrupt the supposed convergence. More disturbing, the disruption could be embedded into the convergence process itself if one considers that convergence is not a pure economic process – as expressed in a GDP to capita ratio – but also reflects centre–periphery and first–second rank hierarchies among countries and the hegemonic situation of one or several political powerhouses financial structures. In short, some crises could have ended convergence not accidentally, but because being provoked by the challenge to the world order, i.e. to the dominant political and financial power(s).[20]

The System of Finance

A second issue, related to the convergence story, derives from the fact that financial system literature asks 'what is finance' rather than 'what is a system?' This question is seldom addressed while it lies at the heart of the significance of the expression 'financial system'. Many conceptual frameworks and expressions have been forged to describe, classify and define financial organizations, institutions and mechanisms. One of the main issues in this effort for labelling derives from the conception of what finance is: are these organizations, institutions and mechanisms structurally linked one to the other so as to form a system, or are they just a loose set of rules and practices built more or less randomly over time?

One could propose two polar views of what a system is. On the one hand, a system could be defined as a dense web of interrelations between various elements, meaning that a change in one element or one interrelation starts a chain reaction on all the other elements until a new version (equilibrium) of the system is reached. If the magnitude of the necessary change is set high, then different systems will follow one another, each time a sufficiently powerful shock affects the system: we have here a financial system version of the structural changes brought by scientific revolutions according to Thomas Kuhn.[21] Between two major shifts, the system would evolve without changing its dominant traits. If the magnitude of the necessary change is set low, there is no longer any real difference between 'evolution' and 'revolution', and the system can experience dramatic changes by simply accumulating a large number of minor modifications. Such a systemic approach, i.e. the very idea that all parts of it are interrelated, means that no institution or area can shield itself from the general evolutions of the system. There is no stability at another level than that of the system itself. But we know that many institutions have in fact been designed to shield participants from evolution and risk. Such a conception of systems can lead to analytical shortcomings, because it becomes very difficult to separate causes and consequences.

From a more general point of view, if one defines a financial system as a risk-sharing and risk-processing system, the fact that it is a closely interrelated could sometimes appear contradictory with its goal of distributing risks along individual preferences patterns without jeopardizing all participants through an increased systemic risk – but the 2007 crisis demonstrates such contradictions may occur in the real world.

On the other hand, a financial system could be more loosely defined as a collection of a few specific structural traits (i.e. the market-based and banks-based financial systems). A minor or even a major shock will not necessarily affect the overall structure of the system, which reacts to much more 'long term' determinants: political and cultural traits, legal structures, etc. The big advantage of this approach is to break up the whole of society into a series of subsystems, each of them becoming the object of more specialized, and as such more competent, academics.[22] Besides, each subsystem would be defined by exogenous and endogenous variables, most exogenous variables actually being elements from the other subsystems. In doing so, most social scientists indulge in a degree of 'hypostasis', i.e. they transform historical processes which manifest themselves in a variety of traits and institutions, to a large extent not related through necessity or even contradictory between them, into '*personas*', actors in their own right, guiding and giving sense to the flow of time, but themselves almost perfectly stable: national character and prejudiced perceptions of a hierarchy between human races once played this exogenous role. Today, 'progress' and its quantitative translation (GDP/capita) is still the main 'hypostasis' and the main ground of this finalism, even when dissimulated behind the veil of 'the one best way'. A good example of such a persona is 'modernization': economic modernization is very often associated with market development and the reduction in political risks (wars, civil strife, revolutions). But as advocated for example by Raymond Aron or Peter Katzenstein, modernization[23] tends to have two opposed consequences: from an economic point of view, it leads to enlarged product and services circulation and deeper economic interdependency but from a social point of view, it leads to more social and economic (revenue) cleavages and can disrupt political or cultural links and cohesiveness.[24] From an international point of view, one can also show that the usual link long established between foreign exchanges and peace is at best dubious.[25] As such, one should be careful in assessing the long-term effects of a single but complex factor.

Linking Sub-State, National and International Stories

In order to propose some answers – we do not pretend they are definitive! – we collectively built a case collection that would address the convergence of financial systems at different geographical and time scales. Indeed, by putting emphasis only on national systems convergence, we forget that national financial structures are not that much more homogenous than financial systems among states. In many ways, what is true of financial convergence at the international level holds true at the sub-state level, except that the 'natural law' of pure power, in the absence of an international regulation, does not apply except in times of civil war (Chapter 8, Pablo Martín-Aceña, Elena Martinez Ruiz and María A. Pons). Thus, convergence at a sub-state level (Part I) can occur in two different but non-contradictory patterns: either an attempt to seize regulation or through social patterns. Jean-Luc Mastin (Chapter 2) shows how a regional financial pattern is embedded into a social and industrial structure in which the area can resist Parisian interferences but with the major drawback of reinforcing conservatism. Kim Oosterlink and Angelo Riva (Chapter 3) tell us of the extraordinary attempt to capture the fate of doom: in 1940, with France defeated, and its state stunted and moved to a remote third-rank city, Lyon brokers tried to seize the opportunity to reverse the trend of their own marginalization in an increasingly homogeneous/converging national security market. Patrick Verley (Chapter 1) shows a parallel story: that of the social distinctions and permanent concurrence between the official market and 'curb' market brokers in Paris. What made the Parisian market thrive during the nineteenth century is not its organizational qualities or the securities diversification, but rather the 'competition' between regulated and unregulated actors and activities. In that respect, too much convergence impedes dynamism.

On the national level (Part II), long-term analysis helps to uncover some semi-permanent features, but when thoroughly analysed, the result is to stress the importance of the context. A same set of institutions or practices can yield different results, as shown by the contrasted impacts of crises on Swiss banks (Chapter 6, Dirk Drechsel) or the divergent evolutions of German, French and Italian mixed banks (Chapter 5, Carlo Brambilla). Moreover, the very meaning of convergence – integration or complementarity? – starts to get blurred (Chapter 4, David Le Bris). Pure convergence could mean product or services substitutability and increased concurrence ending in centralization – and as such in central or peripheral domination (see also Chapters 1 and 3), while complementarity, by providing a wealth of varying products, processes and services, might lend resilience to the system but also provide convergence in another sense, that is fuel flows of capital, labour and ideas between regions, sectors and countries.

This difficulty of ending up with a univocal definition of convergence appears more clearly when historical shocks (Part III) are taken into account: as such, they should not be part of the process, since shocks are short-term events, when convergence is a rather long-term trend and process. Nevertheless, the long-term impact of large shocks, for example wars, given the path-dependency of financial structures, appears too strong to be overlooked (Chapter 7, Patrice Baubeau and Anders Ögren). This has long been recognized by most historians who tend to define long-term periods by initial events, either national or international. The civil war in Spain (Chapter 8, Pablo Martín-Aceña, Elena Martinez Ruiz and María A. Pons) is especially relevant because it shows that facing the same constraint, financing the war, albeit with different resources, both camps tended to rely on one major resource: monetary emission. Given the very different conceptions in law, property rights or public accountability borne by the opposing camps, one can figure out how fragile general conclusions on the role of legal systems or property rights enforcement on financial structures appear. In London, the dominant financial place towards which other financial systems seemed to converge before WWI (Chapter 9, Richard Roberts), the war outbreak delineates the characteristics of the system, at both national and international levels, but also the weaknesses of the City in the ensuing competition with Wall Street.

In fact, as one can see from this short introduction, one cannot separate financial structures from monetary matters, which is precisely what Part IV addresses. For example, Kalina Dimitrova and Luca Fantacci (Chapter 10) show how Bulgaria's convergence to the Gold Standard is at least a two-sided story, whose determinants are not solely monetary, because the goal is not only to provide 'a seal of good house-keeping', but also to shield the national economy from deflationary pressures and to enhance national independence by relying on the far powers (United Kingdom and France) rather than on the close ones (Ottoman Empire, Russia). The ability to play on the two sides – national and international – of currency is also what drives Antoine Gentier (Chapter 11) in showing some paradoxical consequences of the Gold Standard: it provide rules but also incentives to break with them for internal motives, with direct consequences on the financial structures. Jeroen Euwe (Chapter 12) kind of link together several lines of the previous arguments by showing how an event – World War I – shaped the financial fortunes of the Netherlands first as an escape route and a haven for German capitals and then as a European financial powerhouse during the Interwar period, part through the diplomatic skirmishes of the time, part through shrewd strategy. But what a war did, another could undo.

1 ORGANIZATION OF NATIONAL FINANCIAL MARKETS AND CONVERGENCE OF PRACTICES: INSTITUTIONS AND NETWORKS OF PARISIAN BROKERS IN NINETEENTH-CENTURY PARISIAN FINANCIAL MARKETS

Patrick Verley

Contemporaries and historians have always contrasted two modes of organization of the financial market, that of London and that of Paris, as antimonic references – whereas other markets are akin to one of these models or mixes of both. The opposition criterion is the public or private character of the brokers. The London market was labelled as 'free', since *brokers* and *jobbers* were title merchants without connections to any official function, whereas the stockbrokers of the official French market were ministerial officials appointed by the Finance Minister. Such difference resulted from the political and economic heritage of both countries in the eighteenth and early nineteenth century, since France had been governed by an absolute monarchy which had borrowed a lot, thereby conferring a major role to State *rente*[1] whereas London was negotiating private securities and foreign funds. During the last quarter of the nineteenth century in France, admiration for the English model and increasing liberalism tended to question the legitimacy of the stockbrokers' monopoly by diverting the debate towards an opposition between security brought by State-guaranteed monopoly and efficiency on the other hand: the London organization seemed to be the most favourable to business dynamism. It is this debate, leading incidentally to a large number of articles, which gave rise to the Act which recognized and reorganized the coulisse[2] in 1898, an Act which only half-satisfied those standing for liberalism:

> Anyway, the controversy seemed to be closed for the time being and the protagonists as a whole were seemingly content with a solution which was nothing but a compromise, whereas any new debate stood little chances, one must admit, to harmonise to any extent. It left to monopoly a territory well-deserved by all the services rendered as

> well as those it is still providing ... Freedom on the other hand was not really banished from the Stock Exchange. Freedom had become firmly established and could deploy its propelling role therein. It acquired, by the way, a guild-like organisation which was a tribute to law and order requirements, which ought to govern any financial market ... There was hence certain equilibrium, for a while at least, in Paris between two contradictory conceptions regarding the organisation of the financial markets.[3]

The opposition between monopoly and 'freedom' was somehow ideological, since, in fact it concerned at most a regulation provided by law or the government on the one hand, and on the other hand a guild-like self-regulation.

Indeed, all markets had to fulfil three functions; to protect the public, to stabilize their operation and to secure the best loan issued by their governments. Since public safety was the first concern of the governments, it implied the selection of the brokers, the regulation of the forward transactions, an expertise as to the viability of the securities and hence the listing which acted as a protection barrier as well as a moral guarantee. The difference was expressed by an alternative solution between rather strict a corporate control exercised by the Managing Committee and a Numerus Clausus in London and a corporate control also exercised in Paris by the Stockbrokers Association, then by the unions of bank brokers when they were founded during the last years of the nineteenth century, a control exercised within a legally defined framework. In Berlin, the financial market was totally private and corporate until the 1896 Act set a strict framework to forward transactions. The stability of the market and the placement of public loans involved the existence of market-makers, either professional like the *jobbers*, or illegal operators such as the official stockbrokers who were not entitled to this type of operation but nevertheless carried them out more often than not until the 1882 Krach and the *coulissiers*[4] who, up to 1898, were not recognized legally. On the other hand, the London Stock Exchange was also seeing competition from outsiders 'outside brokers, advertising, as designated by the Stock Exchange members, with a certain condescendence, in opposition to themselves, since it was forbidden to fish for customers via newspaper adds ...'[5] Stronger regulation set in London or Berlin by the practices or the laws, more flexible monopoly in Paris by the recognition of the 'free' market, that of the *coulisse*, the efficient operation of the financial markets involved *de facto* convergence among seemingly quite different systems, as well as the banking models, interacting with the financial markets, were not so strongly opposed in their operating modes as believed in the past[6] and that, more generally, the economic structures of the advanced industrial countries saw a convergence process[7] during the second half of the nineteenth century.

Institutions and Networks

This first observation remains insufficient, since it does not take agents' networks into account. The function fulfilled by the market institutions and the networks is identical or complementary, according to the objective sought. A firm may rely on either of them for financing, widening its goodwill and finding loans, reducing its vulnerability to conjunctural uncertainties and cash-flow problems.

The brokerage companies of the financial market form firms of a very peculiar type. For them, the aim of raising capital was not investment, which they hardly needed apart from paying for the rental of offices and purchasing very limited equipment. In fact the raised capitals guaranteed their solvency, towards clients as well as other brokers and large-scale operators, semi-professional and professional bankers, which formed a considerable portion of the clientele during the nineteenth century where the average savers market remained a small niche for a long time. The brokers wanted to diminish the vulnerability factor and to establish trusting relationships that are the very foundation of the financial community. Unlike an industrial company which manages techniques and minimizes its costs relative to the market prices, the activity of the financial brokers was first of all threatened by two interrelated risks: the insolvency of clients who had invested in forward transactions, and the insolvency of their professional partners. Both institutions and networks might at first combine to reduce such vulnerability: the professional and family networks helped raise capitals and provide a mobilizable reserve in case of danger, they helped strengthen the trusting and solidarity relationships between practitioners, but the institutions were also useful in formalizing such solidarity by rendering them compulsory, in imposing rules on the recruitments of people and the guarantees for reducing the aleatory portion and thereby increasing market visibility. Finally the objective of developing business and widening goodwill could only be met by people's networks. The structures of financial intermediation were hence halfway between those of the activities of public legal officials, such as notaries, where the institutional rule, which was the guarantee for the clientele, was of paramount importance, and that of business companies where the role played by the networks superseded the market institutions. The specificities of the operations conducted in the Parisian market and of their evolution contribute to explain the articulation modes between institutions and networks.

The Parisian Financial Market: A Highly Institutionalized Market

The French financial market was highly institutionalized, since it had developed for managing the debt of the State which had increased rapidly during the eighteenth century and the first three quarters of the nineteenth century. Whereas the First Empire had not borrowed but financed its wars with the tributes paid by the vanquished, the loans contracted in 1816, 1817 and 1818 intended for paying the Allied the indemnity foreseen by the second Paris treaty, increased the weight of the public securities in a capital market which was still hardly up and running. Then came the loans to finance the successive wars of the Second Empire, in Crimea, Italy and Mexico, then finally the Franco–Prussian war which required a series of increasingly large loans, intended for paying the 5 billion Francs indemnity imposed by the new German Empire. The last great public issues amounted in 1881 to one billion Francs allocated to great public works for boosting the economy, then in 1883 and 1884 for 1.2 billion Francs with a view to consolidate the floating debt. This market for State debt was hence highly centralized in Paris and closely monitored by the government which considered that the *rente* prices, as a barometer of the State credit, indicated its capacity to issue new loans successfully. Throughout the nineteenth century, along less developed Provincial markets, oriented towards regional industries, the Parisian market remained first of all a public funds market, limited to French funds for a start, before gradually extending to foreign funds.

Table 1.1. Distribution of the French securities listed according to the issuer (rated value).[8]

	1820	1830	1840	1851	1861	1880	1891	1902	1906	1913
State-collectivities	96.8	96.1	92.0	74.7	53.3	50.2	53.0	47.7	48.8	44.5
Railways	0.0	0.0	3.2	12.2	35.3	33.2	29.2	33.2	33.7	33.3
Transports, others	0.2	0.6	0.6	2.9	3.6	1.8	5.0	1.9	2.0	2.4
Banks-finance	3.0	3.3	3.2	5.2	4.4	12.3	10.3	9.6	10.9	13.3
Mines	0.0	0.0	0.9	1.0	0.7	0.4	0.2	0.5	0.5	0.6
Misc.	0.0	0.0	0.1	4.0	2.7	2.1	2.3	7.1	4.1	5.9
Total	100.0	100.0	100.0	100.0	100.0	100.0	100.0	100.0	100.0	100.0

This enormous weight of the State debt not only provided one of the essential macroeconomic data of the French economy in the nineteenth century, but also a reference as regards the actors' practices, like the Parisian bankers elite (*haute banque*) whose 'important' transactions were associated with the submission of public loans, a technique which they then used to the benefit of railway companies and foreign States.

Figure 1.1. Stock value of the French public funds.[9]

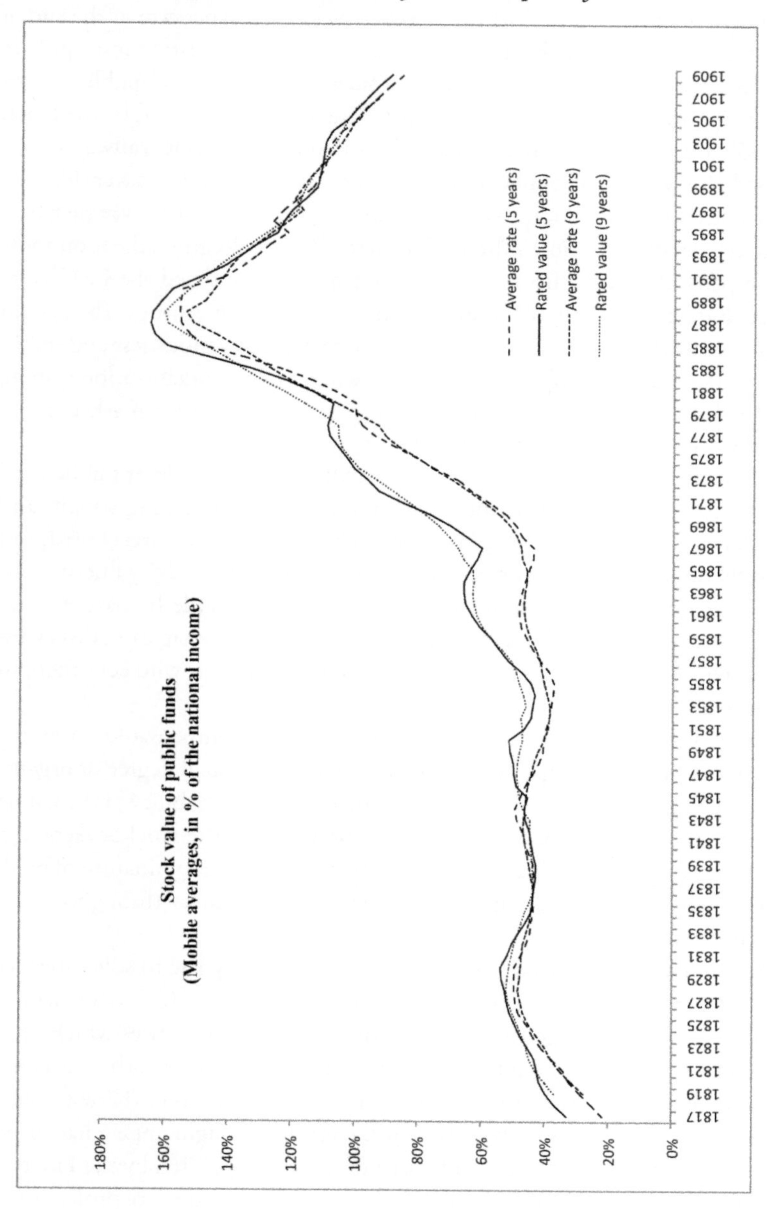

In 1840, the public funds still accounted for more than 90 per cent of the capitalisation of the French securities listed in Paris; close to 50 per cent at the end of the century. Nevertheless, the market kept the same characteristics: most private securities were railway securities, which, *de facto*, were rather semi-public securities than private securities. The interest payment guarantee offered by the State, as of 1857, for private railway companies bonds, outside the state railway sector, increased this weight of public securities accordingly, since the saver, like the financial advisors' handbooks,[10] classed them so. This peculiarity was met by a specific type of organization, inherited from the 'Ancien Regime', the monopoly of a company of Royal officers, who, just like notaries, outlived the Le Chapelier Act, and became legal public officers in the nineteenth century. The system should have provided the Finance Ministers with control, seriousness and stability guarantees indispensable to public credit, whereas a free organization system, as in England, seemed more appropriate to private securities market, more affected by the economic conjuncture than by the State policy.

Even if the stockbrokers limited their activity to a strict role of public legal officers, they could ensure neither market stability by balancing supply and demand, nor support public securities on which the finance ministers relied, and they could not adapt the fixed-costs firm they headed to the activity fluctuations of a market operating with securities which are quite volatile by nature, inasmuch as due to their small diffusion they were long held by big capitalists who were interested in capital gains rather than by small capitalists who kept them in their portfolios.

The rigid organization of the market was necessarily compensated for by the development of a long illegal, free market, which, with a small degree of organization and plagued with high risks, could contribute to the stability of the whole financial market, by dampening economic fluctuations. The stockbrokers and the *coulissiers*, who became legal operators later under the denomination of bank brokers,[11] remained competing and complementary partners throughout the nineteenth century.

The activity of the official stockbrokers was limited by law to sole intermediation on securities which essentially had long remained public loans, whose tradition required a change in denomination in the State registries which only they could certify. They were entitled to buy securities only once they had received funds, and to sell securities only once they had accepted delivery thereof. Their activity, similar to notaries in the field of real estate sales, might appear harmless. Their number was limited to sixty in Paris; they were appointed by the Finance Minister, after cooptation. The recruitment rules were a guarantee of professional competence and probity, since the candidates must be over twenty-five years old, have worked in a stockbroker's practice for four years at least, in a notary's practice or still a banking or business company, not have been convicted, which excluded former bankrupted, destituted brokers and illegal brokers already convicted for violating the official stockbrokers' monopoly. The Chambre Syndicale (Stock Exchange Committee) was the self-regulation authority, with the power to enforce the regulations it generated. The Common Fund, created in 1819, provisioned by various duties paid by agents, played the part of mutual insurance: it enabled lending to failing agents who could not deliver securities at term nor pay their creditors. Proving the solidarity of the official Stockbrokers Association, it demonstrated its efficiency since never during the nineteenth century had a single official stockbroker's client, engaged into legal transactions, suffered losses from a failing debtor. The rigidity of the institutional frame was such that the official trade should not have been risky in any way.

A High Risky Official Market: The Weight of the Professional Networks (1800–82)

However, in spite of strengthened corporatism and the establishment of semi-annual audit checks as of the 1840s, the profession remained highly risky until the end of the 1860s, because the stockbrokers acted as market-makers or made transactions for their own account. The regulation was then finding its limits. Paradoxically in the London Market, with its strict separation and its work division between *brokers*, simple brokers with the public, and *jobbers*, professional market-makers and operators for their own account, was more 'organized' than the Parisian market.

According to the Stock Exchange Committee, among the 114 stockbrokers who had quit the Company between 1815 and 1843, 44 would have left penniless and 39 completely ruined.[12] Due to professional hazards, the average practice duration of the stockbrokers was short. Some could hardly maintain their practice even for a short while: among the 319 stockbrokers who proceeded to the Ring between 1818 and 1860, 27 remained in activity less than a year, 43 less than 3 years, 74 less than 5 years, 170 less than 10 years.

The hazards of this trade were associated with problems specific to an emergent financial market which the operators were starting to learn by doing: that of the forward market[13] legality, unlawful but financially necessary, that of market-making and that of the division of labour between the official stockbrokers and the *coulissiers*. The forward market – forbidden by the letter of the law, was supposed to stabilize rates, which otherwise would have been unstable day after day due to the random fluctuations of the sales and purchases volume. First and foremost the State needed it for placing its loans. Since the firm demand for securities was scarce in a society characterized by high inequality in wealth and income which limited the number of potential buyers, and where the latter were unfamiliar with security investment, the government could certainly not contemplate selling them quickly to savers. Their flow depended on forward transactions conducted by large professional or semi-professional operators. But the unlawfulness of the forward market, which was nevertheless indispensable, left, during the first half of the nineteenth century, the brokers without any legal recourse against unlucky or unscrupulous operators. If they relinquished these operations, the stockbrokers left the whole benefit to illegal brokers.

The other problems raised the same issue, either to accept risks and extend profits by operating outside the institutional protection, or pass the risks onto illegal operators by dividing the tasks, which meant recognizing *de facto* their existence and their usefulness, as well as relinquishing a portion of the commissions to them. The stockbroker was not entitled to act as a market-maker, but the position of the market was the more unbalanced on a daily basis as the market niche was increasingly narrow. The illegal operators provided for the compensation of the *rente* market: they were the best clients of the stockbrokers. When the multiplication of the capital societies enabled numerous private securities to access the transaction market, in the 1840s, with the railway shares and even with stock options, either the stockbrokers accepted risks while claiming for all transactions – on more or less reliable securities whose rates could collapse together the companies issuing them, or they focused on sure securities, forsaking the other securities to the *coulisse*, hence acknowledging the existence of a second market. In the 1840s, certain agents, or some of their employees or associates engaged even openly in the placement of novel securities and were paid a commission by the issuing company.[14]

Up to the 1860s, the stockbrokers' policy remained undecided. In 1859, they obtained the conviction of the main *coulisse* companies in a spectacular trial, which disorganized the illegal market, but also made the official market rather dull. They accepted a portion of the market risks from which their corporatist organization could not protect them completely: which explains the amount of accidents and bankruptcies. But the vulnerability was limited by the high cohesion of the people's networks.

If among the stockbrokers operating on the Ring between 1810 and 1830, close to one in four was a broker's son, it was because certain dynasties had been formed below the Ancien Regime as the trade was not so hazardous. But between 1830 and 1890, this proportion shrunk to less than 10 per cent, whereas it was going to climb back to 26 per cent between 1890 and 1914. Indeed the instability of the trade and the rapid turnover of the holders between 1830 and 1870 hardly enabled families to get the upper hand in the Ring.

Table 1.2. Average practice duration of the stockbrokers and parenthood with their predecessors.

Date of appointment	Average duration in years	Proportion of parenthood marked* with the predecessors such as sons		
From 1/1/1820 to 31/12/1829	10.5			
From 1/1/1830 to 31/12/1839	10.1	Between 1820 and 1850	6 per cent	1.7 per cent
From 1/1/1840 to 31/12/1849	10.4			
From 1/1/1850 to 31/12/1859	10.6			
From 1/1/1860 to 31/12/1869	13.8	Between 1850 and 1880	17 per cent	2.5 per cent
From 1/1/1870 to 31/12/1879	18.3			
From 1/1/1880 to 31/12/1889	24.2			
From 1/1/1890 to 31/12/1899	24.8	Between 1880 and 1914	35 per cent	12.8 per cent
From 1/1/1900 to 31/12/1909	23.9			
From 1/1/1910 to 31/12/1914	21.4			

* it is hence a minimal proportion.

Conversely, the solidity of the professional networks was very high throughout the nineteenth century. As regards the brokers, whose former career could be reconstructed, 85 per cent were working in a practice, the 15 per cent remaining, especially during the first half of the nineteenth century, from banking societies: 46 per cent before proceeding to the Ring were proxy holders or main commercial agents in a practice and very often sleeping partners to their boss, 28 per cent fulfilled a less important function, 11 per cent were only associates, which did not mean that they obligatorily played a passive role as lenders, since the associates, when they had no regularly remunerated employment in practices, were, especially during the first two-thirds of the nineteenth century, often business providers, who were not called '*remisiers*'[15] as yet, or operators working for their own account, since they did not any brokerages. Their personal transactions increased the risks run by the practice. The career of most stockbrokers followed a progression inside the professional framework of a practice or of several practices; it started with a modest employee's work which evolved rapidly towards a main commercial agent's or cashier's position, which enabled, in case of reshuffle by the practice's holder, the joining of a profit-sharing scheme in said firm, then after some ten years' work in the Stock Exchange to become a proxy, and finally to seize the opportunity of applying for the first vacant partner's position. The recruitment of the new agents, only with the resigning partner proposing a candidate who must be admitted by his peers, promoted the constitution of a professional network. This system tended to exclude hardly known candidates from scratch, since originating from outside the trade. In case of vacancy, the broker's associates enjoyed a tacit right of pre-emption on the practice of which they partook.

A Cautious Official Market: The Weight of Family Networks (1882–1913)

After the Second Empire, the stockbrokers' role was defined better and more strictly limited to their intermediation function. Even advice to the clientele – *de jure*, were prohibited.[16] Since the 1870s justice considered the forward market as *de facto* legal even if an Act to that effect was not passed before 28 March 1885. The stockbrokers were henceforth protected against unscrupulous clients, which reduced their risks tremendously. The sequels to the 1859 trial had proved the usefulness of the *coulisse*. A division of the work between both types of operators was then admitted tacitly. The *coulisse* practices specialized in the *rente* forward market, as indispensable partners of the Ring and operators indispensable to placing public loans, were never victims of criticism. As regards private securities or foreign securities, the arguments were then narrowed to delineating the fields of activity. The Stock Exchange Committee endeavoured to enforce task-sharing, claiming for a monopoly on the securities it had elected to list, and leaving negotiations for securities to the *coulisse*, about which said Committee was not sufficiently informed, securities which did not appear reliable enough or which did not appear to attract a sufficient number of transactions to make their official listing profitable. By relinquishing to the *coulisse* the negotiations on hardly known or brand new securities, by leaving the market information and acclimatization process thereto, the Ring reserved the right to recover proven securities for its own good. It therefore passed on the risks and the costs of the introduction of a security on the market to the *coulissiers*, while leaving them the whole benefit of the commissions in case of speculative bubble, such as that on the goldmine shares in 1895. The recognition of the *coulisse*, promoted by the government, and even encouraged, with a view to making it pay the tax on transactions, was officialized in 1898. Even the risks and the costs associated with prospecting new customers were outsourced by the official market, since it accepted from then on to rely on the bank brokers as business providers and it then increasingly resorted to the services of *remisiers*, to whom it relinquished a portion of the brokerages.

The activities of the stockbrokers, which were strictly limited to brokers', were hardly risky anymore. The 1882 Crash, which had put a few practices in a tight spot and revealed that some agents were trading for their own account, was the last major stock exchange accident: from 1882 to 1914, only three stockbrokers were led due to their own carelessness to bankruptcy, forced resignation or suicide. These mutations of the clientele strengthened such evolution. A narrow and speculative market of major operators, private clients or bankers taking risks, was added in the 1870s a vast clientele of average savers who bought securities on a firm basis to invest their capitals instead of operating on credit while hoping to gain on the rate variations. These orders, less voluminous but more numerous, were also more expensive to process, more staff-demanding, but they provided regular influx of brokerages. The risks were hence reduced and the transactions less irregular, but the counterpart was a decrease in the profit rate (Figure 1.2).

The stockbrokers were becoming passive brokers, content to draw a commission without providing any additional services to the clientele. No external competition could contribute to lower their tariff since they enjoyed a monopoly situation. There was no competition among them, since minimal tariffs were fixed and the Committee saw to it that no reduction was granted; the prices of the practices were even fixed uniformly, regardless of the level of the turnover. Consequently, during the last years of the century, a portion of the public, who hoped for an evolution towards a free market, and who were taking the London market as a model, opposed this privilege which appeared unjustified henceforth.

The trade recruitment which ensured the training of the stockbrokers and contributed to mutual acquaintance of the market operators was going to be, during the last quarter of the century, superimposed with family networks, which did not question said recruitment, but were simply added thereto. Sons or son-in-laws henceforth succeeded their fathers or father-in-laws at the head of the practices, but only after they had worked therein and generally occupied functions as proxy holders. Several practices thus remained in the same family for several generations, even sometimes over more than a century.[17] Different members of the family were working in the practices, since the high remunerations of the employees make such jobs extremely attractive. At the same time, in stockbrokers' societies, if the portion of professionals remained significant, either predecessor stockbrokers who maintained their capitals – large contributions generally, in the practice, or for certain practices with more modest turnovers for the employees who had helped raise funds, the place of the holder's family sleeping partners was also increasing: holder's mother when she had inherited from her deceased husband, brothers, sisters, who had inherited a share of the society and whose husbands did not always work in the Stock Exchange, uncles or cousins. The weight of the families was even more significant among the sub-sleeping partners who lent the stockbroker a portion of its contribution.

Figure 1.2. Average benefit relative to the turnover.

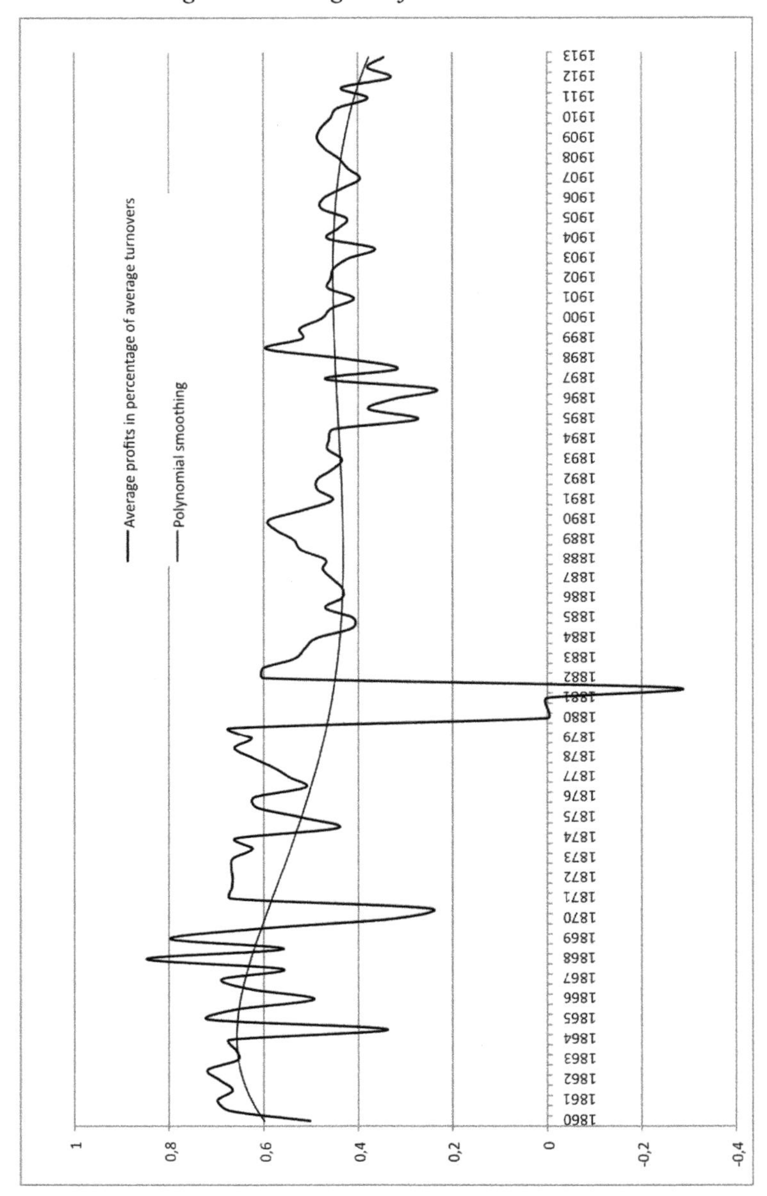

The members of the family were hence rather passive sleeping partners who were well advised to leave their capital in the society, because high profitability was offered, much higher than real estate, land or security investments. The family network was hence not fulfilling any longer a positive function for the operation of the firm (acquaintances, lessened vulnerability, financing): the institutions protected from risks and guaranteed financial solidarity in case of difficulty, the professional networks ensured mutual acquaintance of all market operators and favoured trusting relationships. Rather passive, the family networks were the consequence of a strategy which consisted in reserving the advantages of a trade, which tended to close up.

Due to this fallback on a risk-free intermediation function, the prospection of new clients, French or foreign, relied increasingly on the half-commission men. The latter were auxiliaries who multiplied when the business conjuncture became favourable again, as of the 1890s. Their number quadrupled between the 1890s and 1900s. Their role was to canvass new clients in relation to their address books and to provide them with the financial information and advice which the stockbrokers were not entitled officially to give the clientele. The meshed network of people that the agents had created to protect themselves then to reserve business niches was then opened up to the outside to gain a new clientele, new orders indispensable for maintaining the financial equilibrium of companies whose staff-related costs were increasing with the number of purchase or sales orders, more numerous but regarding lower amounts. In the 1890s, these half-commission men were mainly practices' employees working for themselves[18]. Then an independent trade started to emerge, employing a large number of people on the eve of war, probably close to 1,000 in Paris alone.

For the penetration of the different social circles from middle bourgeoisie to aristocracy to be effective, one had to turn to beaters of various origin, high society, mob and foreign half-commission men or of foreign origin enabling to recruit clients hardly addressed by the stockbrokers' network. These half-commission men were close to the circle of the bank brokers. Many of the latter had started as half-commission men. The family links are attested between both occupations. Unless highly unexpected, the *remisier* Felix Aghion, employee in the Giraudeau practice, was surely related to the banker Jules Aghion, of Egyptian origin, Paul Alphandéry, a *remisier* in the Adam practice, probably came from the same family as Numa Alphandéry, a bank broker in the 1890s whose son took part in the foundation of the Alphandéry, Crémieux, Franckel et Cie in 1907. The stockbrokers' *remisiers* compensated for the very 'official' character of the Ring as private and foreign financial activities were developing, activities where the status of the stockbrokers kept them in a situation of inferiority as regards information and recruitment of clients, purchasers and sellers. The centralization of numerous public issues on the Paris marketplace, among which some, like the Russian ones, for political reasons, did not imply that all said securities be subscribed to and classed by French savers definitely. Foreigners would buy in Paris and, due to the institutional weakness of the stockbrokers' network abroad, would buy through half-commission men and bank brokers.

Figure 1.3. Employees and remisiers: average number per stockbrokers' practice.

(i.e. 60 practices up to 1898, then 70).

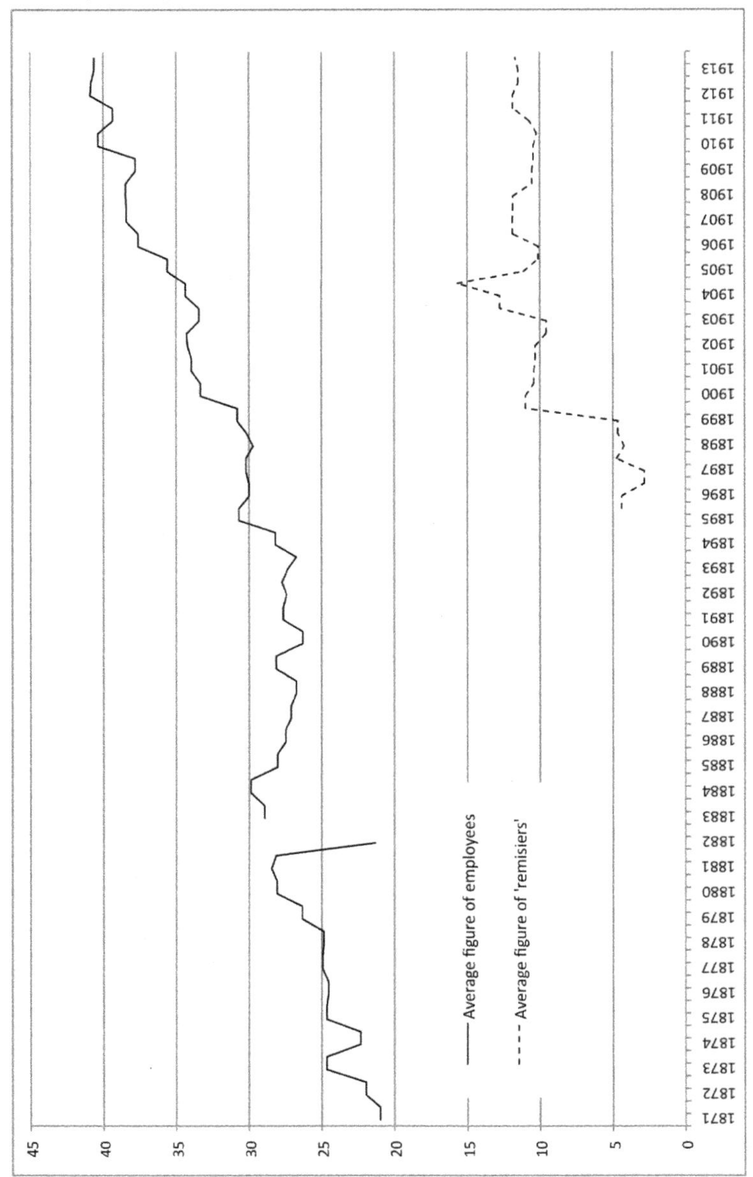

The withdrawing of the stockbrokers' network into itself, which seemed contrary to the dynamics of financial business that enticed operators to converge towards the London model, ought to have toppled the monopoly situation: the trustee of the *Compagnie des agents de change* himself had drawn out a reform bill of the Ring which never came through although it had been approved by the *Chambre*.[19] Nevertheless the institutional structure of the Ring remained the same, the development of the half-commission men, who formed a kind of link between the staff of the official market and that of the free market, and the recognition of the free market of the *coulissiers* was leading *de facto* to a convergence between the Paris and the London intermediation. *Remisiers* and *coulissiers* were hence providing more audacious networks to the defensive and closed network of the stockbrokers, the better to support the marketplace dynamics.

The Bank Brokers: National Networks Open to Foreign Countries

These brokers, illegal until 1898, bore enormous risks. They could not turn to Justice to make reluctant clients pay. They were, by law, as defenceless before their peers: nothing enabled to distinguish between serious, trustworthy, partners and little reliable speculators who ought to be avoided at all costs. Although it was impossible to create a union *de jure*, thereby enabling its members to make such differentiation easier, a draft thereof was available as of the second half of the nineteenth century: certain societies, registered 'in the *rente* or security sheet', provided guarantees which the others could not claim in any way.

The *coulissiers*, before the 1898 reform, mainly focussed on credit transactions, in particular on the *rente* or speculation securities as the Italian 3 per cent annuity, which enabled them to operate on large volumes of securities without investing a very significant capital which they did not possess. The relative significance of the operations and of both markets is not known precisely before the end of the century. A study by a registry civil servant suggested an approximate evaluation as an average of the years 1894–5.[20]

Table 1.3. Negotiations in French rente in millions of FF.

	Ring	Coulisse	Total
Spot exchange transactions	2,596.8	8.9	2,605.7
Forward exchange transactions (carry-overs excepted)	13,994.1	45,940.0	59,934.1
Total	16,590.9	45,948.9	62,539.8

For former time periods, the overwhelming predominance of the forward market, especially on the *rente*, left no doubt to contemporaries, although they were not able to back this assumption with figures.[21] Option deals, carry-overs and security arbitrages became frequent as of the first half of the nineteenth century. The put and call option conversely, a transaction imported from London or Vienna, only developed in the banking market during the last years of the century. The relative weight of the negotiations on the Ring or on the *coulisse* has undoubtedly varied during the century, but the significance of the Parisian free market in the operation of the system is indisputable. Both these institutional characteristics of the Parisian market were due to its nature as a State fund market, whose issue required an active forward market, and whose official brokers were ministerial officers and not just security traders.

Failing any official organization and unable to turn to Justice for protection, the *coulissiers*' risks could only be limited by strong trusting relationships between parties. Up to 1914 approximately, the family networks remained embryonic. The names of outside brokers appearing during the Second Empire cannot be found at the end of the century, which excludes any direct filiation among companies' chairmen and suggests far-reaching renewal of the trade.

Whereas father-to-son successions and kinships between active and sleeping partners of bank brokers' firms remained scarce until 1914, the number of societies managed by brethren was nevertheless significant.[22] But the network whereon the reliability of the *coulisse* transactions rested was a professional network. Almost all bank brokers had made a career in the *coulisse* where they had known each other for numerous years. They were bound by a common culture, revealed by books[23] that described the customs of this small, original and jointly liable group, which they simply called the 'Stock Exchange Operators' – in fact professional operators and not clients from the financial market. The resistance of this professional network was increased by the cross-participations to the social capitals of the firms: certain sleeping partners were common to several firms,[24] certain bankers were sleeping partners not only of their former firms when they retired, but also of competing, and hence also friendly, firms.

Another type of network was characteristic of the *coulisse*. Many foreigners came, in the 1870s, 80s and 90s, in successive waves – in relation to the large issuances of each period, French State loans, then foreign State funds and foreign industrial securities, often imported from the London market, to settle down in Paris for making contact between the French financial market and the banking or financial community of their original place of abode. In the 1870s, Germans, among some were related to firms across the border, came to Paris to facilitate, as brokers, the placement of redemption loans in German-speaking countries. Others came from Spain, Italy, the Ottoman Empire, bringing with them sound knowledge of their national securities which were subject to issuances in France, and especially of the capitalist clientele of their countries, desirous of taking part in the transactions made on the Parisian market. The latter asserted itself from the beginning of the 1890s as an active market, especially on the *coulisse*, the second largest in Europe, more focused on fixed-income securities and continental securities than the London market. The drop in the brokerage tariff in 1898 attracted orders from foreign countries, since henceforth the cost of intermediation was lower in Paris than in London or Berlin. A portion of the community of the bank brokers maintained a link with abroad upon which the European role of the Parisian market rested, a link which the official market was unable to provide.

Table 1.4. The foreign origins of the firms of bank brokers.

		Before 1903	From 1904 to 1908	From 1909 to 1913
Number of known birth-places		81	61	56
Frequency of foreigners		47 per cent	23 per cent	16 per cent
among which	*Germany*	*22 per cent*	*11 per cent*	*7 per cent*
	the Ottoman Empire, with Romania	*5 per cent*	*4 per cent*	*5 per cent*
	Austro-Hungarian or Russian Empires	*6 per cent*	*2 per cent*	*4 per cent*
	Italy or Spain	*2 per cent*	*3 per cent*	
	other (Switzerland, England, Holland, Belgium ...)	*11 per cent*	*2 per cent*	

More characteristic still were the origins and the places of abode of the firms' sleeping partners, who gave rise to certain firms specialized in relationships with the Italian or Ottoman markets, such as *Hazan, Penilleau et Cie*, or with the London market like the *Rodolphe Herz* firm, with German banks like the *Singer brothers*, *Goldschmidt et Cohen* and many others, with the Brussels marketplace like *Albert del Porto et Cie* with two branches in Belgium.

But as soon as their activity was officially recognized, the bank brokers hastened to found two unions in 1898, that of the *Bankers on forward securities*[25] (85 firms in 1901) and that of the *Bankers on spot securities*[26] (105 firms in 1901), jointly liable and guarantors of their reliability and their solvency. The *rente coulisse*, conversely, was still illegal and formed a *de facto* association only, the *Compensation Chamber of French Rentes*.[27] These unions were supposed to reduce the risks by mimicking the institutions of the official market, by establishing joint liability among the members, by edicting rules, by requiring company managers to be of French nationality, requirements which were easily met to the satisfaction of chairmen of firms already established. They forced their members to formally waive to act as market-makers. The *coulissiers* registered with the unions engaged themselves to offer brokerages which were roughly the same as the Ring's, whose they became dependent auxiliaries to a certain extent. Admission to the *Market Listing of the Bankers on Spot Securities*[28] then followed a procedure close to the admission to the *Official Listing.* This institutionalization of the trade reduced the risks but, eventually, also reduced the dynamics of the *coulisse.* The notion of complementarity had superseded the relation of competition, but to the detriment of an optimal division of the tasks between the different brokers. In spite of the respectability gained by their official recognition, the 1898 reform was indeed detrimental to the *coulissiers* whose transactions stepped back whereas those of the Ring increased by the look of the Stock Exchange tax evolution:

Table 1.5. Stock Exchange Tax, in millions of FF.

	1898	1899	1900
Tax collected by stockbrokers	2.409	4.325	4.446
Tax collected by other brokers	2.405	2.181	1.981

Such evolution could only give rise to a new category of firms, outside unions. The temptation to rise to institutional establishment through convergence over the structures and the transactions of the Ring immediately developed a third outside-union free market. This was only possible inasmuch as the banking occupation was not regulated[29] and consequently anybody could join the trade. The large banks which issued foreign securities on the market also benefited from the institutionalisation of the *coulisse.* The volume of orders placed to them by their clients on the same securities enabled them to present 'applications', i.e. to perform transactions without resorting to the official brokers. The stockbrokers revolted against these practices, but put up with them since said banks were, for some practices, their best clients.

Conclusion

The example of the organization of the Parisian financial market suggests that the analysis of the people's networks cannot be conducted unless in the framework of the forms of institutionalisation of the trades or the functions they ought to fulfil or still the roles they seek to play. Three types of networks, different in their structures and functions, could be highlighted. The professional networks of stockbrokers and of bank brokers were closely linked:[30] each of the individuals knew most of the others and was related to them via various links: employer to employees, active partner to sleeping partner, or simply through years of working together. This type of network, highly exclusive, with a tight mesh, offered the greatest resistance, but had limited contacts with the outside world. Its function was defensive: to establish trust and reduce vulnerability. Up to the 1882 Crash, such meshing had fairly effectively ensured its protective function through supporting the solvency of often careless brokers. But its grounds for existence were not so obvious later on, if only to preserve the advantages of the trade for the group. Superimposing onto these cross-networks of stockbroking families at the end of the nineteenth century, juxtaposing exclusive lineages, thereby accepting few new outsiders, through marriages, consolidated this function of monopolising the advantages of intermediation. Whereas the financial transactions became increasingly international and the Parisian market was breaking away from transactions on public loans to turn to securities associated with the productive economy, such a monopoly appeared unjustified and even archaic to many. But the multiplication of the *remisiers* provided the correction which enabled stockbrokers' practices to develop their activities.

On the contrary, the foreign networks of bank brokers which represented the dynamic portion of the financial market, as introducers of new securities, as links with foreign countries, showed a lower density, whereas each individual was in contact with his own myriad of relations, bankers or brokers from the same country and domiciled in Paris or abroad. This network morphology enabled to be globally in contact with a large number of people, i.e. to gather and diffuse information at best, to address the maximum of clients. Their function consisted in intensifying relationships with the outside world, hence to develop the power of the group on its environment: it was offensive economically in order to increase the operations on foreign securities in Paris and extend the goodwill abroad.[31] But the unconscious mimicry relative to the stockbrokers which induced them to be organized into a similar corporate system led to a new group of non-recognized brokers, a third market, under development on the eve of war. Finally, whereas the so-called 'free' foreign markets were evolving towards stricter regulation, the interweaving of the different networks and professional groups enabled the Parisian market to fulfil its functions and to monitor the development of the financial transactions probably as efficiently as the London market. Conversely, regulation in the aftermath of the First World War required that not only the firm chairmen but also all the sleeping partners should be French, was going to contribute to reducing the international role of the Parisian marketplace.

2 THE RESISTANCE OF THE LILLE MARKETPLACE TO NATIONAL CONVERGENCE: A REGIONAL FINANCIAL SYSTEM BETWEEN AUTONOMY AND SCLEROSIS, 1880–1914

Jean-Luc Mastin

When switching from national scale to regional scale, the convergence is far from obvious; the same goes for the existence of a true national financial system in France in 1914. It is exactly what the example of the Lille region shows. Controlled by the 'grand families' of the commerce and textile industries (which were the dominant activities), this marketplace centralized the capital of a large Northern region (departments of the Nord, Pas-de-Calais and Somme), far beyond the Lille district. Lille was the only regional stock exchange market, and the main banking marketplace, but not the only one. Roubaix, where the Banque de France opened a branch in 1871, sought to emerge as an autonomous banking marketplace relative to Lille (for example, in 1893, the Crédit Lyonnais[1] turned its sub-branch in Roubaix into a full-fledged agency). Nevertheless, it relinquished that role at the beginning of the twentieth century. In consequence, it is moreover significant not to study the regional financial system as a homogeneous whole, but using local peculiarities, in particular in terms of credit. Nevertheless, Lille was one of the first French provincial banking and financial marketplaces with Lyon and Marseille, and powerful enough to resist, if not integration into the national financial system, at least the standards which the Parisian centre tried to impose upon it. In 1881, the branches of the Banque de France in Lille and in Roubaix respectively ranked fifth and sixth on national scale (after Lyon, Marseille, Bordeaux and Le Havre) according to the total volume of their transactions. In 1900, they respectively ranked third (after Lyon and Marseille) and sixth (after Le Havre and Bordeaux). In 1900, the Lille Stock

Exchange had become the primary stock exchange among French provinces in terms of stock capitalization, ahead of Lyon.[2]

Still, on the basis of the analysis of the investment flows realized in the region between 1850 and 1914, obtained from the analysis of a sample of company charters filed with the registries of the commercial courts in Lille, Roubaix and Tourcoing, it appears that the Lille region only witnessed very relative industrial diversification at the beginning of the twentieth century. This happened in spite of the growing profusion of the capital available locally from 1880 on, as indicated by the volume of bank deposits, and notwithstanding the abilities of the textile managers to be organized and to engage in collective action. The Roubaix, Tourcoing and Lys valley areas even witnessed strengthened textile specialisation. At the same time, investments in new technologies – i.e. electrical, organic chemical industries, etc. – had been made by external capitals, mainly from Paris and Belgium. The long-preserved, regional financial autonomy was thus weakened by the first developments of the second industrialization wave. This phenomenon reflected the weaknesses of a regional financial system unable to adapt to the financial requirements of the new industrial sectors.

How can this sclerosis be explained? What is the portion ascribed to endogenous factors, i.e. factors of the regional financial autonomy, associated with the predominance of family capitalism? How did the marketplace resist convergence and what part did that resistance play in said sclerosis? And what is the weight of the exogenous factors – integration of the marketplace into the national financial system, and competition with the Paris and Brussels marketplaces?

Through the analysis of the 'social' embedding of the regional financial system we shall see first the resistance factors of the marketplace to convergence. We will then analyse successively the evolution of Lille's banking system and financial market.

A Financial System Held by the 'Grand Families'

The Private Sphere of Credit: the Keystone of the System

The main component of the regional financial system was outside the market: it was the private sphere of credit. Far from being limited to family circles (which were nevertheless still playing a primordial part in the constitution of the initial capitals, when financing the cash flow and mobilizing the resources necessary for saving the credit of a relative entangled in ill-fated speculations and thereby saving 'the honour of the name' i.e. the value of a signature), these financial circuits organised a 'credit mutuality'[3] which took in particular the form of (always personal) quasi cross-participations between family groups (organized into constellations of legally independent sister-companies) and quasi common branches with limited responsibility companies or joint-stock partnerships with locked capital.

It underlined the fundamental ambivalence of the competition–cooperation relationships between these family groups. In a circle where independence was hardly a virtue and where indebtedness was promoted socially as a sign of social power, these groups strengthened in this way the solidarities resulting from interlaced family links created by zealously followed endogamy, which acted as a reduction mode for asymmetric information between creditor and debtor – 'breed will tell'. The closed character of the marketplace was even more blatant.

There was still the double issue of the limits of this private sphere of credit (where did it stop? were its resources sufficient?), and consequently the issue of its relations with the 'public' capital market. It may be observed on the one hand that what did not belong to the private credit networks appeared to be weak (numerically and financially). On the other hand, in the balance sheets (liabilities) of textile companies, at the beginning of the twentieth century, the portion of the current accounts tended to decrease whereas banking indebtedness was on the increase, especially as of 1907.

A Banking System 'Embedded' in the Family System

But the capital market for its own part did not escape the grip of the private sphere. Controlled by the 'grand families' who were the shareholders and the main clients thereof, the three regional banks (Verley, Decroix & Cie; Crédit du Nord; H. Devilder & Cie) and the powerful local banks (Joire; Scalbert; Woussen-Castrique, and the Banque Régionale du Nord in Roubaix) appeared as the institutional extension of the 'credit mutuality' aforementioned. As their shareholders controlled the key sectors of the regional economy (textile, sugar, colliery, mineral chemistry), they formed a 'regionalist' pool seeing to the preservation of the regional financial autonomy. Thus the Crédit du Nord (the only regional bank to be publicly incorporated) formed a constellation whereof the core, composed of groups like Kuhlmann (chemistry; a promoter of the bank since 1848), Agache (flax textile industry; a family allied to the Kuhlmanns since 1873), and the Mines de Lens,[4] extended, in the 1890s, to the Mines de Carvin and to the wool industrial activities of Roubaix-Tourcoing ... while strengthening the family character of the Board of Administration.

In parallel personal links had developed since the 1860s, incorporating local banks and regional banks into an increasingly tight family system: the core of common shareholders and administrators had expanded; the matrimonial alliances between managerial families of competing banks had multiplied (between the Verleys and the Scalberts for example). There was no issue outside this system: Devilder remained isolated until his sons entered into 'rich and honourable marriages' around 1895. The weakness and the failure of the small local joint-stock banks and of the 'discounters' – small local banks that specialized in commercial paper discounting – in spite of the support of the Banque de France in the 1880s, contrasted with the prosperity and the power of the 'private' local banks such as Joire or Scalbert.

At the same time the Lille marketplace grew to fuller integration into the national banking system. A branch of the Banque de France opened in Lille in 1848, then in Roubaix in 1871, while the large national banks started to open branches as soon as 1865 (the Société Générale, in Lille), followed by the Crédit Lyonnais (1881). But it remains questionable whether this integration had loosened the grip of the family system on the market of banking credit. For example, board and auditor positions at the Banque de France's local branches were naturally allocated to the main shareholders of the local and regional banks, and even more to the managers of the banks themselves.

Stockmarket under 'Local Influences'

In the Lille Stock Exchange, equipped with a ring since 1861, the recruitment of the stockbrokers was also under control. It became completely restricted, as of the 1880s, to candidates having entered into marriages in the Lille business bourgeoisie or who originated therefrom, and who could then claim their rights to present a hereditary successor. This applied to Alexandre Crouan: of Breton origin (born in 1849 in a family of lawyers in Brest), he was admitted in 1882 to succeed a bankrupt stockbroker. It should be added that his father had worked as a proxy for the State General Payer of the North in Lille since 1850, and that his sister Léonie had just married Charles Verley, manager of the Verley, Decroix & Cie bank, in 1880. In 1885, Pierre Liagre, son of a doctor in Roubaix, took over the practice of his uncle Emile, a short time after entering into the powerful Descamps family in Lille. His son, who succeeded him in 1912, married Charles Verley-Crouan's grandniece. In July 1899, Léon Leys, from Dunkirk, was recruited just after he married Marie-Louise Fauchille, daughter of an old and powerful Lille family of spinning industrialists. In April 1900, Charlemagne Fauchille-Boone took over a practice: he was the cousin of Leys' spouse. In 1911, he transferred his firm to his brother-in-law, Lucien Alphonse Boone. In total, the recruitments in the 1880s and 90s restricted the brokerage practices to two Lille families: in the Spring of 1900, the Fauchilles controlled three firms, whereof the holders were cousins (Leys, Liagre, Fauchille); the Verleys, directly or indirectly, two other firms (Crouan, Denoyelle).

The corporation was then locked. In 1912, while the list of shares and the activity of the Lille Stock Exchange were in full swing, the six stockbrokers opposed the project of the Minister of Finance to recreate the three firms left vacant since 1832. Paradoxically, Lille, which was then, with Lyon, one of the first two provincial stock markets, had the smallest ring in the province[5].

Finally, the tight relations between the Ring and the Verley, Decroix & Cie bank, as well as the flax textile families, had naturally led them to do a few favours to one another[6]. This may account for the 'local influences' denounced by Parisian shareholders of coalmining companies listed in the Lille stock exchange, who complained about the underrating of their securities and the abnormal fluctuations in prices of their stock values[7]. Anyway, it seemed difficult, for an external broker, to operate in such tightly controlled market.

A Powerful Banking Marketplace which Defended its Usages against the Parisian Standards

Resistance and Expansion of the Regional and Local Banks

Up to the mid-1890s, the resistance of the marketplace translated first into implantation and development difficulties for the local agencies of the national branching banks. The Société Générale opened in Lille one of its very first agencies as early as in 1865, then in 1872, in Roubaix, a sub-agency which became a fully-fledged agency in 1874, but their directors, recruited outside the local market since 1869, resigned one by one: they felt bridled by a centralized and overcautious policy.[8] The Comptoir d'Escompte de Paris (CNEP) opened an agency in Roubaix in 1872, but had to close it down two years later. The reason for this failure leaves no room for doubt: 'a banking company which does not grant any overdrafts has no justification in operating in Roubaix'.[9] It reopened no sooner than in 1893, whereas the CNEP only set up in 1901 in Lille. Only the Crédit Lyonnais, which opened an agency in Lille in 1881, with a sub-agency in Roubaix, which became a fully-fledged agency in 1893, was successful, by adopting conversely a very local strategy and reducing its charges, without however developing loyalty among top-rank clients.

After 1895 however, as prosperity returned, the agencies of the national banks have developed durably: in Roubaix, the Société Générale conquered a 'very attractive goodwill', similarly to the Crédit Lyonnais which recorded 'sizeable profits'.[10] Successes are even more remarkable given that inter-bank competition became substantially harsher on the market at the beginning of the twentieth century, and even more so around 1913, through the irruption of numerous Parisian and foreign banks setting up agencies or branches, or simply entering into business relations with the larger groups in the region. In fact, the position of the Crédit Lyonnais on the marketplace seemed more fragile after 1905. First, its commercial portfolio was sagging. Second, the progression of its deposits was very slow, compared to those of the regional banks and, last it was interrupted by massive withdrawals, far more significant than in the regional banks. These indices highlight the resistance of the local customers, who benefited from the advantages offered by the Parisian competition, without ever being disloyal to the local and regional banks.

Building on the expansion of their branch networks, including Paris (Crédit du Nord, 1889) and Brussels (Crédit du Nord, 1896), local banks resources became considerable: the growth of their deposits accelerated after 1885 and even more after 1895. They strengthened their reserve funds in consequence, supplied after 1910 by the high issuing premiums drawn from the Devilder and the Crédit du Nord capital increases. Meanwhile the latter fought vigorously and successfully against the national banks' competition. On the eve of the war, the Crédit du Nord and Verley, Decroix & Cie concentrated, in their books, 80 per cent of the deposits collected on the marketplace: 282 million FF out of a total of 350 million FF.

Where did Convergence of the Banking Policies Stem From?

According to Michel Lescure, the competition of the national banks after 1895 should have led the regional banks, which had become multiple-branch deposit banks, like the national banks, to match their policies, i.e. raise their safety and liquidity thresholds. This matching, qualified as 'technical mainstreaming of the bank', would mark the beginning of the 'fixed capital disengagement' of the regional banks.[11] In the Lille region, this hypothesis ought to be nuanced for two reasons.

On the one hand, it is mainly in the post-war era that the regional banks clearly fell back on bill discounts and secured loans. Before 1914, the chronology and the specificities of each bank ought to be taken into account: in the 1890s, they all had developed overdrafts, thus promoting post-depression investment recovery. But it remains that after 1904, Verley, Decroix & Cie and the Crédit du Nord secured their engagements by giving secured loans precedence over overdrafts, the former, obsessed by liquidity, even specializing in bill discounting, while the latter added to this trade that of securities-backed loans. On the contrary Devilder & Cie, controlled by the wool merchants and industrial of Roubaix-Tourcoing since 1877, embarked vigorously and up to 1913 on an overdraft policy.

On the other hand, and from a local point of view, it was especially national banks that bore convergence. It was in particular the case of the Crédit Lyonnais that adapted its strategy to the local specificities, as the differentiation of its positions in both its local agencies makes it plain.[12] In Roubaix, it provided personal loans as any other local bank and granted large overdrafts, in particular by acceptance, to the textile groups, the latter being far more frequent than secured loans, especially in the 1890s and again after 1907. In Lille, its policy was more in keeping with its liquidity and security principles – predominance of secured loans – although more deeply immobilized than Verley, Decroix & Cie.

In fact, the powerful marketplace imposed its work practices to the allogenous banks. The concentration of the capital, particularly high in Roubaix-Tourcoing, and the banking competition provided the family groups with a negotiating power which enabled them to impose the form of loans, their amounts and to decline to prove their financial standing. All the more so, attached to banking pluralism, they endeavoured to maintain competition on the marketplace. Thus, in the Summer of 1913, as the Crédit du Nord absorbed Devilder, the Roubaix industrialists promoted the implantation of the Banque Suisse et Française. Which enabled them to increase the profusion of capitals on the marketplace, and consequently, to obtain affluent and cheap loans. Thus, Figure 2.3, representing the difference between assets and liabilities of both agencies of the Crédit Lyonnais, shows that after 1895, whereas capitals were already overabundant, the net flows from Paris increased considerably, especially in Roubaix-Tourcoing. The Lille region hence largely benefited from the centralisation of capitals organised by the main banks at a national scale.

When the Banque de France Relinquished his Lending Standards

The resistance of the marketplace to national convergence is even more blatant when examining its relations with the Banque de France (BDF). As everywhere in France, the latter saw its portion in regional lending decline[13] and its profits dropped after1875.[14] But in its branches in Lille and Roubaix, its strategy to develop its lending and profits forced the BDF to giving up on its own standards.

In a first step (1875–95), this strategy consisted on the one hand in supporting and encouraging the small local joint-stock banks and other 'discounters' who depended on rediscounting to a vast extent, and – such policy being risky and of limited efficiency – on the other hand in attracting large commercial bills to direct lending, while tolerating finance bills. It nevertheless was a semi-failure, since the discount conditions and rates had become so low on the marketplace that industrial and merchants started to desert the tills of the Banque de France, except for remitting large finance bills. And in fact, after the decrease in the 1880s, the proportion of local paper[15] increased in Roubaix as of 1888 and in Lille as of 1895. The portfolio of the Roubaix BDF's branch then purged itself of the large prime commercial bills to be replaced by finance paper, whose proportion increased a great deal up to 1900. Said paper came essentially from a few large 'direct endorsers' who presented effects drawn on other firms, often in the same group, on associates and / or relatives, and more and more on employees, secured by securities deposited in the vaults of the branch and family guarantees, renewed over several years, and intended for financing wool purchases, partnerships and speculations of all kinds (stock values, raw materials or agricultural products).

Figure 2.1. Crédit Lyonnais's branches in Lille and Roubaix, 1894–1914: [Overdrafts / (debit secured current accounts + secured advances)] ratio.

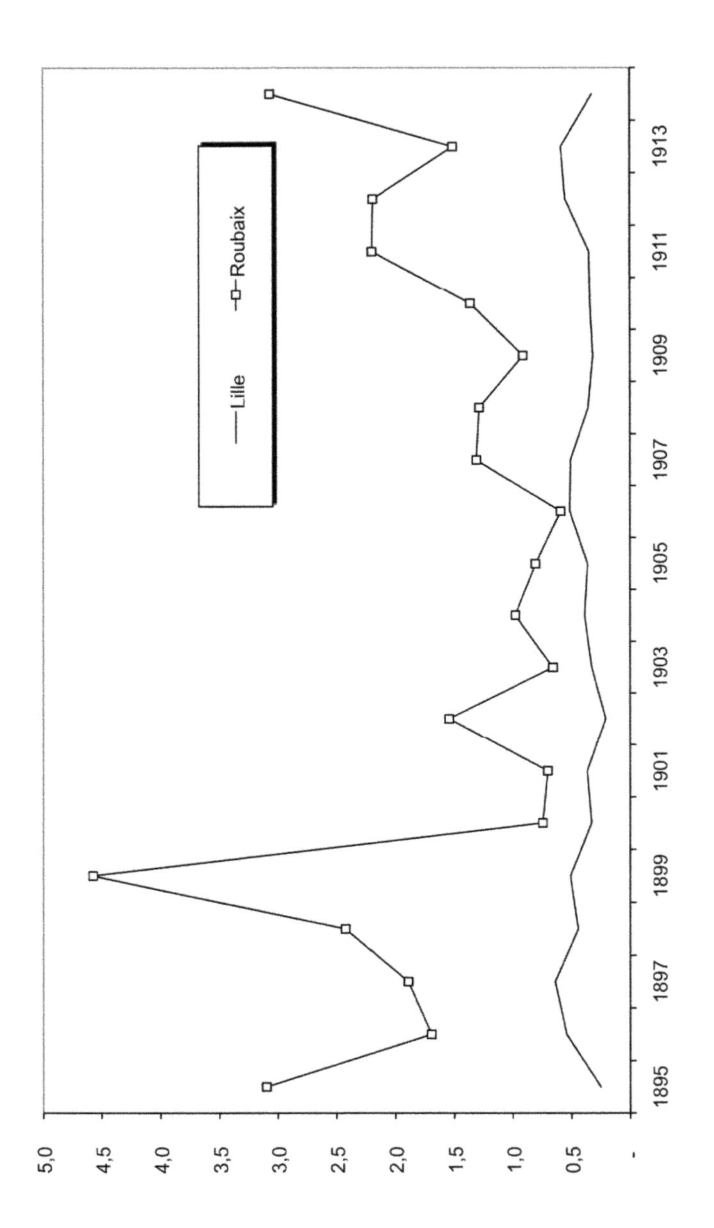

Figure 2.2. Crédit Lyonnais's branches in Lille and Roubaix, 1894–1914: secured advances (millions French francs – MFF).

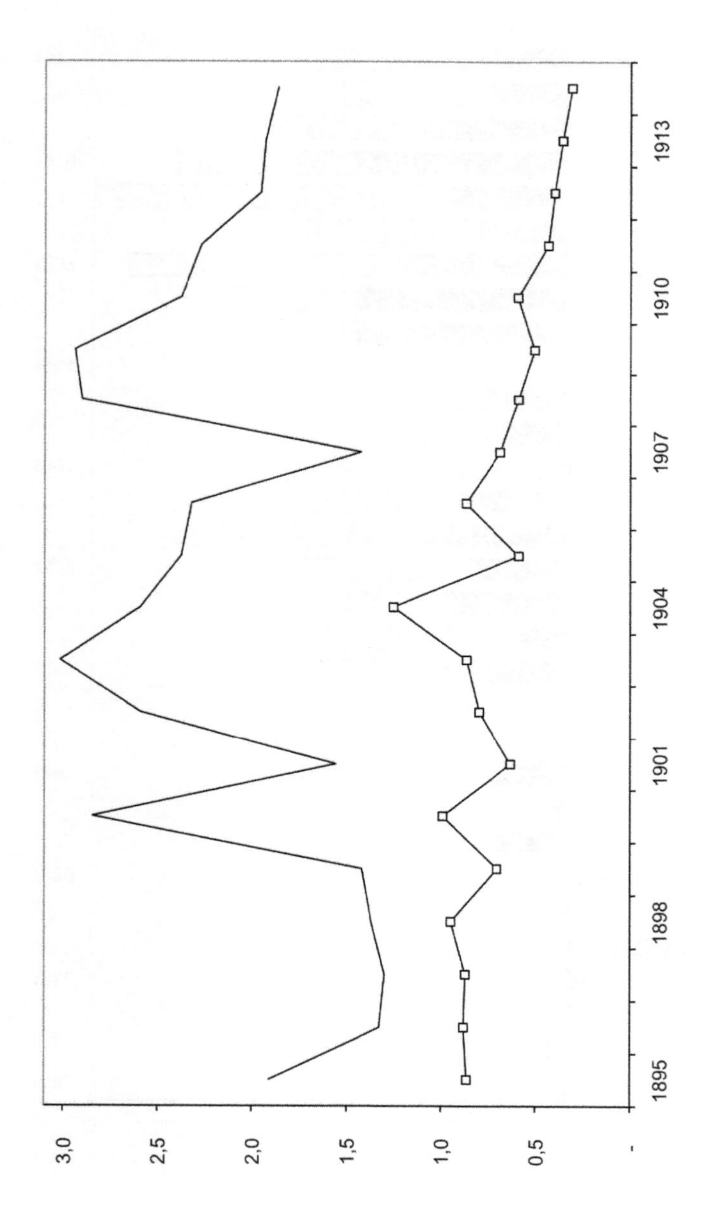

Figure 2.3. Crédit Lyonnais's branches in Lille and Roubaix: [deposits-credits] in MFF, 1883–1914.

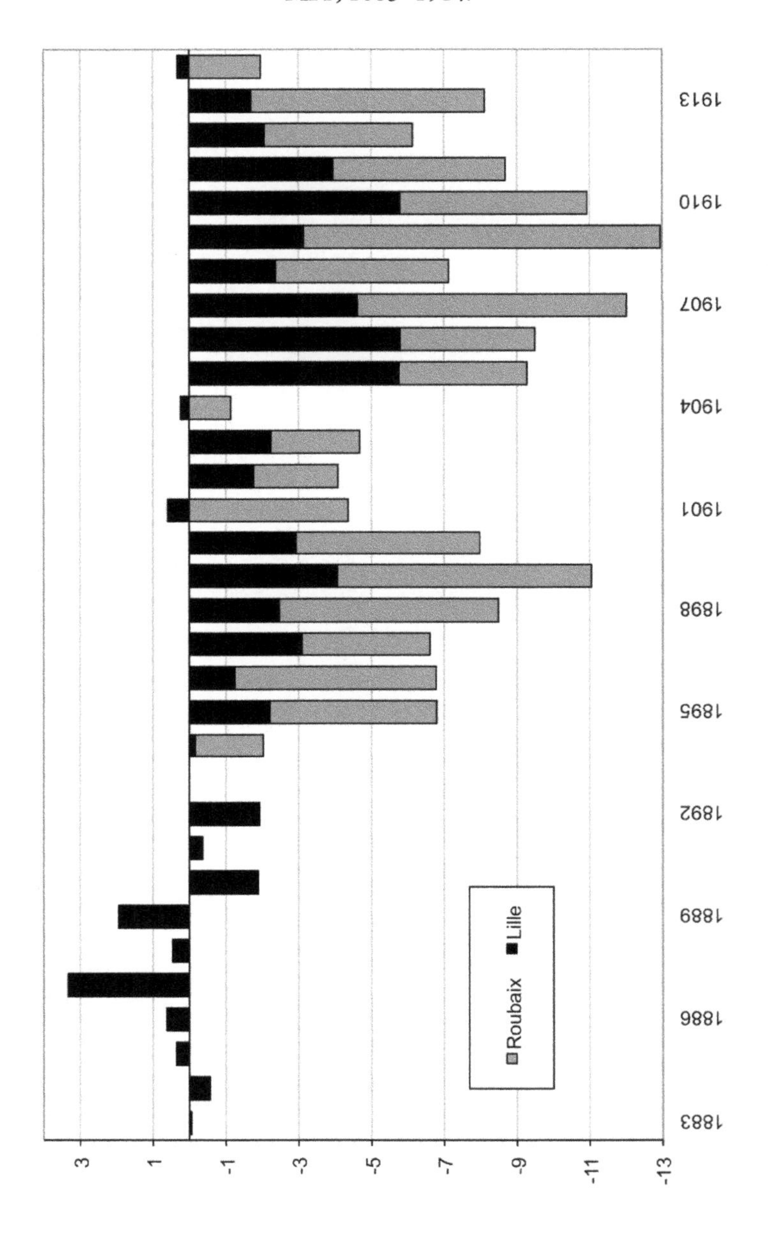

Figure 2.4. Crédit Lyonnais's branches in Lille and Roubaix: [(deposits- credits) / credits] ratio, 1883–1913.

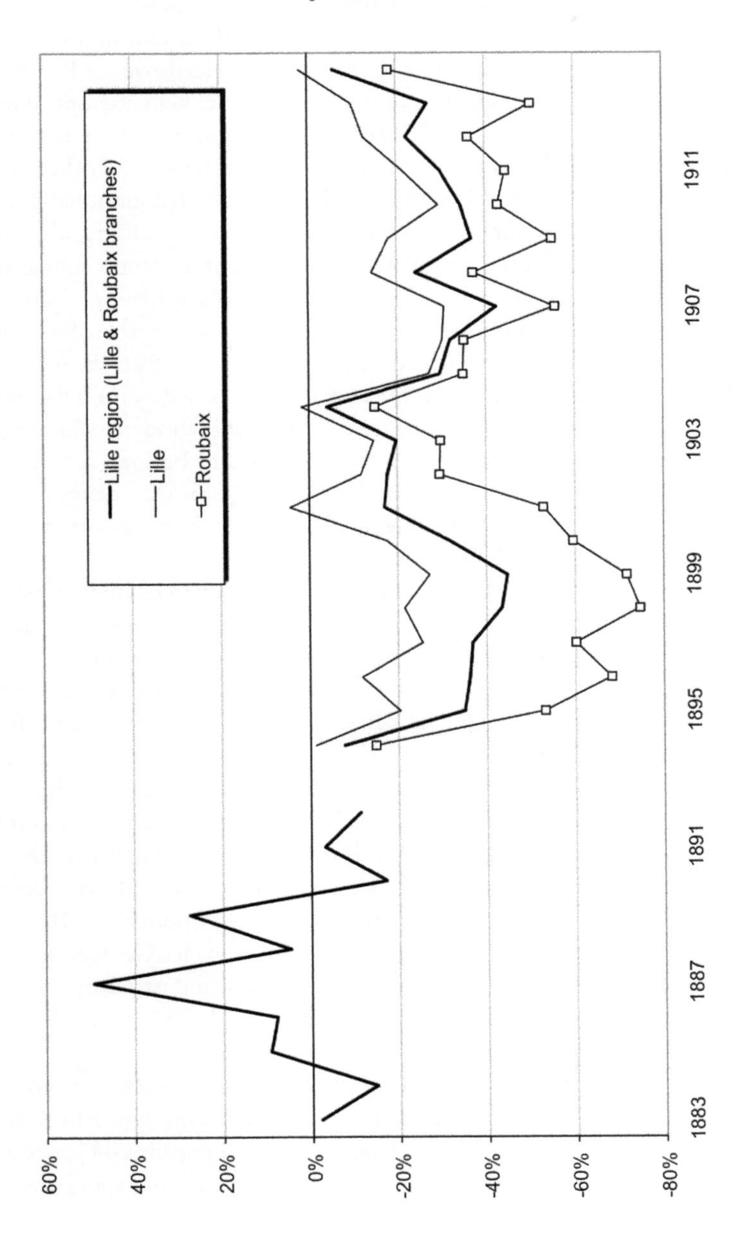

In Paris, the Banque de France started to worry about that situation, and especially about the 'ardour' of the Roubaix manufacturers, about their 'adventurous and entrepreneurial spirit' and they deplored that 'the heads of the financial societies tended to use their employees' signatures with certain flippancy'. But one had to acknowledge rapidly that the crisis of its profits drove the Banque de France to impotence: it would be 'undoubtedly very tricky' to attempt to react against these local habits; and, unable 'to change this trend' or 'to limit the extension' of certain abuses, the Banque could not but adapt to the local rules. At the same time, the headquarters acknowledged that the risks were minimal in view of the securities presented: impressive wealth of the parties involved and of their spouses; matrimonial alliances carefully selected; force of the family solidarities; strong meaning of the commercial honour. The marketplace thereby imposed its usages to the Banque de France, led to compromise with its own terms. Said terms even went through an awkward local deformation: thus, in 1891, the inspector of the Roubaix branch remarked that the finance paper issued by the Tiberghien Frères firm (an integrated company specialised in wool fabric manufacture, in Tourcoing) with a view to purchasing wool, 'refers to true business activities', as if it were an authentically commercial bill! It is true that the direct endorser was 'the largest establishment in Tourcoing' and its associates, representing 'a ten-million wealth at least', were 'of perfect report'.

In a second step (1895–1914), the Banque de France stepped up efforts to turn around the curve of its profits. First, it developed advances on securities (especially in Roubaix, where they were few in number). In accordance with the guidelines of Governor Pallain (1897), it also strengthened its network of bankable marketplaces by creating auxiliary offices in Armentières and Tourcoing (1899). Last it developed direct lending, to compensate for its declining rediscounting function activity. Nevertheless, the growth of direct lending in the Lille region does not result so much from the headquarters guidelines as from initiatives shown by the managers in both local branches, under the variable pressure of the administrators and of the clients: in force since 1869 to meet the demands of the local commerce, it had already seen a first boom in the 1870s. In Roubaix, its development since 1888 resulted from manager Georges Thoyer's solicitude (1884–1909) regarding wool merchants and industrialists, while in Lille, the Pallain guidelines remained a dead letter until 1905 (conversely, those of 1908 and 1909 had visible effects).

Still the weight of the direct endorsers in the amount of presentations progressed, in Roubaix, of 12 per cent in 1894 to 30 per cent approximately in 1895–6, then floated between 20 and 30 per cent, before reaching 48 per cent in 1908, and even 58 per cent in 1911. In Lille, it progressed from approximately 5 per cent in 1905 to 35 per cent in 1908 and to 68 per cent in 1912. Peculiarities to Lille and Roubaix: these proportions are vastly greater than the average of 16.5 per cent calculated by Michel Lescure for the first 14 branches of the Banque de France.[16] But far from democratizing direct lending and opening it up to retailers as wished officially by the headquarters, in the Lille region, the Banque de France sought large bills presented by the most prestigious signatories.[17] Thus in 1911, the average amount of the discounts to direct endorsers was FF 312,000 in Roubaix (it was in excess of FF 507,000 in 1897) and of FF 444,000 in Lille. Thus, a few firms concentrated the majority of the paper discounted into a small number of bills of enormous amounts. Still, even more than during the previous period, the presentations of these large direct endorsers consisted of financial paper:

Table 2.1. Proportion of financial bills among two-signatures discounted bills at the BDF's branches (per cent of the portfolio, at the precise moment of the inspections of the branches).

	1895	1896	1909	1910	1911	1912	1913
Roubaix	65	91	96	87	85		
Lille				98	62	62	99

In Roubaix, this circulation stemmed for over 80 per cent from only four to five groups[18], among which the Motte-Bossut Fils group, which presented every year a constantly increasing 'family paper'.[19] Sure to be more indispensable to the Banque de France than the other way round, and most of them being administrators or administrators' relatives of the local branches, these large direct endorsers pushed audacity and artifice a little further every year in the form of paper presented. Thus in 1906, Louis Duvillier (a 'capitalist' with an 'approximately FF ten million wealth increasing every day', 'more than thrifty' to top it all; uncle of three 'all millionaire' cotton weavers; consequently classed as 'prime 1', i.e. the highest level, which is exceptional) did not waste any time in looking for an acceptor's signature, and presented single-signature bills, thereby combining drawer and drawee positions on his own person. The inspector then signalled to the headquarters 'this fully exposed, and really difficult to accept, form of a direct loan' in spite of the quality of the endorsements and 'eloquent figures' (fortune).The headquarters then asked the manager 'to reach an agreement with the transferor' at least to comply with the conventional form of commercial bills. Four years later (October 1910), in what will appear as an excess of zeal, the inspector signalled another infringement, which was far more widespread: the Amédée Prouvost & Fils SNC (société en nom collectif) presented a draft on its accountant, endorsed by the manager himself.

Figure 2.5. Banque de France's branch in Lille: percentage of bills payable locally, in Paris, and in other provincial branches, on the total amount of discounted bills, 1848–1913.

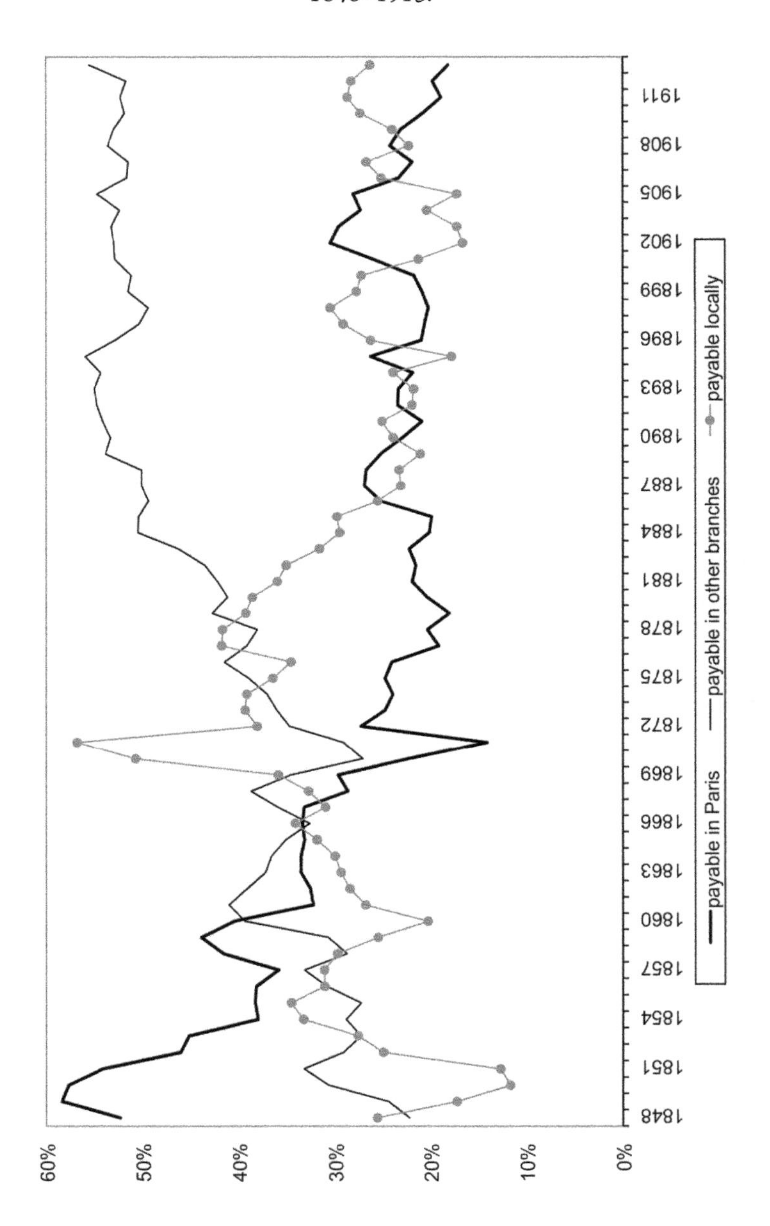

Figure 2.6. Banque de France's branch in Roubaix: percentage of bills payable locally, in Paris, and in other provincial branches, on the total amount of discounted bills, 1872–1913.

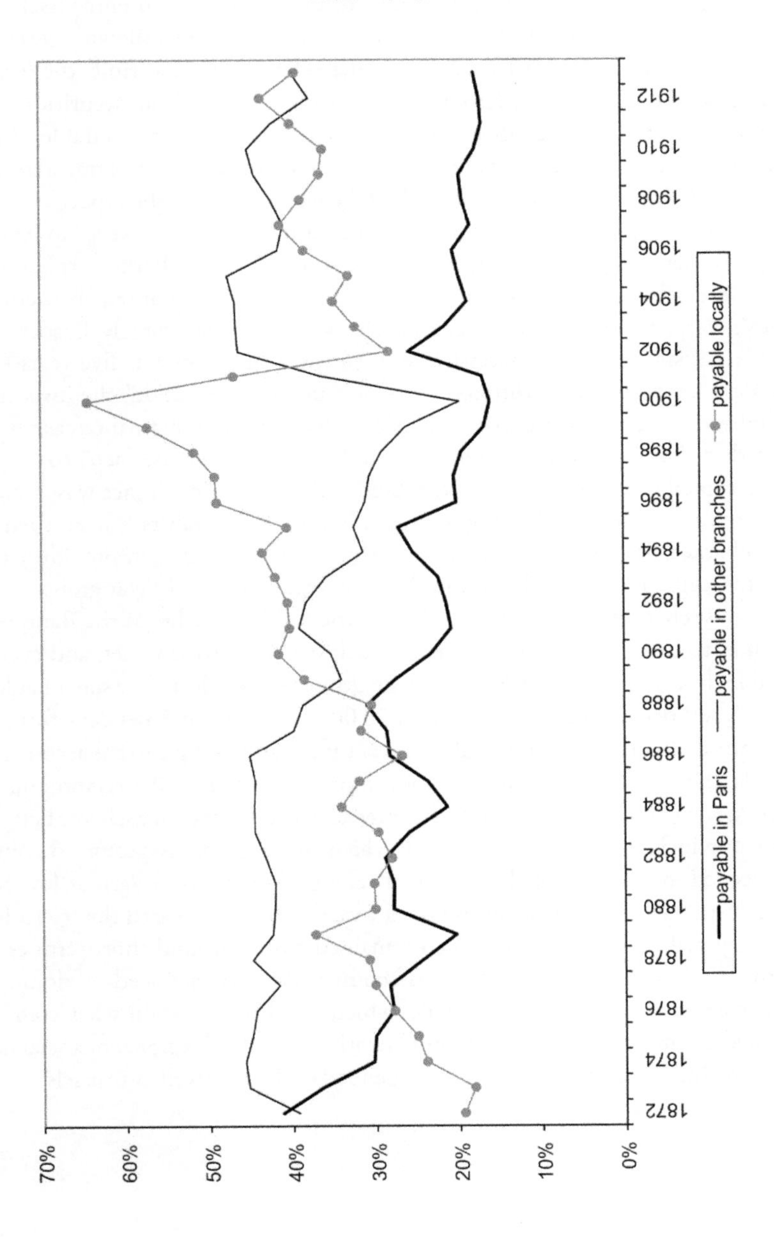

And then went on to say: 'for the sake of regularity, the third signature ought to have been supplied by a person with interests distinct from the transferor's, one of his brothers for example', a curious prescription which showed that, while granting 'disguised advances', the Banque de France clearly contented itself with seemingly compliance with 'regularity', i.e. lending. The following year, the same company committed a second similar offence, but that time, the inspector remembering the transferor's quality, made amends: 'The securities being overabundant, it does not appear necessary to insist with our honourable administrator to obtain a third signature with interests distinct from the transferors, as requested, for the sake of "regularity", by the latest sequel to the report.'

In reality, the Banque de France bothered less and less to keep up lending appearances, and gave up on its own terms. As of 1909 it embarked explicitly on an 'overdrafts' policy, often called 'campaign overdrafts' (granted theoretically for six to nine months), whose seasonal character was in fact largely illusory. And while refusing to see in successive renewals over three, four or five years (and in some cases twelve or thirteen years) a 'true immobilization', the inspection admitted more than once that such 'overdrafts' did not only finance cash flows, but that they had been granted, with full knowledge of the facts, to finance fixed capital investments. Forty years before, the Banque de France was afraid of becoming the indirect sleeping partner of textile industrialists;[20] from then on, it embarked on a direct limited partnership. In reality, far from providing productive capital only (fixed or rolling) to the large textile and sugar groups in the region, such 'overdrafts' also served, with the full knowledge of the Banque de France, to fund financial investments, stock speculations, dowries, and even to enable the associates of the Motte-Bossut group to earn the paltry sum of at least FF 12,000 per annum, by paying FF 600,000 borrowed at 3 per cent from the Banque de France, to their social 5 per cent interest-bearing current accounts.

At the end of the day, the relationships between the Lille region and the Banque de France reflect perfectly the reversal of the dependence scheme between that provincial marketplace and Paris, which the large family groups in control succeeded in setting. But that influx of capitals drained from Paris at low cost, which strengthened the profusion on the marketplace, increased the sclerosis of the regional banking system, which remained frozen around short-term credit forms, i.e. based on the exclusive satisfaction of the financial needs of dominant and mature sectors, especially textile, which had become again what could be termed as a merchants' activity. Consequently, the 'public' regional financial market remained small and increasingly depended on Paris as well as Brussels.

A 'Public' Financial Market Increasingly Dependent on Paris and Brussels

The Lille Stock Exchange: a Specialized and Narrow Market

After a dull period in the 1880s, the growth of the stock activity after 1895–1900 turned Lille into one of the three largest provincial stock markets at the beginning of the Twentieth century. According to the tax revenue derived from stock transactions (created in 1893), the department of the Nord progressed from the fourth to the third rank a little before 1900, then, in 1912, to the second rank behind Rhone (Lyon) and ahead of Bouches-du-Rhône (Marseille). From 6.2 per cent of the total tax collected in provinces in 1902, it reached 21.5 per cent in 1912.[21] The growth of the Lille stock exchange also resulted in the increasing number of listed companies,[22] of the volumes of issued shares and listed bonds,[23] and of the average number of quotations per stock market session.[24]

This booming regional stock-exchange activity at the beginning of the twentieth century was essentially the consequence of the impressive multiplication of transactions on colliery stock values (not only in the Nord-Pas-de-Calais), which constituted the specialty of the Lille marketplace: in 1900, they accounted for 32 per cent of the stock values listed in Lille (against more than a half in 1861) but 80 per cent of the stock capitalization and of the dividends paid, and two-thirds of the stocks listed; in 1912, 76 per cent of the stock capitalization and at least 85 per cent of the stocks listed between 1900 and 1910. The stock market activity hence focused on these values more extensively: induced by the growth of the dividends paid by colliery companies, the Lille marketplace raced out of control after 1900 thanks to the generalized subdivisions of their shares into tenths and hundredths, and absorbed the novel flows of their bond issues. And in 1913, the inflow of oil stock values from Central Europe[25] still strengthened the specialization of the Lille marketplace in mine stock values, and conferred a new momentum thereto, for a short while.

Both main other sectors in the list, around 1900, related to the metal industry (Denain-Anzin, but also the steel industry in the Sambre, Lorraine and Ardennes basins: twenty-three stock values in 1900, thirty in 1913). The regional and local banks (five stock values in 1900) accounted for the last important sector. Other important stock values were also present: gas and electricity, railways and tramways, operated in the Nord. In reality, except for banks, most of these stock values were also listed in Paris and in Brussels: Lille was for them only a very second-rate marketplace. After 1900, the diversification of the Lille official list (by the strengthened sector of the metal stock values and the inrush of various stock values: food industries, superstores, real estate companies ...) was illusory to a vast extent.

Figure 2.7. Tax revenue on stock exchange transactions in the first four provincial departments, 1897–1913 (thousand FF).

The stock exchange list on the other hand highlighted the deficiencies in the regional financial market. The stock values of the new technologies operated in the Lille region were totally out of its control. Thus, the major portion of the production and of the distribution of electricity in the Lille region, organized as of 1907 by Parisian (Giros-Loucheur) and Belgian groups (Union des Tramways de Bruxelles), whose securities were listed in Paris and Brussels. Conversely, out of six listed electrical companies, there were (as of November 1912) three branches of mine companies from the Pas-de-Calais (held by the textile capitals of the Lille region).

The pillars of the regional economy also did not appear in the official list, or hardly. In spite of the growing success of the incorporated society[26] in textile after 1895, this sector only included four stock values listed in 1899, and seven in 1914. This sector was dominated by three large Roubaix stock values representing external investments in the Russian Empire: a wool company listed since 1884, the C.G.I.T. (Compagnie Générale des Industries Textiles) member of the Allart group; and two jute spinning-weaving companies of the Motte group, listed in 1910 and 1912.[27] Even more capitalistic sectors such as mineral chemistry, represented by the Lille Kuhlmann firm (one of the national heavyweights in the sector) and the sugar industry, remained steadfastly aloof from the public financial market.

Apart from the mine, considered speculative stock values, the global liquidity of the Lille market was very scarce: exchanges were very few and highly irregular, except for the Crédit du Nord and Denain-Anzin shares, other leading stock values, with the collieries, in the portfolios of the Nord.[28] This scarce liquidity was obviously restricted to the Lille marketplace: P. C. Hautcoeur insisted upon the 'significant competition' entered into by large banks with national agency networks against provincial stock exchanges, 'which compensated for the securities transactions with their clients and centralized their transactions in the Paris stock exchange, causing protests at the beginning of the twentieth century among (provincial) stockbrokers'.[29] Nevertheless, local factors might have been involved. Some of them were associated with overwhelming family capitalism: the poor offer of regional securities, in particular the low proportion of 'floating' capital associated with the particular behaviour of the regional savings. The latter were concentrated into large portfolios consisting mainly of shares and bonds of regional companies controlled by one or several 'grand families', in opposition to the savings in the department of the Bouches-du-Rhône, avoiding shares and seeking fixed revenue investments (bonds and annuities above 80 per cent at the beginning of the twentieth century), and in the Rhône, where portfolios were more balanced, with a slight preference for bonds.[30] The Mines de Lens, the first value in the Lille stock exchange at the beginning of the twentieth century, offer nevertheless a good example of a limited flotation of capital: from 1883 to 1900, the proportion of their shares being transferred by way of sale (and not by way of succession or other), accounted for 3 to 4 per cent of the capital at the very most, and the actions circulated twice as much by conveyance after death. After 1900, although such calculations could not be made any longer, the division into hundredths certainly did not change much, since, on 1 October 1912, the 6,425 registered shareholders (that is to say 7.4 per cent of the shareholders) still hold two thirds of the capital, while the 79,924 holders of bearer securities shared the remainder.

But another reason for this poor market liquidity was the 'poor commercial dynamism' of the brokers' company in Lille, in particular their refusal to organize a forward market for fear of excessive speculation, held responsible for the five bankruptcies among brokers between 1861 and 1892.[31] And even if the prohibition of forward transactions, which had never been popular among the Lille brokers, was not rigorously adhered to,[32] it mostly turned said brokers into *remisiers* for their Parisian counterparts for all forward transactions.[33]

Finally, and especially, asymmetrical information, protected passively by the stockbrokers themselves (simply because they belonged to the 'grand families' who controlled the most important stock values of the Lille Stock Exchange[34]), and which contributed to the preservation of these stock values in the portfolios of the Nord, renders the intervention of foreign operators more difficult, and hence the opening-up of the market. Still, as of 1901, further to the prolonged drop in their securities (associated with the wool crisis in 1900), numerous colliery companies of the Nord and of the Pas-de-Calais, on the brink of large bond issues, then blamed the Lille market for its 'sometimes excessive, narrow-mindedness', responsible for the under-capitalization of their stocks (in view of the expected effects of their policy of growing dividends and of the share subdivisions) and then, one by one, asked for official listing in Paris. Bitter to note what was a break in market solidarity to them, the stockbrokers then attempted to talk them out of their project:

> A great disadvantage would result for the Compagnies from being listed officially in Paris, it would mean forced publicity for the companies' accounts, the discussion of their reports in all financial papers, sometimes with a dose of malevolence or passion. We believe that the Compagnies had no grounds for complaining about the relative silence observed by the press regarding their situations as long as they were in Lille only where the public gleans inquiries from other sources than newspaper columns; but once they are listed in Paris, they will not be able to prevent the publication of their profits currently recorded and of their annual reports, the discussion in certain, forewarned or ill-willed articles, of the legitimacy of the profits thus exposed, thereby constituting new weapons or new pretexts for rabble-rousers and Compagnies' foes. Needless to dwell on this score; we know that the shortcomings of too large publicity have been tabled in shareholders' meetings of certain of our Compagnies, and we understand the political, economic and social reasons thereof perfectly.[35]

Nothing helped, since two-thirds of the coalmining companies had kept the hybrid status of non-trading joint-stock companies which dispensed them from publishing their accounts. In total, in 1913, the Lille Stock Exchange lost exclusivity for ten collieries of the Nord Pas-de-Calais out of the listed stocks, i.e. 37 per cent of their total number. It had no exclusivity or no any longer for fourteen stock values (out of a total of thirty), that is to say 46.7 per cent of the total number of the category. After the War, the oil stock values listed in Lille followed the same path.

The Banking Market under the Increasing Grip of Paris and Brussels

The banking market is not known as well, since the sources are limited. On the primary market, the regional banks, rejecting immobilizations (to which they preferred personal participations of their managers or administrators), seemed, according to the works conducted by Pierre Pouchain on the Crédit du Nord,[36] to prefer over-the-counter loans to firm underwritings. At least when they operated on their own, since according to J. Laloux, they would not hesitate to constitute 'pools ... with the agencies of the national banks in order to secure issues'.[37] And within the framework of their being affiliated to the Union of Provincial Banks (created in 1885), the CIC[38] transferred to them a portion of the issues in which they participated, thereby disposing of a portion of the securities issued in the province, and conversely, the CIC supported them in investing into regional stock values, whereof a portion may be invested in Paris.

The relationships between the regional banks and the national banks are, admittedly, ambivalent: as soon as it set up business in Lille in 1881, the Credit Lyonnais embarked on a fierce competition in the securities services, especially in stock exchange orders. But, after 1900, the regional banks became associated with national banks (Crédit Lyonnais, Société Générale) for selling bonds issued for coalmining companies. Conversely, in large metal companies (with most companies operating in the Nord funded by Belgian capitals), the influence of the Parisian establishments was undermined by the Belgian banks properly speaking (Société Générale de Belgique and its French branches), and the Crédit du Nord regained, via its Belgian branch founded in 1896, a significant rank among underwriting syndicates.[39]

The 1880s, and the beginning of the twentieth century, saw the proliferation of small local financial establishments indistinctly offering 'banking, stock exchange and stock broking operations', and more especially commission-based purchase and sale of securities (very seldom for their own account), a quarter of which approximately were, at the beginning of the twentieth century, agencies for Parisian and Brusselian financial establishments. They were not sufficiently numerous to engage into financing new industries, and, through lack of support by the 'grand families' who controlled the regional economy, they remained in a weak position. This absence of powerful local financial establishments favoured the increasing grip of the Parisian and foreign finance (Anglo-American and from Antwerp) at the beginning of the twentieth century.

Still, the overabundance of capitals on the marketplace was then illustrated by increasing exports of regional capitals, which, especially as of 1907, stepped across the border massively: transiting over accounts opened in the Belgian agencies of Joire and of Verley, Decroix & Cie, and in the Belgian branch of the Crédit du Nord, they were invested in stock values listed in Brussels, which, as a whole, reflected the predilection of regional capitals for investments into mining values.

But as of 1911, Lille emerged as an inescapable financial marketplace for oil-related business in France: from June 1911 to June 1914, four groups were constituted, by the creation of eighteen oil societies operating in Galicia (Austro-Hungarian Empire) and in Rumania, around the sole three major banks in the marketplace (Clairin & Cie, Banque du Nord et des Flandres, Consortium du Nord).

Conclusion

On the eve of war, the grip of the 'grand textile families' on the financial system of the Lille region was characterized by its sclerosis: by resisting the standards of the Parisian banking institutions, including the Banque de France, they forced them to give in to their requirements. While maintaining a dual financial market, with powerful private circuits, limited to older industries (especially textiles), and a narrow public financial market, specialized in mining stock values, and moreover not very accessible due to ongoing strong asymmetrical information, they hardly promoted local financing of the new industries.

This sclerosis, which essentially benefited the textile groups, seemed to be the fruit of conservative collective strategies expressed, in private, at the beginning of the twentieth century: the reasserted choice of the specialization (textile), the single way enabling to acquire 'a true superiority', was then justified by the will to preserve deep-rooted positions ('not to ruin the achievements of the past'), which also meant, at a time when social struggles became harsher, the will to preserve social control over a whole region. For that matter, the Lille financial marketplace bear witness that convergence is a power-related phenomenon.

3 COMPETITION AMONG THE FRENCH STOCK EXCHANGES DURING THE SECOND WORLD WAR

Kim Oosterlinck
Angelo Riva

Introduction

Relationships between stock exchanges have gained a renewed interest in view of both the mergers (and merger attempts) of the last two decades,[1] and the Mifid Directive in the European Union framework. According to theory the economies of scope and scale, as well as the positive externalities, should push towards concentration of both trading and listing in a unique exchange, which amounts to a form of institutional convergence. In practice however, several stock exchanges coexist and there thus seems to be a 'network externalities puzzle': why isn't there just one market? Several explanations have been suggested to address this puzzle. Informational frictions could stop concentration because traders in a distant exchange cannot obtain (low-cost) information about issuers located near the rival exchange. Within this framework, informational frictions are a decreasing function of both improving information technologies and the growing size of the issuers. Moreover, organizational heterogeneity could explain the resilience of a multi-polar stock-exchange industry. According to this literature, traders and issuers choose the venues matching their heterogeneous preferences. In an integrated zone, similar exchanges should however be viewed as a waste of resources.

The modern literature is usually unaware of historical episodes of competition.[2] Even though stock exchanges did not face as much competition in the past as nowadays, historical evidence suggests that competition has existed for a long time. One question is whether competition implies convergence, either on norms or on efficiency, as many theories state. For example, the French and German stock exchanges were competing to float Russian bonds in the 1880's.[3] In France, Hautcoeur and Riva explore the 'coopetitive' dynamics between the *Coulisse* (the Curn of Paris) and the *Parquet* (the official market) during the nineteenth century.[4] For the US, Brown *et al.* show that between 1885 and 1925 the Consolidated Exchange was a major actor, at some times beating the NYSE in terms of volume of trades.[5] Eventually, White explores the competition between the NYSE and the Consolidated and regional exchanges for the period 1900–33.[6]

In the early 1930s seven provincial stock exchanges existed on French soil. Most provincial exchanges followed a similar pattern during the interwar period. First, a sharp increase in trade during the 1920s and the early 1930s, then a dramatic decline in activity after 1933. Obviously one may wonder whether this decline was specific to regional exchanges or affected also the Paris Bourse. Dubost[7] provides data on the taxes paid on stock market trades for the years 1927 to 1937; a proxy to describe the activity on the market. Their evolution suggests that the Paris Bourse was severely hit in 1929–30, experienced an all time low in 1932 from which it had already partially recovered by 1937. The crisis strongly affected the Parisian market but since its activity was so much higher than on provincial exchanges, it never threatened its existence.

The regional stock exchanges were in direct rivalry with the Paris bourse. At the end of the 1930s, local stock exchanges were blaming their reduced activity on this competition.[8] In some cases, trades had been reduced to such an extent that contemporaneous commentators described provincial markets as moribund. Their mere survival was seriously questioned even for some of the largest such as Lyon. In view of these elements, it seems surprising that the merger of provincial stock exchanges would only happen in 1991. This chapter suggests that the Second World War and the regulations set into place under the occupation favoured provincial stock exchanges and brought many benefits to the ones located in the so-called Free Zone. Since policies differed between the two zones, competition between stock markets was seriously altered by the war. Furthermore, the racist laws imposed by the occupier had a much more dramatic impact on the *Coulisse*, which experienced a drastic reorganization during the war. We argue that this reorganization helped pave the way to the absorption of the *Coulisse* by the *Parquet* in 1961.

The chapter proceeds as follows. Section 2 presents the organizational changes that occurred during the war. Section 3 analyzes the long-term impact of these measures on basis of quantitative and qualitative evidence. Section 4 concludes.

Reopening the Markets after the Occupation

The quick victories of April–June 1940 let the Nazis in charge of a huge part of Western Europe. New laws were soon promulgated in all occupied countries. The ruling authorities imposed a series of market-specific restrictions which completely changed the pre-war equilibrium. Reopening authorization differed from one market to another. Meanwhile, the economics of occupation, and notably its financing, created a favourable environment for the French bourses. Indeed, the successive French finance ministers followed a policy they labelled the 'politique du circuit'. Occupation costs were covered by issuing money which had to be eventually redirected towards (and sterilized thanks to) state bonds. In their view, this all amounted to a circuit: print money to pay occupation costs, let Germany spend the money in France and then 'convince' French holders of money to buy state bonds. In order to be successful, this policy required functioning exchanges and rules that rendered alternative investment opportunities uninteresting. Taxation, price caps on equities and registration were used extensively.[9]

Since no consensus regarding the economic exploitation of the countries under their control existed amongst Nazi rulers it is no wonder that regulations regarding stock exchanges differed from one country to the other. The French case would be especially complicated because of the partition of the country imposed by the Armistice. France lost part of its territory to Italy, the area surrounding Lille fell under the control of the German administration located in Brussels, Alsace-Lorraine came under direct German control, whereas the remainder of France became partitioned into a 'free' and an 'occupied' zone.

In view of the German advances, most provincial stock exchanges had closed by June 1940, following the example given by the Paris Bourse on the 10th.[10] When the seat of the French government moved to Bordeaux, the volumes traded there experienced a dramatic increase. During the time that Paris remained closed, trade volumes had been multiplied by fifteen.[11] Following the fall of Bordeaux, trades moved to Marseille. Soon the Toulouse stock exchange reopened, whereas the Lyon Bourse, which had been closed because of the German occupation, resumed its trade as soon as the German troops left the city. Contemporaneous accounts provide diverging stories as to the exact closing and reopening dates. Table 3.1 provides these on basis of both archival evidence and secondary sources.

Since the bourses located in the free zone (Lyon, Marseille and Toulouse) were subject to French law, their reopening was quickly agreed upon. Minor changes were enacted: only the spot market was allowed to resume and trading methods were altered by the introduction of reduced demand and supply orders. Eventually, while sales of foreign securities remained the same, buying was subject to a strict control.[12] However, arbitrages between 'free' and 'occupied' bourse disappeared and large price discrepancies became frequent.

Table 3.1. Stock exchange closing and reopening dates.

	Closing date	Reopening date
Bordeaux	October 10, 1940	May 15, 1941
Lille	June 1940	June 4, 1941
Lyon	June 17, 1940	July 16, 1940
Marseille	Never closed	Never closed
Nancy	June 1940	Remained closed
Nantes	June 1940	June 18, 1941
Paris Parquet	June 10, 1940	o October 14, 1940[13] for bonds o March 19, 1941 for shares from companies active in metropolitan France o September 8, 1941: all French shares readmitted
Paris Coulisse	May 1940	October 1942
Toulouse	Never closed (?)	Never closed (?)

Sources: ACACL, ACACM, ACACP, AN, Guillorit (1946).

Fleeing the Germans, the members of the Paris bourse had started to move their activities to the South and transferred securities to Châtel-Guyon. The unexpected rapidity of the Armistice signature caught the Agents de change while moving. Many of them chose to return to Paris to start lobbying for the stock exchange reopening. Meanwhile the German occupation forces had imposed a series of measures related to the stock exchange's activities: securities denominated in a foreign currency had to be deposited and declared to the *Devisenschutzkommando* and all safes located in banks were to be blocked.

After long debates, the German occupant allowed resumption of trades but only for a limited number of securities: French rentes (with as exceptions, the 4 per cent, 1925 and the 4.5 per cent, 1937 rentes and French bonds issued in the US), French treasury bills and bonds as well as various corporate bonds. For the Parisian brokers this new regulation represented a first step in the desired direction but certainly not the ultimate goal. During the following months, complaints regarding the privileged position enjoyed by the Lyon stock exchange were voiced. However, brokers would have to wait for the implementation of new laws regarding trades to see the ban on shares trades lifted on 19 March 1941.

The provincial stock exchanges located in the occupied zone suffered from the same restrictions as the Parisian market. However, while there were rational reasons to reopen the Parisian bourse because of its size and activity, few provincial markets could make a similar claim. Their reopening became conditional on the reopening of the Paris Bourse. By July 1944, six provincial stock exchanges had reopened: Lille, Nantes Bordeaux, Lyon, Marseille and Toulouse.[14] Nancy remained close up till the end of the war despite numerous attempts made by its Syndic (Head of the Bourse) to resume trading.[15]

Even though stock markets were all subject to the same laws, a *de facto* segmentation of French stock exchanges existed. For the bourses located in the occupied zone, the agreement of the German occupation forces was requested in all matters. The implementation of the laws was thus followed there by the representatives of both the Vichy and the German government. In the free zone, the Syndics only had to cope with the Vichy government, which was more open to discussion. Besides the different reading of the laws, markets also became more isolated because of communication issues: depending on the periods, communications could either be almost normal or totally inexistent. Furthermore the demarcation line prevented any transfer of securities from one zone to the other. Trades were somewhat hampered in Paris since many securities had been transferred to Châtel-Guyon in June 1940. These securities would only come back to Paris in 1943, after the Germans invaded the free zone. Refugees fleeing the German advance had also brought their securities with them. Most of them left these securities in the Vichy zone because no declaration was required there.[16] Even between stock exchanges located on the same side of the demarcation line, arbitrages were limited because of the insurance costs the brokers would have had to pay to transfer securities. Stock exchanges in the occupied zones were only allowed to trade some of their pre-war securities whereas the free-zone ones had kept all their pre-war privileges. Eventually, the changes in reopening dates led to the creation of temporary monopolies on some securities.

Competition and Changes in Stock Exchanges' Organization

The economic and legal environment in which the French stock exchanges were operating during the war created a segmented market and brought to a halt the concentration pattern observed before the war. Several measures may be used to determine the impact of this new environment on the stock exchanges' activities. To assess the decrease or increase in terms of competition, a common measure is to examine the changes in levels of bid/ask spreads[17]. Since French bourses were operating with order books this is hardly feasible. An alternative is to measure the evolution of the differences existing for cross-listed securities. Another option is to determine the relative share of each stock market in terms of volume: if the war led some bourses to benefit from privileged positions, then it is reasonable to assume that their market share should increase. A third way to compare the relative position of each exchange is to examine the number of listed companies and the number and size of IPOs or SEOs.

Due to data limitation, this essay focuses on changes in volume. Volumes are only directly recorded for Marseille (from 1936 to 1946) and Lyon (from 1938 to 1942). These volumes are reported in Table 3.2.

As shown in Table 3.2, both Marseille and Lyon experienced a huge increase in activity after 1939. Starting from a meager volume of 100 million FF a year in 1938, the Lyon Stock Exchange reached a 35 billion FF volume in 1941. After 1942 volumes decreased, probably as a consequence of two effects: an increase in competition with Paris (following the invasion of the free zone by the Germans and the reopening of the Coulisse) and a reduction in trades due to the limited number of investors willing to sell.

Table 3.2. Volumes of spot transaction in Lyon and Marseille (1936-1946), in 1 000 FF.

Date	Lyon	Marseille
1936		230 294
1937		266 872
1938	100 000	221 650
1939	130 000[18]	279 029
1940	19 500 000[19]	1 556 329
1941	35 000 000	17 989 654
1942	28 600 000[20]	21 795 930
1943		17 137 822
1944	16 900 000[21]	11 375 309
1945		10 170 900
1946		9 669 874

Sources: ACACL, AN and ACACM;

In view of the incompleteness of direct records of volume, proxies of volumes, based on archival data, have had to be computed for Paris, Lyon and Marseille. Two sorts of proxies could be considered: the fiscal revenues from the trade taxes (*impôt sur opérations de bourse*) or the revenues from the 'internal' stamp tax on turnover (*timbres syndicaux*). The second proxy has been chosen because it was the one used at the time by the brokers themselves to gauge the activity on the market and therefore probably the most reliable. Table 3.3 reports the revenues of the internal stamp tax on turnover for the three markets. Even though these stamps were not exactly collected in a similar way in all exchanges, we consider them as comparable to get a first approximation of the changes in each stock exchange's market share.

Figure 3.1 provides the respective market share of each exchange (not taking into account the other provincial exchanges and the Coulisse). The figures for each exchange are thus upper bounds. Figure 3.1 clearly shows that before the war outbreak the French financial markets were completely under the domination of Paris. Marseille and Lyon barely accounted for a couple of percentage points up till 1939. Following the occupation, the importance of the provincial bourses started to increase. By 1940, they had a combined market share of close to 12 per cent, which increased to more than 50 per cent in 1941. Once the Germans invaded the free zone and reopened the *Coulisse*, the trends started to reverse and both Lyon and Marseille saw a decline in their relative importance. By 1944, their joint shares had fallen to 20 per cent and would fall further to 11 per cent two years later.

Table 3.3. Revenues from internal stamps for Lyon, Marseille and Paris (1936–1946), in 1 000 FF.

Date	Lyon	Marseille	Paris Parquet	Paris Coulisse
1936	224	100	10 908	
1937	387	145	21 657	
1938	314	115	17 237	
1939	278	156	16 261	
1940	361	167	7 652	NA
1941	7 300	2 965	8 589	NA
1942	8 048	3 451	15 781	343 (2 months)
1943	8 432	2 965	21 278	2 657
1944	3 565	1 988	22 254	2 228
1945	3 582	1 525	27 584	3 545
1946	4 829	2 955	66 859	12 694

Sources: ACACL, ACACP and ACACM.

For the other bourses, the analysis mainly relies on reports issued during the war. The volumes of trades for these bourses are less complete and allow us only to provide an impressionistic view. The bourses located in the occupied zones seem to have suffered the most as their reopening was conditional on the reopening of the Paris bourse. This meant that they could not benefit from a 'first-reopened' advantage as had been the case for the 'free-zone' bourses. Furthermore, this also implied that they would immediately face stiff competition from Paris. Lille reopened in June 1941 but trades would remain limited. For June–July 1941, they amounted to approximately 5.35 to 6.8 million FF a week but the investors from Lille were starting to sell their local securities to buy national ones which were perceived as less risky,[23] a situation that tended to favour portfolio diversification.[24] The Nantes stock exchange seems to have done reasonably well up till February 1943. At that time, and according to contemporaneous sources, the activity was almost non-existent.[25] Bordeaux was the most successful of the provincial bourses located in the occupied zone. However, the volumes traded there never came close to matching those in Paris or Lyon.

Figure 3.1. Respective market shares of Paris, Lyon and Marseille.[22]

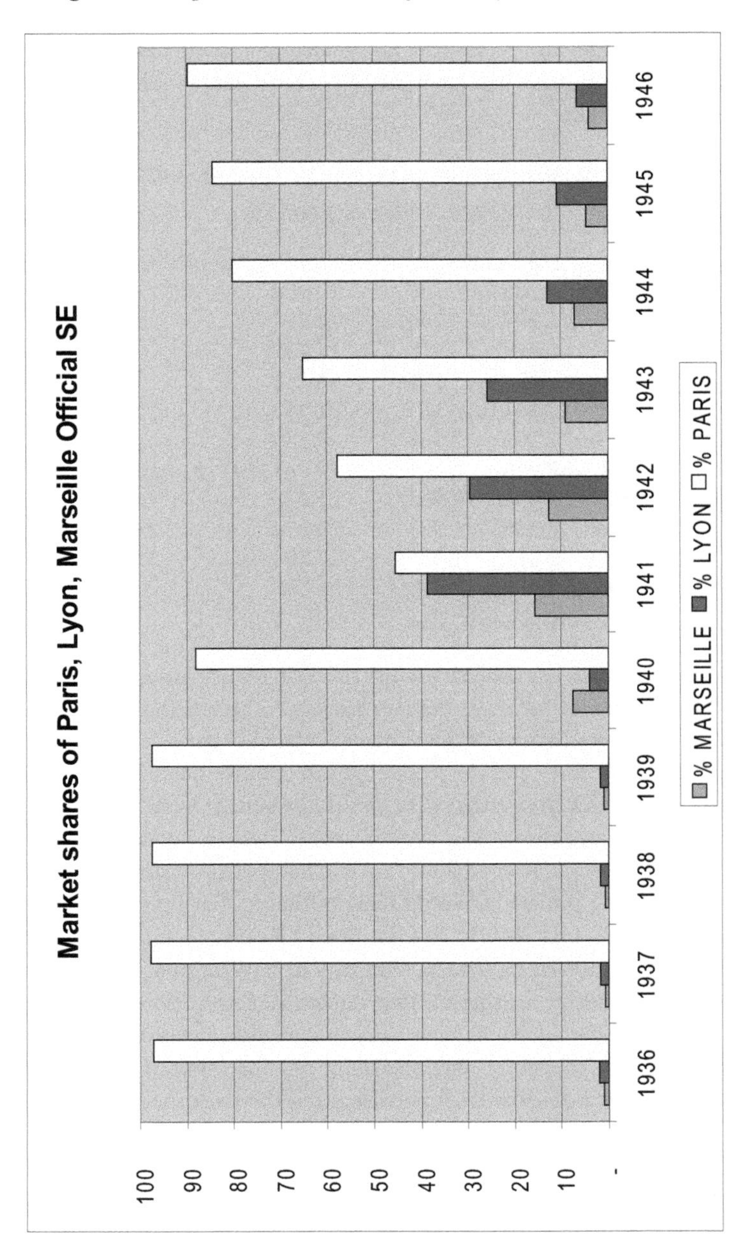

Sources: ACACL, ACACP and ACACM

Organizational Changes

During the war, major organizational changes were imposed by a series of laws that reframed the whole governance structure of the exchanges. Besides these main legislative innovations, other organizational changes, mostly local in nature, were also implemented at the initiative of the stock exchanges.

Comité des Bourses de Valeurs

The ideological views of the occupant inclined it to favour corporatist structures. The banking and financial sectors were considered to be so close that they were to belong to the same structure: the *Comité d'organisation professionnelle des banques, des établissements et entreprises financiers,*[26] which was created by a law passed on June 13, 1941. The fate of the stock exchanges was thus closely intertwined with the banks' future. Despite the seemingly equal status of bankers and brokers, the law provided that brokers would be subordinated to bankers. This was of course hard to swallow for the agents de change. Following protracted discussions between brokers, bankers and the Ministry of Finance, a consensus would be reached at the end of 1941[27]: a new organisation named '*Comité des bourses de valeurs*'[28] (CBV) would represent the brokers' interests.

By law, the CBV would extend its authority on all brokers, including *Coulisse* brokers, and on whoever, company or individual, acted as financial intermediary.[29] The constitution of the CBV was also clearly defined: its president would be the Governor of the Banque de France,[30] the Syndic of the Paris Bourse would act as its vice-president, and two more members, belonging respectively to the banking sector and the French bondholders' association, would be designated by the French finance Minister. For matters concerning them, the Minister of Finance could designate one representative of the brokers active in provincial bourses and one for the *Coulisse* brokers. The first representative of the provincial brokers would be the Syndic of Lyon.[31] The government had a dominant say in this new structure since the Finance Minister nominated most of the persons admitted to the meetings. Furthermore, the state could always make appeal to any decision and force a new meeting within four days.

The competences of the CBV were very broad: it was meant to resolve any matter pertaining to the overall organization of the stock exchanges; it was the ultimate instance resolving eventual conflict between official brokers and *Coulisse* brokers; it was entitled to suggest legislative changes regarding the exchanges or the organization of trades and could, if asked by the Minister, provide advices regarding the market rules[32].

Brokers' New Legal Status

In most cities where a stock exchange existed, parts of the trades were actually handled outside the main market (Parquet). New regulations did forbid trading outside organized (and then supervised) exchanges: every kind of free market was then prohibited. In Paris a longstanding hatred opposed the Parquet and the *Coulisse*.[33] The latter had many reasons to fear the occupant since most of its trades (60 per cent)[34] were forward trades accused to foster speculation, its economic significance was of lesser importance and many *Coulisse* brokers were Jews. The *Coulisse* was severely hit by the racial laws as out of ninety-four curb houses, thirty-three were run by Jews[35] whereas only four out of seventy agents de change were considered to be Jews[36].

Coulisse brokers in Paris lobbied as soon as the Armistice was signed to be allowed to reopen. In view of its specificities, the reopening of the *Coulisse* was not viewed as a priority by the occupying forces. Soon, the *Coulisse* brokers became accused of fuelling the black market.[37] This accusation forced the legislator to intervene. A law passed on 14 February 1942 made the coulissiers' legal status very similar to the official brokers'. Renamed '*courtiers en valeurs mobilières*',[38] their number would be limited to forty.[39] They would list securities that were not listed on the Parquet, but the Parquet was entitled to ask to remove any stock from the curb to add it to its own lists.[40] An additional law passed on 3 August 1942, provided that they would be allowed to trade securities that were neither listed on the Parquet nor on the *Coulisse*.

In practice the new legislation would only be effective in Paris since the provincial stock exchanges successfully lobbied the government to prevent the creation of any '*courtiers en valeurs mobilières*' in the provinces.[41] Despite this measure, the provincial exchanges would suffer from the competition of the Parisian curb. Its brokers added to their lists securities which were not traded on the Paris Parquet but well on provincial ones. Despite the provincial brokers' protests at the end of 1943 no solution had been devised. The reorganization of the profession was kept after the war. Guillorit, at the time working for the Banque de France, viewed this measure as one of the main success of the legislator.[42]

Lyon

As soon as it reopened, on 16 July 1940, the Lyon Bourse experienced a dramatic increase in traded volumes thanks to the huge deposits of securities which had fled to 'free' France and the closing of the Paris Exchange. The order flows from regional state-linked financial institutions, which were previously centralized in Paris but took refuge near Lyon, were now redirected toward the Lyon Bourse. Even though the Lyon Stock Exchange was only allowed to handle spot transactions, it benefited from an appreciated privilege: trades on all kinds of securities were still permitted.

The Lyon brokers' association was 'forced' to reorganize its market to accommodate all the securities that were previously listed in Paris. The Paris stock exchange remaining closed, the Lyon Bourse became almost overnight the biggest French stock exchange.[43] According to the Syndic, the listing of the Parisian securities represented both a national duty and a huge opportunity. More precisely, this provided a chance to revive the activity on the market to such an extent that it would remain once the division into two zones would disappear.[44] At the end of 1940, reviewing the past year and the privileged situation of its stock exchange the Syndic could only view the future with optimism: thanks to the war, 'a new life was about to start at the Lyon Bourse'![45]

The actions of the stock-exchange committee from the end of 1940 on would be directed towards one objective: manage to find a way to maintain the activity on the stock exchange even if the demarcation line was to be suppressed. The means employed would come into two forms: a lobbying action and an internal reorganization.

Lobbying actions started as early as 1940. The geographical proximity existing between Vichy and Lyon and the fact that Lyon was by all accounts 'Free' France's first stock exchange certainly helped. The Syndic made regular visits to Vichy and suggested that the regime's new decentralizing policy be applied to stock markets. The headquarters' localization of a given company would determine on which regional stock exchange its shares had to be listed and regional order flows would have to be directed towards local exchanges and only if necessary forwarded to the appropriate market if the requested securities were not listed there.

In order to get a favourable ear in Vichy, the Lyon bourse decided to set into place regulations which would please the government and this even before they were required to do so. Knowing that the Vichy government was opposed to sharp rises in equity prices because of the *politique du circuit*,[46] the stock exchange committee decided, at the end of 1940, that daily price increases would no more be limited to 10 per cent but to 5 per cent.[47] To further please the government, the Lyon bourse decided to regulate more strictly the market for unlisted securities ('*marché hors cote*'), where illegal practices were more likely to happen. These proactive actions brought them immediate rewards. First, the Lyon Bourse was entitled to become correspondent of the Crédit National,[48] which favoured it for new issues from this institution. Soon after, this privilege was extended to other public companies but also to State bonds. Furthermore, the Lyon Bourse obtained almost a monopoly on the orders from 'Free' France public financial institutions. Last, but not least, the Lyon bourse managed to have a branch of the Caisse centrale des dépôts et virements de titres (CCDVT) created in Lyon, eliminating delays and risk in the delivery system.[49]

Besides lobbying actions, the stock exchange committee worked hard to improve customer satisfaction and the competitiveness of the exchange. The Syndic urged the brokers to speed the delivery process and to perfection the brokerages services. The stock exchange committee created a new structure, the '*Service des rachats officiels*', whose role was to ensure punctuality in terms of settlement. Most notably it forced unable (or unwilling) brokers to execute their part of a deal. This new procedure helped reduce the delays which had appeared because of the sharp increase in activities. The Exchange's Committee also forced brokerage houses to propose a securities' deposit service. This measure was expected to yield two long-term gains: on the one hand, it could retain the clients' securities, offering a solid base for the after-war brokerage activities and, on the other hand, it could convince clients of local banks to directly use the services of the official brokers for their stock-exchange transactions.

Better service also required more human resources especially since the number of trades had experienced a dramatic surge. In just a few years the number of employees of the stock exchange increased from eleven (before the war) to thirty (December 1940), fifty (December 1941) and eventually sixty (end of 1943).[50] At the same time, the number of cockpits on the *Parquet* jumped from two to six and even seven in 1941. The market however never came close to being equilibrated, the huge demand for securities facing a decreasing supply. Brokers were, most of the time, unable to find a counterpart for the less liquid securities and could not determine the securities' prices. In order to address these issues, a new parallel market, the '*marché fermé*' (closed-shop market) was created. In this market brokers' clerks guaranteed the orders' matching not with the traditional open outcry, but by acting as 'specialists'. Eventually, the stock exchange committee decided, for the sake of competition, to keep its pricing structure: its commissions were to remain lower than the ones required in Paris, and its commissions to order collectors higher than in the capital.

To strengthen its chances as the main market, measures had to be devised to better fund the brokerage houses since Lyon brokering houses were relatively illiquid. The increased activities required huge sums to complete the clearing and settlement processes in an efficient way. Three tools were used to limit this problem. First, the banks located in Lyon were allowed to clear their operations directly with the brokers, therefore diminishing the need for treasuries. Second, the rate of the internal tax on the brokers' turnover was increased to create huge reserves to be used in case of distress (from 3 million before the war, up to 9 million in 1941, and to 25 million at the end of 1944[51]). Third, the committee obtained from the general assembly the authorization to borrow from local banks, if its reserves were to become insufficient. The committee pushed the brokers to maintain in the case of a broker's default the *de facto* collective guarantee *vis-à-vis* investors, distinguishing the Lyon Bourse from the other regional stock exchanges since 1930. This guarantee, as well as the minimal risk associated with spot transactions, attracted the capital of the wealthy bourgeois of the region.

In November 1942, the German marched into the free zone to regain a direct control over the whole country. Even though Lyon would eventually keep its pre-reunification privileges, the stock exchange committee suspected competition would soon resume. They feared a dramatic impact on the volumes traded because they expected the Parisian brokers to fight by all means to regain their clients. Knowing that in peacetime they would not stand a chance against Paris,[52] they decided to exploit the war situation to list and trade even more Parisian securities, while at the same time trying to attract a larger number of regional issues.

1943 was characterized by a sharp decrease in the traded volumes. The total commissions perceived by the brokers fell by 50 per cent between the last months of 1942 and the first ones of 1943. As this decrease coincided with the removal of the demarcation line, it would seem logical to blame this change to an increased competition with Paris. Even though competition certainly increased in 1943, it is likely to explain at most a part of the observed decrease since the Parisian brokers registered the same changes in performances at the time. The poor state of telegraphic and telephonic communication between Paris and Lyon on the one hand, and, the non-abrogation of the ban on trades in foreign securities in Paris on the other, implied that both markets were still more insulated than they were before the war. This allowed Lyon to keep relatively high volumes of trades, especially if compared to the pre-war situation.[53] Lobbying actions were of course continued. The strengthening experienced thanks to war, led the Syndic to envision future negotiations with optimism.[54] The creation of the CBV was, paradoxically in view of the enthusiasm shown by the Parisian brokers, believed to provide a better balance of powers between Paris and the regional stock exchanges.

Facts would soon show that the Syndic had been overoptimistic. Even though trade remained high during 1944, most of the year's success was due to the flotation of the *Emprunt de la Libération* (Freedom Loan). During the second semester of 1944, some clients began to ask to get their files transferred to Paris. At the same time, trade in some securities disappeared. In a gloomy mood, the Syndic would state at the end of 1944 that they were 'to expect the worst';[55] a statement in strong contrast with 1943's optimism. To strengthen the Lyon *Parquet* and its creditworthiness, the Syndic suggested implementing a legal form of collective guarantee, but lack of insurance on the securities deposits convinced the brokers to postpone the measure. At the end of 1945, and in view of the France's complicated political situation, the Syndic would wonder to what extent there was a future for regional stock exchanges.

Marseille

In contrast to most other exchanges, the Marseille Bourse remained open during the summer of 1940. The closures of the Paris and Lyon bourses, in June 1940, as well as the interruption of communications with Bordeaux and Toulouse, led to a huge increase in trading volumes. To limit any excessive price rise, the stock exchange committee immediately voted and enforced measures to limit daily price changes. A few months later, the committee would welcome the reopening of the Paris and Lyon bourses,[56] while at the same time setting into place measures to reorganize the functioning of the exchange.

As in Lyon, brokerage houses had been capitalized years before when volumes were minute and liquidity soon became one of the major issues. Traded volumes of November 1940 were twice as large as the volumes exchanged during the whole year 1939! Several innovations were agreed upon to ameliorate the existing situation. First, banking institutions located in Marseille were admitted to the clearing system from January 27, 1941 on. At first, this measure was limited to the major incorporated banks such as the Société Générale or the Crédit Lyonnais. Soon however, in 1942, the spurt in trading volumes would force the admissions of private bankers and small incorporated banks. Meanwhile, the stock exchange committee managed to obtain bank credits to finance the brokerage houses' clearing and delivery activities. Whereas the Lyon banks had requested few guarantees, the Marseille bankers demanded the stock exchange committee guarantee for both credit and default risks.

The Marseille brokers followed the same strategies as their colleagues from Lyon to maintain the exceptional order flow. On the one hand they tried to be viewed favorably by the government; on the other they transformed the organization to increase customer satisfaction. During the frequent stays of the Marseille Syndic in Vichy, the government gave him detailed instructions on how he believed the Bourse should be functioning. Armed with this knowledge, the committee then informally enforced all of Vichy's wishes. Despite their proactive approach, the Marseille stock exchange remained considered as a second tier bourse. As stated by the Syndic himself, he was often received in Vichy by the Ministers but in the presence of the Syndics of Paris and Lyon.

The Marseille Syndic tried to keep good relations with his peers from Paris and Lyon believing that it would have a positive impact on the Marseille Bourse. His approach was attacked by some brokers who tried, at the end of 1941, to dismiss him because he accepted the domination of Paris and Lyon. His main opponent claimed that his submissive attitude was harming the Marseille Bourse. Instead, he called for more autonomy from and more competitiveness vis-à-vis other French exchanges. The Syndic's defensive arguments relied on the size of the Paris and Lyon exchanges but also on the proximity of their committees to the governmental power. In fact, the Marseille Syndic considered the Lyon Bourse as the natural 'vicar' of the Paris Stock Exchange in Free France because of its position as largest regional exchange and because of its location near Vichy. The elections, which took place at the end of the year would confirm the Syndic and reject the opponents. It is noteworthy that this kind of opposition was almost unheard of before the war.

As in Lyon, measures were taken to modernize the exchange. In order to cope with the rocketing volumes, the committee hiked up the number of cockpits from one up to three during 1940 and up to five afterwards. The efficiency of this move remained however limited because of the scarcity of skilled employees and the size of the Stock Exchange building. Rules were also devised to manage the disproportion existing between supply and demand. The reserves of the brokers' common funds were increased and a higher working capital was required from the brokerage houses. As in Lyon, a '*service des rachats officiels*' (official buying service) as well as a service centralizing the files concerning the Marseille brokers and the new CCDVT located in Lyon were created and implemented. Eventually, the committee set into place rules regulating the distribution among brokers of the traded securities.

In view of the stock-exchange development, the Syndic believed a bright future lay ahead of its Bourse, stressing that it would be both legitimate and necessary to keep the current level of activity and even develop it.[57] The lobbying action had proved fruitful since the government had guaranteed that the 'new *Coulisse*' would not be authorized in regional financial centres. Despite these advances the Syndic had nonetheless to regret that the order flow generated by Free French public or semi-public financial institutions were regularly directed toward Lyon. The Marseille Syndic had only managed to obtain that in the case of large differences in the Paris and Marseille public bonds' prices, the Governmental Treasurer of the Marseille Department could direct orders towards the Marseille Bourse.[58]

Following the suppression of the demarcation lines between the two parts of France, volumes traded at the Marseille Bourse experienced a clear decline (see Figure 3.1). The Marseille brokers were still able, in 1943, to keep their private clients, but they were losing their institutional investors, which were redirecting their orders toward Paris. Besides the externalities and the diversification available in Paris, the decrease in the rebates given by the Marseille brokers to the banking institutions (which fell from 35 per cent to 25 per cent of the commissions after 1 July 1943)[59] provided an additional incentive to resume trading with the capital. This reduction had been agreed upon for three raisons: first, the commission rates were higher in Paris and stayed so even after rebate rates were reformed in Marseille, limiting the competitive impact of the reform; second, the *Comité des Bourses de Valeurs* had expressed the wish that Marseille would align its rebates on the other regional exchanges; third, the rise of the employees' wages was pushing the brokers to retain a higher rate of gross commissions. This reform was followed by a further decrease in commissions given to both order collectors and employees. If it is unlikely that the latter diverted their order flows from Marseille, it is possible that the former ones accepted sending their orders to Paris.

Because of the growing centripetal force of the Paris Stock Exchange, the stock exchange committee decided to organize a centralized back-office service. This centralized service was meant to reduce the time it took to receiving the accreditation of an operation executed in Paris through the CCDVT.[60] At the same time, the regional exchanges tried to react to the loss of business through a collusive agreement. The Marseille and Lyon Bourses decided to act together to lobby the government in defence of their common interests. They also signed an agreement by which the brokers from the Marseille Stock Exchange would send to Lyon their orders for national securities that were listed there; reciprocally, the brokers from the Lyon Stock Exchange would send to Marseille their orders for securities cross-listed in Marseille and Paris.

In 1944, the Marseille Stock Exchange put in place huge organizational changes to limit the fall in volumes traded and its impact on brokerage houses' profitability. First, the evolution of military operations on the French soil, and the fear of being cut from Lyon, convinced the committee of the need to organize a local settlement-delivery system. The committee asked for the support from the CCDVT, but to no avail. However, and thanks to the intervention of the banks located in the financial centre, a new institution, eventually recognized by the CCDVT, was created. At the same time, the Nazi authorities ordered the centralization of the foreign securities held on the 'Mediterranean coast'. In order to comply, the committee organized a service of central deposit for these securities. The pattern toward a progressive centralization of the services needed by the brokerage houses, imposed by both the new regulation and Nazi instructions, pushed the committee to study a complete integration of the stock-exchange organization: in other words a centralization of all the services still run by the brokerage houses. In this framework, the committee first created new collective funds to increase the reserves of the Bourse, then a service centralizing the orders from all the brokers' private and institutional clients. This new service, replicated a couple of year later by the Lyon Bourse, eliminated the notion of the professional secret among brokers, but allowed huge gains in productivity and precision, two important issues to survive in a changing environment.

Conclusion

Most provincial stock exchanges were, just before the war outbreak, in dire straits. The Second World War would dramatically alter the French stock-exchange scene and represent for some of them a period of extreme prosperity. The war, however, imposed a geographical division between the French free zone and the one occupied by Germany. Stock exchanges which were directly competing before the war became more insulated: the war had brought a *de facto* segmentation of the French stock exchanges.

Several elements reinforced the segmentation which would in practice favour the stock exchanges located in the free zone. Allowed to reopen early, they kept the right to trade almost all form of securities. By contrast, the stock exchanges located in the occupied zone, were only authorized to reopen much later and were banned from trading foreign securities. In the case of Paris, the reopening was gradual, beginning with bonds (October 1940), followed by shares of French corporations active in metropolitan France (March 1941), and eventually by all French shares (September 1941). The separation into two zones had additional consequences. Since securities had been transferred to the South as the Germans were marching on Paris, most of these were physically in the non-occupied zone after the Armistice. Fearing to bring these securities back into the occupied zone, investors turned themselves to regional exchanges. The war further exacerbated the division since it led to a huge decrease in terms of communications.

The segmentation of the stock exchanges had several impacts. The provincial stock exchanges located in the occupied zone remained subject to the competition from Paris and saw no improvement in their overall situation. One of them, Nancy, remained closed since its location meant that its future was to be determined once the Reich was victorious. By contrast, the stock exchanges located in the free zone experienced a huge increase in activity. The spot transactions at the Lyon stock exchange jumped from 100 million French Francs in 1938 to 35 billion in 1941. Brokers from the favored stock exchanges realized that the benefits created by the war could easily be endangered. In order to protect these, they set into place new organizational measures to increase their competitiveness while at the same time lobbying the French government to obtain more favours. Even though part of the lobbying proved successful, the invasion of the free zone by the Germans in November 1942 came probably too early for the exchanges to completely consolidate their position. At the end of 1944, competition had already resumed with Paris leading to a noticeable loss of clients for these markets.

Besides the impact of the segmentation, the competition between French stock exchanges was also altered by a series of laws passed during the war. These laws led to a complete reorganization of the *Coulisse* (curb), which was forced to adopt an organizational framework very similar to the one prevailing on the Parquet. The *Coulisse* was further weakened by the racial laws which led to the exclusion of a third of its members. The creation of the *Comité des Bourses de Valeurs* also revolutionized the stock-exchange environment. The provincial stock exchanges managed to get guarantees regarding their representation for all matters concerning them.

In a sense the war had a double impact in terms of convergence and divergence. On one hand, it probably led to some form of international convergence in Europe. Indeed some rules or organisms set into place by the occupying forces were kept after the war because they made economic sense. For example, the existence of an institution such as the CCDVT, a war creation influenced by the German stock exchange practice, was not questioned at the Liberation because it improved trade efficiency. Thus, in a sense, the occupation brought some form of convergence amongst French and German exchanges. At a very local level, the reorganization of the exchanges also facilitated the eventual merger of the Paris Parquet and *Coulisse*. By abolishing the heterogeneities between the Parquet and the *Coulisse*, they facilitated their merger, which took place less than fifteen years later, a sure indication of strong convergence. On the other hand, however, the separate treatment of bourses located on each side of the demarcation line induced a strong reversal. The pre-war converging trend all but disappeared overnight. By reviving provincial stock exchanges and by giving them a say in the CBV, the war may have delayed the process of national merger, well underway by 1938, which only occurred as late as 1991. Regarding stock exchanges, the war thus acted both as a converging and as a diverging force.

4 SHOCKS IMPACT ON LONG-TERM MARKET CORRELATIONS: PORTFOLIO DIVERSIFICATION AND MARKET INTEGRATION BETWEEN FRANCE AND THE UNITED STATES

David Le Bris

Introduction

In this chapter, convergence and divergence of financial systems is addressed through the point of view of the investor. This study points out the difference between the international integration of financial markets which means an equalization of prices of risk and the correlation among them indicating that assets are affected by similar events. Each of these aspects follows his own path. Stock market correlation is measured since the middle of the nineteenth century to 2008. Tools offered by Modern Portfolio Theory are used to analyse incentives to diversify. To achieve a consistent result these tools require high-quality data. Indeed, even a slight default in the construction methodology of the data is magnified with time. High-quality data imply dividend series since dividends were the major source of return before 1914.[1] Unfortunately, these kind of data are not easily available. Consequently, this study focuses only on markets with high quality data: France and the United States.

To be correlated, two markets first need to be integrated and that integration has to be measured. Such a study is made possible by the fact that West European savers invested a large part of their portfolio in foreign securities before 1914, although distance-related costs seemed to be stronger than today. The price of risk in US and French stocks is used to test the integration of these markets before the First World War. Since we observe an equal price of risk we cannot reject the hypothesis of financial integration. But this integration is characterized by a low level of stock market correlation.

This *a priori* contradiction is very consistent with exportation of capital: with an equal price of risk the incentive to buy foreign assets can only be low correlation. Optimal portfolio theory indicates a part of US stocks coherent with what was really observed for French savers. But it also shows that convergence is a multifaceted concept: whether one chooses to focus on market integration or on market correlation, this will lead to different conclusions. Thus, this paper aims at a more comprehensive approach to that question.

After the First World War, the correlation level increased strongly despite the end of stable gold-based currency rates and a gradual limitation of a free international capital market in France. A stable and high level of correlation is observed during the 1930s but falls with the Second World War. From the 1950s on, the correlation increases gradually to a historical high value in recent years. A higher correlation means that traded assets (French and US stocks) are more similar. A stock similar to another one means a similar risk or more exactly an identical time-distribution of risks. A large part of the risk on futures payments depends on variation of GDP: one major reason for the increase of French and US stocks correlation can thus be the rise of GDP correlation. But the correlation does not follow a stable trend. Some violent changes caused by special events like financial crises or wars are identified.

Section 1 presents a test of international markets integration before 1914. Section 2 shows that an optimal portfolio before 1914 should and did include a large part of foreign stocks thanks to a low correlation between national markets. Section 3 measures a gradual increase and several short-term jumps in stock market correlation after 1919, building evidence on the changing nature of financial convergence before and after the First World War.

A Test of the Capital Markets Integration before 1914

Previous Studies

International integration means equalization of prices on different markets. The 'law of one price' was formally defined for the first time by Cournot. An integrated market is 'an entire territory of which the parts are so united by the relations of unrestricted commerce that prices take the same level throughout with ease and rapidity'.[2] O'Rourke and Williamson[3] focus on two kinds of convergence: production factors (capital, work, land) follow product prices. They show a first convergence movement until 1914 followed by a regressive period which stopped at the end of 1950s. The spread in the price of wheat between London and Chicago decreased from 57.5 per cent in 1870 to 15.6 per cent in 1913, leading to the full integration of the British and Ukrainian markets for the grain in 1906. The same movements are observed for textile or cotton. The spread between US and British prices for cotton textiles, iron bars, pig iron and copper fell from 13.7 per cent to -3.6 per cent, 75 per cent to 20.6 per cent, 85.2 per cent to 19.3 per cent and 32.7 per cent to -0.1 per cent respectively.[4] The same phenomenon occurred between Europe and Asia, with the London–Rangoon rice price gap falling from 93 per cent to 26 per cent, or the Liverpool–Bombay cotton price spread falling from 57 per cent to 20 per cent. This equalization of prices was due to a decline in transportation costs: –50 per cent between 1870 and 1913. This trend to equalization in prices is also observed for labour prices across eight countries during the same period.[5] But does this kind of spread calculation provide a correct measure of international financial integration?

Price equalization of identical securities quoted in different markets is not enough to test international financial integration. Such easy arbitrage does not need important capital flow and can be realized within the context of weak international exchanges. The equality in the prices of identical securities only demonstrates the existence of a free market and a correct information flow. For example, from the middle of the nineteenth century onward, correct communications meant wire telegraph: by 1860, three lines linked England and the Continent. The first fully successful Atlantic cable was completed in 1866. The price lag between London and New York for a same stock (New York and Erie railroad) decreased from ten to zero days in a few months after the first transatlantic cable was operational.[6] Kaukiainen[7] found the same effect of cable introduction comparing colonial dispatch times to London before and after the introduction of the telegraph in the colonies. For example, the dispatch time between London and Bombay decreased from 145 days by post in 1820 to three days in 1870 by telegraph.

The market integration can be evaluated by quantifying amount of foreign assets. Feldstein and Horioka[8] find a strong relationship between investments and savings in different countries in the 1960s and 70s. This relationship implies a low capital mobility, so that foreign savings cannot fill in the gap of a high national investment level. Before the First World War, this same test shows that low domestic saving rate could coexist with a high investment rate for a panel of countries. This difference is the necessary result of capital imports. According to Obstfeld and Taylor,[9] foreign assets were just 7 per cent of world GDP in 1870 and 20 per cent before the First World War. This ratio fell to a low point of 5 per cent in 1945, and, in recent decades, rose quickly to 25 per cent in 1980 and 62 per cent in 1995. However, this macroeconomic observation does not measure only globalization since the role of financial markets (measured by the market capitalization on GDP ratio) varied across time. In France, the stock market capitalization on GDP ratio was above 20 per cent in 1914 but less than 2 per cent in 1950 and not above 20 per cent again until 1997:[10] the role of financial markets in the economy respects a perfect U-shape. Rajan and Zingales find the same variation in financial development for a panel of countries.[11] Thus, the foreign assets on world GDP ratio measures both globalisation and the financial markets role in the economy. The problem is then to distinguish between the respective impact of these two trends.

Other authors address the international integration by analysing the returns of a same class of assets around the world. For example, Obstfeld and Taylor find a low spread between US and British Bills,[12] while Flandreau and Zumer use the spread between foreign and British bonds as an indicator of financial integration.[13] Unlike previous studies, they show that no direct relation existed between gold standard countries and declines in spread in bonds rate: more accurate variables reduced the explanatory power of gold standard adherence. Mauro, Sussman and Yafeh compare state bonds spreads in emerging countries today and during the first rush of globalization. They found a current average correlation coefficient of 0.77 wheres it was only 0.45 on pre-1914 period.[14] Ferguson and Schularick argue that members of the British Empire benefited from their colonial status through substantially reduced interest rates.[15] Edelstein uses a set of 566 common and preferred stocks and bonds, domestic, colonial and foreign prices, between 1870 and 1913 and computes realized rates of return (without dividends or coupon). He finds a higher return adjusted for risk (1.58 per cent) for overseas investments as compared to English ones.[16]

Another way to measure international integration is to analyse the foreign part of portfolios both empirically and theoretically thanks to the Modern Portfolio Theory. For British investors, according to Edelstein,[17] 32 per cent of their wealth was held overseas. Clemens and Williamson[18] provide econometric evidence that British capital exports went to countries with abundant supplies of natural resources, immigrants and young, educated, urban populations and not to where labour was cheap. Thanks to the Modern Portfolio Theory, Goetzmann and Ukhov[19] focus on diversification benefits for British savers using a panel of security prices.[20] They find a strong incentive to export capital, even if foreign assets have the same return as British ones. According to Michalet, French savers held about one third of their wealth invested on financial markets in foreign securities,[21] a close match to their British counterparts. Parent and Rault use annual domestic and foreign prices index (without dividends) to build an optimal portfolio for French savers before 1914,[22] which allowed French savers to extract a profit from low correlation rather than higher return.[23]

To analyse financial integration in mean/variance framework using the Modern Portfolio Theory we use high-quality data. By high quality we mean higher frequency – i.e. monthly prices – and information on dividends. Taking dividends into account is essential since they constituted the major part of stock returns before 1914.[24] A new database for French stocks, spanning the years between 1854 and 1996, is used and US data is employed as a proxy for international investment since only this country provides data of an equivalent high quality, by linking Old Nyse[25] (1854 to 1870) and Shiller's S&P.[26]

Sharpe Ratio of French and US Stocks are Compared

This study assumes that international market integration means equalization of price of risk since the risk (on future payments) is the real product traded on financial markets. Risk can be measured by the standard deviation of returns. It is always difficult to measure the risk especially since we talk about the anticipated risk. In a classical way, risk can be estimated by the standard deviation of total return. It is not a perfect model since assets returns are not Gaussian but a correct approximation of the reality. It is important to measure the standard deviation of total returns and not only quotations variations since dividends or coupons constituted the major part of total returns before 1914.

A classical method for estimating the price of risk is the Sharpe ratio. The Sharpe ratio is the return of the risk of one asset divided by the quantity of its risk. The return of the risk is the total return minus the return of the risk-free asset. This return is divided by the quantity of risk (the standard deviation) to have the price of each unit of standard deviation. It is the price of 'each unit of risk'. The price of risk, the Sharpe ratio, is calculated for French and US stocks using a rolling window of ten years between 1854 and 1914. Risk free assets are T-Bills in the US market and 'taux de l'escompte de la Banque de France[27] 'in the French market. These annual data are interpolated for monthly value. Each monthly price variation of stock is added to the dividend yield divided by twelve and standard deviation of this total return is calculated on the ten prior years. We choose the ten prior years and not a centred average just to help the lecture of the graph. The risk-free return of one month is the average rate of 120 months before. Returns are nominal in local currency,[28] they are converted in annual value (multiplied by 12) as standard deviation (multiplied by square root of 12).

Formally, French and US markets are integrated if:

$$Sharperatio^{F} = Sharperatio^{US}$$

$$\frac{r_S^F - r_f^F}{\sigma_S^F} = \frac{r_S^{US} - r_f^{US}}{\sigma_S^{US}} \qquad (1)$$

with, r_S : average total return on stocks, r_f : the risk free asset and σ_S: standard deviation of total return on stocks

Results are mixed. The average Sharpe ratios over January 1854 to December 1913 are both 0.31[29]. The price of risk is the same over the period 1854–1914 which would mean that a perfect integration existed between US and French financial markets. But, the ten-years rolling Sharpe ratios give somewhat different results. These ratios are on Figure 4.1.

Figure 4.1. Sharpe ratios of US and French stocks over 1854–1914.

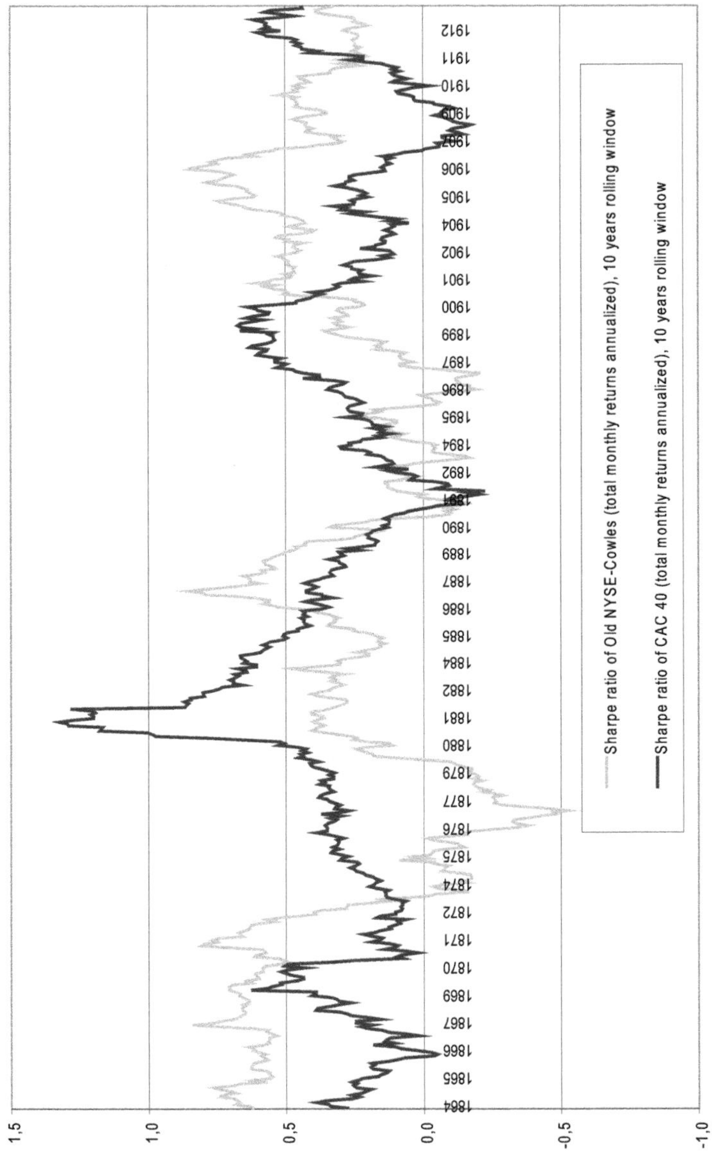

Sources: Goetzmann, Ibbotson, Peng (2000), Cowles, S&P, Homer and Sylla (1998), Banque de France, author

The Long-Term Price of Risk in Various Assets

The relation between risk and return among various assets can be showed in a graphic way. Since Black, Jensen, Scholes[30] study on NYSE stocks from 1931 to 1965, different studies found a consistent securities market line. Using data between January 1854 and December 1913, a clear international securities market line appears.[31] Total returns are measured using price variations and dividend or coupon revenues for stocks and bonds. For short-term rates, the total return is the interest rate only. These returns are calculated on a one-year holding period. All these returns are computed nominal in their respective currency, due to the very low inflation and almost perfect stability of the rates of exchange between the French franc, the US dollar and the British pound. The average return of one asset is scaled on the Y axis and the standard deviation of this return on the X axis of the graph.

The computation of this international risk line leads to two straightforward conclusions. First, the observed line constitutes a validation of the theory that links risk and return: the relative position (X/Y) of each category of asset is relevant to the usual assessment of risks and returns of these assets. Second, French, US and British financial markets were integrated during this period, and this integration seems to have been fairly strong, as shown by the very close position of the different asset categories from the risk line. Despite the limited signification of a regression including only eight assets, it is interesting to note the high level of R^2 (0.93).

Optimal Portfolio before 1914

When international market integration is achieved, incentives to buy foreign assets should not exist since the integration means equalization of prices. Assuming a strong international market integration, and then an equalization of the price of risk, exportation of capital before 1914 can only be motivated by a weak international correlation.

International Diversification Generates Profit Thanks to Weak Correlation

As Goetzmann and Ukhov assume, 'assets return does not just indicate a different rate but can also show the degree of correlation between different investments thus the diversification benefits available to individual investors'.[32] A general explanation of the benefits of diversification is to avoid putting all one's eggs in one basket, meaning that by spreading the wealth between different assets the risk is reduced. The modern portfolio theory is built on this idea.[33]

Figure 4.2. Risk line for various French, Bristish and US assets over 1854–1914.

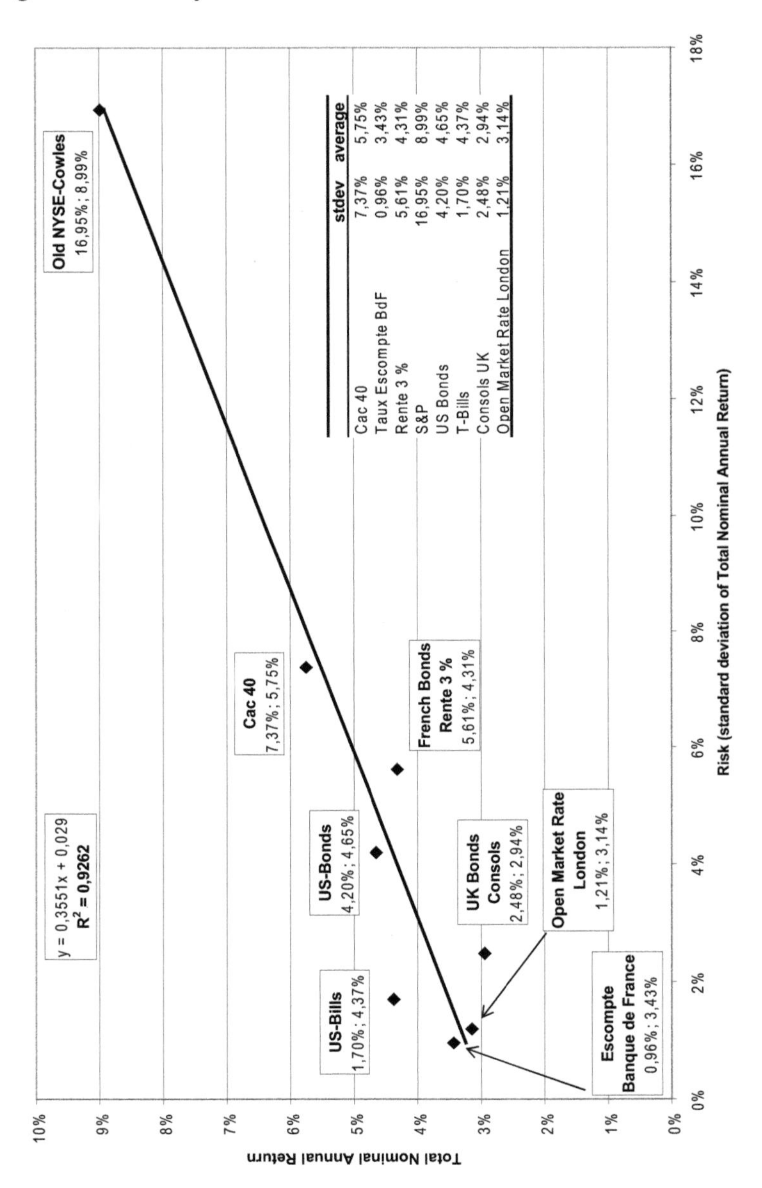

Sources: Goetzmann, Ibbotson, Peng (2000), Cowles, S&P, Homer and Sylla (1998), Banque de France, author.

To invest in low-correlated assets reduces the volatility of the portfolio leading to a better risk-adjusted portfolio return. Diversification cannot achieve a better return since the portfolio return is the weighted average of each asset return. But diversification allows a decrease in the risk level for a given level of return. Consequently, the return paid for each unit of risk increases. For a fixed level of risk, a better return is achieved.

US stocks are used as a proxy for the international stock market since high quality data do not exist for other countries. French savers' portfolio diversification into US stocks is a far cry from actual history since less than 5 per cent[34] of French foreign assets were invested in the US. However, the risk reduction in a portfolio is not linear: the marginal gain of adding one extra asset to reduce risk in the portfolio is decreasing.[35] This means that adding an extra asset to a portfolio of ten assets does not reduce the risk as much as adding an extra asset to a portfolio consisting of one asset. Therefore, the use of US data (or any another one) as a proxy to international portfolio strategies probably demonstrates a significant part of international diversification profit. Moreover, using US stocks allows for a long term comparison which is impossible with non-existant data, Russian for example.

The next figure shows risk/return of portfolios exclusively composed from French and US stocks, in order to measure their relative performances. Nine portfolios combining US and French stocks are calculated. The first one is constituted by a constant 10 per cent of US stocks and 90 per cent of French, the second one of 20 per cent of US stocks and 80 per cent of French stocks, and so on. All possible combinations between French and US stocks in one given portfolio are thus computed on the curb between a 100 per cent French stocks (Cac 40) porfolio and a 100 per cent American (Old NYSE-Cowles) one.[36] It allows us to draw a very simple, efficient frontier.

Theoretically, average and standard deviation are obtained by the following equations. Given

X the weight (in per cent) of one market, with $X_F + X_{US} = 1$

r the total return

σ the standard deviation

σ_{FUS} the covariance between French and US stocks

The total Return of the Portfolio is: $r_P = X_F r_F + X_{US} r_{US}$ (2)

Standard Deviation of the Portfolio is:

$$\sigma_P = \left[X_F^2 \sigma_F^2 + X_{US}^2 \sigma_{US}^2 + 2 X_F X_{US} \sigma_{FUS}\right]^{1/2} \qquad (3)$$

The profit extracted from international diversification (Φ1 and Φ3) is high, thanks to a low correlation between the French and the US markets. This correlation over the 1854–1913 period is 0.063 using only monthly price variation or 0.23 using annual total return (price variations and dividends). The gain achieved by international investment can be measured by several statistics. The first one, Φ1, measures the expected return benefits of international diversification. This measure follows Kandel, McCulloch and Stambaugh and can be interpreted as the profit of international diversification after controlling for risk:[37]

$$\phi_1 = Max\left\{r_P - r_F \middle| \sigma_P^2 \leq \sigma_F^2\right\} \qquad (4)$$

Φ1 can thus be seen as the gain in returns (percentage per year) obtained by international diversification for a level of risk equal to the French market. From 1854 to 1913, Φ1 is about 0.58 per cent and implies a portfolio with 18 per cent of US stocks. The average return of such a portfolio is 6.33 per cent, 0.58 per cent better than a pure Cac 40 portfolio, with the same exact level of risk. A second figure, Φ2, measures the gain in percentage of return relative to a 100 per cent French stocks portfolio return. The increase in return for a French investor through US diversification, is 10,45, free of extra risk.

$$\phi_2 = \frac{r_P - r_F}{r_F} \qquad (5)$$

The third measure of the gains from international diversification concern the decrease in risk allowed by diversification. Φ3 is the decrease in standard deviation provided by the minimum variance portfolio relative to the French benchmark. This minimum risk portfolio implies 9 per cent of US stocks and achieves a risk reduction of 0.15 points of the standard deviation or, in percentage, 2 per cent.

$$\phi_3 = \sigma_{MP} - \sigma_F \qquad (6)$$

with MP, the portfolio with the minimum standard deviation

Figure 4.3. Efficient frontier between US and French stocks over 1854–1914.

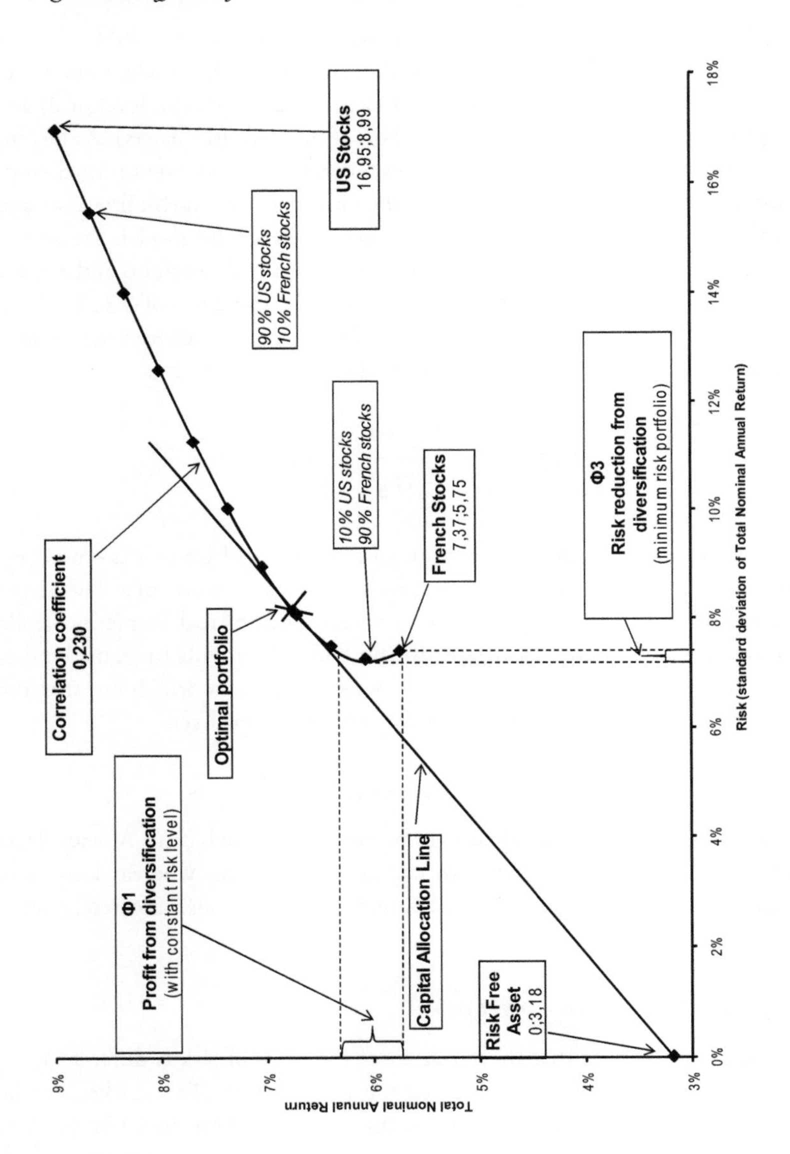

Sources: Goetzmann, Ibbotson, Peng (2000), Cowles, author

Optimal Portfolio

Using US stock returns as a proxy for foreign securities and Cac 40 for French ones, it is possible to build the Capital Allocation Line. All efficient portfolios are on this line joining the risk-free asset (with an artificial risk level of 0) and the optimal portfolio (optimal combination of the two risky assets). According to his risk aversion, one investor chooses a combination of the optimal stock portfolio and risk-free asset. This line is the tangent between risk free asset and the efficient frontier, it is the line with the higher slope. This slope is the Sharpe ratio, *(ro-rf)/So* with r_O, the total return of the optimal portfolio and r_f, the return of the risk-free asset. Thus, from an equal Sharpe ratio of 0.31 for both French and US stock market, international diversification increases the value of the risk to 0.40 for French saver. Equation of this line is given by:

$$r_P = r_f + \left[\frac{(r_O - r_f)}{\sigma_O} \right] \sigma_P \quad (7)$$

This optimal portfolio indicates an optimal proportion of US stocks – used as a proxy for all international stocks – in a French saver's portfolio of about 31 per cent. This proportion is very close of all observations of real French portfolio hold overseas at this time.[38] Goetzmann and Ukhov[39] provide the same kind of analyse for several countries whose stocks were available to British investor and find an optimal portfolio including 38 per cent of foreign assets.

Changes and Shocks on Correlations

But stock market correlation appears to be unstable through time. At a low level before 1914, it was consistent with capital exportations, whereas long-term changes may be following GDP correlation. Correlation is also affected by some special events.

Long-Term Changes in Correlation

It is important to note that the variation of the price of risk is different from correlation. Market integration does not mean correlation. Two markets can be integrated without any correlation if the products traded on these two markets are completely different.[40] For stock markets, integration means correlation only if stocks quoted on the two markets are the same. Thus the question becomes: When are French and US stocks an identical product?

We saw that a main incentive to buy foreign stocks was their low correlation with domestic ones. But what is the variation of the correlation among international markets? Longin and Solnik show changes in correlation over the

1960–90 period and reject the hypothesis of the stability of the correlation.[41] Mauro, Sussman and Yafeh use correlation coefficients to analyse emerging markets[42] both in modern and in historical times. The average correlation coefficient is 0.77 in modern times compared with 0.45 in historical times for the full sample, and 0.42 for the high-quality-data sample. Goezzmann, Lingfeng and Rouwenhorst[43] using stock prices from the Global Financial Database, the Jorion and Goetzmann sample of equity markets, the Ibbotson Associates database of international markets and the IFC database of emerging markets built a five-year rolling window correlation, through international markets. They find four peaks in price correlation: around 1860, just before 1914, during the 1930s and after the 1970s. And the level of correlation reached during the 1930s is higher than the current one. Obstfeld and Taylor, using a ten-year rolling window, show a weak correlation before the beginning of the twentieth century, a quick increase just before 1914, a low correlation during the First World War, another time of high correlation during the 1930s and a gradual increase since the low level observed at the end of the Second World War.[44]

A low correlation before 1914 is consistent with a period characterized by important capital exports. If stock markets had displayed a strong correlation, there would have been almost no incentive to buy foreign assets. If the price of risk is equal between several countries, the only motivation to export money is to choose markets with a weak correlation. French or English savers probably found incentives to export overseas rather than in Western European countries after 1880. Perhaps, traditional countries of capital exportation were more correlated with French and English markets after this date, thus pushing savers to look for more exotic countries. High-quality data are not available to make a correct comparison among several stock markets but the correlation between France and the US, as we have already stressed, is a good example.

Three different correlation coefficients are calculated on monthly stock-price variations on a ten-year rolling window. Monthly price variations are used to calculate the correlation coefficients presented in Figure 4.5. This choice makes comparison possible with a prior measure of long-term correlation.[45] However, these monthly variations are more sensitive to a gap in the exact date of the price during the month or to the unknown date of payment of the dividend than a coefficient obtained from annual total return. The first one comes from nominal price variation without any attrition for inflation or currency changes. The second uses one annual jump for the exchange rate. The last adjusts currency exchange rates monthly through a linear interpolation from annual exchange-rate data. All these correlation coefficients are underestimated since a permanent lag exists between French and US data: French one is based upon the first Friday price of each month, while the US one comes from the last day of the month. But since this lag is constant over time, it should bear no impact on the observed variations.

The main result, as shown in Figure 4.4, is that the correlation is obviously stronger today than before 1914 and that it varied to huge proportions in over 150 years. Despite the gold standard and consequently a stable currency rate between 1878 and 1914, the correlation was very low at this time. The 'first' and the 'second' globalizations are totally different in this respect. This weaker correlation before 1914 is a consistent explanation to massive purchases of foreign assets.

Does Long-Term-Correlation Follow GDP Correlation?

A higher correlation means that the products traded (in this case French and US stocks) are more similar. A stock similar to another one bears the same risk. A part of the risk on future payments depends on GDP variations: one major reason in the increase of French and US stock correlation can be the rise in their respective GDP correlation. Dumas, Harvey and Ruiz theoretically link together stock market correlation to national output correlation[46]. Were French and US national outputs correlated before 1914? Figure 4.4 shows that, unlike today, there was a low stock market correlation before 1914 and thus that US and French stocks differed in nature, probably because national outputs were also different. This is the point we now investigate.

Using annual data[47] (interpolated to achieve monthly value), the correlation coefficient between US and French change in GDP is calculated on a ten-year rolling window. The correlation level of GDP – Figure 4.5 – seems to be correlated with the correlation level of stocks. The current higher stock correlation is probably partially due to a stronger integration of real economy. Therefore, the incentive to export money decreases when economic integration increases.

Shocks on Stockmarket Correlation

It is possible to look for major monthly shocks on US–French stock correlation since long term changes in correlation are accompanied by many short term fluctuations. The level of the correlation is measured without any adjustment for currency value since monthly data are not available. Correlation coefficient is calculated over the prior ten years using a rolling window and we compute monthly changes in the correlation. This correlation coefficient needs to be adjusted since volatility is not stable over time. As pointed out in Forbes and Rigobon,[48] the standard correlation coefficient is vulnerable to heteroskedasticity bias. Non-adjusted correlation coefficients mislead both the results and their interpretation. This bias can be important because, after the gold standard, the volatility of the French stock market increased threefold.[49] In order to suppress the heteroskedasticity bias, the correlation coefficient should be adjusted to account for the increased variability during the month.

Figure 4.4. Correlation between US and French stock markets over 1854–2007.

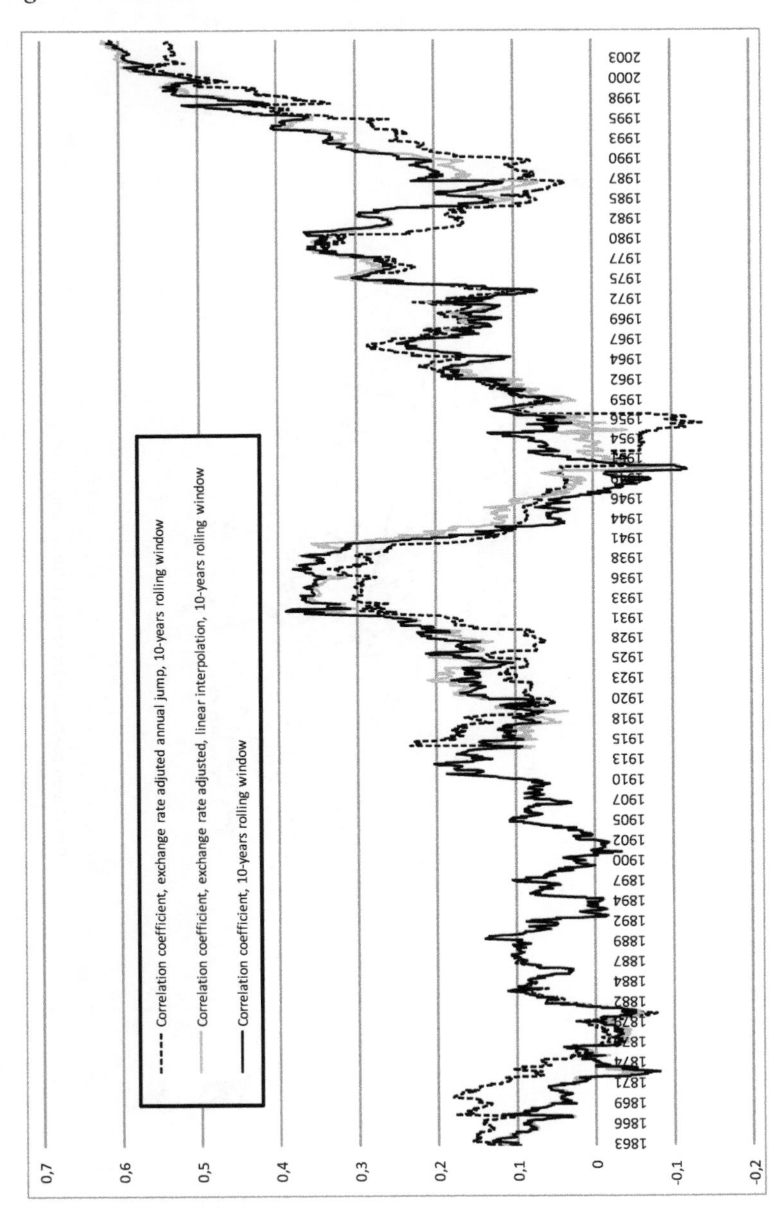

Sources: Goetzmann, Ibbotson, Peng, Cowles, S&P, author

Figure 4.5. Correlation between US and French stock markets correlation and US and French GDP correlation, over 1854–2007.

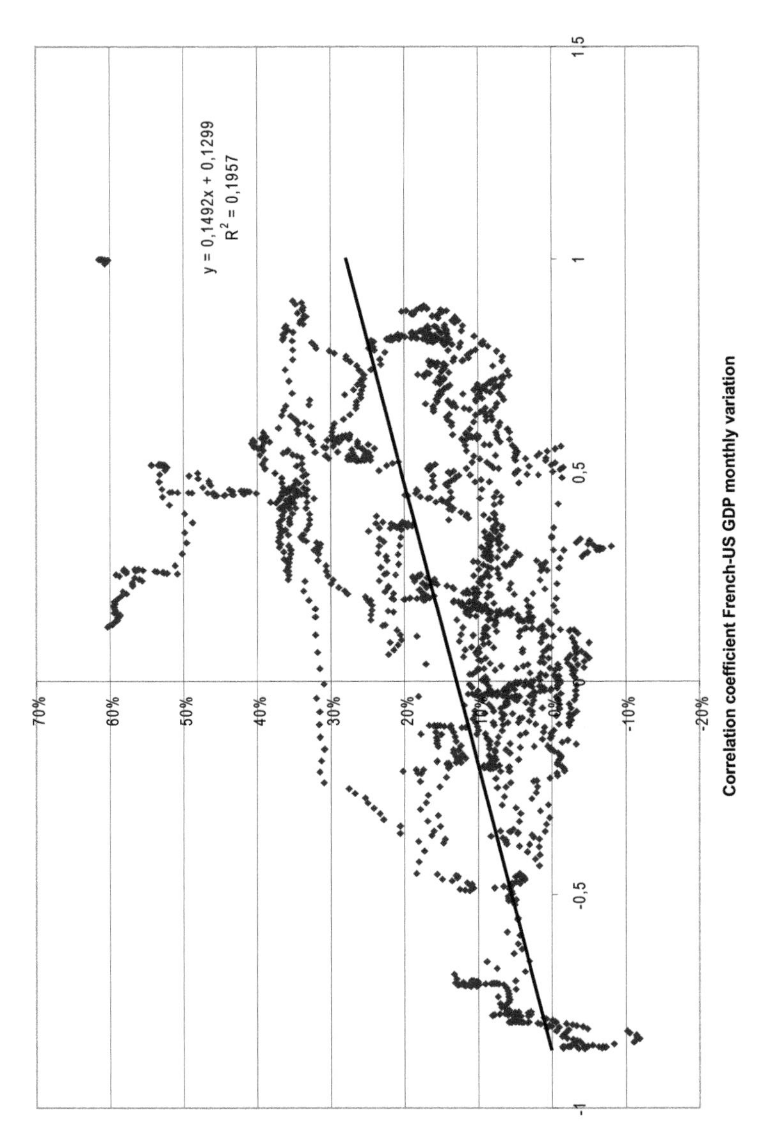

Sources: Goetzmann, Ibbotson, Peng (2000), Cowles, S&P, INSEE, Lévy-Leboyer & Bourguignon (1985), StatUS, author

The adjusted correlation coefficient is obtained by adjusting for the increase in variance of France from the month *m-1* to the month *m*, according to equation (8).

$$\delta = \frac{\sigma^{m}_{France}}{\sigma^{m-1}_{France}} - 1 \qquad (8)$$

The heteroskedasticity adjuster for France, *d*, is used to adjust the standard correlation coefficient using equation (9) following Forbes and Rigobon.

$$\rho^{*} = \frac{\rho^{u}}{\sqrt{1+\delta(1-(\rho^{u})^{2})}} \qquad (9)$$

where r^{*} is the adjusted correlation coefficient, and r^{u} is the standard correlation coefficient.

Monthly changes of the adjusted correlation coefficient are displayed on Figure 4.6. These changes are those borne by a French investor in US stocks or the reverse. They can be caused both by an important currency rate variation or by a fundamental change in correlation. But the period of the gold standard with a constant parity between the French franc and the dollar (1878–1914) does not appear to be specific when compared to later periods.

Nevertheless Figure 4.6 shows that exceptional changes in the correlation occurred especially outside the period of the gold standard. Table 4.1 reports the ten major increases and decreases in the correlation coefficient and proposes explanations. A financial shock can cause both increases (October 1987, November 1873) or decreases in correlation (Asiatic crisis). It is the same for war events. German and inter-allied debt agreements produced strong decreases in correlation.

Table 4.1. Major shocks on adjusted correlation coefficient of French and US stocks over 1854–2007.

Major changes in adjusted correlation coefficient		
1 september 1997	-6.92%	*Asiatic crisis*
2 april 1950	-5.39%	*Korean war starts*
3 july 1932	-5.30%	*Lausanne conference*
4 may 1955	-5.14%	*Vasovia pact*
5 july 1956	-5.13%	*Suez nationalization*
6 july 1984	-4.76%	*Fabius premier ministre,communists ministries outsted ?*
7 march 1943	-4.17%	*See Riva and Oosterlick in this book*
8 april 1972	-3.68%	*Monetary crisi in Europe*
9 november 1952	-3.53%	*Eisenhower president ?*
10 june 1929	-3.38%	*Young plan*
1 september 1867	8.42%	*Juglar cycle - European crisis*
2 october 1987	7.88%	*Wall Street krach*
3 june 1974	6.33%	*Chirac Premier ministre*
4 april 1965	6.21%	*March 1965 French elections won by opposition – Vietnam war escalation plus intervention in Dominica*
5 december 1949	6.02%	*?*
6 november 1973	5.10%	*Oil shock*
7 july 1949	4.82%	*Berlin blocus*
8 december 1914	4.67%	*end of movement war – US market opens again*
9 february 1920	4.16%	*?*
10 november 1873	4.05%	*Financial crisis*

Sources: Goetzmann, Ibbotson, Peng, Cowles, S&P, author

Figure 4.6. Changes in correlation coefficient of French and US stocks over 1854–2007.

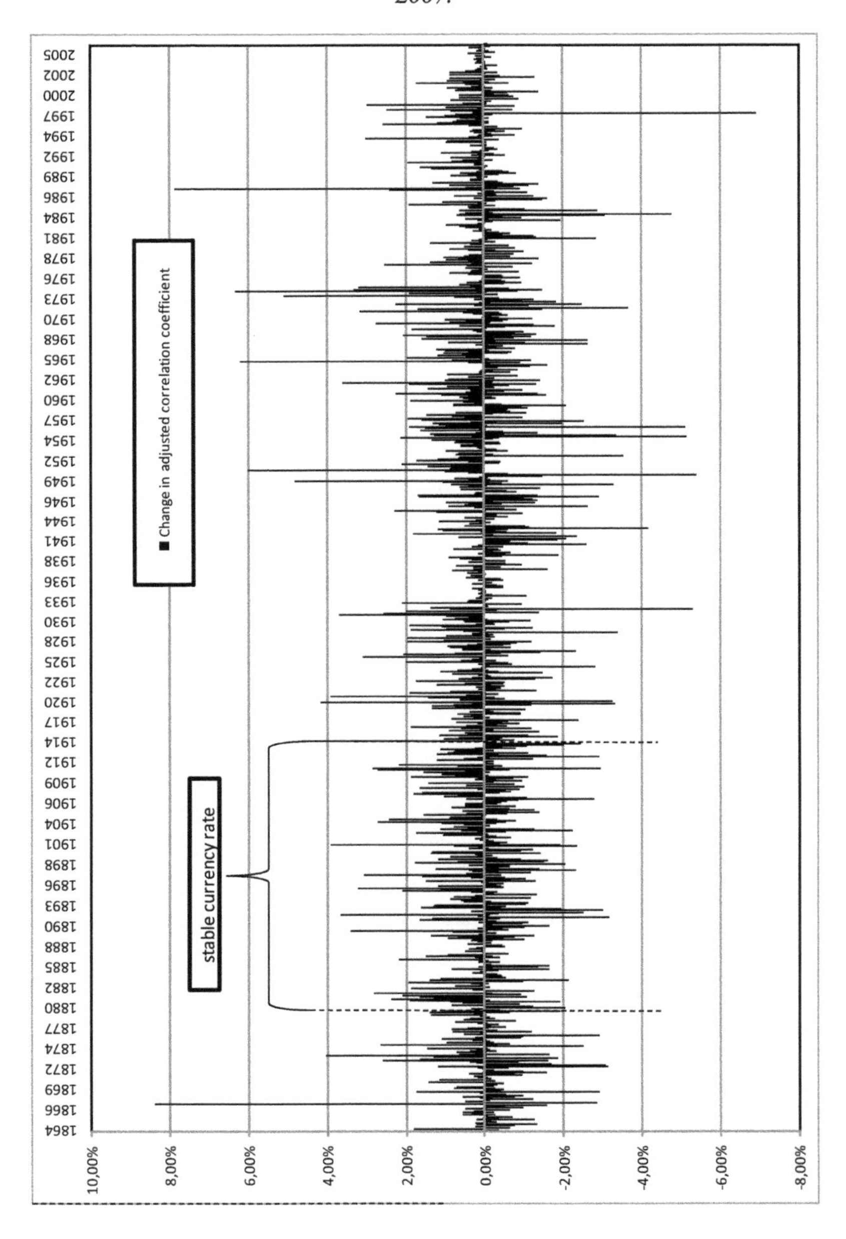

Sources: Goetzmann, Ibbotson, Peng (2000), Cowles, S&P, author

Conclusion

Before 1914, financial markets appear to have been integrated, as risk/return of international assets were consistent with each other. In other words the price of risk was the same across different markets and assets meaning that these markets were integrated. This integration was accompanied by a low level of stock market correlation between US and France. This distinction between integration and correlation is very consistent with capital exports. If the price of risk is the same across the world the only reason to explain capital exports is this low correlation. Before 1914, a French investor could achieve an important diversification gain through US stock purchases thanks to this very low level of stock market correlation.

Since the end of the international gold standard, stock market correlation increased strongly to a top floor during the 1930s. After the low point reached in the wake of the Second World War, correlation increased again to achieve an exceptional level in the recent years. Maybe these movements follow 'real economy' correlation. On a monthly view, some specific events, such as financial crisis or war, affect stock correlation, highlighting that correlation does not follow a stable linear trend.

The distinction between the international integration of financial markets and the correlation among them allows us to draw a more subtle story than the common knowledge of the first and second era of globalization just interrupted by the historical twentieth century characterized by state regulations and wars. The first era of globalization appears to be a first step with an integration of financial markets which authorize large capital flows. But before 1914, real economies kept following specific paths as indicated by the low level of asset correlation. An integrated market combined with low correlations motivate investors to export capital to benefit from a strong diversification effect. The second globalization, as we know, gradually has permitted an integrated market with the end of legal restrictions. On this aspect, it is just a return to the first globalization. However, today real economies seem to be also integrated and evolving together, leading to a high asset correlation. This leads to a paradoxical result: with the real integration today observed, the incentive to export capital decreases.

5 ASSESSING CONVERGENCE IN EUROPEAN INVESTMENT BANKING PATTERNS UNTIL 1914

Carlo Brambilla

Introduction

In continental Europe, the advent of railways, public utility companies and other capital-intensive industries took place from the mid-nineteenth century onwards as the progressive diffusion of a new wave of innovations, characterizing and giving shape to the energetic and technological paradigm known as the second industrial revolution. The affirmation and consolidation of this new paradigm stemmed from imitation and adoption of the new technologies throughout European industrializing countries, fostering convergence in the long run both in their economic and social structures, and eventually in income. Such a process, nevertheless, required the adoption of a financial innovation, which appeared around the 1850s and consolidated in the following decades, the joint-stock investment bank. As pointed out by a vast literature on economic development, starting from Gerschenkron's works, these banks were able to mobilize and rise large amounts of capital, and to allocate it to those 'new combinations of means of production' – the (big) business enterprises – characterized by high capital intensity, differed profitability and high degree of risk. Moreover, by creating and issuing tradable securities representing those investments and by organizing secondary markets wherein to trade them, the new banks increased industrial assets' liquidity, thus enhancing investors' willingness to buy and to hold them. Incorporated investment banks had often a common origin and fulfilled the same functions in continental Europe, starting a financial revolution and fostering both financial and industrial growth in second- or late-coming countries.[1] This notwithstanding, while a certain degree of economic convergence can be observed in those countries as their growth went on, it seems to be questionable that their financial systems, and especially their financial intermediaries, experienced that same degree of convergence. The observation of their structures, organization and activities suggests, in fact, that these investment banks were not all the same, but that they often adopted different patterns and degrees of specialization.

Retracing the financial revolutions which took place in continental Europe in the nineteenth century, this work focuses in particular on investment banking patterns' comparison in France, Germany and, especially, Italy, over the long run. Besides supporting the industrialization process, in fact, major large investment banks probably represented the most important financial innovation after the establishment of issuing banks and of standardized tradable public debt. As such, they had a relevant role in building and shaping those countries' emerging financial and credit systems, giving birth to modern banking. The paper considers great banks' evolution between the 1860s and the Great War, verifying and assessing differences and similarities among them, taking into consideration the structure of single banks. Quantitative analysis, indeed, shows that relevant differences emerged in the evolution of investment banking patterns in the three countries before 1914. The deepening of these differences during the period supports the hypothesis that divergence, rather than convergence, characterized investment banking patterns in continental Europe. The paper eventually tries to give reasons for such an outcome referring to institutional frameworks' peculiarities, rather than relying on classical explanations involving the permanence of economic growth differentials among countries or of different speeds in their economic convergence.

The Rise of Joint-Stock Banks in Europe

Though its origins can be traced back to the second quarter of the nineteenth century – when, first in France and then in Belgium, a number of pioneering projects were promoted in order to set up big financial institutes aimed at fostering industrial enterprises - the establishment of joint stock investment banking in continental Europe took place successfully around the mid of the century.[2] Pioneer of this financial revolution that rapidly diffused throughout the Continent was the Crédit Mobilier, promoted by the Pereire brothers who were able to gather a group of bankers, financiers and industrialists around the project of a huge joint-stock investment bank, devoted to finance railways, public utilities and the related industries. As is well known, the foundation of the Crédit Mobilier in 1852 was rapidly followed in the succeeding years by that of several other institutes, such as the Crédit Industriel et Commercial and the Société Générale in France, or the Darmstädter Bank and the Disconto Gesellschaft in the German states. All these new institutes were big joint-stock banks, with huge amounts of share capital, whose charters tended to very much resemble those of the Crédit Mobilier in relation to the kind of activities they were allowed to carry out. In fact, their statutes all provided for the widest range of financial activities, such as promoting new firms and companies, and investing in public securities, but also underwriting, issuing and placing new shares and bonds on behalf of both firms and governments, making loans and advances in a variety of forms, and, not least, raising capitals through the collection of deposits and by issuing bonds of various kind and maturity. In this sense, they were multi-purpose banks, free to choose any kind of activities they preferred: specific banking regulation were still far to come and they were only subject to corporate laws,[3] as any other commercial or industrial company. Moreover, all these banks originated from the association of prominent banking houses – known in France as the *haute banque* – that the Pereire brothers caught off-guard when they launched their bank at the beginning of the 1850s. Those bankers, indeed, quickly understood the potential that the new banking pattern could have in both assuring endless and growing funding for new technologies and in making capital investments more liquid, therefore enlarging the audience of prospective investors, and thus they moved into the new business, promoting or becoming shareholders of these initiatives.[4]

The diffusion of this new pattern of investment banking throughout Europe has been widely discussed, alternatively underlining the pivotal role played by the Crédit Mobilier, not only in accelerating the financial revolution in France, but also in exporting it to the Continent, either serving as a model for new banks in the German states, or directly establishing new Crédit Mobilier-like banks in many countries; or emphasizing the presence of a class of bankers in different national contexts, already aware of the transformations that were taking place and that simply were able to do what the Pereires and the *haute banque* were doing in France.[5] What seems to emerge from the literature, however, is the presence in continental Europe of a relevant community of 'old' merchant-bankers which occupied the high segments of finance and was often cosmopolitan in character. They collaborated in many *affaires*, such as issuing, underwriting and launching government loans and railways bonds and shares in various countries, and tended to establish and develop personal relationships with each other, often enhanced by marital strategies, thus forming a wide financial network of bankers and financiers, to one or the other of its branches the founders of the new investment banks often belonged to.[6]

The evolution of the financial and credit systems in Europe accelerated in the following decades with the adoption of these banking features in almost all European developing countries. In Italy, for instance, great 'new' joint-stock investment banks arose after the example of the Crédit Mobilier. From the 1870s, Credito Mobiliare Italiano and Banca Generale[7] emerged as giants in an environment of dwarf or local banks. Although multi-purpose banks according to their charters, they were primarily committed to market activities and collaborated with the major note-issuing bank, Banca Nazionale nel Regno d'Italia, in placing Italian public debt securities, in emitting bond issues by provinces and municipalities, and in underwriting and placing railways companies' bonds and equities. After the financial crisis of the early 1890s had swept them away, two newly founded German-style universal banks, Banca Commerciale Italiana (Comit) and Credito Italiano (Credit), took their place as top rank investment banks[8]. During the two decades preceding the Great War, universal banks answered to the growing demand for investment banking and industrial financing induced by the upturn trend of the Giolittian years, committing themselves in financing especially new industries to which they offered a vast range of financial services.[9] While there is generally a certain agreement on the fact that new great banks tended to evolve towards unspecialized patterns, in particular following the German model of universal banking, the French case has been described as a peculiar one, in which the early disappearance of the investment banks' ancestor Crédit Mobilier, in 1867, and other shocking episodes such as the bad experience suffered by Crédit Lyonnais in the 'affaire Fuchsine' and the crack of Union Générale in 1882, convinced big banks as the Société Générale and the Crédit Lyonnais itself to accelerate the realization of a nation-wide network of branches and to rapidly specialize in safer activities, such as deposit and commercial banking, while only few big institutes, first and foremost Paribas, devoted themselves to 'pure' investment banking.[10]

In this sense, high segments of the emerging credit systems in continental Europe can be roughly described as dominated by great unspecialized investment banks, with possibly the partial exception of France, whose credit system experienced the articulation in several layers of specialization already from the late 1880s.[11] As both historians and banking scholars have shown, what defines banking patterns is what banks did and the way they did it. In other words, banking patterns are concerned with the kinds of activities these banks carried out, and in which proportion, as compared to their total assets. Therefore, a comparative quantitative approach is adopted here to verify and assess whether divergence, rather than convergence, characterized investment banking patterns in the Continent before the First World War.

Comparing Investment Banking Patterns: Balance Sheets and Assets Composition

In order to compare investment banking patterns, balance sheets of prominent great investment banks from the three major continental European economies, namely those of Germany, France and Italy, have been collected and analysed. Banks are chosen according to their relevance in investment banking, in fostering industrial development and for their significant role in the development of their respective financial systems. Therefore the paper considers the French Crédit Mobilier, Crédit Industriel et Commercial, Crédit Lyonnais, Société Générale, Paribas, and Crédit Commercial de France; the German Bank für Handel und Industrie (Darmstädter Bank), Disconto Gesellschaft, Deutsche

Bank, Dresdner Bank, Commerz und Disconto Bank; and the Italian Credito Mobiliare Italiano, Banca Generale, Comit, Credit.[12]

Balance sheets are often regarded as unreliable or inaccurate sources, as window-dressing and profit concealment are indeed quite well documented practices.[13] Nevertheless, such customs, especially as hidden profits and reserves are concerned, were principally aimed at preserving 'the trust of the public', i.e. to 'normalize' short-term fluctuations in earnings that could affect the perceived robustness of the bank, having indeed the effect of strengthening its capital structure. It has to be noted, then, that a relevant part of banks' assets and liabilities items (sharecapital, deposits, loans and advances) are expressed at nominal values and, as such, cannot be easily manipulated. Generally, then, assets liable to subjective valuation (securities and participations) were given prudential estimates, in order not to show excessive profits or constitute (hidden) reserves for coping with non-performing loans and other risks. Deviation from 'normal' habits could have happened, but if they persisted in the medium to the long term, they would have affected banks' soundness, eventually leading them to bankruptcy. Balance sheets, giving accounts on the development of a business over time, were also the primary form of self-representation of the firm itself – at least in the early stages of business enterprises' development – and a device managers have often used as an important signalling tool towards stakeholders. Indeed, even the economic press' reports on businesses' performance relied upon such kind of public sources. Thus, although accounting records could be hazy or blurry as for the quality of some of their items, they are still able to provide reliable information as for the choices and policies of bankers, and thus about banks' structures and patterns of specialization.

Balance sheet items from the aforementioned banks have therefore been collected, reorganized and standardized in a common grid. Assuming that similar balance sheet structures imply the adoption of the same banking patterns, raw figures have then been used to calculate financial ratios – such as liquidity, solvency, assets and liabilities composition, and so forth – and employed in the quantitative analysis to assess long-term convergence (divergence) among great investment banks. First, some of these ratios have been used to chart scatterplots in order to compare banks' assets and liabilities composition. Then a multivariate analysis method, cluster analysis, has been applied to all the ratios, to check for similarities among the banks. Cluster analysis permits to group objects of similar kind into respective categories, and to build taxonomies. Different kinds of clustering exist: in this work hierarchical clustering based on the single linkage method and the Euclidean distance – which adopt a 'friend to friend' clustering strategy – has been used. Thus each bank (object) is assigned to its own cluster and then the algorithm proceeds iteratively, joining at each stage the two most similar clusters according to their characteristics (financial ratios), continuing until there is just one single cluster. Groups resulting from computing represent similar banking patterns among the banks considered.[14]

The first two scatterplots (Figures 5.1 and 5.2) show assets composition for all banks considered, permitting to verify which kinds of activities each bank choose to privilege. The X axis refers to 'direct loans' (loans, advances, discounts, etc.), while the Y axis concerns 'investments' (industrial shares and bonds, securities and other marketable instruments purchased by banks): 'pure' investment banks are then expected to dispose in an upper left area (high investments, low direct loans), while specialized commercial ones would place themselves in the opposite corner; the central area identifies banks with fairly relevant, though variable, shares of both direct loans and investments, that is universal banks. Figures 5.1 and 5.2 are relative to two subperiods: the first plots data concerning the Crédit Mobilier (1856–65)[15] and all banks existing in the 1876–85 period; the other plots data concerning all banks (but the meanwhile failed ones) in the 1895–1912 period.

What emerges from Figure 5.1 is that the Crédit Mobilier is the only 'pure' investment bank in the sample, while both Italian Crédit Mobilier-style banks tend to slide towards the central area, overlapping with Paribas and other banks. In the right corner, with relatively high shares of direct loans and quite a low proportion of investments are the Crédit Lyonnais and the Crédit Industriel et Commercial, to which Deutsche Bank, Dresdner Bank and Commerz und Disconto Bank tend to get close. Société Générale and Banca Generale tend to concentrate right in the central part of the graph, with very balanced proportions in their assets, while both Paribas and the Darmstädter Bank, though positioned in the same area, show higher shares of investments to their total assets. In Figure 5.2, while pure investment banking disappears, all banks tend to glide towards a composition in assets with lower amounts of investments and higher proportions of direct loans, suggesting a certain convergence did take place along the period. This notwithstanding, at a closer look some relevant differences emerge among these banks. While Crédit Lyonnais seems to have adopted a commercial banking pattern, with the highest share of direct loans and the lowest in investments, Crédit Industriel et Commercial, Société Générale and Crédit Commercial de France, though retaining only a small proportion of investments, show lower shares of direct loans as compared to the former. Also the other banks show some differences in their policies. Although most of Italian and German banks group in the same wide area, which would imply the adoption of similar unspecialized patterns, Comit and Darmstädter Bank tend to stay in the same subarea clearly separated from the others to the left, with lower shares of direct loans. Paribas, then, with the highest proportions of investments, tends to find a position alone in the central upper end of the graph. That seems to suggest the presence of different patterns of investment banking, casting doubts on convergence.

Figures 5.3 and 5.4 plot solvency and liquidity ratios for the same periods and banks. At first glance, these scatterplots seem to suggest that a certain degree of convergence in banking patterns emerged between 1870s and 1910s. In fact, in both graphs most of the banks tend to form a 'cloud' in the same area, denoting the adoption of similar proportions of capital and liquidity ratios.

Nonetheless, also in this case some differences can also be noted. In Figure 5.3, for example, Crédit Lyonnais, Société Générale and the Crédit Industriel et Commercial tend to depart from the other banks, showing higher liquidity ratios; nonetheless, Banca Generale too can be found in the same area, though with higher solvency ratios. Moreover, in Figure 5.4, while Société Générale and Crédit Industriel et Commercial have mantained the same policy as before, the Crédit Lyonnais has shifted left (lower liquidity) towards the other banks. The 'cloud' of bank is now tighter than in Figure 5.3, with banks grouping around lower values both of liquidity and solvency, even though Darmstädter Bank has probably moved up on higher solvency ratios. Though perhaps suggesting a certain tendency towards specialization, at least as far as some banks are concerned, it seems however that no clear-cut answer on investment banking patterns' convergence emerges from these outcomes. The next section then tries to deepen this study using cluster analysis.

Figure 5.1. Banks activities 1856–85.

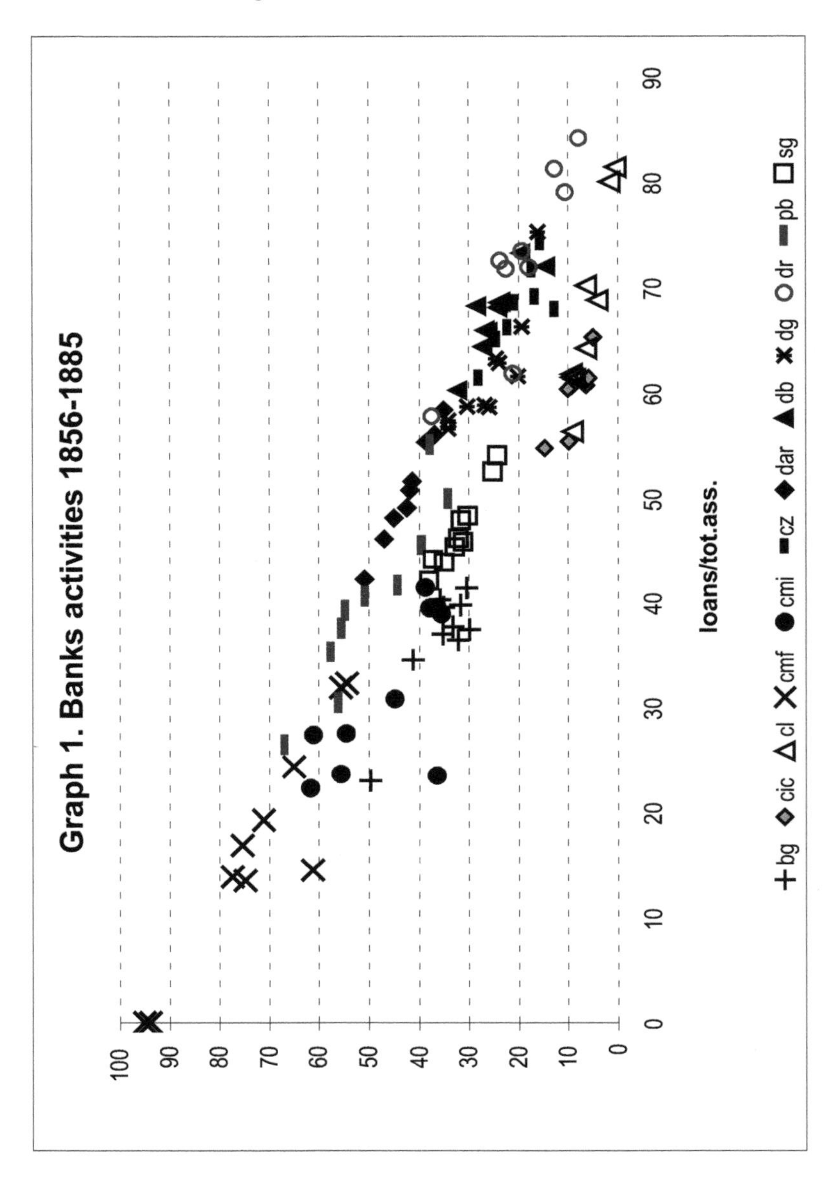

Figure 5.2. Banks' activities 1895–1912.

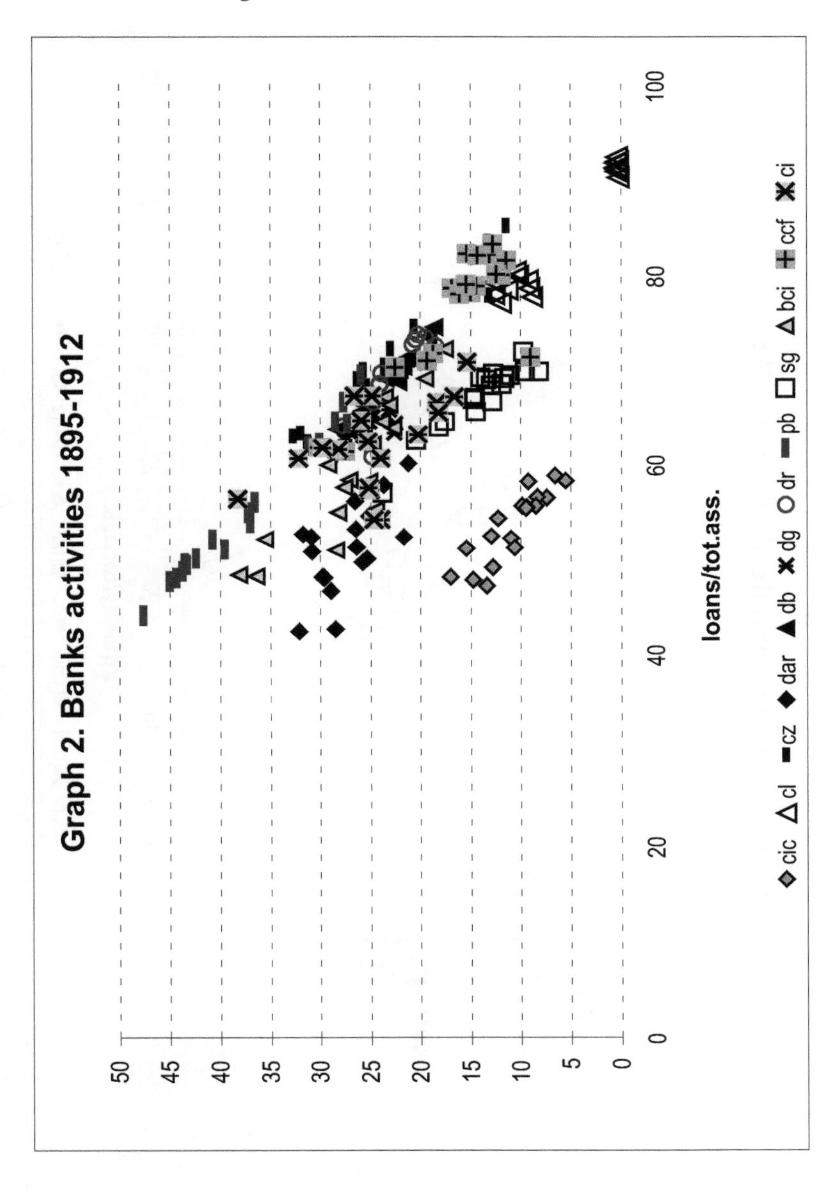

Figure 5.3. Solvency and liquidity 1856–85.

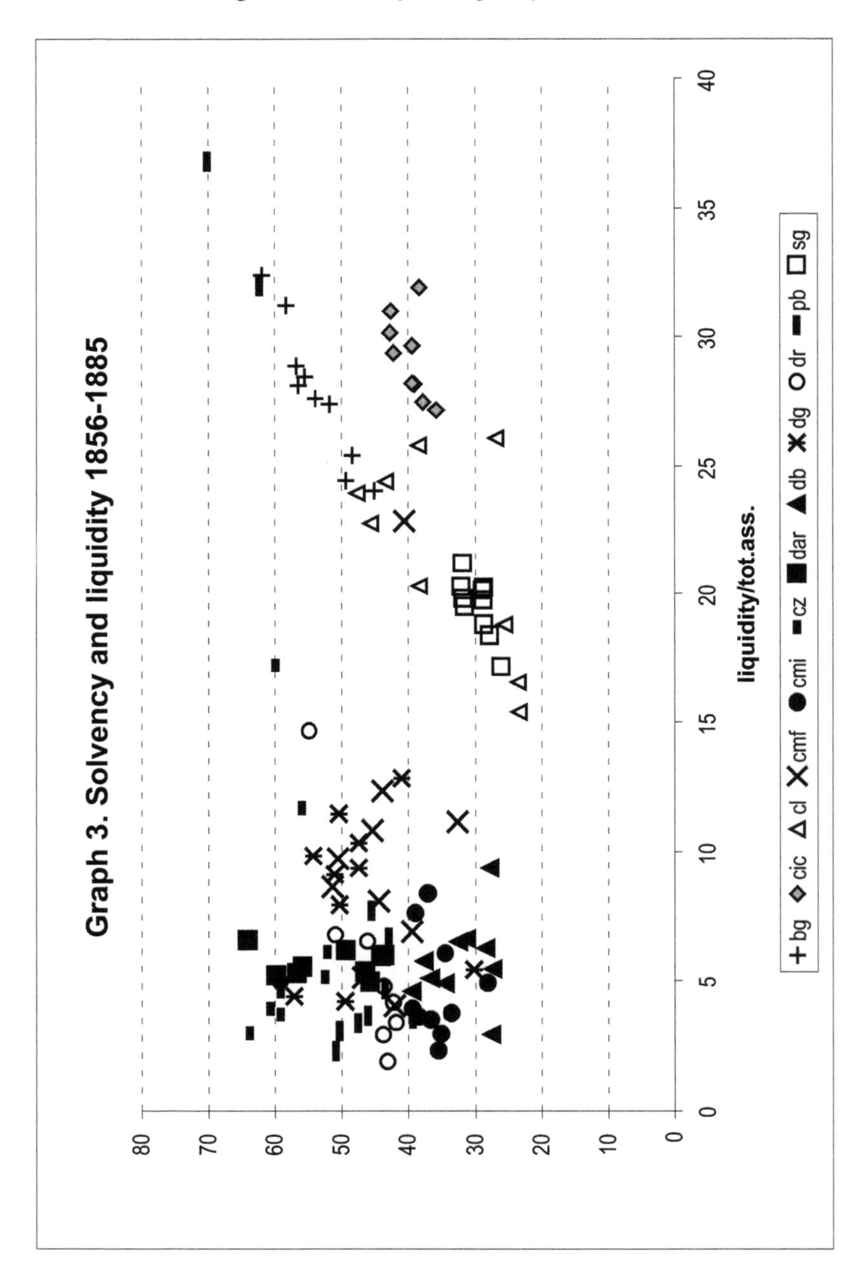

Figure 5.4. Solvency and liquidity 1895–1912.

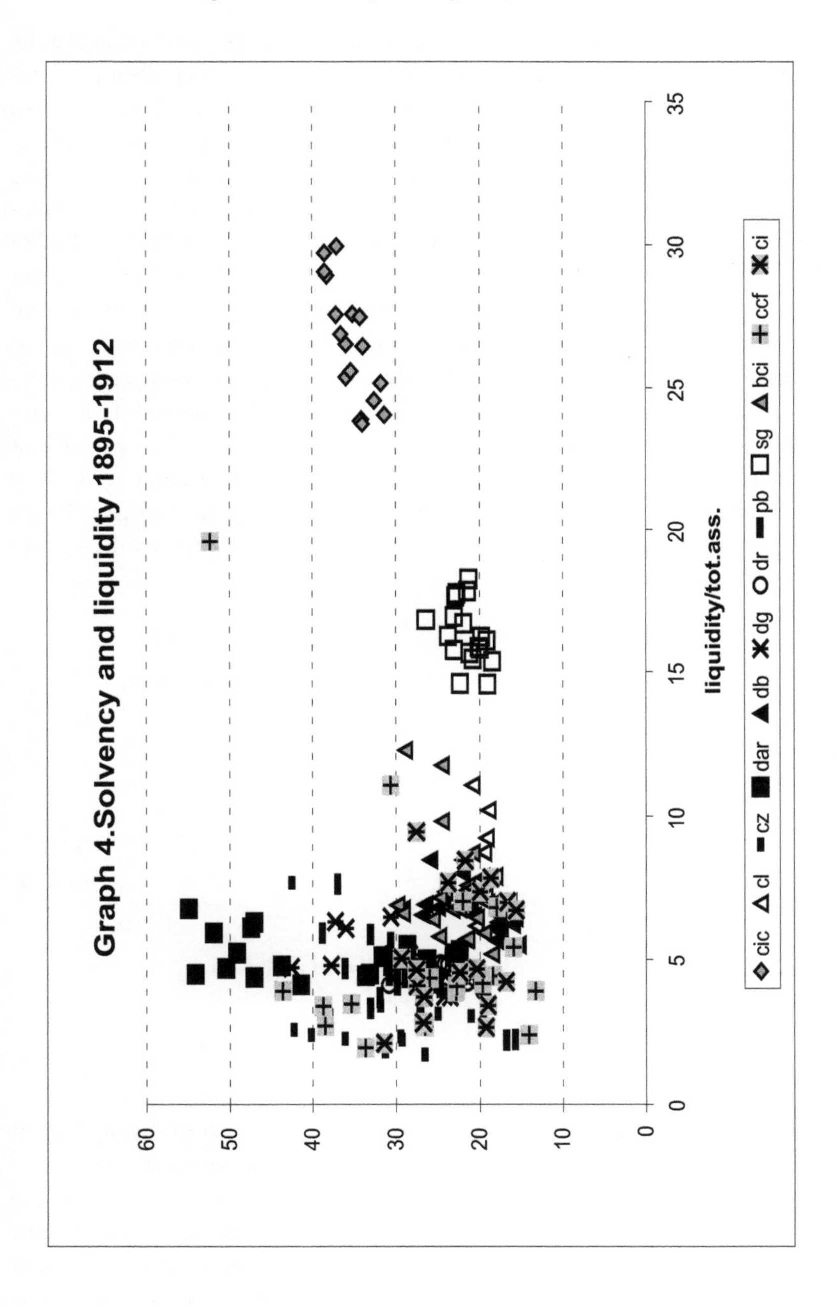

Assessing Divergence: Evidence from Cluster Analysis

Cluster analysis, as recalled above, permits us to make comparisons among banks, or other objects of study, taking into consideration many of their distinctive features at the same time. In this case, eleven financial ratios for each bank were used to compute a series of clusters for the entire period, from the 1850s to the 1910s. Figures that follow (5.D1 to 5.D5) represent a few relevant and typical examples of incorporated investment banks' behaviour in the period and of their evolution in the long run. Figures 5.D1 and 5.D2 show clusters for 1877 and 1885 (data on the Crédit Mobilier are relative to, respectively, 1857 and 1865). What seems to be clear is that the Crédit Mobilier doesn't group with any other bank in the sample, and, moreover, that the distance between the Pereires bank and the other European investment banks is always very high, thus suggesting quite different behaviours between the former and the latter. In other words, it seems questionable that this bank – often considered a precursor and an ancestor of joint stock investment banking on the Continent – represented a model for later experiences. Or, perhaps more likely, that in just a decade the other great banks developed different patterns of functional organization. Moreover, these latter seem to be quite similar to one another.

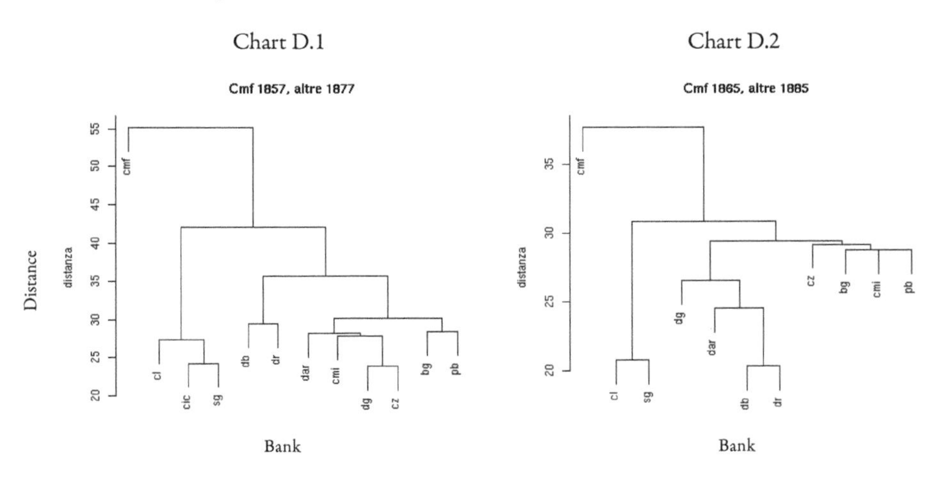

In fact, in both charts, the only other clear cut cluster is that of the big French banks Crédit Lyonnais and Société Générale, which soon developed a massive multi-branch and deposit collection strategy: they group together at the second iteration at most, and at very low distances. Paribas, the Italian Credit Mobilier-style banks and the German banks tend to group together at various stages between the third and the fifth iteration, at small overall distances, thus suggesting quite high degrees of similarity. Inside this cluster, a closer look to its components suggests the presence of two patterns, one emerging from the stronger similarity among second-generation German banks, especially as for Deutsche Bank and Dresdner Bank, and the other highlighted by quite rapid convergence among the first generation Italian and German banks and Paribas.

Considering these first two charts altogether, therefore, suggests that divergence rather than convergence in European investment banking patterns is already emerging in the 1870s and 80s. On the one hand, in fact, we can observe three quite well-defined clusters already in the 1870s: that of the French great deposit banks, the ancestor – whose model is already abandoned by the others at a decade from its introduction – and that of all other investment banks. On the other hand the emergence of a cluster grouping together the most relevant second generation German banks suggests the process of divergence being likely to deepen in the following decades.

And in fact, between the 1890s and the 1910s, the situation evolved even further (Figures 5.D3 to 5.D5). At a first glance to these clusters, it is immediately clear how Italian universal banks have developed their own pattern, which distinguishes them from any other great European bank.

Chart D.3

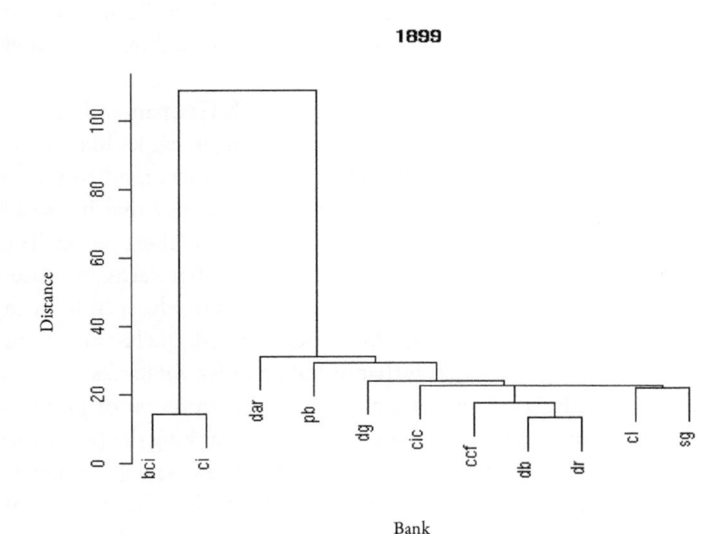

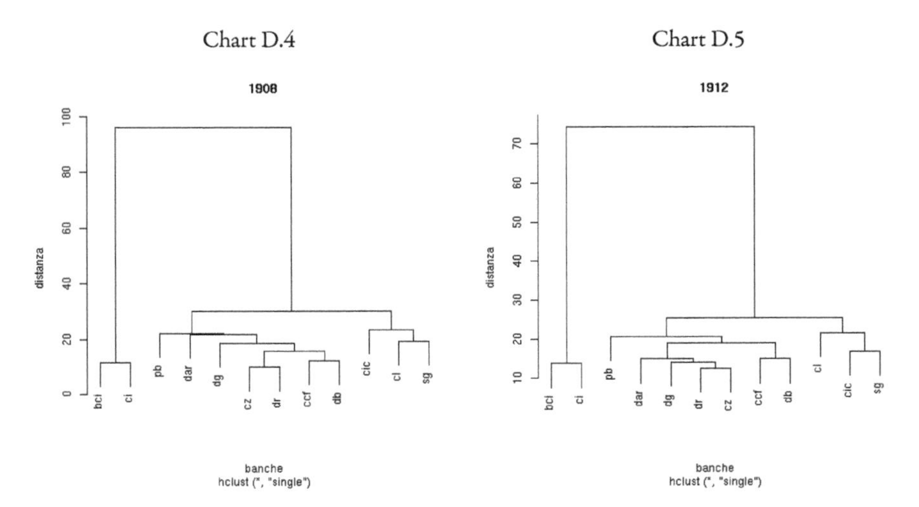

Comit and Credit, indeed, group in the same cluster immediately, at very low distances in the whole subperiod. In Figure 5.D3, Crédit Lyonnais and Société Générale already adopted deposit banking and show a similar structure, grouping together at a certain distance from the other banks forming the second large cluster; this tendency is confirmed and accentuated in Figures 5.D4 and 5.D5, where the cluster made by the former and Crédit Industriel et Commercial is even more clearly shaped, revealing a fairly well-defined model, different to that of the other European great banks.

In all three charts, a larger cluster comprehends both German and French universal or investment banks. Quite interestingly, younger banks like Deutsche Bank, Dresdner Bank and Crédit Commercial de France, tend to group together at the first iterations and at short distances, a tendency that increases in the new century, suggesting a similar pattern characterizing these banks. The other German banks and Paribas gather to them shortly afterwards in subsequent iterations, forming a larger and fairly cohesive cluster which in its turn groups with that of French deposit banks. As already noticed, the last cluster to join the tree, and at very high distance, is that of Italian universal banks.

What emerges over the long term, then, seems to be a process of progressive divergence in the experience of European investment banking development. Starting in the middle of the nineteenth century, this process saw great investment banks spreading through the Continent following at first the example of the French Crédit Mobilier. A certain differentiation, then, took place already during the 1870s, with the early specialization of some great French banks in deposit banking, while other French, German and Italian banks remaining on an investment banking pattern, though quite different from that of their French ancestor Crédit Mobilier. Divergence became deeper in the following decades, when French deposit banking pioneers went on specializing in this business and developing a huge network of branches; along with them, other banks, as Paribas and Crédit Commercial de France remained – to a higher or lower degree – on a universal banking pattern, together with German ones. Even in universal banking did emerge divergence, as the case of the Italian banks clearly showed.

Explaining Divergence

These results seem to question classical explanations relying upon degrees of economic development as determinants for the adoption of specific patterns of financial organization. Although in those countries a process of financial modernization did take place and several kinds of financial institutions did emerge along the period, in fact, universal banking was not abandoned in any of them, but continued to characterize many of their larger and most prominent banks; moreover, these latter clearly adopted differentiated universal banking patterns. As emerged in quantitative analysis, this divergence depends on differences in banks' balance sheet structures, hence on the way continental investment banks decided to make use of the variety of tools they had at their disposal, or in other words on the adoption of a peculiar set of activities in which those financial tools were used in different proportions. Why was that? What are the reasons why similar financial institutions, blossomed from the same seed, quite well interconnected to each other and working on fairly open markets, decided to diversify their activities to the point that this resulted in banking patterns divergence?

Investment banks' ability to carry out their functions is related to the existence of proper institutional frameworks, such as the functioning of organized financial markets, the legal enforcement of contracts, and so forth. In Germany, indeed, universal banking enjoyed support and protection from the institutional context. The central bank supported universal banks providing a fairly stable system, as compared to the Italian or even the French one; connections between great banks and savings and cooperative banks helped the former raise funds and cope with up- and downturn trends more easily; and company laws passed from the 1870s permitted universal banks to better monitor debtor companies. In France, though the central bank showed less friendly or even sometimes hostile attitudes – as in the case of Crédit Mobilier – towards great banks, larger, deeper and less volatile financial markets encouraged small investors to hold bonds and shares, thus helping banks to channel investments to industrial companies with no need for maintaining large portfolios of securities.

As cluster analysis has shown, divergence in universal banking patterns is mostly due to Italian banks' behaviours, as compared to Central European ones. After reunification, the commercial code of 1865[16] tended to privilege the protection of entrepreneurs' rights and properties from possible speculators, however somehow sacrificing minority shareholders and creditors' rights to those of promoters.[17] Indeed, though till the introduction of the new commercial code in 1882 the government authorization for establishing limited liabilities firms and companies was needed, very weak measures were set up to ensure companies' and administrators' accountability.[18] The segmentation of the credit system, on the one hand, and the characters of the institutional framework, on the other, can explain the strong ties Credito Mobiliare Italiano and Banca Generale established with Banca Nazionale, which sustained them whenever downturns or crises threatened their liquidity.[19] Their primary commitment to market activities can then be seen as an attempt to preserve their own stability in an economic context in which creditors suffered a lack of information. Most of these activities indeed concerned either risk-free securities, or public utilities and basic industries, these latter being basically projects of national interest, hence offering high guarantees. In this sense, the similarities between the Italian and (especially) the first generation German banks (Figures 5.D1 and 5.D2) are coherent with the establishment of gerschenkronian banks during the early phases of financial development and of infrastructural modernization in later comer countries.[20] When great infrastructural projects came nearly to an end, during the 1880s, the two banks started investing heavily in the real estate boom connected with the renovation of main cities like Rome and Naples, relying upon a patrimonial concept of credit. Unfortunately this was not sufficient to avoid bankruptcy when the bubble burst. Frozen assets in real estate and industrial investments, non performing loans and persisting economic depression, eventually led to their failure in 1892–3.[21]

The new commercial code of 1882 presented several novelties which ameliorated both the information disclosure on the part of companies and the minority shareholders' and creditors' rights as compared to the privileges of promoters and majority shareholders, improving corporate governance tools in joint-stock companies, so bringing Italian institutions closer to those of the other main European countries.[22] The new code, in fact, fixed a few stricter rules on bookkeeping and made annual balance sheet publication as well as a statutory board of auditors (*collegio sindacale*) compulsory. However, the law only prescribed that balance sheets reported the exact amount of profits and losses, of capital and of reserves, but did not fix rules on the quality and quantity of information to be given on other items, in contrast with other European legislations, such as those introduced in England, Belgium and Germany, which indeed provided for more precise and accurate bookkeeping practices.[23] The statutory board of auditors, then, was elected by the same majority that expressed the board of directors; moreover, the law was very soft about shareholding syndicates, interlocking and pyramidal shareholdings; and shareholders maintained the right to withdraw from the company at any time, a threat that can be used to oppose strategic decisions such as new capital issues, mergers and acquisitions, changes in the company objects, etc.[24]

Comit and Credit had to cope with a framework in which the newly founded Banca d'Italia was unable, and unwilling, to maintain the same strict, friendly relations and generous attitudes Banca Nazionale had had with the failed great banks.[25] Compared to their Italian ancestors, they showed stronger abilities to raise funds from customers, to manage multi-branch banking, particularly from 1900 onwards, and to maintain friendly and stable relations with international financial circles: that allowed them to more easily manage demand for funding and investment banking services through the organization of larger pools and syndicates, thus preventing too rapid exhaustion of their means and helping preserving their liquidity.

This notwithstanding, cluster analysis has shown how Italian universal banks' pattern was quite different from that of German ones. This suggests that they indeed developed peculiar strategies and adopt different sets of tools in performing their activities. In Germany the legal context provided several measures to discourage speculative behaviours: higher face value of stocks; a clear separation between common and privileged stocks; a balance of power between managing bodies – such as the board of directors and the executive board (*Vorstand*) – on the one hand, and controlling bodies – such as the supervisory board (*Aufsichtsrat*) and the auditors appointed by local authorities – on the other; wider information on companies situation and deeds; and more precise provisions on managers' responsibility in case of frauds.[26] By putting their own representatives in supervisory boards, German banks had a pretty effective means for overseeing and monitoring debtors, thus lessening their risks and guaranteeing for effective intermediation between savers and investors. The new law on the stock exchange of 1896, then, having banned future contracts for most securities and assured a stricter supervision over the stock exchange, brought a large share of securities' trading 'inside' the banks, hence fostering a stricter control by banks over the market, which enhanced their ability to assure long lasting commitment in industrial companies' financing. In Italy, the legal framework shaped by the commercial code of 1882 left important issues, such as that of the protection of minority shareholders' rights, or that of full information disclosure, still unresolved; moreover, the stock markets were smaller and more volatile, characterized by higher speculative behaviours which discouraged the diffusion of stock investments.[27] In such a context, then, Italian banks tried to cope with information asymmetries and to strengthen their position as creditors and/or minority shareholders first and foremost by acquiring enough voting rights in general meetings as to assure themselves one or more seats in the board of directors of the debtor companies and getting effective supervision over them.[28]

This practice implied, however, a careful tuning in order not to excessively burden banks' securities portfolios, hence endangering their own liquidity. And indeed balance sheets data suggest that Italian great banks did not maintain significantly higher participations in industrial companies than German ones. What, on the contrary, seems to differentiate Italian banks' balance sheets from the others, is the amount of *contangos* and, especially, of third parties' securities deposits (*conti titoli*), this latter being very tiny in French banks and absent in German ones. Comit and Credit securities deposits, on the contrary, amounted on average to two thirds or even more of their total assets.[29] In most French banks, *contangos* amounted to small proportions of total assets, while on average German ones invested more on them, but still to a lesser extent than Comit and Credit, which on average show figures in the order of 20 per cent of their assets.[30] Both *contangos* and securities deposits are indicators of proxy voting rights acquisition by Italian banks, a strategy that enabled them to maintain and extend supervision and control over companies, hence securing their position as creditors or minority shareholders, at a fraction of the cost that they would have had to bear for taking stakes in them. The variety of patterns and degrees of specialization that cluster analysis outcomes show are likely to be explained, then, by the different strategies each bank adopted in channelling funds to industrial undertakings while coping with a peculiar institutional environment. In this sense, French banks' ability to develop a greater division of labour, and a higher degree of specialization during the period was perhaps also due to the character of international financial centre and of prominent Continental market enjoyed by the Paris stock exchange, which, enhancing securities' liquidity, lessened needs for banks' direct industrial investments.

The international liquidity crisis of 1907 hit the Italian stock exchanges and interrupted financial markets development, which never recovered completely nor grew broader till the last decades of the twentieth century, thus leaving industrial capital supply entirely on banks' shoulders.[31] This had relevant consequences on the universal banks' ability to fulfil their functions while preserving their own liquidity and 'freedom of movement', since it compelled them to higher commitments towards industrial financing, and hence to eventually accept heavier portfolios of securities and illiquid loans, soon determining an involution in universal banks' patterns. This notwithstanding, there is no evidence of that in cluster analysis, nor in balance sheet ratios, before 1914. It was, in fact, after the war that universal banks saw their balance sheets progressively burdened both by industrial participations and illiquid assets. Comit and Credit found it more and more difficult to renew their assets and preserve their liquidity both because of the weakness of the Italian financial market, and of the shrinking of interbanking funding from European great banks, on which they had relied before the war. In such a situation, and while the segmentation of the credit system still prevented the development of a proper interbanking market,[32] universal banks progressively came to hold higher and higher amounts of industrial and public utilities' shares, transforming themselves in a sort of holding companies at the head of huge pyramidal financial groups.[33] As known, when changes in monetary policy curbed the ephemeral boom of the mid-1920s and general economic conditions deteriorated at the beginning of the 1930s, they eventually failed and had to be bailed out by the government.[34]

Conclusion

Modern banking arose in Europe between the 1850s and 60s to finance public utilities and other capital intensive industries, characterized by differed profitability and high degree of risk. Under many respects, these banks had very similar features: they blossomed from the same seed, fulfilled the same functions, performed the same activities, and were interconnected through a wide international network of bankers and financiers. Nonetheless, they evolved quite rapidly towards different patterns, as cluster analysis has shown. Reasons for such an outcome could have been many: initial similarities could have faded as 'sister institutions' grew up and affirmed their own 'personalities'; in this sense their own growth, leading to big bureaucratic businesses, may have weakened personal networks and relations among bankers; moreover, the international position of the hosting country may have accelerated the national path of development, as well as growing nationalistic sentiments, which interested large part of European new powers of the time, and could have affected the cosmopolitan attitude that characterized their original promoters.

A perhaps better explanation, though, is to be found in the evolution of institutional frameworks in hosting countries. Financial innovation, indeed, is not always attended and steered by 'regulative' innovation; thus banks have to adapt their strategies to the specific kinds of guarantees and risks they can rely upon and have to cope with. This affects the composition of the set of activities, the peculiar 'crafts', they can opt to use for performing their allocative functions. In Germany, indeed, the choice for universal banking found support in the evolution of the institutional and legal framework. On the one hand, central bank policies were aimed at protecting banks from overly sharp fluctuations and shocks; on the other, laws on companies and on the stock exchange, enhanced banks' ability to manage riskier activities. Though heavily inspired first by French and then by German ones, Italian banks choose instead a different pattern of development. The institutional framework, in fact, proved unable to sustain and foster the widening of credit and capital markets and to promote the integration of a segmented system. That prevented banks from specializing, as happened in France, but also to adopt a 'classic' universal banking pattern, as in Germany. In Italy, indeed, the legal system neither enhanced minority shareholders' rights – providing, for instance, for stronger controlling bodies and institutions as in Germany – thus limiting information disclosure by companies, nor limited stock exchanges' speculative attitudes and prices volatility. All this led to higher degrees of opacity as for investment projects' quality and industrial undertakings' performances, and to higher degrees of risk connected with capital investments. As a consequence, Italian great banks, whose monitoring and controlling strategies implied the acquisition of larger voting rights, were more exposed to liquidity risks and to financial crises, as the experience of Credito Mobiliare Italiano and Banca Generale showed. New universal banks addressed these issues trying to overcome credit markets segmentation by developing stable relations with European great banks and bankers, and to minimize their commitments towards industry by relying upon proxy voting, as large shares of securities deposits accounts and *contangos* in their balance sheets show, thus developing a distinctive universal banking pattern. Though these strategies proved effective in the medium term, they tended to increase capital markets weaknesses and instability, and after the 1907 crisis shook the system, banks' involvement in industrial companies grew, leading to their transformation in quasi-financial holdings during the 1920s, and eventually to their failure at the end of the decade.

6 SWISS BANKING CRISES DURING THE GOLD STANDARDS, 1906–71

Dirk Drechsel

Introduction

Switzerland participated in the varying gold standards in the period 1871–1971. Switzerland backed its currency to gold and committed itself to fixed gold exchange rates from 1878–1914 and from the end of 1924 until 1936. After the Second World War Switzerland returned to gold convertibility until 1973. In order to understand the implications of the gold standard regimes for the divergence and convergence of international financial systems it is important to investigate the outcome for the banking industry. Using a new data set on Swiss banking it becomes possible to study banks' balance sheets over a long time period from 1906 until 1971.

During these times Switzerland had to cope with three banking crises, the first being a consolidation of the banking industry in the years 1911–14 and the second one a result of the First World War in the years 1920–1. Last, a very severe banking crisis occurred in the wake of the Great Depression in the years 1931–5.

In this chapter, the three Swiss banking crises in the period 1906–71 will be analysed with respect to gold standard membership. The gold standard regimes might have helped European financial systems to converge and to prosper growth due to the reductions in exchange rate fluctuations during normal times. At the same time increased international interdependencies might have made the Swiss financial industry more vulnerable to foreign shocks in times of crises.

An indicator measuring the output gap between the potential return on equity and actually achieved return on equity is proposed, instead of using the traditional measures such as return on equity, Tier I ratio or cost–income ratio. By including the profit and loss accounts as well as balance-sheet data in the investigation, it becomes possible to reduce a comprehensive data set to one single measure. If a banking group strongly deviates from its potential output it is considered to be under distress. Potential output is measured by a profit function with return on equity as the dependent variable and balance sheet and profit and loss account data as independent variables. The output gap is determined by applying stochastic frontier analysis. Broadly speaking, the theoretical potential output as estimated by the profit function is compared with the actual output. The ratio of the two is the output gap and indicates how close a banking group is to realizing its potential return on equity.

The remainder of the chapter is structured as follows. Section two briefly outlines the Swiss banking system. Section three gives a short introduction to the applied stochastic efficiency analysis. The results are described in sections four and five. While section four gives an overview over the entire observation period 1906–71, section five looks into the banking crises in detail. Section six concludes.

The Swiss Banking System

Roughly speaking, the Swiss banking system can be divided into three major groups. The first group is formed by the big universal banks, the second by the cantonal banks, and the third by various smaller banking sections such as the savings and regional banks, private banks and foreign banks. In terms of the size of balance sheets, the Swiss banking system is dominated by the 'Big Two', the UBS and the Crédit Suisse.

The origins of the modern Swiss banking system lie in the early nineteenth century when a great number of savings banks were founded. In the middle of the century, the economic elites of Zurich, Winterthur and Basel created several commercial banks from which emerged the big universal banks. The creation of the cantonal banks started in the 1830s, but the breakthrough occurred in the 1860s, when owners of small and medium businesses demanded banks for their own needs, as the big commercial banks were limiting themselves to giving credit to the large Swiss industrial firms and railway companies. Ultimately, the foundation of the cantonal banks was a result of a political movement which explains why this Swiss banking group is the only one with explicit state guarantee. The most important cantonal bank is the Zürcher Kantonalbank operating since 1870.

Figure 6.1. Categories of banks' market shares as percentage of balance sheets total, 1906–2007.

Figure 6.2. Balance sheet total by bank categories, in million Swiss Francs (2005), 1906–65.

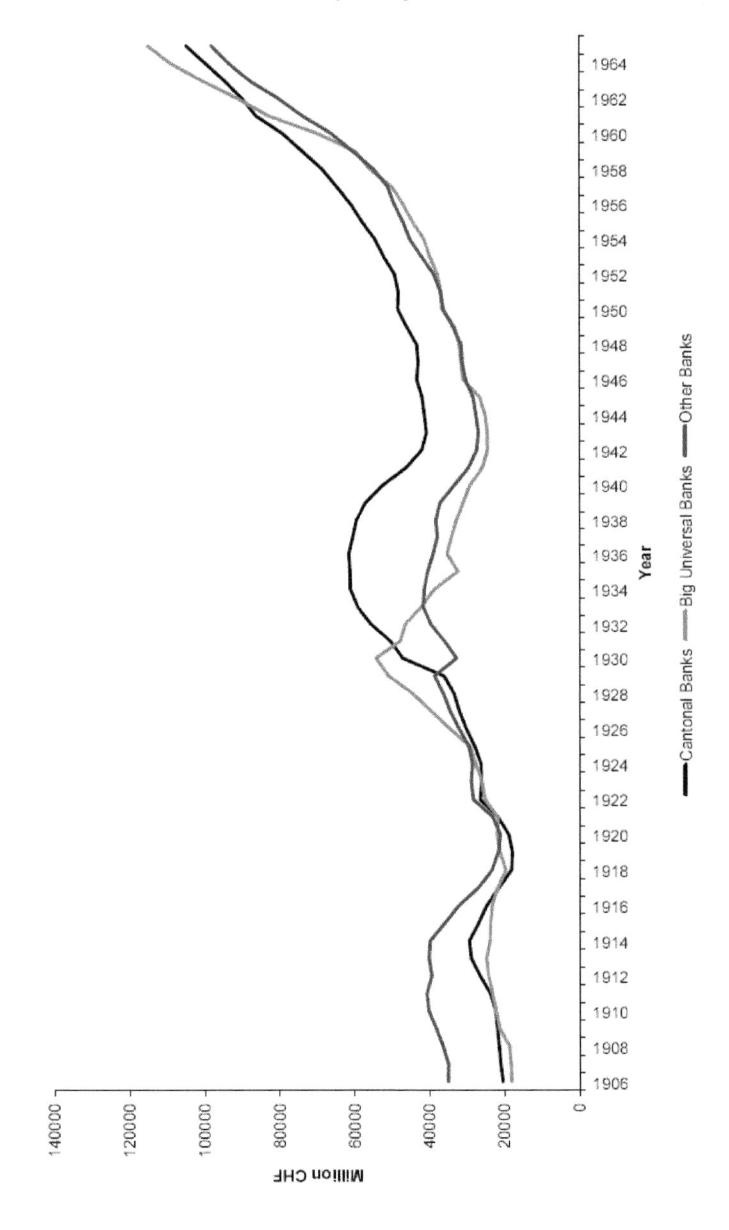

Up until the 1960s, the size of the balance sheets of the big banks and the cantonal banks was roughly the same.

Identification of Banking Crises

Stochastic frontier analysis has been pioneered by Aigner *et al.*[1] and Meeusen and Van Den Broeck.[2] The approach helps to distinguish between productivity changes, input factor accumulation and technical efficiency. Stochastic frontier analysis is a parametric method, i.e. it requires the specification of a functional form for the production or cost function. In the context of the present paper output gaps will be measured as profit intermediation efficiency.

A frontier profit function describes the maximum profit (in this case Return on Equity, ROE) which is achievable with a given set of inputs. Profit intermediation inefficiency occurs if a bank uses more resources than necessary for a given level of production, i.e. produces below the frontier. If banks perform below their potential ROE, the deviation can be used as an information about the bank's distress based on balance sheet data. The procedure follows Coelli and Battese.[3]

The deviations from potential output (return on equity) have been estimated utilizing stochastic frontier analysis. For the exercise, commercial bank balance sheets collected by the Swiss National Bank have been used. The Swiss National Bank aggregated single banks' information into banking groups (big banks, cantonal banks, local banks, co-operatives, wealth management banks, foreign banks, commercial trade banks, customer loans banks, private banks). Balance sheet data on return on equity, salaries, interest payments, write-offs, customer loans, stocks and securities, mortgages, interbank loans, physical capital, risk and money market claims have been used.

Figure 6.3 describes a profit function. The profit function indicates the maximal possible ROE a bank can realize. If the actual achieved ROE lies below the profit function, i.e. below the maximal possible ROE, a bank produces below its limit. The difference between the actually achieved ROE is the ineffciency or output gap measure used in this paper. The larger the output gap the less a bank realizes its profit potential. The profit function is parameterized by a Translog function.[4] In general, the setup for the profit function is:[5]

$$\begin{aligned}
\ln \pi_{it} &= \alpha_i D_i + \sum_j \beta_j \ln W_{ijt} + \sum_j \delta_j \ln Y_{ijt} + \sum_j \rho_j \ln Z_{ijt} \\
&+ 0.5 \sum_j \sum_k \lambda_{jk} \ln W_{ijt} \ln W_{ikt} + 0.5 \sum_j \sum_k \vartheta_{jk} \ln Y_{ijt} \ln Y_{ikt} \\
&+ 0.5 \sum_j \sum_k \varsigma_{jk} \ln Z_{ijt} \ln Z_{ikt} + 0.5 \sum_j \sum_k \varphi_{jk} \ln W_{ijt} \ln Y_{ikt} \\
&+ 0.5 \sum_j \sum_k \eta_{jk} \ln W_{ijt} \ln Z_{ikt} + 0.5 \sum_j \sum_k \phi_{jk} \ln Y_{ijt} \ln Z_{ikt} \\
&+ v_{it} \quad u_{it}
\end{aligned}$$

Figure 6.3. Method: Stochastic frontier analysis.

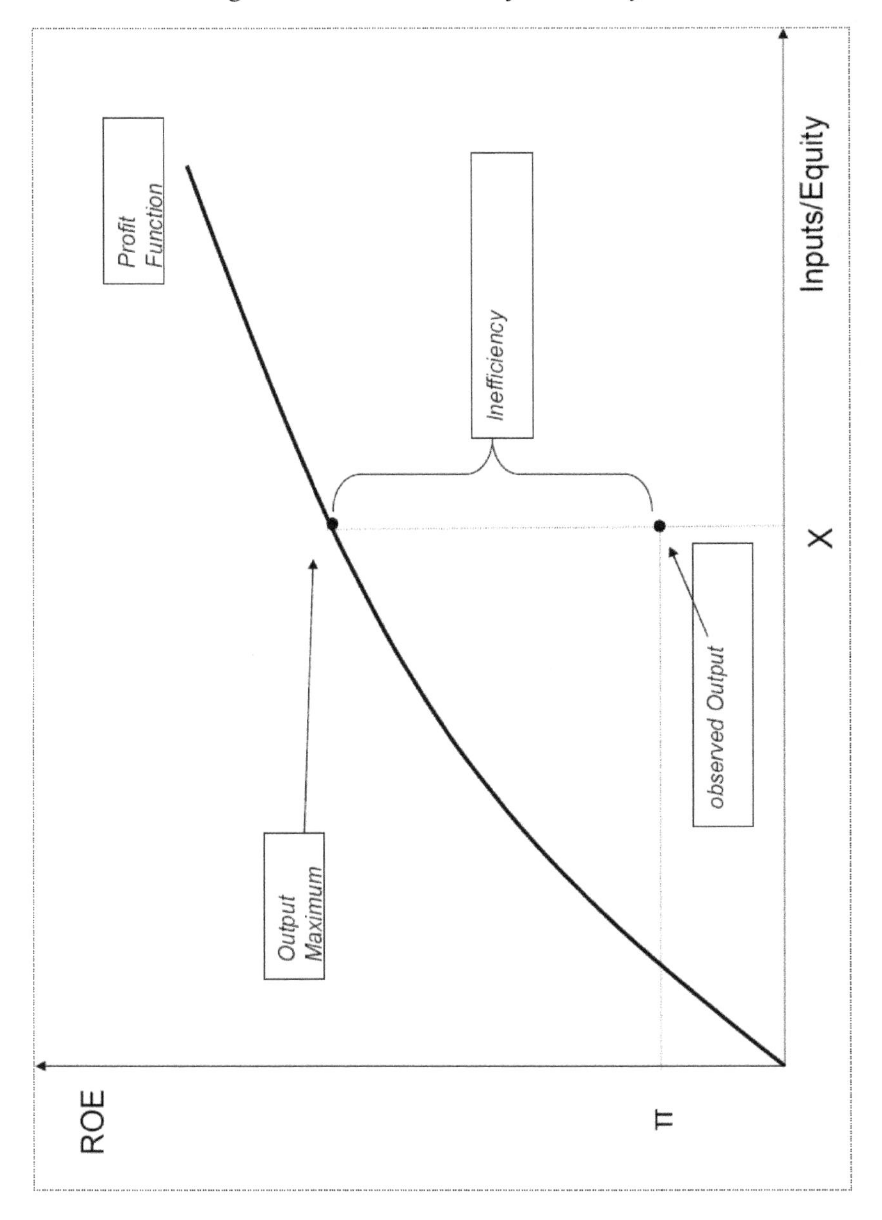

The index *i* represents a banking group, *t* time and *j, k* the entries in the respective vector. π_{it} is return on equity, W_{ijt} are inputs, Y_{ijt} are outputs, Z_{IJT} netputs and D_i dummies for the different banking groups. α and β are parameter vectors. The random disturbances v_{it} are assumed i.i.d. $N(0, s_v^2)$ of the output gaps u_{it}.

The output gaps *uit* are truncated normal, $u_{it} \sim N^{+}(\mu_{it}, \sigma_{u}^{2})$. Symmetry restrictions apply for $\lambda_{jk} = \lambda_{kj}$; $\vartheta_{jk} = \vartheta_{kj}$ and $\varsigma_{jk} = \varsigma_{kj}$. Following the literature,[6] all variables have been divided by equity capital to cope with the different sizes of the banking groups and to avoid heteroskedasticity. For 1930–71 the output vector consists of loans to customers/equity, interbank loans/equity, mortgages/equity, money market claims/equity and stocks and securities/equity. The vector of input contains salaries/equity, interest payments/equity and the risk measure risk weighted assets (RWA)/equity is based on the Basel II Accord. The construction of RWA follows the Basel II Accord[7] and tries to capture the ex-ante risk of defaults (the ex-post risk of default is given by the defaults themselves). It has been computed as

$$\text{RWA} = \sum_{i} w_i \times \text{Asset}_i \times \text{Equity Requirement},$$

where *wi* are the weights for each asset, calculated by the Bank for International Settlement based on historical default rates. The netput vector contains physical capital/equity and time in order to capture non-neutral technological change between the variables and ROE. Physical capital has been used instead of office expenses due to the unclear composition of office expenses (it contains office consumption like paper and ink cartridges, as well as investments like computers and books, etc.) Group-specific intercept dummies have been used to control for idiosyncratic differences between banking groups.[8] For 1906–29 dummies, output and netput vectors remain the same. Due to data limitations the input vector contains administration expenses instead of wages.

The output gaps for 1906–29 have been taken from estimates for the time period 1906–2005 and equal those used for 1930–2007 except for the input vector, which for 1906–2005 contains administration expenditures and a modified risk measure (due to the availability of data). Further details on the estimation and results can be found in Drechsel and Straumann.[9]

Distribution of Output Gaps

In between 1906–71 three major banking crises can be identified: the bank consolidation 1911–14, the post World War I inflation and the Great Depression. Additionally disturbances after World War II and during the turbulent 1970s are visible.

The bank consolidation of 1911–14 and the real estate and business loans crisis were homemade. The credit risk models and measures were too weak, overconfidence in banking capacities and asset quality led to deterioration of credit quality which could not be overseen anymore. This crisis led to consolidation pressures within the Swiss banking industry, forming stronger banks with higher equity ratios and better risk management by mergers and acquisitions on a large scale.

The crises of 1919–20 and 1931–6 are rooted in external finance shocks hitting the Swiss banking industry.

Figure 6.4. 1906–66 Return on Equity Profit Function Efficiency Scores.

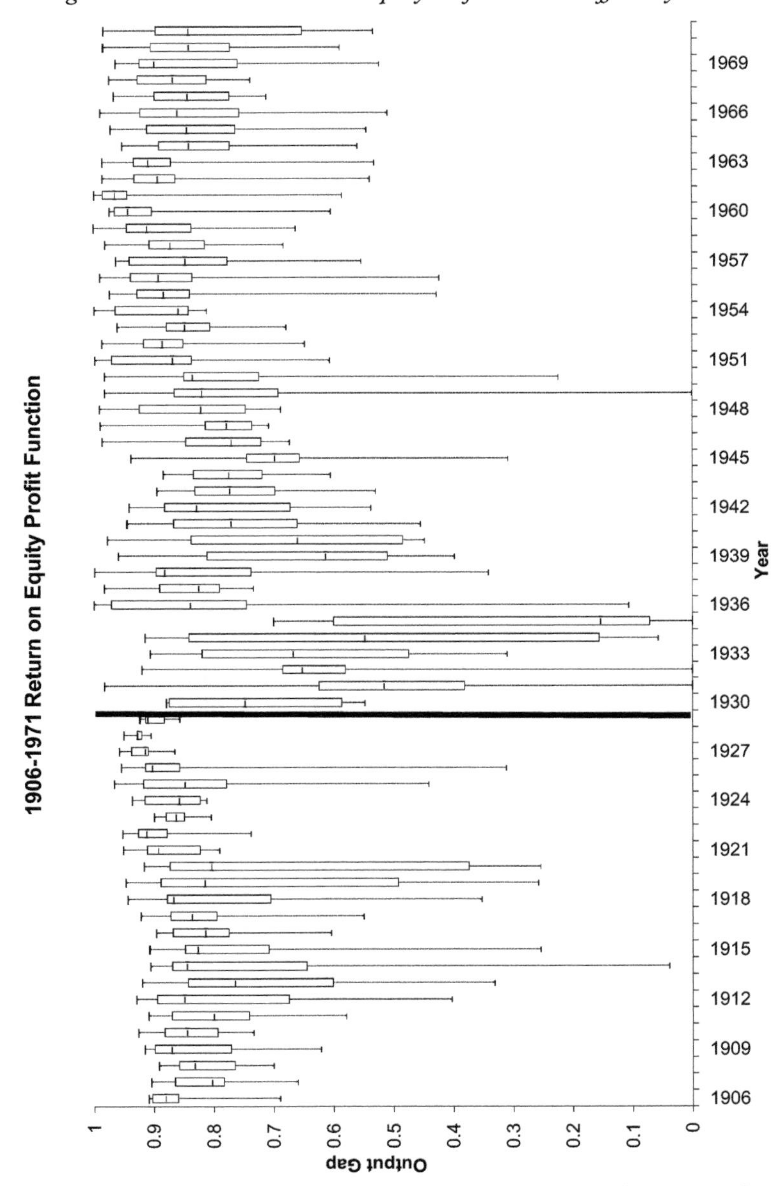

Figure 6.4: The upper and lower twinkers represent the maximum and minimum values, the box in between the 75 per cent, 50 per cent and 25 per cent quantiles. The thick black line is the weighted average. The weights are determined by the relative balance sheet size. The outputs gaps have been estimated by applying Stochastic Frontier Analysis. The estimation period is 1930–2005. Further details can be found in Drechsel and Straumann (op. cit.).

Figure 6.5. Bank Consolidation, 1911–14.

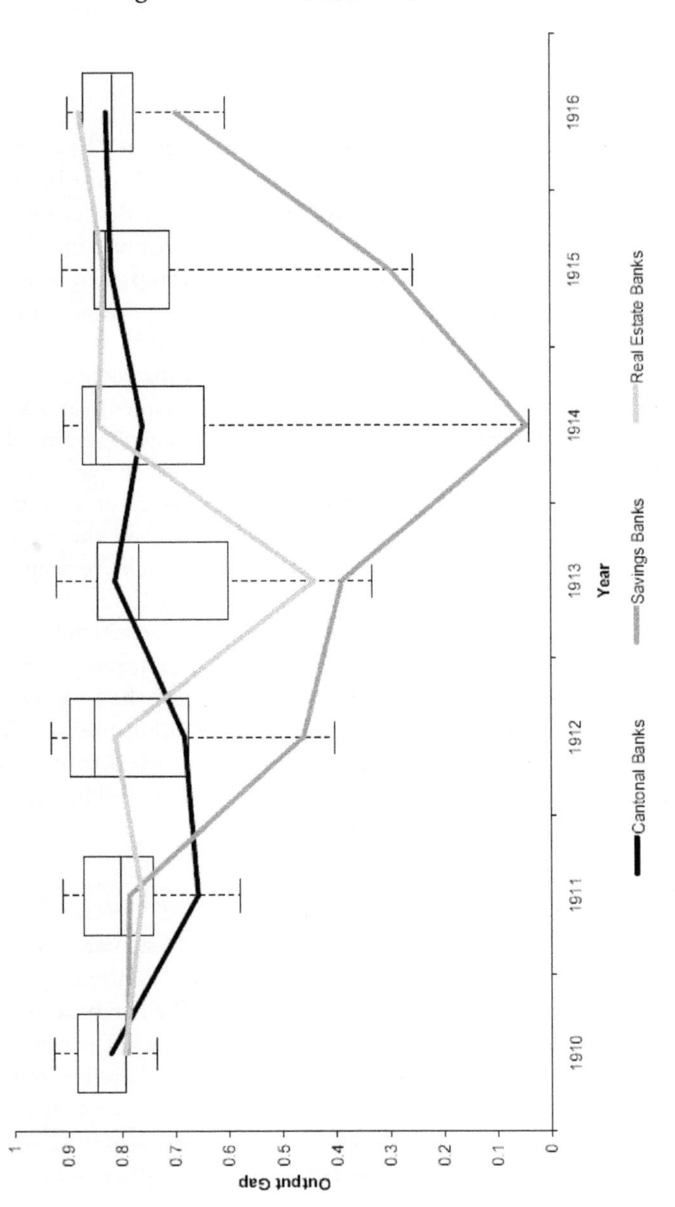

Figure 6.5: Output gaps for selected banking groups The outputs gaps have been estimated by applying Stochastic Frontier Analysis. The estimation period is 1906–2005.

Crises in Detail

Bank Consolidation 1911–14

In the years 1911–14 the Swiss banking system was shattered by a series of low scale bankruptcies of savings banks and real estate banks. Yet the banking crises were confined to certain banks in cantons Thurgau, Zurich, Berne, Aargau, Basle, Ticino, Uri, St Gall, Schaffhausen. The most common cause for the banking insolvencies was a concentration of risk positions, accompanied by insufficient liquidity, a very thin equity base and in some instances nepotism. Roundabout 4 per cent of the entire banking equity base was thus erased.[10]

At the beginning of the twentieth century a growing economy with scale-enhancing companies alongside demanded larger and larger loans. Banks were more than willing to approve those, while unfortunately neglecting their own refinancing potential. An intensifying competition between banks led to lower profit margins and shrinking capabilities to increase reserves and capital stock.[11] As can be seen from Figure 6.5 the years 1913 and 1914 where the years in which savings and real estate banks were the least capable to achieve their potential ROE.

The gold standard with its international capital flows enabled larger banks a wide variety of refinancing options, placing them at better positions in a competitive industry. Small savings and real estate banks lacking the resources to grasp the opportunities of globalized capital markets were losing ground. This led to an increased appetite for risk in order to secure their own part of the growing banking market. Yet these risky strategies did not work out, leading to a consolidation in the savings and real estate banking segment.

Post World War I Deflation/Inflation 1919–20

The gold standard broke down in the first days of the First World War. The war undermined the willingness for international cooperation and coordination necessary for the functioning of the gold standard. The combatants increased their monetary base in order to finance their war activities. The new monetary base-to-gold ratios violated the gold conversion rates, therefore the right to change currency into gold at a fixed rate was abolished in 1914. The increased monetary bases led to inflation in Europe. After the war ended in 1918 the inflationary pressure which was released by establishing a free price system again had its effect on the foreign exchanges.

Figure 6.6. Post WWI Inflation, 1919–23.

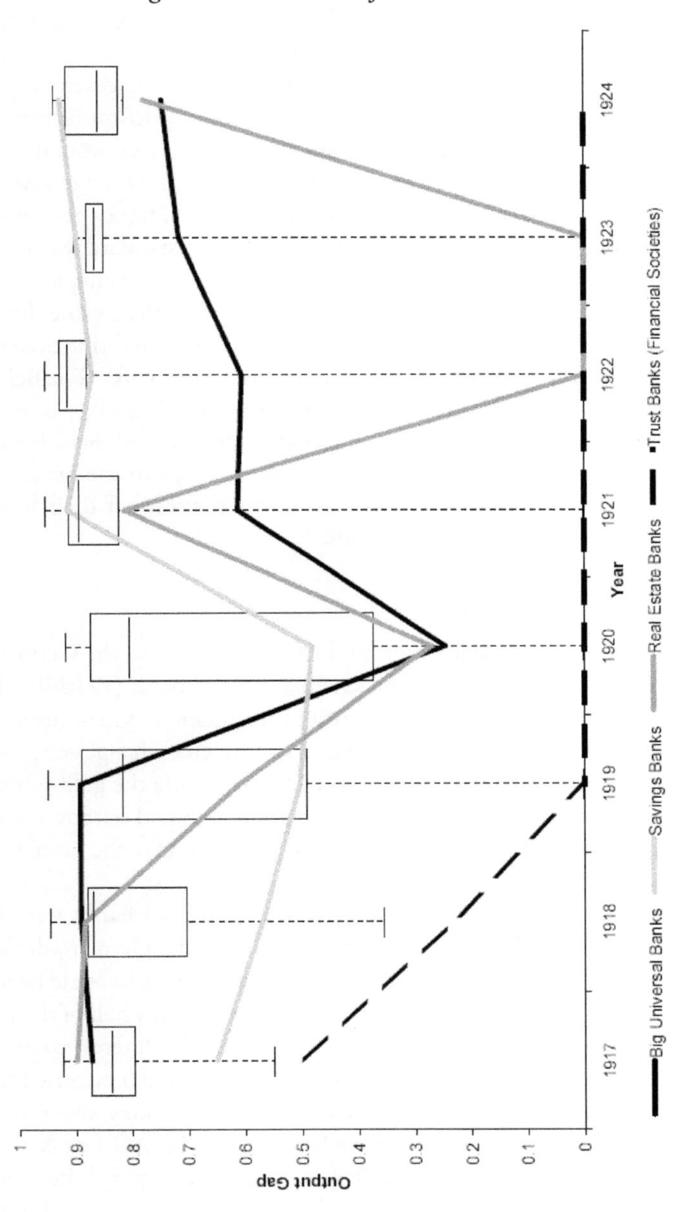

Figure 6.6: Output gaps for selected banking groups. The output gaps have been estimated by applying Stochastic Frontier Analysis. The estimation period is 1906–2005.

Figure 6.7 depicts the exchange rates between the Swiss Franc and the French Franc, Italian Lira, Austrian Krone and German Mark. The exchange rates deteriorated so dramatically that assets denominated in these currencies basically became worthless vis-a-vis the Swiss Franc. Furthermore, changes in the political landscape such as the Russian Revolution led to expropriation of property in Russia by the new communist government. Swiss Banks lost around 93.4 per cent of their Russian holdings. Swiss banks saw their entire foreign assets being reduced from 8 billion francs pre-war down to 2.5 billion francs post-war.[12]

With the beginning of the First World War the gold standard was abolished, most European countries and even the USA announced a banking moratorium. While the assets of Swiss banks were blocked, they lost their value due to the inflation in wartime Europe. As can be seen from Figure 6.6 this time the big universal banks, savings banks, real estate banks and trust banks (Financial Societies) suffered most. The strong linkages in the financial markets prior to the First World War led to large losses at internationally exposed Swiss banks. The strong devaluations of formerly fixed exchange rates due to the breakdown of the first gold standard affected Swiss banks, which wrote-off their losses and returned to normal business quite quickly.[13]

Great Depression 1930–6

The Great Depression probably started for Swiss banks with the German bank moratorium in July 1931, when the German central bank (Reichsbank) recognized a bank-run on German banks from foreign and German investors. To avoid further losses of deposits it declared strict foreign exchange controls.

Swiss banks were affected by the Great Depression via the gold standard in a twofold way. The liability side was affected by inflows and outflows of money into Switzerland via deposits in Swiss bank accounts and the asset side was affected by bank moratoria and domestic borrower defaults.

At the beginning of the 1930s the big Swiss universal banks were heavily involved in short- and long-term lending to Germany. After Germany declared its bank moratorium a standstill agreement on short-term deposits could be reached with foreign investors. Foreign depositors could retrieve only half of their investments in short-term money by September 1933. Reduced interest payments on medium- and long-term debt continued until 1934, afterward they ceased. Similar, for Swiss banks adverse currency exchange restriction measures were introduced in Austria, Hungary and Poland.[14] Some Swiss banks (i.e. AG Leu & Co.) had invested more assets in Germany than they had secured by equity.[15] Besides, some institutes had to write off so many assets that they either had to ask for government aid and renegotiate depositor treaties (Schweizerische Volksbank) or, as in the case of Banque d'Escompte Suisse, had to file for insolvency.

Figure 6.7. Swiss Franc / Foreign Currencies, 1913–23. Source: Swiss National Bank.

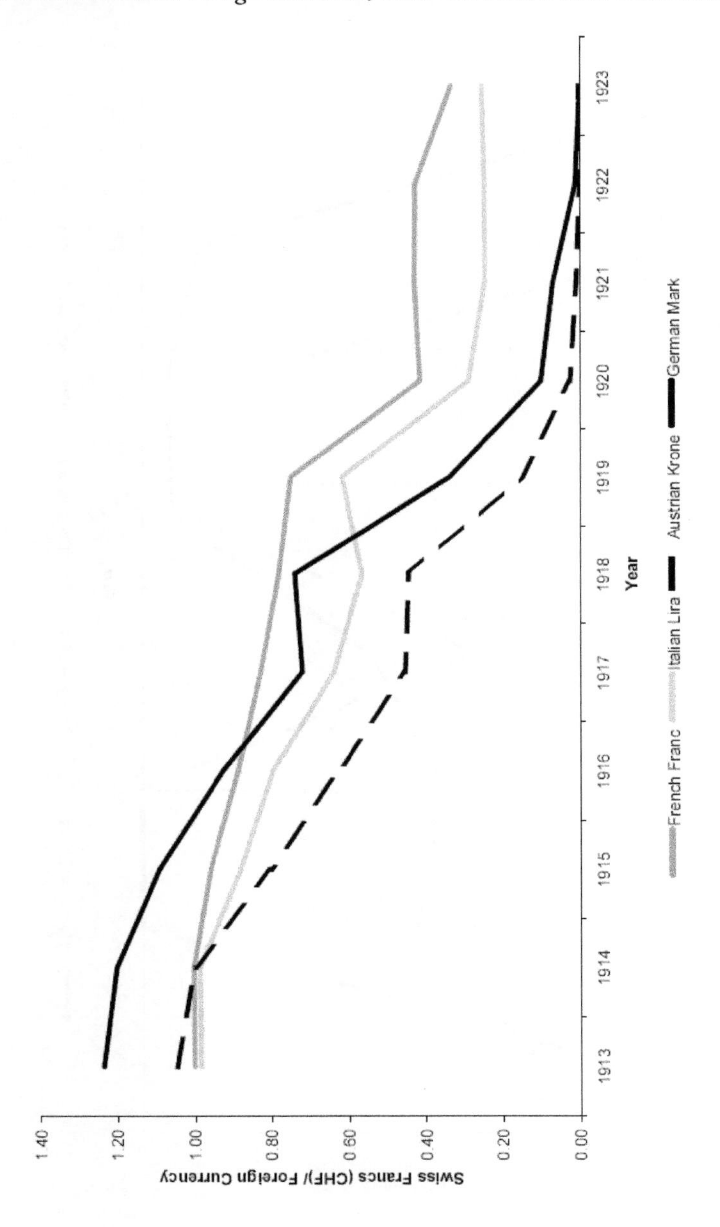

Figure 6.7: Swiss Franc / Foreign Currencies, 1913–23. Source: Swiss National Bank.

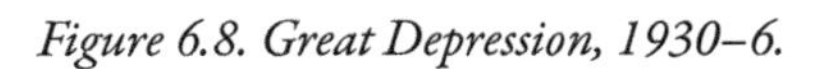

Figure 6.8. Great Depression, 1930–6.

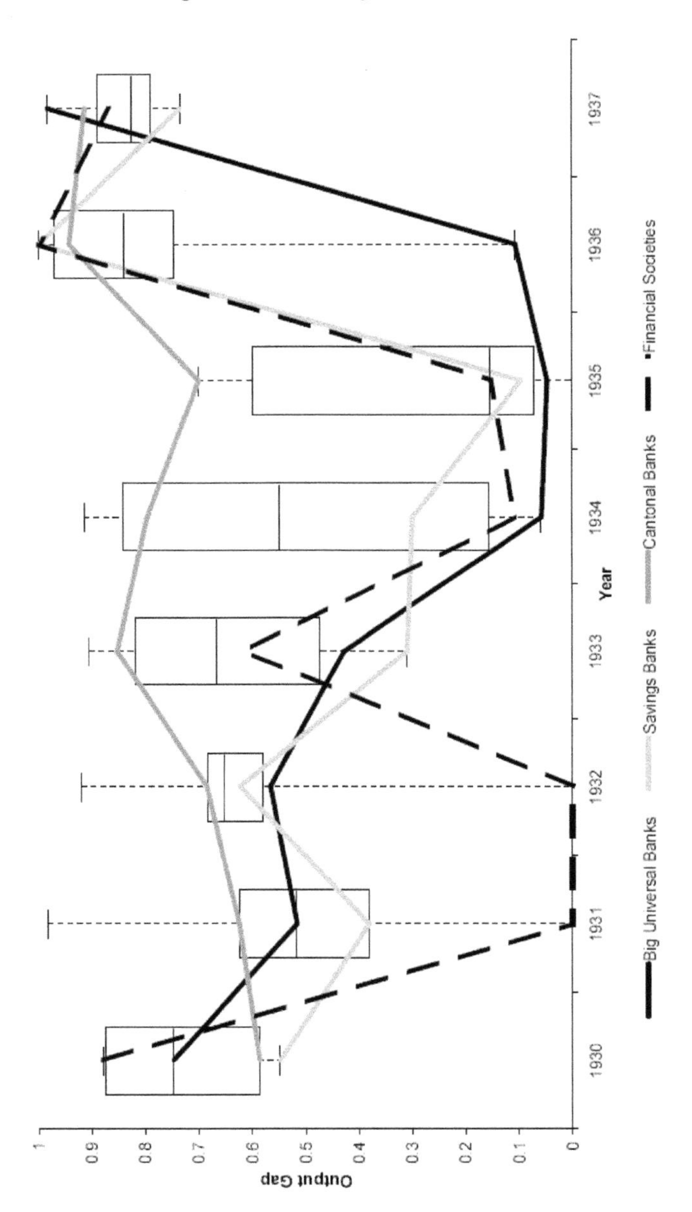

Figure 6.8: Output gaps for selected banking groups The output gaps have been estimated by applying Stochastic Frontier Analysis. The estimation period is 1930–2005.

Customers of those Swiss banks that were heavily involved in business liaisons with German banks and firms (Big Universal Banks and Financial Societies) started to withdraw their deposits from these Swiss banks and accumulated cash. To equalize the balance sheets Big Universal Banks and Financial Societies were forced to sell assets. The strong increase in assets disposal reduced their prices, and banks faced the unfortunate choice between either selling bad frozen assets in Germany with heavy deductions on their value or disposing of good assets in Switzerland, leaving their balance sheets with the bad frozen assets. Additionally the ongoing depression of the economy led to a withdrawal of funds owned by companies and private investors to finance their individual expenditures. Abroad, laws demanding the withdrawal of foreign deposits, also away from Switzerland, increased the pressure on Swiss banks, as well as the fear of Switzerland leaving the Gold Bloc (which actually happened in 1936) leading to a further outflow of deposits from Swiss bank accounts. The capital flight put a large burden on Swiss banks' balance sheets.[16] Balance sheets had to be massively adjusted.

The deposits of clients and other banks declined strongly, as can be seen from Table 6.1. Expressed in current value the deposits at big banks declined from 3790.8 million Swiss Franc in 1930 down to 1445.2 million Swiss Francs. While in the wake of the events of July 1931 foreign money was transferred into Switzerland, the deposits of big universal banks declined since 1930 (Table 6.1). Rumours about a possible devaluation of the Swiss Franc after the devaluation of the Belgium Franc in March 1935 led to a massive capital flight out of accounts at Swiss big banks.[17]

Table 6.1. Client and bank deposits in big bank's balance sheets in current values.

Year	Deposits
1930	3790.8 million CHF
1931	2879.2 million CHF
1932	2473.5 million CHF
1933	2155.2 million CHF
1934	1955.7 million CHF
1935	1445.2 million CHF
1936	2133.1 million CHF
1937	2339.9 million CHF

Source: Swiss National Bank

Swiss big universal banks and financial societies faced heavy reductions on their liability side while having their asset side blocked and their incomes deteriorated. Domestically, the deflationary pressures transmitted via the gold standard, increased lender's debt expressed in price adjusted terms. The ongoing depression led to a strong increase in firms' bankruptcy rates from 1,513 in 1931 up to

3,022 per year in 1936, threatening the existence of their lenders (savings banks, small local banks and cantonal banks). Six out of eight big universal banks had to ask for help, three out of twenty-seven banks in the Cantonal Banks group had to be restructured, and many more small banks had to shut down their business or to merge with financially solid institutions.

As can be seen from Figure 6.8, the mismatch between the potential ROE and the achieved ROE for Swiss banks was greatest in the years 1934 and 1935, when all the described problems of the financial sector culminated. Only after leaving the Gold Bloc in 1936 the performance of Swiss banks improved.

Conclusion

The three major banking crises in 1911–14, 1919–20 and 1931–6 allow for some reflections about banking crises, international financial convergence and the gold standard regimes. Out of the three crises two occurred while Switzerland was part of the first and second gold standard regime (1911–14, 1931–6). The crisis of 1919–20 happened while the Swiss currency was not confined by a gold standard regime. The crisis of 1911–14 was caused by consolidation within smaller banks and was not caused by international transactions. The crises after the First World War and during the Great Depression were initiated by foreign financial shocks. It is interesting to take a comparative look at the causes and developments of these two banking crises to understand the role of the gold standard in promoting or prolonging them.

The crisis of 1919–20 was caused by the dissolution of the gold standard. The war itself and the end of the first gold standard regime at the beginning of the First World War caused heavy exchange-rate fluctuations and depreciations of foreign assets. These losses were written off after the war ended. The post-war recession and the following stress and burden on banks' balance sheets further aggravated the already poor performance of Swiss big universal banks and investment trusts. The regime switch away from the gold standard is maybe responsible for some of the output gap banks had to cover.

Swiss big universal banks and investment trusts suffered during the Great Depression from the losses on their foreign investments, especially in Germany. The bank moratoria in various countries burdened the balance sheets. But the outflow of foreign deposits out of Swiss accounts was even more hazardous for financial stability. Switzerland continued to be part of the Gold Bloc until the end. Together with the severe recession which led to defaults of domestic customers, the weakening of big banks' balance sheets on the liability side endangered the stability of Swiss big banks and investment trusts. In the process of 1935 financial investors reckoned that the Swiss currency would devalue. This finally happened on 25 September 1936.[18] The Swiss currency was under heavy speculative attacks, convincing depositors to withdraw their deposits out of Swiss accounts before a devaluation of the currency would significantly reduce their assets. Membership in the Gold Bloc aggravated and prolonged the problems for the Swiss banks.

7 DETERMINANTS OF NATIONAL FINANCIAL SYSTEMS: THE ROLE OF HISTORICAL EVENTS

Patrice Baubeau
Anders Ögren

'The only true, the only real Oeconomy is Peace'

John, Earl of Stair, quoted by J. Brewer, 1990

Introduction

Studies of today's national financial structures have for a couple of decades been concerned with finding the main factor that lies behind the evolvement of different types of financial system. Indeed, such a factor may help explain why a country would rely rather on a 'bank-based' system that is more geared towards information-gathering and processing organizations, or on a 'market-based' system that is more geared towards competing individual agents that are meeting on an (more or less) open market.

Theoretical and empirical inquiries on such issues have been developing for over fifty years,[1] fuelled by the apparent bank-to-market shift ignited in OECD countries at the end of the 1970s and the return of financial crises, almost non-existent in developed countries during the Bretton Woods era.[2]

Nevertheless one can still roughly divide the explanations for why a country would adhere to the one type or the other into two categories: 1) structural explanations or 2) developmental (or evolutionary) explanations.

The first category of explanations relies on the idea of (almost) permanent influence from certain social factors such as the legal basis, the distribution of political power, the existence of entrenched social or economic powers and so on. These are assumed to exert a constant (or at least an extreme long-term) influence on institutional development and thus serve a key role also for present financial structures. The second category is more concerned with the pattern of economic and financial development over time, and relies on the link between specific difficulties or challenges (regional imbalances, information asymmetry, relative backwardness and so on) and the build-up of institutional solutions to these difficulties. Academic historians tend to rely more on the second approach, which allows them to expand historical explanations and use careful contextual analysis. While academic economists seem to be more prone to the first approach they are searching for more general everlasting explanatory variables behind the emergence of different financial systems.

Nevertheless, these distinctly different types of explanations share two common conclusions in most academic works: convergence of financial systems is not only possible, it is more or less bound to take place given an open international capital market and, second, path dependency is a very strong feature of financial systems.

In a previous work, we proposed a qualitative approach to a third category of explanations, based upon the impact of major events, such as wars,[3] the lasting effects of which are at the start of path-dependent evolutions. The demonstration rested upon A. Demirgüc-Kunt and R. Levine's[4] data relative to the financial structures of a large sample of countries around 1995, and concluded, as Charles Calomiris[5] did from a more theoretical point of view, on the major and enduring impact of the two major twentieth-century wars on financial systems.

We intend here to go one step forward, in order to reconcile the qualitative approach that is still at the heart of historical methodology – and that we believe necessary in order to avoid major anachronistic biases – with quantitative tools, to allow for a more formal demonstration. In the process, we will propose a measure of the impact of wars, a measure we know is still susceptible to further improvements. Such research is not only of academic interest. Indeed, if financial structures are dependent on specific historical events, convergence among national financial systems will only be a theoretical construction since any historical event at any time may disrupt the supposed convergence. Moreover, convergence itself may appear as a political as well as an economic phenomenon, reflecting the hegemonic situation of one-power financial structures and its influence on second-rank or peripheral countries. In short, we intend to bridge the gap between the qualitative approach and the econometric-like analysis tools, and to deepen our understanding of war's impact – causes and consequences.

This chapter starts out with a look at different causes for explaining the differences in national financial systems: the above-mentioned structural and developmental explanations. We then look briefly to the dependent variable: the type of financial system. We analyse their explanatory strengths and shortcomings. We then add a third type of explanation: the historical event (war) and make a qualitative argument for why it is necessary to include this variable. We study what different types of financial systems mean: what are the differences between bank- and market-based financial systems in practice? Can we measure different types of financial systems so that we can grade national financial systems between the two extremes of 'market based' versus 'bank based'? And what are we really measuring when we measure national financial systems in relation to this dichotomy? We proceed with a statistical testing of the impact of war on the type of different national systems in comparison to other explanations. We conclude with a discussion on what the result means for mainstream ideas on financial convergence.

Bank- or Market-Based Financial Systems

The most common way to distinguish among national financial systems has been along the bank-based/market-based dividing line. Most authors recognize the limits of such a gross distinction, and have highlighted the fact that markets do not substitute for banks – but banks evolve such as to retain a major role on markets, while incorporating new trades, like securitization, insurance, domestic services and so on[6] – complicating the simple measure of the relative weight of banks and markets.

Nevertheless, this binary approach proved highly valuable since it authorizes easy classification, and does not reduce the past to the present or vice-versa. For example, by this simple measure, it is easy to show that France[7] as well as Japan[8] were rather 'market-based' before 1914, or at least more than the United States, a relative situation which changed dramatically in the following thirty years, an evolution that led Raghuram Rajan and Luigi Zingales to challenge structural explanations.[9]

The Determinants of Financial Systems

Structural explanations have been very popular in economic and institutional research especially in the wake of the influential work by La Porta, Lopez-de-Silanes, Shleifer and Vishny.[10] The argument in this work is that it all eventually boils down to the type of legal system that is governing economic activities. In short the Anglo-Saxon Common Law tradition is said to yield the best result for economic growth while the French Civil code is the worst. While developing in subtle ways the demonstration made by La Porta et al., Asli Demirgüc-Kunt and Ross Levine fall into the same trap by enlarging what is, strictly speaking, a correlation without causality – all the more so given the very high degree of complexity of all the depicted elements – into a broad causality chain:

> Finally, we analyze legal, regulatory, tax and macroeconomic determinants of financial structure by looking at correlations and simple regressions that control for the level of real GDP per capita. We see that countries with a Common Law tradition, strong protection for shareholder rights, good accounting standards, low levels of corruption and no explicit deposit insurance tend to be more market-based, even after

> controlling for income. On the other hand, countries with a French Civil Law tradition, poor protection of shareholder and creditor rights, poor contract enforcement, high levels of corruption, poor accounting standards, heavily restricted banking systems, and high inflation tend to have underdeveloped financial systems in general, even after controlling for income.[11]

Of course, we do not mean here that Demirgüc-Kunt and Levine do not pinpoint crucial issues, but that following too narrow a methodology, built on pure correlations, the risks of reaching highly biased conclusions are very high, that simply confirm as the 'one best way' the dominant model of the time. Such conclusions are at best anachronistic, since they depend on the idea that a given trait is independent from context or from the varying interrelations with other traits. As remarked by Paul Dunne and Fanny Coulomb, 'As is characteristic of neoclassical economics, which sees itself as the science of the social sciences providing tools with which to analyse any social setting, its approach to analysing war is ahistorical.'[12]

Corruption is a good example of the difficulties of reaching simple conclusions. For example, the development of venality in offices among European Powers, from the sixteenth century onward, cannot be ascribed to a stronger diffidence of this tool of state finance in England than in France or Spain; rather, it is against a similar diffidence but in face of immediate and urgent needs for funds that France and Spain resigned to it. War, here, played the crucial role and 'England's greatest advantage was that it was never put to the sort of gruelling fiscal-military test that year after year drained the nation of its resources and the Treasury of its wealth.'[13] *Ceteris paribus*, that is the point we want to make clear here: if one considers that vested interests and corruptions can be feared in similar terms at the same period in different countries, what are the hidden factors that explain some state will escape the bane, while others not?

This is one of the many reasons that led scholars to develop a more cautious approach when it comes to the past, i.e. considering that a various set of institutions may have different outcomes and represent different levels of efficiency, depending on the context and other phenomenon – such as available technology, military power, etc.

Conversely, whatever the institutional background, 'in higher income countries financial systems tend to be more market-based'.[14] This idea that higher income countries are more market oriented was expressed many decades ago by Alexander Gerschenkron,[15] and paved the way to what one could call 'developmental explanations'. Such approaches are more popular with historians and economic-historians that put emphasis on empirics and context,[16] such as Caroline Fohlin,[17] Youssef Cassis[18] or Georges Gallais-Hamonno and Pierre-Cyrille Hautcoeur.[19] A somewhat intermediary approach can be found in Verdier's work[20], and is well illustrated in the two books edited by Richard Sylla.[21]

Finally, some approaches, often building on political-science concepts, propose a kind of mix between structural and developmental explanations. For example, Richard Carney[22] shows that the patterns and dynamics of votes and vested interests may explain some permanent traits in national financial systems and reaches interesting parallels with Verdier's books. Raghuram Rajan and Luigi Zingales aim at the same goal, by studying the political, social and legal tools used by incumbents to retain their dominant positions in the economic system, using state and rules to their own profit and against challenging newcomers.[23]

In some ways, militarization is a similar tool of analysis, which appears as a specific form of social and economic mobilization, an issue largely debated in political science and that one can trace back to Herbert Spencer's distinction among militant (i.e. socially coercive) and industrial (i.e. contractual) societies.[24]

Using a concept such as militarization means we aim at avoiding time-free, non-historical or anachronistic concepts, and to escape this major sin of historians: the never-ending quest for origins. But what are the bases for using an event – that is something partly random, accidental – as a touchstone to explain structures?

A pure event is something that 'happens in the present', which means that it was not anticipated and could not be (at least not completely in its final outcomes), or, in other words, that is 'new'. If history were made only of such pure events, it would be incomprehensible, since each event would be isolated from any historical fabric and encapsulated into its own meaning. Events, from a historian's point of view, but also in popular wisdom, are usually associated with causes and consequences on the one hand and a degree of uniqueness, on the other. Events are not supposed to be purely random: they can be linked to other events, or actors, forces and trends. They are not completely determined either: assessing the whole past would not make divination much more precise, as in our meteorological world, a five-day forecast is significantly less accountable than a 24.00 forecast but a seasonal forecast is accurate in predicting that summer will be hotter than winter in northern territories. Also, understanding trends, forces and interrelations makes it possible to build economical (or historical) forecasts six months or one year in advance, as it is possible to forecast general weather patterns three to six months in advance. But events are not part of econometrical models, especially forecasting models, even though they bear a much more considerable impact on the overall economic system than meteorological events do on weather patterns: comes a crisis and forecasting becomes dubious. The situation is rather different when it comes to retrospective models: very often, their goal is to separate between structural and eventual factors, and to identify the weight of the structural factors supposed to play a key role. In doing so, eventual factors are given an 'exogenous' label, while structural factors are given an 'endogenous' one.

But this leads to two problems. First, structural factors are usually deemed to be more important than eventual ones. In separating structural and eventual factors, one then dismisses the last as being the correct and meaningful explanations of history. Second, events are impacting our social and economical structures at every moment. Then, from what point of view should events be considered as 'exogenous'? Is that not something everybody knows: that events are occurring? The problem, here, is that events can be assessed only if they are embedded in a pattern, a cycle, a structure. For example, an election outcome is an event (or might be), but the election itself is not, at least in most advanced democratic countries. It means that for the social scientist events are, strictly speaking, merely embedded facts. And the bed is the structure, the endogenous factor, the causal link.

This means that events, however random they might seem to some, largely contribute to the political, social and financial structure. It also means that there is a link between the nature of events and the nature of structures, provided that events can be integrated into a causal chain. Considering war, that is precisely what Jean Jaurès, the prominent French social democrat of the early twentieth century, meant. At the Chamber, in 1895, he declared that

> ... war can be born from any possible chance ... Always your violent and chaotic society, even when it longs for peace, even when it lays in apparent rest, bears the war in itself, as a sleeping cloud bears the storm.[25]

Jaurès made clear that war was at the horizon, not because eventually it could happen, but because the very social system included as a possibility the outbreak of a war, that it was part of its structure – the war being only the element revealing that structural possibility. The analysis by Jaurès is even more striking as he actually was shot dead at the outbreak of the First World War because he opposed the war.

This analysis can be summarized in its most apocryphal form: 'capitalism bears war as clouds bear storm'. Of course, we do not intend here to back the old 'capitalism is war' *motto* – but to stress that national structures, whatever their label (capitalist, feudal, ancient, modern, developed, Western, etc.), do imply the possibility of a war. And war was the most prominent among events, and the most susceptible to being attributed to structural factors (especially in the twentieth century). For all these reasons, war is a reasonable candidate as an 'independent' variable.

Choosing war as an event which is the independent variable when explaining financial structures makes sense for two paradoxical reasons. First, it is not independent – it takes place into a causal chain. Second, it is not an isolated event. Of course, the outbreak of a war is an event, in the above meaning, but in the course of the twentieth century, most wars have been carefully planned, sometimes even expected; budgets and military expenses have been voted and carried on to prepare for it. The war itself, once declared, had to be organized, planned, stocked and equipped as soon as initial plans proved wrong – which actually occurred quite quickly. And coming with war were occupational expenses or spoils, human and material destruction, crime and social and political tensions that exerted a heavy price on the society and its economy. Last, recovering from the war, repairing damages, meant also, sometimes, adapting to a modified territory structure or paying for foreign withdrawal and even, sometimes, for foreign occupation.

Such planning and anticipation also means that war is not isolated from the whole structure of the economy: some institutions acted in ways that were highly influenced by war expectations, as central banks, treasuries, industries, notwithstanding the army. If so, what does this tell us about the role of the two prior types of explanation and the possibility for convergence? As the French economic historian Jean Bouvier stated, 'To the historian, nothing is "exogenous"'.[26]

A Statistical Test

In this section we test for the impact of the two world wars on the degree of market- or bank-based financial systems. We utilize the same dataset as Asli Demirgüc-Kunt and Ross Levine in their extensive World Bank Working Paper[27] and add indexes for the degree of military and economic engagement during the two world wars.

The Key Hypothesis: War leads to Bank-Based Systems

Our main hypothesis is that the fact that countries were more or less engaged in these wars affected their financial system to the degree that we still today (1990–5) can see differences in to what extent they are market- or bank-based. Simply put we expect countries that were more heavily engaged in war activities to be less market-based. The basic assumptions of this hypothesis are very 'orthodox', in that we picked up as many criteria as we could, and tried to figure out whether such criteria would lead to a more bank-based or market-based system.

In short, our assumptions are twofold:

- The development of unbalanced political power leads to a bank-based system, since a completely state-dominated economy will be planned – and markets are not state planning instruments.
- The growth of extra-economic debt (i.e. not related to economic business activities) leads to a bank-based system because the market assessment of a debt value is constrained by the valuation of its collateral (for example the fiscal pool in which to tap).

Political costs of war – territorial, population and reputation losses – may have different effects from a 'bank-based – market-based' point of view. But we consider that when those costs are high, they tend to destroy market systems[28] and then enhance the chances of a bank-based system being implemented. To avoid any threshold effect, we then consider the overall consequences of these costs to lean towards a bank-based system.

Last, the combination between strength of public opinion and war costs tends to promote a bank-based system, because governments have then a strong incentive to avoid the distribution of the costs through market mechanisms, and to implement a system that will be supported by their constituents, such as making the enemy, the richest, the children, pay the bill.

The important thing is then to have as many different criteria bringing specific understanding to the financial effects of war, and including in the variable the direction of its effect, that is in favour of a market-based financial system or in favour of a bank-based system.

We will first see the independent variable criteria, relating to militarization, and then the control variables.

Table 7.1. Criteria for Militarization as Independent variables.

Code	**Developed name**
NWW1	Neutral WW1
WW1	Belligerent WW1
InvaWW1	Invaded WW1
VicWW1	Victorious WW1
EcoMobWW1	Economic mobilization WW1
EEWW1	Economic looting WW1
TGWW1	Territorial gains WW1
TLWW1	Territorial losses WW1
MilPowPreWW1	Militarized power before WW1
DictPreWW1	Dictature before WW1
OccPostWW1	Occupied after WW1
VoteMPreWW1	Universal male voting rights before WW1
VoteMPostWW1	Universal male voting rights after WW1
DictPreWW2	Dictature before WW2
DictDWW2	Dictature during WW2
DictPostWW2	Dictature after WW2
MilPowPreWW2	Militarized power before WW2
NWW2	Neutral WW2
WW2	Belligerent WW2
InvWW2	Invaded WW2
EEWW2	Economic looting WW2
VicWW2	Victorious WW2
TGWW2	Territorial gains WW2
TLWW2	Territorial losses WW2
OccPostWW2	Occupied after WW2

We can present these criteria[29] in three categories: political, military and economic. Three criteria fall into the political categories:

- Dictatorship;
- Militarized power;
- Universal male voting rights.

The dictatorship criterion is quite easy to assess: we define a dictatorship where national votes can take only one form, that of a plebiscite or a referendum and where the actual power was seized through a coup. From that point of view, only one country falls in this category before 1914, and eight before 1939. We assume that, for political reasons, markets are impeded by dictatorship in a warring context: indeed, a dictator would not comply to financial 'realism' if he (there has been no 'she') decides to wage a war. As argued by North and Weingast,[30] government accountability is an important condition to build the confidence necessary to a financial market. But government accountability is also opposed to what a dictatorship means. This is why we consider that there is a contradiction between a market-based financial system and dictatorship.

Turkey is counted as a dictatorship in 1914, because of the coup that brought the 'Three Pashas' to power in 1913. There are three limits to this position. First, Turkey did not exist as such before 1923, only the Ottoman Empire, of which what was to become Turkey was the political and military heartland. Second, the coup occurred during what was already a war – the Balkan war – and in this way, the category is perhaps not well defined for Turkey.

Last, it has been argued that the three pashas – or 'dictatorial triumvirate' – were actually under the control and plots of the CUP, the Committee of Union and Progress deeply influenced by the 'Jeunes Turcs' (Young Turks) movement. That might be so, but then, all dictatorships develop their own counter-powers and factions.

The eight countries counted as dictatorships before WW2 are: Austria, Germany, Greece, Italy, Japan, Portugal, Spain and Turkey. They all comply with the two elements of our definition of a dictatorship, with two reservations. Japan had no formal coup, but, under the pressure of the military, and with the menace of several coups that officially failed, the parliamentary regime progressively vanished and, even sooner, retreated from any control over military matters, as demonstrated the 1931 'Mukden incident'. Hitler's seizure of power is sometimes presented as a parliamentary one. This is basically true as long as one concentrates on his 30 January 1933 choosing as chancellor. But it was not long before he plotted a complete seizure of power, by manipulating to his own profit the burning of the *Reichstag* through the exceptional powers law that followed, as soon as March 1933. All ensuing constitutional measures, in 1933, led to the demise of the checks and balances system, leaving Hitler and the NSDAP the sole powers in place.

Militarized power is a complementary criterion to dictatorship, and acts in the same direction. What we mean by 'militarized power' is either the fact that military matters are not dealt by the civilian government officially in charge (for example the government cannot prevail when military matters are at stake) or that the goals of the government before the outbreak of the war are openly military goals or goals that can be attained only through war. This criterion is not entirely at odds with the previous one and means fundamentally that war is a positive option to the considered country leaders.

Of course, before WW1, the Ottoman Empire fell into the two categories, but as explained before, this is a logical consequence of the challenges faced by the old empire, assaulted by European powers and internal turmoil, at war almost every ten years since the beginning of the nineteenth century. The Japanese case shows the difference between dictatorship and militarized power. Since the Meiji revolution started in 1868, the country developed a civil government based upon a parliamentary-like constitutional law. But military matters were largely shielded from the intervention and even supervision of the civil government. The 1905 war against Russia, the conquest of Formosa (Taiwan) and of Korea were largely military decisions, and the military would accept no interference from the government. The same goes for WW1: it is the military that pushed for strong and quick action against Germany, to seize the latter's colonial possessions in Asia. Japan's case shows that one can have a civilian and constitutional government, and not a dictatorship, but at the same time a strong and relatively independent military power, able to influence the overall political course of the country.

The same applies before WW2 to five 'militarized powers': Austria, Germany, Italy, Japan and Spain. If this is quite evident for the four latter, the case of Austria perhaps needs more explanation. Before the 1938 *Anschluss*, Austria was already a dictatorship, under the rule of Kurt von Schuschnigg, who had a clear record of authoritarian ideas, since 1933–4. The fact that he opposed the German's annexation of Austria and spent several years in jail does not change the nature of the Austrian state before 1938. But then, this shows only that Austria was a dictatorship, not a 'militarized power'. This shift took place through the unification process with Germany, in 1938–9, that is before the outbreak of the WW2 in Europe and not under Schuschnigg's boot.

The last political factor is the universal male voting right. This political issue was very important in Europe before and after WW1. During and after WW2, female voting rights came to the forefront. In short, we consider that voting rights are a good proxy for the incentives governments have to comply to their constituents. In case of a very dire crisis this means that a suffrage-controlled government will give priority to economic intervention over financial soundness or orthodoxy, for example creating specific institutions short-circuiting market mechanisms. This factor is thus considered – in a context of war – more favourable to bank-based than to market-based financial systems.

We streamlined military factors into seven criteria: neutrality, belligerence, invasion, victory, territorial gains and losses, occupation. We count seven because many countries experienced no territorial gains and no territorial losses during the same war.

Those criteria are quite clear and they do not overlap: for example, Italy, Ottoman Empire/Turkey, United States and Belgium were, during WW1, both neutral and belligerent. Italy did not enter the war until 1915. In 1914, it was an ally of Germany and Austria-Hungary, but opted for neutrality before siding with France and the United Kingdom against its former allies. When the war broke out, the Ottoman Empire was considered to be a German ally. Nevertheless, the country did not enter the war before 28 October 1914, siding with Germany. The United States and Belgium where officially neutral states, the United States following out of their own will the Monroe Doctrine (no entanglement in European affairs, following the 1796 Washington's address),[31] while Belgium was created as a compulsory neutral state by the 1839 London Treaty, under the warranty of Prussia (Germany later accepted assumption of this warranty), France, United Kingdom and Russia. In the course of war, both countries came to be considered as belligerent, Belgium because it was invaded by Germany, and the United States because they joined the United Kingdom and France in April 1917. But they kept some peculiarities: Belgium tried, while considering its goals of war, to retain advantages of being both neutral and belligerent, i.e. to get full reparation from Germany, as a neutral state attacked by one of its warrants, and at the same time to get a share of the war spoils, as a belligerent state. The United States came to war but proclaimed it would not take part in war spoils, just as a neutral state would – as expressed in the Wilson's famous fourteen-points speech. We then can conclude that these factors do not overlap and allow us to estimate the effects and results of war with greater precision.

Those factors are interpreted in such a way that, the more a country is entangled into war, the more likely it is to lean towards a bank-based system. This is quite easy to understand, following our 'orthodox' assumptions: as the price of war grows with the resources invested in it, it becomes increasingly difficult to finance it through market mechanisms, because the risks associated with war become too heavy. Empirical research shows how belligerent states tended to create *ad hoc* banking and financial bodies to shortcut markets.

Last, we selected only two economic factors: economic looting and economic mobilization, and it is clear that further research should dig deeper into that area. Economic looting is quite easy to assess, the more so because we do not yet intend to put a threshold: we consider simply whether a country was, or was not, looted, not the magnitude of the looting. Economic mobilization is more difficult to figure out, since it is a domestic decision, which amounts to the question of whether the economy goes on in a more or less business as usual fashion or whether the whole economy is at war. This question had a meaning, apparently, only during WW1. Indeed, during WW2, all belligerent countries, because of the previous war, engaged in a degree of economic mobilization, even if that mobilization varied over time. During WW1 we consider that only six countries have done so, mostly because they were the only ones to be technically able to do it: Austria(-Hungary), France, Germany, Ireland, Italy and United Kingdom. Ireland is counted as economically mobilized since it was still, by then, part of the United Kingdom. Belgium, on the other hand, did not mobilize its economy mostly because over 95 percent of its territory (metropolitan) was occupied by Germany. The other countries, were either engaged in war for too short a time (Japan, United States), were too far away (Portugal) or kept out of the war.

These two factors add to the investment in war, and then reinforce the chances for one given country to lean more on the bank-based side.

The Sample: OECD Countries

Using Asli Demirgüc-Kunt and Ross Levine 2000 paper,[32] we selected twenty OECD countries for two sets of reasons. First, they are the only countries whose historical and financial record is easily available for most of the twentieth century, because most of them have enjoyed political independence during most of the period. Second, using only such countries avoid biases linked to the strong discrepancies in economic structures – which are not fully captured by GDP – since some large raw materials exporting countries or small regional redistribution centres can enjoy high standards of living without sharing the industrial-based kind of prosperity of OECD countries.

Table 7.2 indicates the selected countries and the value of the two key figures used to determine whether they lean rather on the bank-based or on the market-based side. These key figures are bank assets and market capitalization ratios to GDP, which offers two advantages. The first one is that they are broad enough to be resilient to rather large measurement errors, albeit efforts to calculate homogenous figures among countries. The second is that they are based upon a common denominator, which increases the quality of their comparison. In order to do so, the last column gives our calculation of the relative position of each country on the bank-based–market-based axis. The principles of this calculation are very simple and straightforward. Because both ratios are based upon GDP, and to compute a synthetic ratio, the only issue is to normalize the variance and the mean of the two series, by dividing each ratio by the mean of the relevant series and multiplying it by the standard deviation of the series – i.e. using the averaged standard deviation as a normalizing tool. The resulting Financial System Ratio is then multiplied by 100 to make it more readable. Decimal digits, of an illusory precision, are rounded to the unity. The resulting ratio increases with the importance of financial markets activities relative to that of the banking sector, and seems to capture quite well the 'common sense' opinion of most countries (Table 7.3).

Last, we applied to these twenty countries the previously exposed factors of war costs.

Table 7.2. The Twenty OECD Countries Sample and their 1995 Bank-/Market-Based Ratios.

Country name	Bank Assets / GDP	Market capitalization / GDP	Financial System Ratio
Austria	1.26	0.12	14
Belgium	1.18	0.36	46
Canada	0.66	0.59	134
Denmark	0.48	0.34	106
France	1.02	0.33	48
Germany	1.21	0.24	30
Greece	0.41	0.15	55
Ireland	0.36	0.26	108
Italy	0.74	0.17	34
Japan	1.31	0.79	90
Korea (South)	0.55	0.37	101
Netherlands	1.12	0.69	92
Norway	0.69	0.26	56
Portugal	0.79	0.13	25
Spain	0.96	0.30	47
Sweden	0.54	0.62	172
Switzerland	1.77	0.98	83
Turkey	0.19	0.14	110
United Kingdom	1.16	1.13	146
United States	0,73	0.80	164

Table 7.3. Twenty OECD Countries Ranked According to the 1995 Financial System Ratio.

Country name	Financial System Ratio	Country name	Financial System Ratio
Austria	14	Japan	90
Portugal	25	Netherlands	92
Germany	30	Korea (South)	101
Italy	34	Denmark	106
Belgium	46	Ireland	108
Spain	47	Turkey	110
France	48	Canada	134
Greece	55	United Kingdom	146
Norway	56	United States	164
Switzerland	83	Sweden	172

Test and Results

Based on our previous discussions our first two hypotheses are: 1) Both bank-based and market-based financial systems increase in harmony, thus there is no negative relationship between growth in them. 2) The degree of participation in the two World Wars will increase the tendency of one given financial system to lean on the bank-based side rather than on the market-based side.

The results as displayed in table 4 below clearly support these two hypotheses. There are two factors that make these results worth noticing. Despite the fact that we are looking at more comparable countries in our sample and thus have a quite low number of observations we are receiving both highly significant coefficients and a relatively high explanatory value in both cases. First of all we receive explanatory values of around 30 per cent. We can also see that a one percent increase in the war ratio led to a 1.6 per cent increase in bank assets per GDP, and a more than 2 per cent decrease in market capitalization per GDP. At the same time a one percent increase in market capitalization per GDP led to a 0.4 percent increase in bank assets, and vice versa that a one percent increase in bank assets per GDP also meant a 0.7 per cent higher market capitalization per GDP.

Table 7.4. Cross Sectional OLS-regressions on twenty OECD-countries.[33]

	LOG(BA/GDP)		**LOG (MARKCAP/GDP)**
C	**0.181**	**C**	**-0.900*** **
Prob.	0.408	Prob.	0.000
LOG (MARKCAP/GDP)	**0.447** **	**LOG (BA/GDP)**	**0.697** **
Prob.	0.016	Prob.	0.016
LOG (TOTRATIOWW)	**1.662** **	**LOG (TOTRATIOWW)**	**-2.019** **
Prob.	0.028	Prob.	0.033
R-squared	0.387	**R-squared**	0.374
Adjusted R-squared	0.310	**Adjusted R-squared**	0.296

* 10 percent, **5 percent and *** 1 percent significance level

We can therefore tell that rich countries do not depend on either bank- or market-based financial systems at all, but that these tend to grow in harmony. This means that the developmental explanation for countries leaning towards one form of financial system or another is not historically valid, i.e. that market-based systems might be the 'natural' outcome of any financial system in a long-term peaceful context, but that no such context ever existed.[34] And more importantly, the fact that countries were involved to a higher or lesser degree in the two world wars made its impact on what kind of financial system the country would lean towards for a long time after these historical events. The results show that the sweeping conclusions of the structural explanations must be considered to be dubious, at best.

A valid remark is of course to what extent these two variables capture what really would be the effect of another variable? This problem seems to be at hand for the measure of monetization (M2 per GDP) and Bank Assets per GDP. These measures are both interlinked since they both influence the size of the banking system (albeit on different sides of the balance sheet). There is also an historical observation that war funding was, at least during WW1, massively linked to monetization. In Figure 7.1 below we can also see that there is a high positive correlation between the two variables. In fact the explanatory value of the broad money supply (M2) per GDP as dependent only on Bank Assets per GDP is 67 percent.

Figure 7.1. Linear regression between Bank Assets per GDP (BAGDP) and the Broad Money supply per GDP (M2GDP) in logarithmic values.

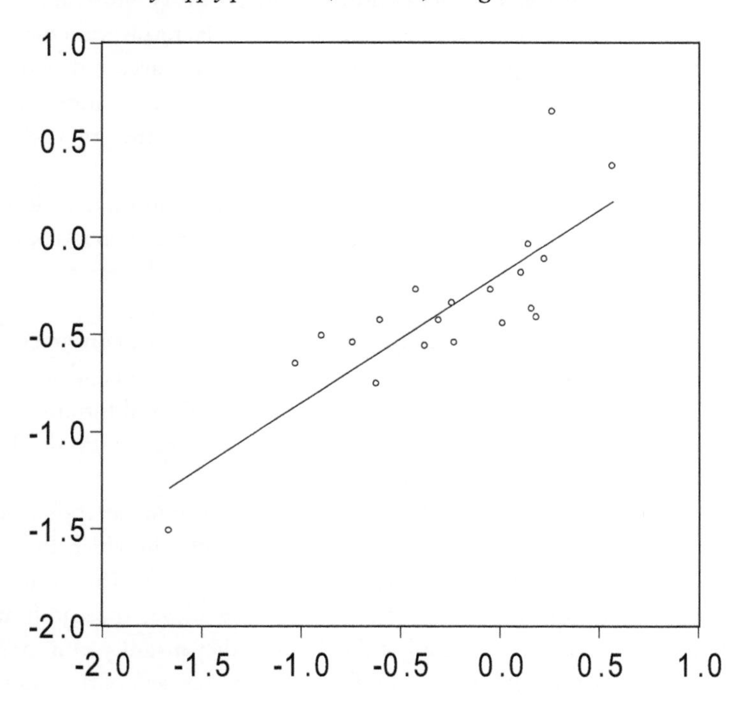

Is Convergence Possible?

Is convergence a mere matter of fact, or a way to interpret history? An initial problem arises when one asks such a question: how to determine endogenous and exogenous factors? We must remember that the difference between exogenous and endogenous factors is very difficult to assess in formal regression methodologies. Indeed, if one considers that crises are fundamentally exogenous events, one avoids linking the structural conditions that may shape the characteristics, outbreak and contemporary perceptions of one given crisis. In short, crises might not just be an interrupting event in the process of a long-term trend in financial systems building – a form of a-historical, anachronistic approach to history that is more or less built into financial system literature since 1989 as critics of North and Weingast approach have shown. Here, we believe that crises take different forms and have different consequences due to the context in which they take place. In doing so, we refute the idea of a monotone trend of financial development, which would dominate history and make it a more or less random collection of events, whose meaning has to be enlightened by neo-hegelian 'zeitgeist' concepts.

The second issue is linked to the fact that most of these studies focus on macroeconomic data aggregated at the national level, which might not make sense a few centuries ago and even during the last two hundred years,[35] first, and which transforms the great variety of local and regional financial forms, structures and institutions in a highly aggregated and rather theoretical averaged structure. One given crisis, by revealing among all different structures, complementary or concurrent, which bear the challenge the more easily, has then two different kinds of impact.

First, it selects the most adapted forms of financial structures and institutions in the new context, not necessarily creating them, but making them looking suddenly more prominent at the aggregated level – it is a high-risk strategy to take a modest shift in figures for a dramatic revolution in structures.

Second, it encourages innovations either from regulators, consumers and financial actors, to reduce the cost of the crisis they bear or to take advantage of the new conditions. Those two kinds of impact are an adapted formula of the 'destructive creation' process highlighted by Schumpeter, but we still think it is necessary to try to distinguish between them.

This means that crises cannot be considered as exogenous or endogenous: they are both. They are provoked in part by the structures in which they take place, leading to unexpected actions and results in consequence. This means also that, beyond the major shifts observed at the aggregated level, the signification of some changes might be misleading, either because they magnify a minor shift (as if in an election, the shift of one party from 49 to 51 per cent of the votes was supposed to change the whole political structure) or hide the perfect continuity in some local or professional segments of the financial structures.

But one has also to remember that, without assumptions, no research is possible. Our objective here is, first, to recall that these assumptions do not come unencumbered – they bring biases with them – and, second, to propose another approach, with its own biases, but with the basic assumption that convergence is not a natural force, rather the result of historical context. To test and study this historical context, we have picked the most gigantic 'events' of the twentieth century: world wars. But to study such an event, one has to make sure it is not reduced to an insignificant alternative.

Conclusions

The objectives of this chapter are threefold: First it is methodological as we argue for the possibility of combining historical events as determinants of present structures without losing out on the importance of contexts and changes in the historical dynamic. Second, it is empirical as we aim to find another more plausible explanatory variable for the division between 'bank-based' and 'market-based' financial systems than what legal system was originally adopted. Third, it is theoretical in that, in light of the finding that historical events are major determinants for financial structures, we may define what convergence means. The world is neither frictionless nor perfect, and historical events continue to challenge the existing social, political and economic structures and thus convergence is not, and should not be regarded as a shaping force in the real world, but rather as an empirical result of that world, related to ideology, shared practices, prejudice and, over all, power.

We believe we have established in this essay the casual link between main historical events; the degree of participation in the world wars, and the structure of financial systems. Of course there are a number of other explanatory variables that might be added to the list as reasons for the different countries' financial structures. But we do believe that wars are one of the most, if not *the* most important explanatory variable. And this deserves to be pointed out as most academic studies, economical as well as historical, tend to regard them as anomalies and thus take wars out of the equation.[36]

8 THE FINANCING OF THE SPANISH CIVIL WAR, 1936–9

Pablo Martín-Aceña
Elena Martínez Ruiz
María A. Pons

The Civil War was one of the most significant events in the history of contemporary Spain. The war lasted nearly three years, from July 1936, when a military coup attempted to overthrow the government of the Second Republic, to March 1939, when General Franco's Army claimed total victory over a demoralized Republican Army. The sorry legacy of this tragic episode were the 300,000 lives lost, the 300,000 exiled, the 300,000 political prisoners, and the ensuing dictatorship endured by the country for forty years until the death of Franco.

This chapter addresses the 'financing of the civil war', a subject that until very recently has received little attention in the literature, although it is widely accepted that once a war begins it is economics as much as military strategy that decides the outcome. This neglect of the general financial aspects of the war is partly due to the lack of reliable data, with most studies relying on a handful of reports that the victorious Francoist authorities produced after the conflict was over, especially the so-called Larraz report published in August 1940. However there are exceptions that have advanced our knowledge of the financial aspects Spanish Civil War.[1] Building on this research and using new quantitative information, we revise the established view of how the war was financed and the amount of resources available to each of the contenders. Section 1 introduces the economic context of the war, section 2 examines how the Republican Treasury met the cost of the conflict, while section 3 does the same for the so-called 'national Treasury'. We conclude with a reassessment of Spain's war finances and some conclusions.

Spain at War

Historians and political scientists have viewed the civil war as a major turning point in Spanish history.[2] It was not only a military conflict but also a political, social, ideological and religious confrontation. From its onset the Spanish conflict became an international affair. Hitler and Mussolini openly supported the military rebellion from its very beginning, while Stalin helped the Republicans after several weeks of hesitation. France and Great Britain tried to keep the Spanish civil strife within the territorial limits of the Peninsula and so promoted a non-interventionist policy that blocked the sale of arms to the Republic, to the despair of democrats all over the world. In Washington the Roosevelt administration simply followed whatever policy London adopted.

The military uprising split the country's territory in two halves and as a consequence two ideological factions and antagonistic states emerged. The Republican government remained in Madrid until November 1936 when, under the threat of a possible conquest of the capital by the rebel Army it removed to Valencia on the Mediterranean coast; a second removal to Barcelona took place in September 1937. The pilgrimage of all central offices, the headquarters of major companies and banks, as well as that of other organizations and institutions such as the Bank of Spain, the Supreme Banking Council and the Foreign Exchange Control Centre followed the relocation of the government. The so-called 'national administration' chose Burgos, 250 km north of Madrid, as its official site. The rebels' generals established a Technical Committee composed of military and civilian personnel with the task of organizing a new and parallel State that was ready and in full operation when on 1 October 1936 Franco was appointed head of the government.

The war ruptured the financial and monetary union of the country. Although the headquarters of the main banks and saving banks remained in the territory controlled by the Republican authorities, many branches and a large number of regional and local financial institutions operated independently in the area occupied by the military forces commanded by General Franco. Two central banks – one in Madrid and another in Burgos – and two 'pesetas' coexisted during the war. Financial institutions on both sides of the divide were subjected to close supervision and regulatory bodies were transformed or newly established. In the Republican zone the Supreme Banking Council was put under the control of the Ministry of Finance, while in the 'national' zone it was suppressed and replaced by the National Council for Credit. The operation of all Spanish stock exchanges was suspended, the redemption and payment of interests on public debt were deferred and a moratorium on bank mortgages declared in all Spain. Moreover, rigorous foreign exchange controls and strict measures to regulate the financial system were enforced. Altogether these stipulations disturbed and in some cases interrupted the normal mercantile activity of firms, corporations and financial institutions because, although only provisional, they remained in place during the three years of the war. The Franco administration adopted similar measures: price and exchange controls were introduced, trade unions forbidden and the industrial sectors militarized.

The currency also suffered the consequences of the war. A decree of November 1936, the 'national authorities' declared illegal all banknotes issued by the Republican Bank of Spain after July 1936. All series in circulation before that date had to be stamped and provisions were taken to put into circulation new banknotes issued by the Bank of Spain operating from Burgos. Also, an official mint was opened to coin donated or confiscated metals. Later, in August 1938, the country's monetary division widened when Burgos prohibited the possession of enemy money. This included not only the banknotes issued since the date of the uprising, but also the silver certificates issued by the Treasury in Madrid and the paper money issued by the regional and local governments. Although the Republican authorities responded with delay to this cascade of national acts, they too prohibited the circulation of enemy notes, but no measure was taken with respect to bank deposits.

How the Republican Government Financed the War

The initial position of the Republican government at the outbreak of the war was of relative advantage mainly because they held the Bank of Spain's gold reserves. However, despite this apparent financial supremacy the Republican government did not go on to win the war, in the early stages of which the growing 'weakness' of the Republic led to a change of government. In September 1936 Largo Caballero became the new President and the socialist Juan Negrín the new Minister of Finance. From this moment Negrín became the great statesman of the Spanish Republic. He tried to recover part of the Republic's lost power by centralizing its financial and banking institutions, and in May 1937 he became Prime Minister of the Republic and Minister of Economics and Finance.

The government had to look for funds to finance the war. In the Ministry of Finance archives there is a summary (dated 1 February 1939) of the Spanish budgets carried out by the Ministry of Finance.[3] This internal document, never published, summarizes the budgetary expenses for 1936, 1937 and 1938. The budgets for those years distinguished between ordinary, extraordinary and undisclosed credits; of these, only the first two were published in the *Gaceta*, the government's official bulletin. The picture that emerges after including the undisclosed credits is completely different from that presented in the official figures. According to this new evidence, the Republic's public expenditure multiplied five-fold from 5,752 million pesetas in 1936 to 21,335 million pesetas in 1938, with more than half being set aside to finance the war: in 1937 the Ministry of War received 54.38 per cent of total public expenditure, a percentage which had increased to 66.76 per cent by 1938.

Table 8.1. Budgetary expenditures in 1936, 1937 and 1938 (in millions of pesetas).

	1936	1937	1938
War expenditures	1,089	7,187	14,244
Total Expenditures	5,752	13,217	21,335

Source: Archives of the Ministry of Finance reproduced in Pons (2006).

How did the government manage to finance this increase in public expenditures? Taxes, credits from the Bank of Spain and money issues were the main mechanisms of the internal financing of the war. The Bank of Spain reserves were the main external source of finance. These mechanisms of finance shall now be examined in detail.

Internal Financing

When it came to paying for domestic goods and services, the principal source of internal finance was taxation. The government approved new taxes and tried to introduce a new fiscal reform, but it failed and revenues from taxes dropped abruptly in the first few months of the war. Any attempt to introduce fiscal reform in wartime was bound to fail since there were significant falls in income, rents and profits and, moreover, a loss of central governmental power. However, contrary to the received view in the literature, the main objective of this fiscal policy was to finance the war, not merely to contribute to their 'revolutionary project'.[4]

Unfortunately, no aggregated data for taxes is available for the Republican zone. We know that the Republican fiscal administration collapsed in the first months of the war and that it took time to rebuild it. Moreover, the revolutionary organizations suppressed what they considered 'capitalist taxes', blocking the collection of land rents; and the confiscation of private property and of many industrial companies and service firms interrupted the payment of corporate and other taxes.[5] An official report released on 8 February 1938 by the bureau of the Prime Minister, Juan Negrín, showed the fall in total revenues from taxes in the first months of the conflict, although later there was a slightly recovery.[6] Income from all taxes during the second semester of 1936 was around 420 million pesetas, a far cry from the 2,000 million pesetas collected in 1935 over the same period. This figure improved in the second semester of 1937 when tax revenues increased to 550 million pesetas. For 1938, some other fragmentary information indicates that the government was able to collect 1,200 million pesetas at most, way below the 4,140 million pesetas of the 1935 budget in the same semester.

We also have some partial data for Valencia and Catalonia that indicates the sharp drop in Republican wartime tax revenues. In Valencia, the last major city to remain in the hands of the Republicans the government obtained around 44 million pesetas from the *Contribución de utilidades* (a tax on profits and rents) in January 1936. This amount fell to only 2 million pesetas in January 1937 and further to below 1 million pesetas in January 1938 and January 1939. In Catalonia the revenue from taxation fell dramatically from 45 million pesetas in 1935 to 9.4 million pesetas in 1937.[7]

The only successful tax was 'inflation', as a consequence of continuous monetary issues. Thanks to Bank of Spain loans, the Republic spent more than 24,000 million pesetas. As a consequence the money supply grew from 6,595 million pesetas in July 1936 to 17,053 in December 1937 and 26,613 million pesetas at the end of 1938.[8] The main problem in the Republican zone was that, in addition to the government's monetary issues, civil society institutions (local authorities, trade unions, cooperatives, etc) were also printing money and thus breaking the Bank of Spain's monopoly. The printing of money on such a huge scale in the different Spanish regions (in Catalonia alone there were more than 10,000 different kinds of local bills) had a dramatic effect on inflation, which verged on hyperinflation by 1938. Thus, for the Republicans, printing money became an essential mechanism for the internal financing of the war.

Another such mechanism was public issues. However, lack of confidence and the high risk associated with these issues meant that the Republic was only able to obtain very limited funds from this source. A case in point was Negrín's failure to place public bonds in July 1938.

To these instruments of finance, other emergency measures such as confiscation were passed in order to increase revenues. The Republican government declared it a duty to hand in all metals and jewellery to the Bank of Spain and proceeded to the requisition of properties belonging to declared enemies of the Republic, namely those that would have joined sides directly or indirectly with the rebels. There is no data about the total amount of funds collected by this means, or the use to which these funds were put. In the first few months of the war confiscations were made illegally; but from December 1936 the General Director of Security became responsible for formal confiscations through the *Caja de Reparaciones* (War Reparations Fund). According to Viñas, the Republicans obtained between 9 and 11 million dollars from sales of the Fund's assets. However, the bulk of these funds was not used to finance the war but was put aside with a view to helping in the reconstruction of the country after the war.[9]

In addition to the central administration, thanks to their respective laws of the autonomous governments, the Basque country and Catalonia had their own administrations. Basque autonomy was very shortlived, lasting from July 1936 to June 1937, when Bilbao fell into the hands of the Francoists, who expunged all legislation passed by the Basque authorities. By contrast, the role of the Catalonian authorities was more significant in terms of the actions the government undertook and the amount of funds they controlled. The *Generalitat* of Catalonia, constituted after the 1931 elections, had assumed control of the central government's financial delegations in Catalonia and introduced new taxes. The Catalonian government's chief sources of finance[10] were taxes (initially it controlled a percentage of the taxes raised by central government, and later on it introduced new taxes);[11] the resources obtained from the central government's financial delegations in Catalonia (the Catalan authorities confiscated the resources from branches of the Bank of Spain and Ministry of Finance delegations); and some financial support from central government.[12] Arias Velasco estimates that the total wartime expenditure of the Catalonian government was between 1,750 and 1,850 million pesetas.[13]

Gold Sales and Foreign Loans

The main external means of financing the war was the Bank of Spain reserves. The Republicans controlled most of the Bank of Spain's gold and silver reserves. At the outbreak of the Civil War the volume of bullion in the Bank of Spain that could be mobilized in order to finance the war stood at about 635 tonnes of fine gold, or 715 million dollars. These reserves were the fourth largest in the world and had been accumulated during the First World War, when Spanish neutrality resulted in considerable inflows of foreign exchange that was converted into gold in the international markets. The Republican government used these reserves to purchase military equipment, ammunition, food and raw materials abroad. The Bank of France acquired 27 per cent of the gold (around 174 tonnes of fine gold), with the Republican government obtaining in exchange 3,922 million francs (around 196 million dollars).

Table 8.2. Sales of Bank of Spain gold to the Bank of France.

	Amount of fine gold (in kg)	In millions of francs
Bank of France	34,478.7	549.5
Stabilization Fund	142,535.9	3,372.5
Total	174,535.9	3,922.0

Source: Martin-Aceña (2004).

The rest of the reserves were sent to the USSR, the only country that had been genuinely willing to help the Spanish republic after Stalin had decided as early as September 1936 to send the first ship with Soviet arms, which arrived at the city of Cartagena on 4 October; from then on, the Soviet government maintained its unequivocal support of the Republic throughout the conflict. As indicated above, through the 'non intervention accord', also adopted in September 1936, the Western democratic powers agreed not to provide large-scale material support to the legal Spanish government, so the Republic had to look elsewhere to obtain military equipment and Moscow was considered the best option. Martin Aceña, however, considers that the Republic might have been too hasty in its decision about where to send the gold and, under the pressure generated by the rapid victories of Franco's troops and the shortages in war material, did not consider other possible options, such as France, the UK or the USA.[14]

The Negrín 'dossier', an extraordinary report that Negrín's son gave to the Spanish consul in Paris in 1956, provides detailed information about the gold operations carried out in those years. 510 tonnes were sent to the USSR; equivalent to 460 tonnes of fine gold with a value of 520 million dollars at 1936 prices (its real value was probably higher, this figure overlooking, for example, the numismatic value of a large number of the gold coins). The Republican government obtained 245 million dollars, 42 million pounds and 375 million francs. Of these sums the Soviet government retained 132 million dollars as payment for supplies, and the rest was transferred to Paris to different accounts in the Banque Commerciale pour L'Europe du Nord, a Paris-based Soviet bank. Out of these accounts the Republic paid for all types of war supplies (aircraft, tanks, artillery, rifles, etc.), as well as foodstuffs and raw materials. The purchases were made in Brussels, Prague, Warsaw, New York and other parts of the world. The Republic issued nineteen orders to sell between 19 February 1937 and 28 April 1938: in fourteen months, 426 tonnes of fine gold were spent.

Table 8.3. Sales of the Bank of Spain gold to the Gossbank.

	Alloy gold (in Tm.)	Fine gold (in Tm.)	Million $
Sale orders (1–15)	415.0	374.0	394.6
Sale orders (16–19)	58.0	52.0	75.0
Credit guarantee gold	35.0	31.2	70.0
Total	508.0	458.0	469.6

Source: Martin-Aceña (2004)

By April 1938 most of the Moscow gold had been spent and in February, at Negrín's request, Stalin gave additional credit of 70 million dollars at 3 per cent interest, 31.2 tonnes from the gold deposit being assigned as guarantee. By the end of the year the loan had been completely used up, and the Soviet authorities informed the Spanish government that the deposit was depleted. While it cannot quite be said that the Soviet authorities cheated the Republic, the Spanish government was certainly not given any preferential treatment. The Kremlin was not generous at all but charged for all the financial services proffered (melting, refinery and transport costs, and so on), as well as applying abusive exchange rates for all the – extremely poor quality – materials sent to the Republic.[15]

Lastly, after selling the gold, in 1938 and 1939 the Republic sold 1,225 tonnes of silver to the US Treasury and the Bank of France in exchange for around 15 million dollars. It also sold silver to private French and Belgian firms, obtaining around 5 million dollars in return. To sum up, if we add together all the funds obtained from the sale of gold in Paris and Moscow, silver in New York, and some small credits obtained for the Republic, the Republic collected around 710 million dollars.

Table 8.4. Total sales of gold and silver.

		Alloy gold (Tm)	Fine gold (Tm)	Dollars (million)
Gold	1936	194	174	195.8
	1937	415	374	394.6
	1938		67.5	75
	Total		615.6	665.4
Silver	1938		s.d.	20
TOTAL				685.4

Source: Martin-Aceña (2004).

How the Francoist Administration Financed the War

Internal Financing

The division of the country into two separate areas made the collection of taxes very difficult for the Francoists. A tax administration was hurriedly created with limited effectiveness.[16] The main problem was that the lion's share of sources of taxation was located in the territory controlled by the government, which controlled the main ports and borders and the main financial and industrial centres. The Francoist economic authorities took several measures to make sure that all the agents operating in their territory paid taxes there. So, the deadlines for paying certain taxes, such as land and utility taxes were shortened, and manufacturing guilds, responsible for collecting certain taxes, were dissolved. Perhaps the most important measure taken was the creation of independent companies by seizing the productive assets and plants of firms with headquarters in Republican territories. A byproduct of this process was the creation of a management class that was loyal to the cause of the military uprising.

This does not mean that the Francoist authorities planned to rely on taxes to finance their rebellion. On the contrary, they made no changes to the tax system, neither raising the rate of any of the main taxes nor introducing any new taxes until July 1938, when duties on sugar, beer and chicory were levied, along with postal tariffs and stamps. The most significant tax policy decision was taken as late as January 1939, when a tax on extraordinary war profits was introduced. The new tax took retroactive effect as from July 1936 and obviously provoked strong opposition among businessmen. Controversial and short-lived, the new tax was scrapped in September 1943. Studies of this tax conclude that it was blighted by tax evasion on a massive scale, which has yet to be estimated. At any rate, the revenues from the war profits tax were not used to finance the war but the later reconstruction.

While the Francoist authorities did not intend to finance the war through taxes, they did introduce new taxes and raised existing tariffs in order to finance social assistance schemes. At first, the revenues were used to develop a basic and limited welfare system, composed of social canteens, orphanages, childcare centres and the like. As the conflict went on, the Francoist authorities' goal of supporting soldiers' families took priority, and so the revenues became a complement to the soldiers' remuneration, generally known as pro-combatant subsidies. To finance those benefits a whole range of new taxes was introduced including indirect taxes on tobacco, theatre tickets, perfumes and alcohol; a tax levied on real estate owners; and diverse taxes on hotels and restaurants. An important feature of these new taxes is that they were not administered by the Treasury but by the Home Office, which made it very difficult to coordinate tax policies and detect tax fraud. This contradicts the received view of an efficient, well-organized and smoothly functioning administration on the Francoist side, as opposed to a chaotic one on the Republican.[17]

There are practically no data available to analyse the effectiveness of these tax initiatives, the total revenue raised or the total benefits provided. The only data about tax revenues in the Francoist zone during the war comes from the report presented in 1940 by the Francoist Minister of Finance, José Larraz. This report provides data regarding the total annual income, presumably total tax revenues, of the Francoist Treasury. The figures are shown in Table 8.5.

Table 8.5. Annual income and expenditure acknowledged by the Francoist Treasury (million pesetas).

	Income	Expenditure	Deficit
2nd semester 1936	396	819	423
1st semester 1937	552	1,291	739
2nd semester 1937	680	2,252	1,572
1st semester 1938	791	2,602	1,811
2nd semester 1938	847	3,208	2,411
1st trimester 1939	418	1,722	1,304
TOTAL	3,684	11,894	8,260

Source: Ministerio de Hacienda (1940).

According to this report, tax revenue increased from 396 million pesetas in the second semester of 1936 to 847 million in the second part of 1938. In total, during the thirty-three months which the war lasted, the Francoist authorities were able to collect 3,684 million pesetas through taxes, a relatively small amount compared with the 4,336 collected in 1935 alone. Thus, taxes did not constitute the chief means of financing the military effort but played only a secondary role, funding at most 30 per cent of acknowledged expenditure, as may be inferred from Table 8.5.

Nor did the Francoist authorities resort to issuing debt in order to finance the war. According to the few documents that have survived relating to decisions made regarding the financing of the Francoist military effort during the war, and according to the literature on the subject, public debt was never even considered as an option to finance war.[18]

Money creation was the main source of finance for the Francoists. The internal financing of war by the Burgos-based Francoist Bank of Spain led to increasing advances from the Bank to the Treasury; these were formalized in twenty credit lines issued under the Banking Act, of which all but the last were signed in Burgos. By 1937 the Francoist Treasury had already received 2,500 million pesetas. Those advances increased afterwards until they reached the amount of 10,100 million pesetas. In his 1940 report, Larraz recorded a figure of only 7,200 million, as the last 4 lines of credit were signed immediately after the war. Money creation was consequently the main financial source of the Francoist Treasury. According to official data, the deficit on the revenue account during the war amounted to 8,260 million pesetas, 7,200 of which were covered by advance payments from the Bank of Spain in Burgos, the remaining 1,060 million being covered by debit balances on different Treasury accounts at the same bank. Thus, the Bank of Spain in Burgos helped to take care of almost 70 per cent of the internal expenses of the Francoists during the war.

The Francoists used other revenue-raising instruments too, which mainly consisted in requisitions and voluntary contributions, although it is difficult to establish the extent to which contributions were truly voluntary.[19] With respect to requisitions, these commenced shortly after the outbreak of the war given the lack of financial resources available to the Francoist military. Part of the cost was also raised from political opponents: fines and confiscation of assets in retaliation for political opposition were a constant source of revenues for Francoist authorities, even long after the war had finished. Although it is likely that such measures were not motivated primarily by the need to raise finance, nonetheless a certain economic profit did accrue on political repression. But not only opponents were expropriated: General Queipo de Llano, for instance, who commanded the Francoist troops in Western Andalusia, requisitioned all property and assets, ranging from motor vehicles to the output from mines, which he determined useful to the war effort. The British firm Rio Tinto was one of the first to suffer this type of requisition.[20] Unfortunately, however, while the existence of these requisitions can be established, the absence of any reliable data or estimates makes it impossible to quantify their magnitude.

The deferral of payment for military supplies was of greater financial significance. In August 1936, the Junta, the highest administrative body in the Francoist-controlled territories, established that payments corresponding to the war budget could, at the discretion of the authorities, be deferred until the end of the war, with the exception of personnel costs. As a result the financial burden of the war effort fell to the military suppliers since close to 60 per cent of purchases were subject to deferral.[21] Larraz's report estimated that total deferments amounted to 800 million pesetas. However, it is likely that the total amounts deferred were much higher, in view of the broad powers of requisition. In fact, in the official government budgets for the years 1940 to 1946, the administration included 8,060 million pesetas to cover debts and expenditures whose payment had been postponed; of these, 22 per cent corresponded to the interests and principal of the public debt and more than 50 per cent to military supplies.[22]

Foreign Aid and Loans

The Francoist authorities resorted massively to external sources in order to finance the war effort. The most important element in this financing on account for its magnitude and military significance was the aid received from the Axis powers, which included sending troops and military experts, military supplies and credit. The form of aid and terms under which the aid was given varied considerably from one country to another. However, there were some features in common: the accounting and control of the aid received was entrusted to the countries providing the aid, and the total amount to be paid by the Spanish authorities was established in bilateral diplomatic negotiations after the war.

In the case of Mussolini's Italy, the total amount of aid has been calculated as standing between 7,000 and 8,668 million lire (377 to 467 million dollars).[23] This figure can be broken down as follows (Table 8.6).

Table 8.6. Italian aid.

	Value
Military supplies until 31.July.1938	3,627 million lire
Expenses of voluntary troops (January-April 1939)	3,300 million lire
Revolving credit	300 million lire
Financial expenses	68 million lire
TOTAL	7,295 million lire (393 million dollars)

Source: Martínez Ruiz (2006b).

Nevertheless, from studies on the negotiation of the debt it can be concluded that some factors were missed out, such as the supplies made in the second semester of 1938. In fact, even the Spanish authorities raised the volume to 8,300 million lire, the figure considered by the Ministers' Council at its meeting of 25 June 1940, where the matter of the debt with Italy was discussed. It is difficult to choose between these figures, above all because subsequently the Italian government agreed to a substantial reduction in the Spanish debt, which was finally set at 5,000 million lire. In any case, the figure proposed by the Ministers' Council might be the more acceptable on the following grounds: the average volume of Italian supplies in the first four semesters of war had a value of approximately 907 million lire; if the volume of help received between July and December, 1938 was similar to that of the previous semesters (i.e. approximately 900 million), once that volume was added to the 7,295 million which can be vouched for, the total amount would reach approximately 8,195 million lire, an amount very close to the figure mentioned at the Ministers' Council.

The case of German aid is much more problematic. Different studies offer a wide range of figures, from 430 million to 580 million RM, for the debt contracted by the Francoist authorities, but none for the total amount of aid received from the Nazi regime.[24] All these reconstructions are based on documentation generated at different levels of the Nazi administration in the course of the subsequent bilateral negotiation the function of which was to determine the volume of the debt contracted by the Spanish authorities. Hence the main objective of those reports, notes or estimates was not to establish the total amount of aid provided, but to determine which of the items might be considered to be a debt, what part of that debt could be subjected to the 4 per cent interest rate agreed in 1937, and how the debt was to be paid back.

It is possible, however, to detail the items and amounts proposed by the Germans in the subsequent negotiation of the debt. The total amount of 560 million RM ensues from the sum of all possible concepts, ranging from supplies to three armies through commercial obligations to the expenses of the Legion Condor.[25] However, the German authorities included in their calculation some items that can hardly be qualified as military aid. For example, they claimed 45 million RM as compensation for the damages suffered by properties belonging to German citizens during the civil war. On the other hand, in order to ascertain the total amount of aid, to the amount of the debt would have to be added the volume of payments made by the Francoist authorities during the war. These payments were partly devoted to the anticipated payment of the debt and partly to other expenses such as the maintenance of the Legion Condor. Once these payments are included, the total amount of Nazi aid reaches 629 million RM (253 million dollars).

Table 8. 7. German aid.

	Value
Maximum amount of debt claimed by Germany in 1939	558,53 mill. RM
Items not considered as aid	45 mill RM
Payments during the war	115 Mill RM
TOTAL	628,53 million RM (253,44 million dollars)

Source: Martínez Ruiz (2006b).

In addition, the Francoist authorities received loans from several Spanish and foreign institutions and firms, notably from Portugal. Table 8.8 summarizes the available information, which is to be found in an incomplete list. We do not have any information regarding the commercial loans granted by foreign companies, for example Texaco or Standard Oil. However, we do know that other sources of foreign finance were used. Thus, during the course of the war obligations were established on Spanish citizens with respect to international means of payment. Spanish firms and nationals had to turn over to the State all minted gold and coins, as well as shares in internationally traded companies. Between March and December 1937, 1.43 million pounds, 3.46 million Argentinian pesos in shares and 8.54 million pesetas in gold were deposited. These assets were used as guarantees for the securing of some of the foreign loans mentioned above, while some of the gold pesetas (4.7 million) were purchased by the Francoist authorities at the official exchange rate. There were also voluntary contributions. The drive for funds was initiated by the so-called National Subscription set up on 17 August 1936, through which the National Defence Committee (the military Junta) called for the population to donate foreign currency, jewels and gold. The quantity of these donations has not been determined with any precision, although some estimates exist for particular items.[26] Of course, these quantities are only minimum estimates of the amounts raised by the Francoist; the real amounts may have been considerably higher.

Table 8.8. Other sources of foreign exchange.

	Value
Portuguese credits	4.89 mill. $
Credits from other institutions	10.97 mill. $
Foreign currency donations	6.76 mill $
Gold donations	2.740 kg. (fine gold)

Source: Martínez Ruiz (2006b).

Conclusion

There are four means of paying for a war: taxation, borrowing from the public in the domestic market, borrowing in foreign markets and creating money.[27] How those means are combined to finance a given war varies greatly in accordance with internal and external constraints, institutional factors and the length and intensity of the conflict. The evidence shows that governments finance wars through a mixture of direct contemporaneous taxes, debt and money creation. Moreover, the same evidence shows that all wars have a major inflationary component built in to them since the inflation tax is widely used as a consequence of the resort to money creation.

In two recent books, distinguished historians have reviewed the economics of the two world wars.[28] Both volumes examine the war experience of the main combatant countries and devote special attention to financial questions. In all cases public expenditures increased and governments resorted to all possible means of finance for the war effort. When possible, taxes were raised. Borrowing was intense and, as a result, government debt multiplied. Deficits were unavoidable, the upshot of which was new money being thrown into circulation causing inflation and currency depreciation. The experience of at least three civil wars, preceding the Spanish one, in the nineteenth and twentieth centuries tells the same story. In the American Civil War the Union covered its expenses by raising new taxes, but most of the revenue needed to finance the war came from money creation (the well-known greenbacks) and from debt issuance. Unable to pay for the war effort through taxation, the Confederacy resorted to bonds selling in London or Amsterdam and to currency issuance on a huge scale. Inflation in both the North and the South was the inevitable result of printing money.[29] During the long Mexican Civil War the two armies in conflict tried to raise taxes, borrow from the public and sell bonds abroad. However, as this was not sufficient to meet expenses, the printing presses had to start working overtime. Prices skyrocketed and the Mexican peso depreciated sharply.[30] Revolutionary Russia offers a third, even more extreme, example. The Bolsheviks faced insurmountable difficulties financing the war: the fiscal administration collapsed, the domestic financial market vanished and markets abroad closed their doors on Soviet issues. Paper money became the sole means of financing the deficit caused by the increase in war expenditures. As was the case in other civil or international wars, in Russia, too, prices rose unrelentingly to reach hyperinflationary levels.[31]

What do we know about Spain? How did the Republicans and the nationalists meet the cost of the war? How the two combatants did finance the war? From where did they obtain the resources needed to pay for the war? Which of the two parties managed the resources under their command more efficiently? Did the Republican army lose the war because of lack of financial resources?

The civil war broke up the unity of the financial system of the country. A new central bank was established in the Francoist zone that issued its own currency (the 'nationalist peseta', different to the legal or Republican peseta issued by the Republican Bank of Spain). Moreover, the appearance of local and regional money in various areas of the Republican territory contributed to the fragmentation of the monetary system. Hence, during the three years of the war there was no what can be called a national monetary system. The financial evolution of the two combatants diverged and this posed a challenging problem after the war when the system had to be rebuilt. If the monetary systems diverged, the sources of finance, however, were more alike. This study has shown how the two sides in the Spanish Civil War resorted to all feasible means to raise the finance needed to pay for the conflict: new taxes, public borrowing and money creation. Taxation was limited and neither of the sides was able to collect much of the money needed to meet the huge increase in expenditures entailed by the three years of conflict. Domestic borrowing caused insurmountable difficulties, mostly the lack of a well-functioning and organized capital market, since the stock exchanges were closed in both zones. Furthermore, the issue of government debt was precluded since the two combatants had suspended the amortization and interest payments of the existing debt. Foreign credit, by contrast, was readily available to the Francoists as they received most of the necessary foreign funds on loan from their ideological allies (Germany and Italy) and from friendly Portuguese, Swiss and British banks. This was not the case for the Republicans. They did not receive any foreign assistance from the democratic nations nor did they attempt to float debt in London, Paris or New York despite having a large amount of gold that could have been used as a solid guarantee. Instead, they decided to sell the Bank of Spain's metal reserves to pay for imported military and civil supplies. All in all, measured in dollars, the two sides secured equal amounts of external resources, as shown in Table 8.9.

Table 8.9. External sources of financing (million dollars).

		Republican government	Francoist authorities
Allies credits (aid)		70	749.16
Assets sales	Gold	665.4	
	Silver	20	
	Others	14	10.97
TOTAL		769.4	760.13

Sources: see text.

Money creation was the main resource used by both Francoists and Republicans to pay for the war. At least 60 per cent per cent of all expenditure was financed through the issue of new money. By way of advances and credits from the respective central banks the two parties were able to obtain all the revenue they needed to meet the expenses of the war. There was little difference between the Franco administration and the Republican government on this account. Accordingly, inflation and currency depreciation in both zones was the inevitable result of overworked printing presses. In the Republican territory, prices rose unrelentingly to hyperinflationary levels as the result of political instability, lack of confidence in the military victory, the failure of controls and the loss of most of its agrarian and industrial base. Depreciation and inflation was less acute in the Francoist territory where the administration enhanced its economic base, centralized the use of resources, adopted strict controls and continuously built up hopes of a favourable outcome to the war. As in all previous wars, the two Spanish combatants resorted to various methods to finance their expenditures, and as in all previous conflicts money creation was the main means of meeting the financial requirements of civil strife. The Republican army did not lose the war because of lack of financial resources; in fact, the two armies spent the same amount of money. Rather, political, social, diplomatic and military factors played the decisive role; it is politics rather than economics that best explains the final result of the war.

Acknowledgements

We would like to thank Patrice Baubeau, Anders Ögren, Cristiano Ristuccia, and the participants at the International Conference on War, Money and Finance, Université Paris 10 Nanterre, June 2008 and at the Quantitative History Seminar, Cambridge University, March 2009 for their comments and suggestions. This research has received the financial support of the Spanish Ministerie de C??? e Innovacion, through the project ECO2009-08791.

9 THE LONDON FINANCIAL CRISIS OF 1914

Richard Roberts

On the eve of the First World War London was the world's foremost international financial centre, as it had been for more than a century. Other major financial centres developed from the 1870s, notably Berlin and New York, principally to serve their rapidly growing domestic economies though they also increasingly provided international services, as did Paris and Amsterdam, London's long-standing juniors. However, the operation of first mover advantages and powerful external economies of scale and scope ensured that London sustained a pre-eminent position.[1] Thus the effect of the expansion of international trade and capital flows in the first era of globalization was both greater divergence in the provision of international financial services, but also the emergence of a complex multipolar pattern of convergence with London as the hub of a new financial web. The crisis that engulfed London in summer 1914 shattered the international network of financial relationships and also threatened to destroy the mechanisms of London's operations as a financial centre.

'It came upon us like a thunderbolt from a clear sky,' marvelled financial commentator Hartley Withers. 'The fury of the tempest was such that no credit system could possibly have stood up against it'.[2] Over the course of little more than a week London's key international financial markets broke down, threatening widespread bankruptcy among the specialist firms that operated in London's wholesale financial markets. The crisis also put at risk the domestic banking system and jeopardized sterling's convertibility into gold and its role in the international financial system.

The unprecedented scale and scope of London's financial crisis of 1914 was matched by unprecedented intervention in the financial system by the British state. The authorities mounted a series of novel initiatives to save the banks and revive the markets, including contemporary forms of quantitative easing, the removal of 'troubled assets' from the money market, and partial recapitalization of the banking system by government guaranteed loans at significant risk to taxpayers. The measures proved successful – by early 1915 the City's markets were operating once more and failures among financial firms were minimal. By then Britain was at war and the restored financial mechanisms were being put to work serving their saviour by funding the war effort.

Breakdown of the International Financial Markets

London's financial markets were not even 'ruffled' by the assassination of Austrian heir-apparent Archduke Franz Ferdinand in Sarajevo on 28 June 1914.[3] In following weeks bond yields showed no signs of anxiety: after all, there had been international tensions the previous three summers.[4] War-risk perceptions were rudely transformed by news of an Austrian ultimatum to Serbia that hit the markets 'like a bombshell' on Friday 24 July.[5] Over the course of the following week the key international financial markets – the foreign exchange market, the sterling money market and the London Stock Exchange – broke down.

Foreign Exchange Market

The London money market and capital market, and their participants, were creditors to the world on a huge scale. The scramble for liquidity from 24 July led to the disintegration of the mechanisms of international remittance through the foreign exchange markets.[6] International loans raised in London, whether short-term trade credits or long-term bonds, were provided in sterling and had to be serviced and repaid in sterling, with aggregate payments of millions of pounds being required every day.[7] Before the First World War, the principal instrument for the settlement of sterling obligations by overseas borrowers was the sterling bill of exchange. Sterling bills were created by participants in the London money market, which was the forum in which they were traded. However, so widespread was the use of the sterling bill – it was estimated that sterling commercial bills financed 90 per cent of British trade and 50 per cent of world trade – that they were constantly bought and sold by banks across the world.[8] Overseas recipients of payment by a sterling bill obtained local currency by selling it to a local bank, while those needing to settle obligations in London were buyers. By 1914 telegraphic transfer of funds between banks was a possible alternative form of remittance, but it was relatively costly and in fact little used unless rapid settlement was of paramount importance.[9]

The shipment of gold was a further possible means of international settlement. Under the gold standard each participating currency had a fixed parity against gold, but there was also a market price for gold. If the market price of gold rose above, or fell below, the fixed price *plus* the costs of transport and insurance, it became profitable to ship gold between countries. These so-called 'gold points' provided the usual upper and lower bounds of fluctuations in the gold price, since arbitrage between centres would quickly restore price differentials to within the bands.

In the decades before the war the international circulation of the currencies of the US, Germany, France, Japan and other gold-standard countries, was growing, leading to increased need for foreign exchange facilities especially against sterling. These were provided by the expansion of the foreign exchange markets outside London: in Paris for francs; Berlin for marks; New York for US dollars; etc. Thus, for instance, it was in Paris, not London, that holders of sterling bills sold them for francs, or parties needing to settle in sterling bought sterling bills with francs. This structure worked adequately so long as there was a supply of sterling bills in the world's foreign exchange markets to meet the requirements of debtors to the London financial markets.

Beginning on Friday 24 July, the world's foreign exchange markets experienced a scramble for sterling bills. On Tuesday 28 July remittance to London became impossible, preventing debtors, however solvent and willing, from making cross-border payments to meet their obligations.[10] That day, bidding for sterling in New York pushed the pound above the upper gold point of $4.89 to $4.93; by 1 August the exchange rate had reached $6.50 'a level never seen before'.[11] Bankers who had known nothing but the gold standard were astounded by the gyrations of the dollar and the franc. 'The condition of the foreign exchanges is, we believe, without precedent,' declared *The Economist*, 'and the world (as an experienced banker said to a member of *The Economist*'s staff) seems to be returning to a basis of cash and barter'.[12]

Sterling Money Market

Simultaneous with the turmoil in the foreign exchanges the sterling money market was also experiencing grave difficulties. The unique size and liquidity of London's sterling money market was a key factor in the City's pre-eminence as an international financial centre before 1914. It was a wholesale, over-the-counter market among banks that they used to profitably deploy surplus balances and to meet funding requirements. The unrivalled opportunities provided by the London money market for treasury activities was the foremost reason why a score of foreign banks maintained branches in London.

The key instrument traded in the London money market was the sterling bill of exchange arising out of international trade transactions (typically of three-month maturity). On the buy-side the foremost purchasers of bills were domestic and foreign banks, high quality bills forming an important part of their second line liquid assets. The money market was served by a set of intermediary firms – the discount houses – that acted as brokers and jobbers (combining the roles). They enjoyed privileged access to discounting (purchase) facilities for their holdings of bills at the Bank of England. The discount houses funded their bill portfolios by call loans from domestic and foreign banks collateralised by the bills, such loans also constituting part of banks' liquid assets.

On Saturday 25 July, the discount rate for bills in the London money market was 3 per cent (bank rate). By Wednesday 29 July, buyers were being offered a 5 per cent discount rate and there were reports of transactions taking place in the next few days at 10 per cent or even 15 per cent.[13] The early days of the week saw reductions in call loan facilities to the discount houses by the clearing banks and 'heavy calls' by foreign banks.[14] The discount houses turned to the Bank of England for support, resulting in a trebling of the volume of the Bank's discounts and advances from £13 million on Saturday 25 July to £40 million on Friday 31 July. Money market activity plummeted under these conditions; by the end of Wednesday 29 July market prices had become nominal and the London money market was 'reduced to a condition of paralysis'.[15]

The negotiability of a bill of exchange was enhanced by its endorsement by an 'acceptor' – a firm or bank which guaranteed payment to the holder upon maturity in case of default by the debtor. Acceptance business was the specialization of a set of City firms known as accepting houses (merchant banks) whose outstanding acceptances totalled some £115 million on the eve of war.[16] The accepting houses, such as Barings, Rothschilds or Schroders, had modest capitals, estimated in 1914 at £20 million in aggregate.[17] They depended on punctual remittance from overseas clients to be able to meet their acceptances liabilities.[18] 'Their capital was ample to provide a guarantee fund against any occasional default,' observed Treasury official R. G. Hawtrey, 'but was quite inadequate to cope with a complete breakdown. The City was suddenly confronted with the prospect of a general suspension among the very names which were regarded by the discount market as the most unexceptionable'.[19]

The breakdown of remittance from foreign borrowers in respect of maturing acceptances meant that acceptors had to meet the payments as they became due. Desperate to avoid further liabilities, from Monday 27 July the accepting houses refused to undertake new acceptance business.[20] In effect, as outstanding bills matured London acceptors were withdrawing available international credit at around £3 million each working day, contributing to the dearth of sterling bills.[21] But the retrenchment was too little, too late. On Wednesday 29 July, Frederick Huth Jackson, a leading merchant banker, confided to City editor Sir George Paish that his own firm and seven other accepting houses – one-third of the sector – were on the brink of insolvency.[22] The failure of an acceptor would render worthless its guarantee in respect of all outstanding bills in the market that bore its name, impairing the bill portfolios of the discount houses and banks. The scale of failure foreseen by Huth Jackson conjured the prospect of wholesale ruin among the accepting houses and discount houses, destroying the traditional infrastructure of the sterling money market, and endangering the stability of the banking system.

Capital Market – London Stock Exchange

In 1914 the London Stock Exchange was the largest and most liquid securities market in the world. The rules of the exchange imposed a strict division of activity between two types of member, brokers and jobbers. Brokers acted as agents on behalf of non-member buyers and sellers. Jobbers made a market in particular securities, quoting buy and sell prices to brokers. Brokers had modest capital requirements, but jobbing involved holding a stock of securities that required substantial working capital. These funds, totalling £81 million in summer 1914, were borrowed as short-term call loans roughly-half-and-half from the clearing banks and the London branches of foreign banks.[23] The banks' loans to jobbers were collateralized by the securities they funded, plus an element of margin. The collateral securities were regularly marked-to-market and if the price went down, firms had to provide increased margins or sell the security and repay the loan.

The system operated satisfactorily in normal markets, but, as a banker put it: 'the delicate financial mechanism of modern London had never been put to the test of a European war'.[24] The 'deluge' of selling orders on Continental account sent securities prices plummeting.[25] Confronted by a relentless one-way market, 'bewildered' jobbers stopped dealing.[26] The price falls triggered margin calls from the banks. Moreover, the banks, especially foreign banks, were calling in their call loans to boost their liquidity or transfer funds from London. Either way, jobbers disastrously found themselves being forced sellers in a market without buyers.

Brokers were in trouble too. As chance would have it, the closure of the nineteen-day Stock Exchange account, at which settlement was due from buyers and sellers, fell on Wednesday 29 July in the thick of the emergency. Brokers who had executed transactions for foreign clients who were unable to remit sums due because of the breakdown of the foreign exchanges had to make the payments themselves. Seven firms failed on Wednesday 29 July and several more on Thursday 30 July.[27] To forestall large-scale failures, the management closed the Exchange on Friday 31 July.[28] This halted the ruinous write-downs since there were no longer quoted prices to serve as mark-to-market benchmarks. With the closure of the New York Stock Exchange a few hours later, all the world's major stock markets were shut.[29] (Berlin closed well ahead of London, as did the Coulisse in Paris; the Bourse remained open nominally, but there were no transactions).

The Banks and Bank Rate

The Banks

The market breakdowns threatened the solvency of the banks. On the asset side, the banks experienced drastic reductions in the liquidity and value of their loans and investments: (1) their second line liquid assets – call loans to the discount houses and stock exchange firms, and their holdings of commercial bills – had become unmarketable or unrecoverable; (2) their holdings of securities were unrealizable; and (3) they faced the prospect of having to pay out on account of bills for which they had acted as acceptors but had not received remittance (the same problem as the accepting houses). Sir Edward Holden, chairman of the London City and Midland Bank, one of the biggest, warned the Chancellor that almost seven-eighths of the major banks' assets were 'frozen up'.[30]

The alarming deterioration in the banks' liquidity and their anxieties about their vulnerability to a run on deposits led leading bankers to make a joint proposal to the Treasury on Friday 31 July. To boost their liquidity they proposed that they should deposit £15 million of their gold reserves, plus £30 million of securities and commercial bills (currently unmarketable), in return for £45 million of new Bank of England notes. This would have doubled the £44 million of Bank notes outstanding. The scheme would also have the virtue of substantially increasing the amount of gold at the disposal of the Bank of England. The adequacy of the level of the Bank's gold reserve had been a concern among commercial bankers for two decades, and was a source of considerable friction between commercial banks and the central bank.[31] Lloyd George was apparently 'attracted by it', but ultimately gave way to the combined opposition of the Bank and Treasury officials who regarded the bankers' scheme as a means of advancing their power.[32]

Over the days either side of 31 July, while the bankers' scheme was being formulated and considered, the banks hoarded their gold.[33] The annual summer bank holiday, which fell on Monday 3 August, always generated substantial withdrawals to pay wages or meet holiday expenditures. But instead of paying depositors in gold sovereigns (£1), the everyday circulating currency, the banks paid them in Bank of England notes whose minimum £5 denomination (£430 in 2009 money) was highly inconvenient.[34]

More than 5,000 recipients took them to the Bank of England to be cashed into sovereigns.[35] This resulted in queues outside the Bank from Thursday 30 July, presenting an unfortunate impression – a run on the central bank. Doing his rounds of the City that day, Sir George Paish, editor of the *Statist* an influential business weekly, was told by the general manager of Lloyd's Bank, the biggest British bank with deposits of £107 million, that a general run on the banks was underway. Paish recalled that:

> I hurried round to the Bank of England and there found an immense queue waiting to cash their notes ... Hundreds and hundreds of people waiting as patiently as possible to see if their money was still safe! A taxi took me to Downing Street to see Mr Lloyd George [Chancellor]. 'There is panic in the City,' I said, 'and something has to be done about it.'[36]

Widely reported in the press, the lines outside the Bank of England unnerved depositors. On Saturday 1 August the run claimed a victim, the National Penny Bank, a London bank with a dozen branches and £2.4 million of deposits.[37]

The conduct of the banks during the final week of July came in for sharp criticism by the Governor and by the Chancellor's principal Treasury officials, Sir John Bradbury, Permanent Secretary, and Basil Blackett, who on Saturday 1 August wrote to John Maynard Keynes that 'the joint stock banks have made absolute fools of themselves and behaved very badly'.[38] Keynes subsequently subjected the bankers to public censure and ridicule in a number of articles that attracted considerable attention.[39] He levelled a variety of charges against the banks of pursuing self-serving acts or proposals: failing to support client stock-exchange firms and discount houses; lobbying for suspension of sterling's convertibility into gold; pressing for the general moratorium; and hoarding their gold: 'our system was endangered, not by the public running on the banks, but the banks running on the Bank of England'.[40] Historians have been more sympathetic to the banks' plight, while acknowledging that it was 'not their finest hour'.[41]

Bank Rate

At the onset of the crisis, Bank rate (the rate at which the Bank discounted eligible bills presented by the discount houses) was 3 per cent. Demands on the discount houses led them to discount a huge volume of bills at the Bank. The Bank responded by raising Bank rate from 3 per cent to 4 per cent on Thursday 30 July, and to 8 per cent on Friday 31 July, the highest rate for forty years.[42]

On Saturday 1 August, the Governor sent a letter to the Chancellor warning that unless the government gave the Bank permission to issue notes in excess of the legal limit, the procedure used in the crises of 1847, 1857 and 1866, the Bank would shortly be obliged 'to curtail the facilities which, under present conditions, we regard it as essential to offer to the trade and commerce of the country'.[43] He promptly received a letter signed by the Prime Minister and Chancellor authorizing the Bank to exceed the legal issue conditional on a minimum Bank rate of 10 per cent, following precedent.[44] Thus on Saturday 1 August Bank rate was hiked again to 10 per cent.

The authorities were following orthodox practice for dealing with a financial crisis: make funds liberally available at a penalty rate. But the crisis was by no means an orthodox commercial panic and the sudden and unprecedented 'skyrocket jump' in Bank rate astounded the market and observers.[45] Keynes criticized the 'violent movement' as undermining confidence by causing 'great alarm' to the discount houses and among the general public.[46] Likewise, financial commentator Hartley Withers condemned the authorities' action as ineffective and counter-productive: 'a most untimely shock to the public's nerves ... merely for the sake of blindly following a mouldy old precedent'.[47]

Saving the System

The financial meltdown, against the prospect of a European war, necessitated state intervention to secure the country's payments and credit mechanisms. Crisis meetings took place day-and-night at the Treasury from Friday 31 July to Thursday 6 August, a week that saw Britain's entry into the war at midnight on Tuesday 4 August. Since neither the Treasury nor the Bank of England had a contingency plan for war, on Monday 3 August the authorities' extended the summer bank holiday for a further three days buying time to work out what to do.

The quest for solutions to the financial crisis was energetically led by the Chancellor, supported by Treasury officials and other advisers. Lloyd George was not an expert on banking or financial markets and relied heavily on support from Sir Walter Cunliffe, the haughty but shrewd Governor of the Bank of England.[48] Further guidance was provided by two confidants, Sir George Paish and Lord Reading. Paish, a leading financial and economic commentator, had acted as adviser to Lloyd George on financial issues since 1909.[49] Reading was a barrister who specialized in City cases and had recently joined the Cabinet as Lord Chief Justice.[50] Lloyd George also drew on the expertise of Edwin Montagu MP, Financial Secretary to the Treasury (who hailed from a prominent merchant bank family), and closely involved the Shadow Chancellor, Austen Chamberlain MP. Lloyd George and his colleagues explored potential ways forward with a large number of senior figures representing the banks, the accepting houses, the Stock Exchange, Chambers of Commerce, merchants and industrialists.

Also present at the Treasury during the crisis meetings was thirty-one-year old John Maynard Keynes. Summoned for advice by Blackett, Keynes arrived at Whitehall from King's College, Cambridge, in his brother-in-law's motorcycle sidecar on Sunday 2 August. He wrote several briefing notes on aspects of the crisis that had influence, though his name does not appear among those listed as attending meetings and Lloyd George's memoirs make no mention of him.[51] Moreover, he did not secure the hoped for appointment as economic adviser, the position having gone to Paish. Keynes eventually joined the Treasury in 1915 as Paish's assistant.[52]

Convertibility, Moratoria and Emergency Currency

The Treasury conferences focused on three main subjects: the convertibility of the pound into gold; payments moratoria; and the creation of an emergency currency. As regards convertibility, the bankers favoured suspension but Paish and Keynes argued strongly for its retention and Lloyd George accepted their advice.

Their analysis was resoundingly vindicated – the convertible pound attracted a huge influx of foreign gold seeking a safe haven and the Bank's bullion holdings soared; between 7 August and 15 December, the Bank of England's gold reserve rose from £26 million to a record £73 million.[53] The pound remained nominally convertible into gold throughout the war, but in practice a series of regulations made it increasingly difficult for the public to exercise the right.[54]

On Sunday 2 August, by royal proclamation, a one-month moratorium was introduced on the payment of bills of exchange that relieved the immediate threat to the accepting houses. Four days later, a second 'general moratorium' was introduced by which any payment arising out of a contract made before 4 August could be postponed, with interest due from the debtor. Exceptions included wages and, inevitably, taxes. Cunliffe thought the general moratorium unnecessary, but the bankers pressed hard for it as a further safeguard against a run on deposits: 'they wanted security and more security', observed Clapham, 'and it was given them'.[55] Manufacturers and retailers were soon complaining about the conduct of the banks, accusing them of limiting credit to customers despite the protection provided by the moratorium.[56] 'I have had some complaints that the Banks are not quite playing the game as far as traders are concerned', Austen Chamberlain informed Lloyd George on 11 August, less than a week after the introduction of the general moratorium.[57] As the threat of a meltdown of the financial system began to recede, the economy faced a different challenge – an acute credit crunch stemming from a drive by the banks to boost their liquidity by all means possible.

The issue of currency notes by the Treasury, not the Bank, to meet the banks' need for liquidity to meet a potential run when they reopened was another bold move. Probably the most compelling reason was, as Lloyd George put it, 'an advantage to the Government from a Revenue point of view' – i.e. seignorage.[58] An additional consideration was that the government was told that Bank of England notes would be unacceptable in Scotland and Ireland.[59] Furthermore, the Bank was unable to promise to meet the delivery deadline while printers De La Rue were able to do so in three days using postage-stamp paper.[60] Nevertheless, the Governor was displeased by what he called 'this arrangement of yours' to Lloyd George.[61]

The Treasury's currency note scheme authorized possible drawings by the banks of up to £225 million (20 per cent of their liabilities). This was a hefty fivefold increase on the £44 million Bank of England notes outstanding, and more than doubled the £200 million total of notes and currency in circulation.[62] In fact, the initial circulation was only £4.1 million because of problems with printing and distribution; however, by the end of the year £38 million was in circulation.[63] Like Bank notes, the Treasury currency notes were convertible into gold at the Bank of England. With the Treasury currency notes (known as 'Bradburys') and the general moratorium in place, Bank rate was reduced to 6 per cent on Thursday 6 August.

Reopening of the Banks – Friday 7 August

Friday 7 August saw the end of the extended bank holiday. Their tills primed with shoddily printed new Treasury notes, the banks opened for business. But the feared run did not materialize.[64] The non-event features in H. G. Wells's semi-autobiographical novel *Mr Britling Sees It Through*: 'When the public went to the banks for the new paper, the banks tendered gold – apologetically. The supply of the new notes was very insufficient, and there was plenty of gold'.[65] The following day Bank rate was cut to 5 per cent, where it remained for the next two years. In fact it was purely nominal and 'completely ineffective'; henceforth, short-term rates were determined by the Treasury bill rate and long-term rates by government War Loan bond issues.[66]

Reviving the City

With the banks and the domestic payments mechanisms safeguarded by the moratoria and the emergency currency, Lloyd George's advisers turned their attention to the problems of the breakdown of remission across the foreign exchanges and the paralysis of the sterling money market. Within a week of the reopening of the banks on Friday 7 August, two further initiatives were launched by the authorities to revive activity: the establishment of overseas gold depositories; and a 'cold storage' scheme for pre-war bills of exchange.

A new mechanism for transatlantic payments was created on 10 August with the opening of a Bank of England account to receive and purchase gold at the Canadian Finance Ministry in Ottawa, thereby overcoming the expense and risk of shipping metal in wartime.[67] Depositors of gold at the Ottawa Mint received a sterling credit with the Bank with which they could meet obligations in London; by the end of the year the equivalent of $105 million (£21 million) had been remitted this way. Similar arrangements soon followed with South Africa, India, New Zealand and Australia.[68] By December sterling exchange rates with the US and the major countries of the Empire had become 'nearly normal'.[69]

'Cold Storage' Scheme for Pre-War Bills

The foremost obstacle to the revival of the sterling money market was the large volume of unmarketable bills of uncertain value for which remittance had not been received from foreign debtors – the 'troubled assets' of the day. However, it was expected that the war would be short and that the money market problem was principally one of liquidity rather than solvency. 'Most of these bills are good and were the machinery of credit to be restarted the means of meeting them would soon be forthcoming', Paish told Lloyd George on Thursday 6 August. 'All that is needed is the machinery for and the means of holding the bills until the money is received to pay them'.[70] Six days later, on Wednesday 12 August, the Chancellor unveiled a 'cold storage' scheme by which the Bank of England would buy pre-war bills, being guaranteed against loss by the Treasury.[71] The purchase price was Bank rate – 5 per cent of value to maturity – the Bank's usual discount rate, with no premium to cover the risk of loss being assumed by taxpayers. A further favourable feature of the scheme for sellers – the banks and discount houses – was that they were relieved of the usual secondary recourse on the bill. The accepting houses continued to be liable for their bills on maturity, but the liability was removed from the market and concentrated at the Bank of England. 'A Government guarantee to the Bank against losses on financial operations of a commercial character', observed the *Statist*, 'is absolutely unique'.[72] The effect, reported the *Bankers' Magazine*, was 'of sending holders pell-mell to the Bank of England, not simply to obtain the necessary financial accommodation, but to get rid of all liability on the part of the holder. So great was the pressure on the Bank that it became almost a physical impossibility to deal each day with the mass of bills presented'.[73]

The money market in July 1914 comprised £450 million of finance and commercial bills, plus £15 million of Treasury bills.[74] An estimated £350 million were 'prime' bills – endorsed by an accepting house or major bank – and £100 million so-called 'trade bills'. The prime bills comprised £140 million of commercial bills – 'approved bills' eligible for discount at the Bank of England – plus £210 million of finance bills (issued by banks for funding and normally ineligible for discount at the Bank. Under the cold storage scheme the 'approved bill' category was broadened to encompass also 'good trade bills and acceptances of such foreign and colonial firms and bank agencies as are established in Great Britain'.[75] Thus the total approved bills comprised potentially some £240 million. In the event, the Bank purchased £120 million of bills, amounting to half of extended approved bills or a quarter of the entire money market. This was intervention in the financial system on an astonishing scale – 65 per cent of 1913 central government expenditure; 5 per cent of GDP – and at potentially a substantial cost to taxpayers.[76]

The *Bankers' Magazine* reported that the money market was 'staggered' by the boldness of the move, while the *Statist* hailed it as 'beyond praise'.[77] But there was criticism from manufacturers and merchants that the scheme went 'too far' in its generosity towards the banks.[78] 'I think it may very well be that we shall have to give cash for bills which the banks regard as hopeless', commented the Chancellor, who seems to have privately agreed with the critics. 'I have no doubt we shall have many of their losses dumped upon us. But this is a great national emergency and we have no time to pick and choose ... when we want to get the trade of the country in motion. We shall, of course, make a loss, but the loss will be very much greater if you stop the trade of the country for even two or three weeks'.[79]

Credit Crunch

The Chancellor and his advisers expected the cold storage scheme to promptly relieve the credit crunch in two ways. First, the currency notes received by the banks for the bills sold to the Bank would provide them with the liquidity to start lending again.[80] Second, the removal of the pre-war bills that were choking the money market would make its facilities available for the creation of new credit instruments. But they were disappointed on both scores.

Lloyd George told the bankers that he expected that the removal of their illiquid bills, potentially at taxpayers' expense, would be matched by liberal lending to business. But it didn't happen. 'Banks' position not improved', reported Paish to Montagu on 15 August. 'Things are not improving. Do not find any disposition to do business at all. Joint stock bankers not moving at all'.[81] A week later the *Statist* informed readers that: 'the joint-stock banks are doing little ... complaints reach us from all parts of the country that ordinary accommodation is not given'.[82] Lloyd George was furious. 'If the Government and the country are prepared to take risks, they must take risks as well', he thundered to the House of Commons on 26 August, warning that: 'It may be necessary to take stronger action. A good deal depends upon the banks'.[83]

While the banks were unwilling to make the 'vast sums' they were accumulating available to commercial clients, lending to the state was a different matter.[84] The first wartime issue of Treasury bills was made on 19 August. Applications totalling £42 million were received for the £15 million of bills on offer and the funds were secured for a 3.6 per cent discount, notwithstanding nominal Bank rate at 5 per cent, an 'extraordinarily low average ... so that in this direction alone the Government reaped a very great advantage from its bold policy in coming to the assistance of the money market'.[85]

A poll of 10,000 firms asking whether they favoured an extension of the general moratorium after its expiry on 4 September produced a majority for termination.[86] Nonetheless, it was decided that 'the recovery ... has not been sufficient to justify a termination of the moratorium ... there is much still to be done to re-erect the fabric of credit'.[87] Accordingly, the moratoria were extended for a further month to 4 October. This rejection of the clearly expressed wish of domestic industry and trade has been interpreted as evidence of establishment bias in favour of financial interests.[88] But in the context of the market breakdowns and the requirements for war finance, the authorities were just playing safe.

Advances to the Accepting Houses

Only two days after the launch of the cold storage scheme, Montagu counselled Lloyd George that: 'If I may be allowed to express an opinion, I think that you will have to amend your scheme, and that you will have to put endorsers in the same position as holders if you want the banks and Acceptance Houses to move'.[89] This was because the cold storage scheme left accepting houses ultimately liable for their pre-war bills and thus in no position to give new endorsements.[90] In the meantime, the money market remained idle despite the cold storage arrangements. On 4 September, it was announced that the Bank of England would advance funds to acceptors to pay pre-war bills on maturity, with the government guaranteeing the Bank against loss.[91] The advances would cost borrowers 2 per cent above Bank rate, a steep premium relative to prevailing market rates, but the loans would not be repayable until one year after the end of the war.

In total £74 million – 40 per cent of 1913 government expenditure; 3 per cent of GDP – was advanced to acceptors under this scheme.[92] Most of the funds were used to pay off cold storage bills in the hands of the Bank; by November 1914 the Bank's holding of such bills was down to £12.5 million (from £120 million).[93] Creditworthy acceptors found that it was significantly cheaper to borrow from the banks than to pay the Bank 7 per cent interest, resulting in substantial pay-offs of pre-war advances. By August 1915, the outstanding aggregate of funds provided under government guarantee – (1) pre-war bills bought by the Bank; and (2) advances against pre-war acceptances provided by the Bank – had fallen to £39 million.[94] This was principally the result of the resumption of remittances from abroad, particularly from American and British Empire debtors as well as £8 million on account of Russian bills.[95] Thereafter, the outstanding pre-war debts were largely owed by German and Austrian debtors from whom no remittance could be expected until after the war.

Easing of the Credit Crunch and the End of the Moratoria

The provision of Treasury notes and the discounting of pre-war troubled bills resulted in the banks being awash with cash.[96] From late-September the credit crunch began to ease. 'As confidence revives', reported *The Economist*, 'the banks begin to look around for chances of employing their large Bank of England balances on remunerative terms, the bill market tends to become easier'.[97] However, progress in the development of new commercial bill business was painfully slow; in late October it was estimated that it was just 5 per cent of the normal volume before the crisis.[98] On one hand, the fall in activity was due the disruption of home and foreign trade that came with the war.[99] But on the other, it appears that alternative credit arrangements had replaced the bill of exchange: 'there is no doubt', stated *The Economist*, 'that a large part of our foreign and colonial trade is now being carried on without the assistance of the bill on London'.[100] With conditions still uncertain, on 30 September the moratorium on general payments was extended for further month to 4 November, though the moratorium on bills was continued for only to 19 October.[101] These were the final extensions, both of which lapsed with 'singularly little fuss'.[102]

Reopening of the London Stock Exchange

The difficulties of stock-exchange firms on account of funds owed by overseas clients relented as a number of foreign bourses reopened and remittance across the foreign exchanges eased. Despite the closure of the exchange, cash dealings in securities continued, being conducted face-to-face in City streets, hotels, brokers' offices and via the Extel tape.[103] Enterprising auction houses undertook public auctions of securities, while the *Daily Mail* launched a small-ad section for buyers and sellers. Returning confidence was reflected in the growth of the volume of securities traded by these means. On 18 November, the settlement of the account postponed by the closure of the exchange on 31 July on took place smoothly. December saw a marked rise in the price of securities on the street market, regaining pre-crisis levels. The reopening of the Stock Exchange on 4 January 1915 marked the end of the crisis.[104]

Outcomes

The City Saved

Lloyd George titled a chapter of his war memoirs: 'How We Saved The City'.[105] Under his leadership an unprecedented financial crisis was met by unprecedented state intervention. But, as the Chancellor pointed out, he acted not to preserve the financial markets and their participants just for their own good, but for the common good: to finance food and raw material supplies from overseas; to sustain business activity, especially the export industries, to avoid large-scale unemployment; and to protect the country's payments system and thus, among other things, the government's ability to raise tax revenues. With Britain's entry into the war on 5 August, maintenance of a functioning financial system became a crucial part of the national and allied war effort.

The authorities achieved their fundamental crisis objective. The existing structure – the money market, with its discount houses and accepting houses; the stock market, with its brokers and jobbers; and the banks – was preserved. (Though within that framework there were significant shifts in how business was conducted.) Furthermore, there was a surprisingly small number of failures among individual City firms and banks. The crisis saw the failure of just seventeen stock exchange firms, and a single, small, bank.[106] All the accepting houses survived, though many were mothballed for the duration. After the war several smaller firms combined, including Governor Cunliffe's firm, or were wound up. Again, the authorities' aim of preventing the failure of banks and other financial firms was achieved.

Having saved the financial system, the state promptly made use of it for its own purpose – to fund the war effort. The currency notes and purchases of cold storage bills conveniently provided the banks with the means to mop up the flood of government paper. Between 19 August and the end of October 1914, six issues of Treasury bills of £15 million each were made; in January 1915 outstanding Treasury bills totalled £100 million, and in 1921, at the peak, £1.2 billion.[107] During the war the Treasury bill replaced the commercial bill as the key money market instrument and the daily bread of the discount houses

The Stock Exchange was still shut when the first War Loan bond issue was launched on 18 November 1914. At £350 million – 190 per cent of pre-war government expenditure and 14 per cent of GDP – it was, boasted Lloyd George, 'the largest loan ever raised in the history of the world'.[108] Most of the loan was subscribed for by 'the great financial interests,' though the issue also attracted 100,000 'small people'.[109] The reopening of the Stock Exchange not long after provided a secondary market for this unprecedented army of bondholders and an institutional framework for further War Loan issues, with war finance becoming the core business of the London capital market.

Criticisms and Caveats

During the emergency people were mostly thankful for the 'boldness' and vigour with which the financial crisis was handled by Lloyd George and his colleagues.[110] Yet a number of criticisms or caveats were expressed at the time and later. That despite the extensive military planning for war, there were no financial preparations by the Bank or Treasury. That the general moratorium, insisted upon by the banks, was unnecessary and harmful to domestic manufacturers, merchants and retailers and to London's international financial operations. That hiking Bank rate from 3 per cent to 10 per cent in three days was an extreme and damaging overreaction; an inappropriate orthodox response to a far from orthodox crisis.[111] That, with the benefit of hindsight, it would have been better if the emergency currency had comprised Bank of England notes not Treasury notes; thus there would not have been a handy source of funds to boost the country's circulating currency almost threefold over the course of the war, from £170 million to £470 million, with £295 million Treasury notes outstanding in November 1918, generating an 120 per cent increase in prices – in stark contrast to decades of pre-war price stability.[112] But one crisis decision that the authorities indisputably got right was the retention of sterling's convertibility into gold. The maintenance of convertibility kept faith with the holders of sterling and sterling-denominated securities around the world, even though conversion became restricted in practice. This proved vital for raising loans overseas later in the war.

It was the banks rather than the authorities that were the butt of most criticism. For refusing to pay out gold sovereigns at the end of July. For misguidedly pushing for the suspension of sterling's convertibility into gold. For the various further self-serving proposals or acts catalogued by Keynes. For limiting credit to business despite extensive government assistance through the cold storage scheme, incurring the Chancellor's wrath. 'It is difficult to resist the view,' concluded economist E. Victor Morgan in 1952, reviewing the crisis of 1914 in the wake of a further world war, 'that Government was too much influenced by purely banking advice'.[113]

Epilogues

Paish told Lloyd George that the cost to taxpayers of the cold storage scheme might be as much as £50 million.[114] That was the sum the Chancellor suggested to parliament in November 1914, observing that: 'the total losses upon the whole of these transactions will not be equal to the cost of a single week of carrying on the War, and it saves British industry and commerce from one of the worst panics'.[115] *The Economist* was more pessimistic, putting the downside of the government guarantees at potentially £200 million, depending on whether the war lasted for a short or long period.[116] In fact, no public account of the cost to the taxpayer of the 1914 government guarantees was ever presented. During the war the matter was regarded as secret; afterwards there were other priorities.

In 1915, the Treasury paid the Bank £39.5 million in respect of its holdings of outstanding cold storage bills and advances to acceptors. Thereafter, when the Bank received payment in respect of a discounted bill or an advance to an acceptor, the Treasury received a reimbursement. By 1916 outstanding cold storage and advances had fallen to £31 million.[117] On 31 August 1921, the 'official' end of the war, they were down to £15 million. Provisions of the Versailles Peace Treaty facilitated repayment of the bulk of outstanding German and Austrian pre-war debts (plus interest).[118] A year later, when advances to acceptors became repayable, £197,000 was written off on account of sixteen failed banks or financial firms.[119] By then the total outstanding had been reduced to £4 million, most of which was recovered in subsequent years.[120]

In December 1926, prompted by an inquiry from a financial journalist, the Treasury conducted an in-house computation. It calculated that it had received repayments (including interest) from the Bank totalling £46 million.[121] Thus in the final reckoning, taxpayer support for the financial system, via Bank discounts and advances under government guarantee, during the crisis of summer

1914, netted the Treasury a nominal profit of £6.5 million. An unexpectedly happy eventual outcome.

Wartime disruptions and the focus of the London markets on government war finance meant that London largely shut down as a global financial entrepot for the duration of the hostilities. The closure of the London hub triggered divergence in the pattern of international financial intermediation. New York and neutral Amsterdam were major beneficiaries, the latter emerging as the leading financial centre of Continental Europe through the provision of financial services to German clients.[122] On the other hand, Berlin never recovered as an international financial centre and German banks lost their operations in London, Latin America and Asia. The measures taken to tackle the financial crisis in London in 1914 ensured that the mechanisms of the City survived largely intact, thus allowing London to re-emerge in the 1920s as an international financial centre. But it did not reassume its former dominance. London's markets and institutions played more domestically oriented roles, with the money market dominated by the Treasury bill, the capital market by government bonds, and the merchant banks increasingly focusing on the development of a British client base. New York, having survived its own financial crisis in summer 1914, had become the focus of the international bond market while Amsterdam had become an important centre for international trade finance and capital raising.[123] After the war London and New York were the twin – and often rival – leading financial centres of an international financial system that was soon beset by new crises that proved more intractable than the crisis of 1914.[124]

10 THE ESTABLISHMENT OF THE GOLD STANDARD IN SOUTHEAST EUROPE: CONVERGENCE TO A NEW SYSTEM OR DIVERGENCE FROM AN OLD ONE?

Kalina Dimitrova
Luca Fantacci

Introduction

The first few decades after independence were dedicated by Southeast European states to the construction of a modern political and administrative apparatus. As in other new peripheral states, nation-building was continuously confronted with the model provided by the older countries of the West and with the need to find a place within the global balance of powers. A crucial step in this direction was the establishment of a monetary system compliant with the international standard. It would be, however, too simple and simplistic to believe that it was merely a matter of converging towards a predetermined model – if only because the model was not at all predetermined. In fact, all these changes occurred in Southeast Europe at a time in which their outcome was not at all straightforward: the countries in this area were engaged in state-building, convergence, and monetary reform just as the concept of state, the relationship between centre and periphery and the notion of money were being redefined on a global scale.

The construction of a national monetary system is an element of great symbolic and practical importance in modern state-building.[1] In Bulgaria it was undertaken immediately after Liberation with the establishment of the National Bank in 1879 and the introduction of the lev as the official unit of account in 1880. The compliance of the national money with the international standard was crucial for the integration of the new state into the 'concert of nations'. The Bulgarian monetary system was initially designed along the bimetallic principles of the Latin Monetary Union. Within three decades, the system eventually conformed to the principles of the gold standard, which had emerged in the meantime as the universally accepted regime. Bulgaria was one of the last to join, in 1906, after a tortuous convergence marked by several failed attempts. In order to comply with the gold standard, Bulgaria was required:

- to establish a unique *unit of account* instead of the plurality of reference units, which had been used in private and public accounting;
- to establish a national *means of exchange*, to replace the foreign coins, in particular of Russian silver rubles, which were legally permitted and practically widespread;
- to safeguard the *autonomy of the central bank* against the government's pressures to finance its fiscal deficits through the proceeds of seigniorage;
- to fix the *exchange rate* in terms of an unalterable parity within the international gold standard, after having initially adhered, if somewhat loosely, to the bimetallic standard of the Latin Monetary Union.

Most historical accounts have described the years from the Liberation to the Balkan Wars as a period of 'monetary chaos'.[2] The legacy of Turkish domination, pressure from outside, political weakness and mismanagement simply postponed an inevitable outcome: the homologation, at least *de facto*, to the international gold standard.[3] The story, however, deserves to be revisited in the light of several remarks.

(1) First, what briefly appeared as the definitive and universal monetary system soon proved to be rather fragile and contingent. The gold standard collapsed, together with the other institutional pillars of European liberalism, under the shells of the Great War, and could not be rebuilt afterwards on the same basis. Retrospectively, it was 'a brief experience, a matter of a few decades, a half-century at most. It was only the sense that it was the final step, the ultimate money that made it seem so much older'.[4] Even in comparative perspective, the gold standard was more an exception than a rule: in a number of different periods and regions, the rule was rather a plurality of monies, serving different purposes, rather than a unique standard.[5] Hence, even when the gold standard is the eventual outcome, it should not serve as the only benchmark for an accurate historical assessment of the events that lead to its adoption.

(2) The gold standard was not only followed but also preceded by other systems. An alternative benchmark for the events we are considering is indeed available, if only we trace the story according to its actual course, i.e. from the beginning rather than from the end. The new

order that was eventually established was, in fact, preceded by an older monetary regime that had only recently been replaced even in Western Europe. And this previous, bimetallic system had lasted much longer, dating back over five centuries.[6] In terms of plain duration, the 'classical' gold standard marked not the inauguration of a definitive age of gold after a tentative age of darkness, but rather the transition towards a precarious season of gold from a secular period of gold and silver and other metals.[7]

(3) The gold standard had many virtues, but also several backdrops that contributed to its fragility. A universal money, firmly anchored to a material basis and thus cosseted from political interference, was seen as the necessary pledge for balanced, safe and unhampered cross-border trade. However, even the classical gold standard was in fact a gold sterling standard, in which growing capital movements were not simply an option, but a condition of stability for British and world trade (De Cecco 1974). Despite the appearance of an automatic mechanism, therefore, the system relied heavily on careful management by the leading financial centre, London, and on cooperation by major central banks, in order to ensure the continued acceptance of a national currency in the function of international money and to keep up the expansion required as a condition for stability.

(4) By contrast, the previous regime, i.e. the 'system of imaginary money' that provided the European monetary rule for a thousand years, 'from Charlemagne to Napoleon', was based on the distinction between an internal currency for local exchanges and an external currency for long-distance trade.[8] This made it possible to combine, rather than contrast, internal and external balance, autonomous national policy and free international trade.[9] Over the eighteenth and nineteenth century, this system was increasingly criticized for being too complicated and liable of mismanagement by authorities eager for seigniorage. Eventually, it was completely abandoned. Yet one might question whether it was set aside because its defects had become apparent, or because the possibilities it offered were no longer understood.

(5) In any case, the existence of a previous monetary regime, and not simply of an institutional void, prior to the establishment of the gold standard may help to explain why it took so long, and not only in Bulgaria, for a monometallic standard to be successfully introduced. The apparent disorder and delay in the shift to a new order could depend on the reluctance to renounce the benefits of the old, particularly in allowing for greater autonomy in pursuing objectives of domestic balance.

As all these factors clearly suggest, the establishment of the Bulgarian monetary system occurred at a time in which the meaning of money was undergoing a radical change. What was supposed to serve as a means of international settlement? What was the most appropriate domestic means of exchange? And how should national money be related to international money? These questions accompanied the rise of the international gold standard – and resounded again after its demise. It was only for a brief span of years that they seemed to admit only one plausible answer: a fixed quantity of pure gold, to serve as measure and means for all payments, national and international. The identification of money with a quantity of gold came to be deemed a natural law, despite the tremendous efforts and controversies that had been needed in fact to establish it. Those efforts were particularly troublesome in peripheral countries, such as Bulgaria, where a great number of different monies were used, both as units of account and as means of payment, and with different and variable relations to different metals, before the simple rule of the gold standard was eventually established.

This research will review the various monetary forms used in Bulgaria from the Liberation to the outbreak of the Balkan wars. The purpose is not simply to enumerate and describe them in their variety, but to provide a tentative explanation of the logic underlying their concurrence – without resorting to the comfortable, but scientifically void, assumption that this was an error waiting to be corrected by more enlightened rulers. We shall make, instead, the assumption that there could indeed be reasons for maintaining multiple monies and regulating their relationship, and that these reasons had to do with the desire to preserve autonomy in pursuing objectives of domestic equilibrium.[10] A hypothesis that deserves to be contemplated, in the light of historical evidence, is if and how the distinction between internal and external money, which was typical of monetary regimes prior to the gold standard, continued to operate, de facto if not de jure, in the various, apparently chaotic, monetary phenomena that characterized the first decades of Bulgarian independence. This requires identificating, from time to time, not only which types of currency were used for domestic and for international payments, but also, and more significantly, how they were set into relation.

The different forms taken by internal and external money, and by the relationship between them, may suggest a preliminary distinction in three regimes, covering three successive, if somewhat overlapping, periods of the early history of Bulgaria's monetary system.

I. In the first period immediately after Liberation (1879–85), foreign coins continued to circulate extensively throughout Bulgaria, while the national currency, the lev, was gradually introduced, first as a unit of account and then as a means of payment. The relationship between internal money (lev) and external money (foreign coins) was determined by law, i.e. by a *tariff*, according to the practice employed extensively throughout Europe to manage bimetallic systems over the previous six centuries.

II. Almost immediately, however, foreign silver coins were received in private transactions at a rate which was lower than the official rate fixed by the tariff. The depreciation of silver coins in terms of the unit of account was called *agio*. Throughout the long period in which the agio persisted (1882–1906), it was the variable level of the agio on the market that determined the relationship between external money (gold coins) and internal money (silver coins).

III. In the meantime, in 1885, the Bulgarian National Bank was granted the status of an issuing bank. At the beginning, however, very few banknotes were issued and their value did not substantially exceed the value of the gold reserves kept at the Bank. It was only after the agio disappeared (1906–13) that Bulgaria managed to establish a gold standard system, with banknotes serving as internal money, gold serving as external money, and the relationship between the two being fixed by *convertibility* at a par.

Throughout the monetary history of Bulgaria, from its early beginning to its more recent developments, the subjection to external standards has recurrently appeared as a viable alternative to the subjection to local malfunctioning and political pressures, in view of building a stable monetary system. A retrospect on the longer history of European monetary institutions may serve to question whether the only way to obtain monetary stability was for Bulgaria – and is in general – to renounce monetary autonomy.

Tariff (1879–85)

The willingness to conform to an international monetary standard was apparent immediately after independence, when Bulgaria decided to adhere to the principles of the Latin Monetary Union (LMU).[11] With the law of 27 May 1880, the lev was established as national unit of account on a par with the French franc. All silver and gold coins were to be minted at the same weight and fineness as the French equivalents. The same bimetallic ratio of the LMU (15.5 units of fine silver per unit of fine gold) was thus implicitly accepted.

However, Bulgaria's application of LMU principles had two significant exceptions: it established a state monopoly over minting and it fixed no limit over the issue of silver coins. Moreover, since Bulgaria did not have a mint, coins had to be minted abroad, and until their amount was sufficient to meet the needs of domestic circulation, foreign coins circulated widely throughout the country.[12] All these features, which were certainly to be regarded as defects according to the principles of the emerging gold standard, in fact brought the new Bulgarian monetary system closer to the traditional principles of old bimetallism. This is confirmed by the explicit provision of a tariff, to be promulgated by the Prince, establishing the value at which foreign coins could and should be accepted within the principality. The monetary law of 1880, in fact, established that the Ministry of Finance was entitled to issue a tariff, whenever it found necessary.[13]

The first element of the monetary system that was introduced with the law of 1880 was a national unit of account, and not a national means of payments. Bulgaria coined its first silver coins, for a total value of 10 million leva, only in 1883.[14] Yet this did not mean that Bulgaria failed until then to establish a national monetary system. According to the principle of monetary rule, which was common to most European countries throughout the modern era, the truly distinctive character of a national monetary system was the unit of account, rather than the means of payment. Any coin, even minted abroad, could circulate within a country, provided that it was evaluated in terms of the local unit of account according to the tariff issued by the local authority. In light of this rule, the fact that foreign coins continued to circulate in Bulgaria for years after independence is not exceptional, nor is it a sign of backwardness or marginality. The same was true in many cases, even important economic centres throughout Europe, until the establishment of the metal standard.[15] And in peripheral countries, particularly in Southeast Europe, it remained true even after the formal adoption of the metal standard: thus e.g. throughout the Ottoman Empire, where foreign coins in circulation represented still approximately 8 per cent of total circulation in 1914.[16]

The first tariff was issued even before the introduction of the monetary law, with the decree of 11 July 1879 (Figure 10.1). At this stage, there was obviously no national means of payment: the coins included in the tariff were the Russian ruble, the Turkish lira, the pound sterling, the Austrian florin, and even the Italian lira, but not the Bulgarian lev, since it hadn't been issued yet in any form or denomination. What is perhaps at first more surprising is that the tariff did not mention national money, not even in the form of a unit of account: in fact, the lev had not been established yet and the value of the coins listed was expressed in French francs with a view to complying with the LMU convention. What was then the content of the decree? Can we still say that it established a Bulgarian monetary rule, even when there appears to be no Bulgarian money? The fact that the tariff was issued under the juridical form of a decree and in the name of Kniaz Alexander seems to suggest that authority was indeed at stake. In fact, if this law did not establish a national unit of account or a national means of payment, it did however enact a national monetary rule by establishing a peculiar relation between unit of account and means of payment – a relation, which could be, and actually was, different from those prevailing abroad.

Figure 10.1. Decree of 11 July 1879, issuing the first Bulgarian monetary tariff.

Указъ.

№ 4.

Ный Александръ I.

Съ Божія милость и волята народна

Князь на България.

По предложеніе на Нашътъ Министръ на Финансытѣ направено съ докладътъ отъ 10 юлій 1879 подъ N 3, основанъ на рѣшеніето на Министерскій Съвѣтъ отъ 9 тек., и като взехмы въ съображеніе загубытѣ, които търпи държавното съкровище отъ сѫществующата тарифа на монетытѣ, постановихмы и постановявамы:

1⁰ Да ся издаде една тарифа за разнытѣ монеты които ся употребяватъ въ Княжеството, по съобразна съ истинската стойность на тія монеты.

Испълненіето на това постановленіе възлагамы на Нашътъ Министръ на Финансытѣ.

Издаденъ въ Нашътъ дворецъ, въ Софія, на 11 Юлій 1879 година.

На първообразното подписано:

Александръ.

Приподписано: Министръ на Финансытѣ

Г. Д. Начовичъ.

Тарифа на Монетытѣ издадена отъ Министрерството на Финансытѣ съгласно съ горній Указъ.

Златны Монеты.

	Фр.	Сан.
1 Лира Английска	25	—
1 „ Турска	22	70
1 Полуимпериалъ	20	60
1 Наполеонъ-доръ	20	—
1 20франкъ: Италіанскій и белгійскій	20	—
8 Фіорины Австрийски	20	—
1 Румунскій 20 Леу	20	—
1 Мищъ, австрійска жълтица	11	80
Сребърны монеты.		
1 Фіоринъ Австрійскій	2	30
1 Лира Италіанска	1	—
1 Меджидіе турско	4	30
1/2 „ „	2	15
1/4 „ „	1	7 1/2
1 Леу румунскій	1	—
1 Франкъ французскій	1	—
1 Пятофранкъ	5	—
1 Рубла	3	70
75 Копѣйки	2	77 1/2
50 „	1	85
25 „	—	92 1/2
Размѣнно сребро.		
20 „	—	50
15 „	—	37 1/2
10 „	—	25
1 Кредитна рубла	2	64

Source: State Gazette, year I, No.2, 4 August 1879.

The values of foreign currencies fixed by the tariff were to be considered binding throughout the jurisdiction of the new Bulgarian state, and not only for dealings with the Ministry of Finance (Monetary Law 1880, Art 17).

Even after the law of 1880, the relation between the newly defined national monetary unit, the lev, and the various foreign coins circulating within Bulgaria (such as the Russian silver ruble, but also Serbian, Romanian and Ottoman coins) continued to be determined by a tariff. The local value of foreign coins was not fixed once and for all, and it did not necessarily correspond to their relative appreciation in other countries. The Russian ruble, for example, was evaluated 4 francs in Bulgaria, versus 3.30 and 3.70 francs in Romania and Serbia respectively. The value of the ruble was reduced by the Council of Ministers in 1881 once to 3.70 and further to 3.50 leva, in order to reduce the inflow from Romania and Serbia, where it was valued even less and eventually demonetized. In 1884 the Bulgaria demonetized all Serbian and Romanian coins and a couple of months later, a law was passed providing for the depreciation of silver rubles from 3.50 to 3.40 or 3.30 leva depending on the type of ruble.[17]

Demonetization of foreign silver coins was eventually accomplished only in 1887. On 13 March 1887 a Regent's Decree was passed, allowing a period of 3 months for the payment of taxes with rubles at the cash desks of the Treasury, where they would be received at the value of 3 leva.[18] After this term, they would not be accepted at all. On 21 July 1887 the Ministry of Finance sent a letter to BNB district governors to urge conversion of all rubles by the public at officially fixed rates. Within two months, only Bulgarian coins remained in circulation.[19]

The misalignment in the relative evaluation of foreign coins, and hence their protracted circulation within the country, need not, however, be regarded necessarily as the undesired consequences of inexperienced misconduct. On the contrary, they could be the coherent outcome of a deliberate decision, aiming at attracting and maintaining an adequate amount of silver coins, corresponding to the needs of domestic circulation. To change the value of foreign coins, in terms of the local unit of account, could reflect, not the clumsy attempt to strike the correct assessment, but rather the conscious management of an instrument of monetary policy.

The question remains open. Was Bulgaria unable or unwilling to enforce state monopoly over coinage, accepting that foreign silver coins circulate extensively throughout the country? Perhaps we can at least advance the hypothesis that Bulgaria could be interested in encouraging the inflow of silver coins, even at the cost of exchanging them for gold, and that the overvaluation of foreign silver coins was intended to provide the domestic market with adequate means of internal circulation.

The issue was not confined to Bulgaria, but involved in quite similar terms also other neighbouring countries. Even in Serbia, for example, before independence, the circulation of a great many foreign coins within the territory was regulated through 'currency exchange rate lists' or 'money tariffs', specifying the value of each of them in terms of the local unit of account.[20] The same continued to occur throughout the Ottoman Empire until its eventual demise.[21]

Agio (1882–1906)

When all foreign silver coins were eventually withdrawn from circulation, and substituted with Bulgarian silver coins, the relation between internal and external money assumed a different form. Silver money was now exclusively national money, while gold served as international money.[22]

Within this system, the relation between internal and external money was, in principle, fixed, and it corresponded to the official bimetallic ratio (bmr). However, since 1882, gold was accepted at a premium, in exchange for silver or other goods. 'Agio' is the name of the premium that was paid for the purchase of gold against silver, over and above the official rate. It may also be regarded, symmetrically, as the discount at which silver coins were received, not only for the purchase of gold, but for the payment of any price or debt denominated in gold.

Insofar as silver may be regarded as the national currency and gold as the international currency, agio may be interpreted as the form taken by the exchange rate within the bimetallic system. In fact, 'it can be said to represent an indicator of depreciation of the national currency against gold, as the internationally recognized legal tender'.[23] Agio may be seen, therefore, as the peculiar form taken in Bulgaria, between 1882 and 1906, by the relation between internal and external money. In fact, determined on the domestic money market, BNB starts to report agio figures in October 1885.

Once again, it is worth noting that this particular feature of the monetary system was not peculiar to Bulgaria only. Other countries experienced the same phenomenon in the same period, particularly in Southeast Europe: not only in Serbia but also in the lands still under Ottoman rule, where the premium for gold over silver coins increased over time, as silver depreciated on international markets,[24] and over space, as one moved from Istanbul towards the periphery of the Empire.[25]

The aim of the econometric analysis that follows is to identify possible factors that might have caused or influenced the appearance, the fluctuation and the eventual disappearance of the agio in Bulgaria, between 1882 and 1906. Since the agio is not fixed by authority but by private negotiations on the market, the first direction to look for its determinants is towards the relative supply and demand of gold and silver coins. In fact, since there are no particular reasons to believe that the decades under observation should have experienced relevant variations in the composition of the demand for silver and gold coins respectively, the analysis may be restricted to the supply of precious metals and coins.

Among various possible determinants, it is the relative value of silver and gold coins in circulation which has the closest relationship with the development of the agio.[26] Although there is some data on it, simply adding up those figures would not lead to a significant indication of the coins actually circulating within the country, given the large amount of silver and gold coins flowing across the borders. An alternative proxy may be provided by the coin holdings recorded in the balance sheet of the Bulgarian National Bank.[27] The *ratio between silver and gold holdings at BNB* (SGR) may hence be assumed as a first possible determinant of the agio.

Around the turn of the century, as we have seen, metal currency was supplemented by a conspicuous issue of silver-backed banknotes, while the total value of gold-backed banknotes in circulation was still lower than the value of the issuer's gold reserves. As silver-backed banknotes continued to be accepted at par with coins for the purpose of domestic settlements, the amount of silver-backed banknotes (SBB) could be a significant explanatory variable, particularly for the spike of the agio recorded in the first years of the twentieth century.

On the other hand, gold being used for international payments, it is to be expected that the amount of gold coins circulating within the country should follow the fluctuations of the *balance of trade* (BOT). However, a trade deficit does not necessarily result in a depletion of national gold reserves. Outflows on current account deficits may be compensated by inflows on capital account. For this reason, the cumulative amount of *foreign loans* (FL), increasingly granted to Bulgaria towards the end of the period considered, may be taken into account as a possible explanation for the reduction and eventual disappearance of the agio. A further element of the balance of payments that deserves to be considered is monetary movements driven by arbitrage on the difference between the relative value of precious metals fixed by Bulgarian monetary law and the *bimetallic ratio* (BMR) prevailing on international markets.

The agio, however, concerns the relative value of silver and gold coins, not specie. Since gold coins could be used for international settlements and for the purchase of tradable goods, their relative abundance on domestic markets could depend on conditions of international money markets, reflected in the exchange rates. This is the reason for including *nominal and real effective exchange rates* (NEER and REER) into the picture, and observing how they relate to the agio.[28]

It is, however, important to note that the very existence of the agio is a symptom of the fact that the rules set by monetary law, and specifically the official values of silver coins in terms of the national unit of account, were being bypassed. This fact may be seen as depending on a lack of confidence in the issuer of the coins, i.e. the Ministry of Finance, which could be related, in turn, to the laxity of the Ministry in running public finance. Hence, the *budget balance* (BB) may also be considered as a possible determinant of the agio.

It was possible to collect data for all these variables for the years 1886–1912 as the earliest data for the ratio of silver to gold holdings is available for 1886. Adjusting the series by operating logarithms and first differences, in order to obtain stationarity, reduced the available sample to twenty-five observations. A preliminary test was performed to check for correlation (Table 10.1), before running linear regressions on the variables that resulted more significantly related to the agio. Although all coefficients are quite low, it served at least to exclude those with the lowest correlations, namely NEER and BMR.

Table 10.1. Correlation coefficients.

	BOT	BB	FL	NEER	REER	BMR	SBB	SGR
AGIO	-0.13	-0.11	-0.20	-0.02	-0.20	-0.03	0.29	0.34

All remaining series were used, in various combinations, as possible explanatory variables in OLS regressions. After several estimations, the best fit was obtained by regressing AGIO on SBB, SGR and their lagged values (equation 1). Hence, the agio appears to depend primarily on current and past values of both the ratio between silver and gold holdings and silver-backed banknotes in circulation. There is only one significant dummy variable for 1902 (D_1902) when the development of the agio cannot be explained by the values of the two determinants. In fact, inclusion of this dummy is justified by the specific measurement of the variables. While agio is taken as annual average, the explanatory variables are end-of-year balance sheet data. Hence, while the silver to gold holdings ratio decreases drastically at the end of 1902 as a result of the highest BOT surplus in the sample (18.5 per cent of trade turnover) and 82 million levs increase in the consolidated foreign debt, the decrease of the agio taken as annual average is lower than expected (5.3 percentage points). If we look at the agio monthly data, however, it shows a drastic decrease from 13.1 per cent in January to 2.6 per cent in December 1902.

Equation 1. OLS regression

$$\begin{aligned} AGIO = &- 0.27 + 0.18\, SBB + 0.78\, SBB_{-1} + 0.38\, SGR \\ &+ 1.22\, SGR_{-1} - 5.44\, D\_1902 \\ &\mathit{(-0.98)\ (3.82)\ \ (8.41)\ \ (3.76)\ \ (3.34)\ \ (-16.7)} \end{aligned}$$

(t-statistics are given in parentheses)
R^2 =0.74; Adjusted R^2=0.67
LM test for serial correlation: F-statistics = 0.17 (0.84)
Normality test: χ^2 (2) = 2.69 (0.25)
Heteroskedasticity: F-statistics = 0.77 (0.63)

Taken together, these econometric exercises identify the relative supply of silver coins and of silver-backed banknotes as the indicator of which behaviour is closely related with the dynamics of the agio. Silver currency appears to suffer a discount in relation to gold currency, depending on its relative abundance in domestic circulation, either in the form of coins or banknotes. The agio appears therefore to reflect the conditions of domestic circulation, and to remain rather unaffected by conditions on international money and metal markets, reflected in the bimetallic ratio. Bulgaria's relationships with other countries through the balance of trade, foreign loans, and foreign exchange markets are incorporated by the ratio of silver to gold holdings at the BNB which is in closer and more direct relation with the agio.

Despite the agio, silver coins were still coins, not just silver. They still retained a large part of the value assigned by monetary authorities and were not treated as a mere commodity, not even in private transactions. The agio did not deprive silver coins of all the fiduciary value granted to them by the tariff. If the agio may indeed be regarded as the consequence and measure of a lack of confidence in (and demand of) the domestic currency in relation to the external currency, the data show that the lack of confidence was far from complete, and hence that, by issuing silver coins and by assigning them a nominal value greater than their intrinsic value, the Ministry of Finance was not simply gaining seigniorage but also providing domestic circulation with an adequate means of payment.

Convertibility (1906–12)

In 1906 the agio disappeared completely thanks to a favourable balance of trade, conspicuous foreign loans, abundant gold reserves and a low minting of silver coins.[29] As the agio was reduced and eventually eliminated, the BNB also managed to successfully circulate banknotes backed by gold. Until then, Bulgaria had lacked a system of central banking. Indeed, the BNB had been founded shortly after Liberation, by the provisional Russian government, two days before going out of office.[30] It was established as a State bank. However, it was not an issuing bank, but simply a deposit and discount bank. It could not issue banknotes or provide overdraft facilities.[31]

Several attempts had been made to endow the new state with a modern central bank. Already in 1880, Russian bankers Ginsburg and Polyakov submitted the proposal for a new BNB, to be established as joint stock company, under government control, entitled to issue coins and banknotes and to sign external sovereign debt, in view of enhancing its capacity of providing capital to an ailing Bulgarian economy, in the hands of usurers. The proposal was withdrawn from the National Assembly by Finance Minister, Petko Karavelov, in fear that it would excessively strengthen Russian influence.[32]

On 11 February 1883 new articles of association of the BNB were approved. BNB was to be established as a joint stock company, and authorized to issue banknotes, backed in metal for one-third of their value, and convertible into gold upon request. However, the new statute was not implemented due to the lack of private investors and was eventually repealed by the Karavelov government, which went into office in June 1884. A General Act was eventually passed on 27 January 1885. BNB acquired the exclusive right to issue banknotes convertible into gold at request and backed by a proportional gold reserve of one-third. A broad interpretation allowed credits towards foreign banks to be assimilated to gold reserves. The amount of banknotes issued should not be more than double the capital and reserves of the Bank.[33]

Hence, in 1885, the first Bulgarian banknotes were put into circulation. They were initially of high denomination, from 20 to 500 leva.[34] The main source of banknotes in circulation was the discount of bills.

Circulation of banknotes initially met with a strong resistance on the part of the public, due to the memory of depreciating paper money under Turkish rule.[35] Moreover, banknotes were immediately converted into gold by speculators, who then brought the gold abroad, converted it into silver at the international market bmr, and brought the silver back into Bulgaria to have it minted and evaluated at the more favorable bmr. This arbitrage exerted an upward pressure on the domestic bmr, resulting in an increase of the agio. On the other hand, the persistence of the agio was regarded by the Bank as the main obstacle against the circulation of banknotes.[36] In 1888, the Bank issued banknotes of lower denominations, of five and ten leva, in view of expanding their use. However, circulation of banknotes remained low. They were accepted at a premium against silver coins and hence hoarded. In any case, the value of BNB banknotes did not exceed the value of the gold reserves, and they did not add significantly to the monetary base, until 1906 (Figure 10.2).

In 1890, BNB governor and directors participated in a special committee, chaired by the Finance Minister, and proposed the adoption of the gold standard. Again in 1893, on 3 February a BNB report on coinage urged the Ministry of Finance to establish a gold standard and to withdraw excess 5 leva silver coins from circulation. Losses to the Treasury would be compensated by broader issue of gold-backed banknotes and reduced interest rate.[37] Finally, in 1897, given the rise in agio and the depletion of gold reserves in an effort to contrast it, the BNB called for the abandonment of bimetallism and the adoption of the gold standard. However, the measure could not be implemented until 1906, when the agio had eventually receded and gold-backed banknotes were successfully circulated.

Figure 10.2. Gold-backed banknotes issued and gold reserves at BNB.

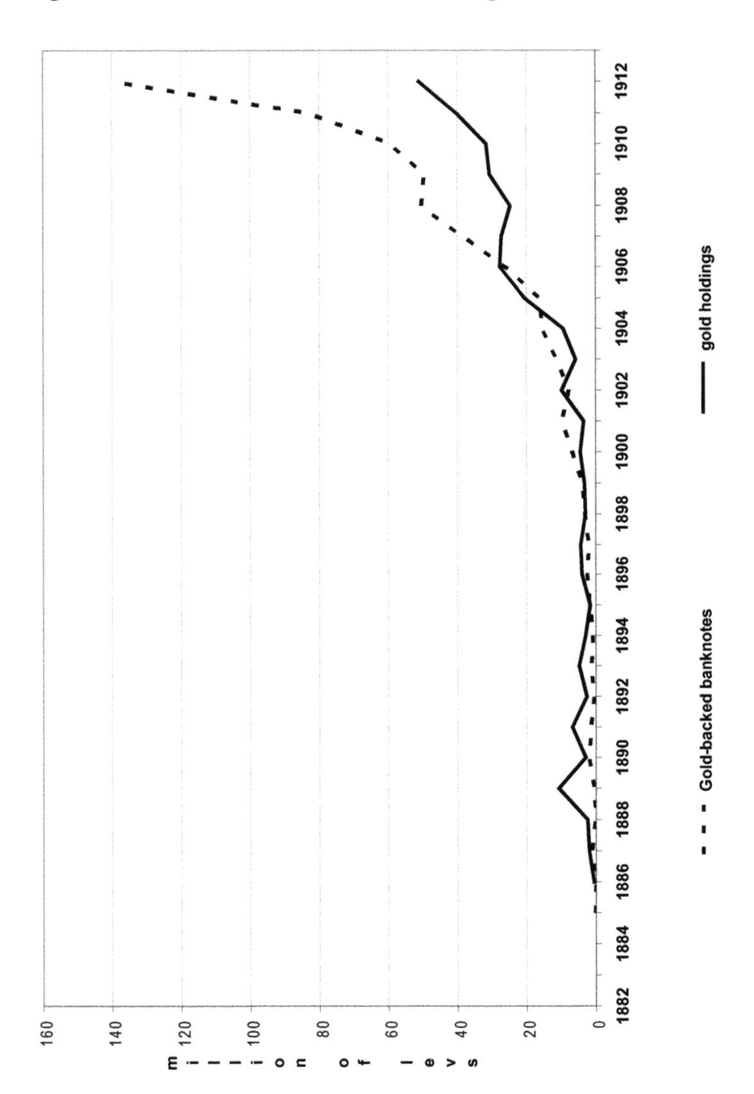

Source: Bulgarian National Bank, Jubileen *sbornik po sluchai 50-godishninata na BNB (Jubilee collection on 50 Anniversary of the BNB)* (Sofia: State Print, 1929).

This inaugurated the third and most modern stage of Bulgarian money in the pre-war period. It complied with the principles of the gold standard, which was then becoming then the worldwide standard. Despite the fact that it was represented and celebrated as the ultimate truth in money matters, it was, in fact, only a peculiar system with its own distinctive characteristics, which would eventually prove crucial to its demise. According to this peculiar rule, the international money was gold and the national money was paper. As the old monetary authority had consisted in the faculty of issuing a tariff that defined the variable relations between internal and external money, the new monetary authority consisted in the faculty of issuing domestic money (banknotes) upon the warranty of its fixed relationship with the international money (gold). The relevant rate between internal and external money became the exchange rate between the lev and foreign currencies.

Both the value and the metal content of the currency were now irrevocably fixed, in terms of an unalterable parity. The unit of account was identified with the means of payment. The national monetary authority was deprived of the faculty of assigning and modifying the value of the currency. Any discretion in this respect was revoked. At the same time, also the agio disappeared.

Was it the issuing of banknotes that put an end to the agio, or was it the end of the agio that allowed to issue banknotes? The agio was responsible for delaying the widespread use of banknotes as a means of circulation. On the other hand, it was by assuring gold convertibility of banknotes that the BNB finally managed to drastically reduce the agio in 1902 and to eventually get rid of it in 1907. Something similar happened throughout Western Europe, where, as Marc Bloch states, monetary alterations through the tariff eventually ended when paper money was issued and circulated.[38] Bloch has no doubt: it was this new form of money, and the possibility of increasing its quantity according to the needs of domestic circulation, that allowed monetary authorities to refrain from other, less expedient policies, such as the alteration of the tariff.

One must not think, however, that the end of the tariff meant the end of monetary authority and discretion as such. Certainly, under the new regime, the relation between national and international money was fixed at par, by a law of convertibility that was conceived almost as a law of nature, as if the identification between money and metal (of a specific fineness and weight) were an eternal truth that had simply awaited to be discovery. In fact, however, the relation between money and metal, between banknotes and reserve, between internal and external money, continued to be a matter of authority, and hence of confidence. The maintenance of the metal parity relied on the fiduciary bond of the convertibility promised by the issuer, which in turn depended on the liquidity of his reserves, and hence on the overall trend of the trade balance and of the public budget, and ultimately on the supply of foreign loans and on the correct functioning of liquid markets.

Even in this regime a lack of confidence was possible. On 10 October 1912, five days after the outbreak of the First Balkan War, a decree suspended the limitations on government loans by the BNB and consequently the convertibility of BNB banknotes.[39] By 1914, gold and silver coins had disappeared, leaving only paper money in circulation. Lack of confidence in the excess paper money would show after the end of the war, not perhaps in the form of an agio, but in the form of an internal and external depreciation of the currency. And, despite the purported automatism of the gold standard, the discretion of monetary authorities turned out to be essential for an active money management by changing, not the tariff, but the discount rate or the reserve ratio.

Open Questions

The three different regimes are mutually exclusive. They respond to irreconcilable principles. The passage from one to the other is doomed to appear chaotic and to involve a discontinuity. What dictates the passage from one set of rules to the other? Can the 'institutional change of the monetary regime' be seen as 'a result of the fight of economic agents', and particular of the struggle between creditors and debtors?[40] Or is the monetary regime the framework for this fight, and hence a dimension that necessarily precedes it? How can the establishment of a monetary regime be interpreted, if not as the outcome of a struggle for survival or for power?

Perhaps the form of a monetary system is not decided by the same forces that can and will legitimately come into play once the system is established. In the establishment of the system, there is something at stake which exceeds the payoffs for the parties involved. To establish a monetary system means to determine the form of monetary authority and responsibility. It implies a series of decisions concerning various aspects that cannot be addressed systematically here, but have emerged through the course of this story. To establish a monetary regime means answer a series of questions that can only be briefly evoked here.

Is it better to identify or to distinguish internal and external money? The problems that the US dollar has had to face, ever since the system of Bretton Woods was interpreted as a dollar standard, in order to reconcile its status of national and international currency should discourage other currencies from taking the lead and encourage the international community to consider if it is really desirable that any currency should perform simultaneously the two functions.

Ought the exchange rate be determined by law or by the market? Within the broad taxonomy of exchange rate regimes envisaged by the IMF, adjustable pegs seem to be the least fashionable. The systems actually implemented tend to polarize at the opposite ends of the scale: most rates are either fixed or flexible. In either case, the possibility of defining and redefining the exchange rate by law seems to be ruled out: if it is not fixed, it is set by the market, and all the authorities can do is try to influence the operation of market forces by announcements or direct intervention. It is common wisdom that authorities are not able to fix exchange rate autonomously. History shows, however, that the monetary system can be designed so that national authorities are not only allowed, but required to define the exchange rate (and this does not mean that they can do so arbitrarily, but on the contrary that they are held responsible for their decision).

Is a rule preferable to discretion? The question is relevant in relation not just to what we are accustomed to considering the key variables of monetary policy, but also to exchange rates. For centuries before the establishment of the gold standard, the tariff was the main lever of monetary policy, like today the discount rate. That the issue is not settled and the option remains open is confirmed, not only by the proposals in this sense advanced by Keynes in the interwar period, but also by the fact that this option was adopted, at least de jure, in the original Bretton Woods system of adjustable pegs. It is questionable whether even the key exchange rates today are in fact determined by market forces.

Is even the dichotomy between national and international money adequate to cover all possible options? Must 'optimal currency areas' be either national or supranational? Could they not be also infranational, regional or local? Must currency areas be intended necessarily in geographical terms? Could it not be conceivable to define a currency area in functional terms, reserving different currencies for different functions? Would it not be possible for different currency areas to coexist, rather than to compete, fulfilling different, complementary tasks? Is it not conceivable to maintain, within one geographical, maybe supranational, monetary area, a certain number of geographical (regional or local) sub-areas, together with several functional sub-areas (with different currencies, e.g., for current account and capital account)?

The period covered by this research is particularly interesting, since it corresponds to the establishment of the international gold standard, and to its diffusion throughout the world, from central to peripheral countries. As the case of Bulgaria shows, however, it is not possible to interpret this diffusion univocally in terms of a process of convergence. Indeed, the Bulgarian monetary system was established along the lines of the bimetallic standard, at a time when the latter was being abandoned by the countries of the centre in favour of the gold standard. And, as we have argued, this cannot be understood merely as the unintended outcome of an alleged backwardness, but rather as a deliberate design in view of the peculiar circumstances and needs of the domestic economy. Moreover, it did not imply the isolation of the Bulgarian economy from the rest of Europe, but rather contributed to set the conditions for its integration. One could speak, in this sense, of a convergence without conformity. And Bulgaria is not the only example of a similar course.

Balkan countries provide other interesting cases in this respect. Bulgarian monetary history of this period should be read in parallel with the largely similar developments in neighbouring countries, particularly Serbia,[41] Romania, Greece[42] and the Ottoman Empire.[43] As we have seen, developments in confining areas are quoted as being responsible for certain monetary phenomena that characterize Bulgaria in this period. In particular, the rise of the agio in the mid-1890s is set in relation with the devaluation of the Russian ruble in Serbia and Romania and with its demonetization in Turkey.[44] The role of Russia should also be considered, since it exerted a great pressure on the area to impose its influence even through monetary principles and policies. Moreover, the perspective should be widened to consider the relations with Turkey and to assess a possible path-dependency from the period of Ottoman rule (e.g. lack of trust in banknotes due to failure of paper money issues by Ottoman state and bank in the mid-nineteenth century; outflow of gold from Bulgaria to Turkey as a payment for the purchase of land from Ottoman owners).

Acknowledgements

This research was undertaken thanks to a contribution of the Bulgarian National Bank (BNB). The authors are grateful to N. Nenovsky for having promoted the initiative, to S. Vladimirova and to C. Ianovsky for hospitality at BNB Library, to M. Amato, R. Avramov, P. Bernholz, M. Ivanov, N. Kiosseva, and S. Pamuk for information, suggestions and encouragement, and to other participants in BNB and Codisyna workshops for comments and questions. The usual disclaimer applies.

11 MONEY CREATION UNDER THE GOLD STANDARD: THE ORIGINS OF THE ITALIAN BANKING CRISIS OF 1893[1]

Antoine Gentier

Introduction

This Italian experience is very interesting from the perspective of analysing divergence and convergence under the Gold Standard (GS). This experience shows the paradox between the common thought on GS (an automatic rule to avoid inflation) and an Italian reality where, in spite of gold convertibility, the economy suffered inflation that ended in an economic crisis.

Common wisdom associates nineteenth-century price stability with the GS rule. This common wisdom is sustained by a change in the perception of the notion of inflation. In fact, price stability does not have the same meaning today as it did in the past.

As a matter of fact, the link between nineteenth-century price stability and GS rules is defined more by the instability of the twentieth century than by its own stability. The Italian case illustrates this point: Italy could participate at the same time in the GS and still experience uncontrolled monetary creation. As such, the GS was not necessarily a set of rules conveying with it the degree of convergence most commonly assumed. Italian monetary difficulties were the direct consequences of the endless financial needs of the government, and no rule was strong enough to reign in the drive for governmental expenditures.

This chapter will show the link between the monetization of the national debt and the destabilization of the Italian banks of issue, and will explain the monetary origins of the 1893 crisis. The main argument rests on the fact that government intervention in the banking industry is one of the major factors of the crisis. The focus on this specific aspect of the crisis does not mean that there was just only one origin of this crisis. Nevertheless the return to the GS did not prevent Italian economy from monetary creation because the government could not meet the commitments of an equilibrate budget. Moreover, the financial commitments of the GS had led the Italian Government to take new measures to prevent a gold flee that worsened the crisis.

This chapter will explain the background of the 1893 banking crisis by exposing the fiscal question (Section 1) and the organization of the bank of issue (Section 2). Then we will focus on the monetization of the national debt by the banking system (Section 3) and the evaluation by the stock market of the banking crisis (Section 4).

Fiscal Question, the Return to the GS and Money Creation

The 1861–1914 period was dominated by the fiscal question.[2] The Italian government was unable to equilibrate its budget. The fiscal base was too poor to finance the governmental ambition in military spending and infrastructure (railways). The military spending had two origins: an arms race and several costly military expeditions (during the last two decades of the nineteenth century, Italy started its colonial policy). The railway construction was seen as symbol of political unification that could not be postponed. The results were a growing national debt, essentially financed by monetary creation. 82 per cent of public deficits were monetized between 1862 and 1914[3], as shown by Da Pozzo and Felloni series (1964) and the more recent evaluation of Vera Zamagni (1998)[4], whose differences are just marginal. The conclusion drawn from these data confirm an increase of the national Italian debt in absolute value, and as a proportion of the GDP. The graph 1b shows that the Debt to GDP ratio increased from 35.8 per cent in 1861 to 117 per cent in 1897. Between 1880 and 1894 alone, the Debt to GDP ratio increased from 80.3 to 113.7 per cent.

Thus the return to the GS had not changed the Italian public spending policy, characterized by public deficits during the whole period. Only five years happened to record budget surpluses (1874, 1878, 1886, 1893 and 1896, for detail see Figures 11.2a and 2b). As a consequence, the Italian national debt rose from 2 419 millions of liras in 1861 to 12 979 millions of liras in 1896, its amount being multiplied by 5.5[5] (See Figure 11.1a). The first three years after the return to the GS (1882, 1883, 1884) had smaller deficits but soon thereafter the Italian state returned to the same pace of borrowing .

Figure 11.1a. Comparison between Da Pozzo and Felloni (1964) and Zamagni (1998) series.

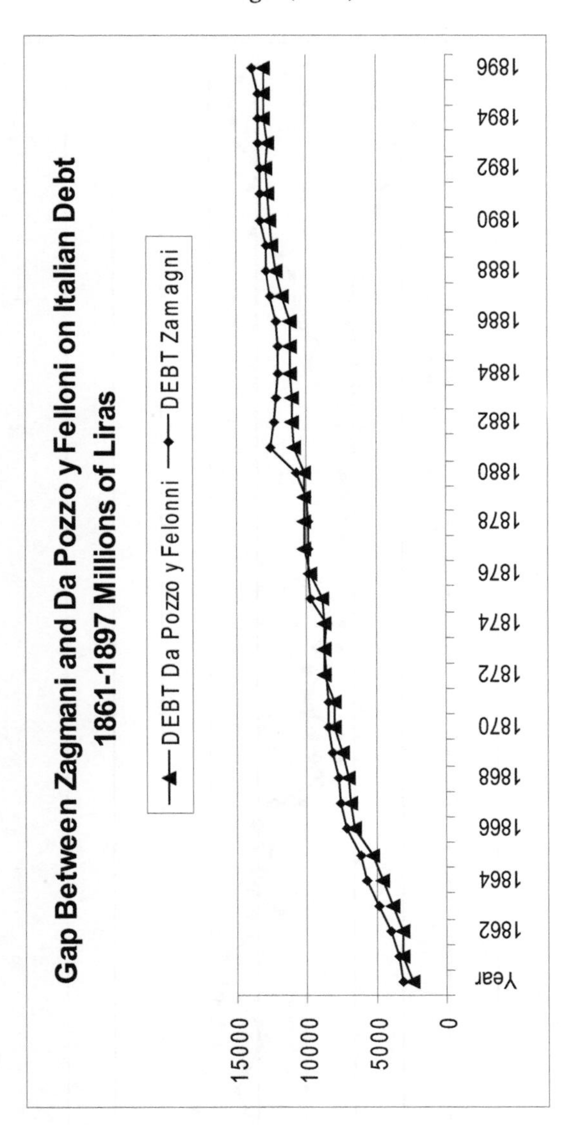

Figure 11.1b. Ratio Debt/GDP (1861–1914).

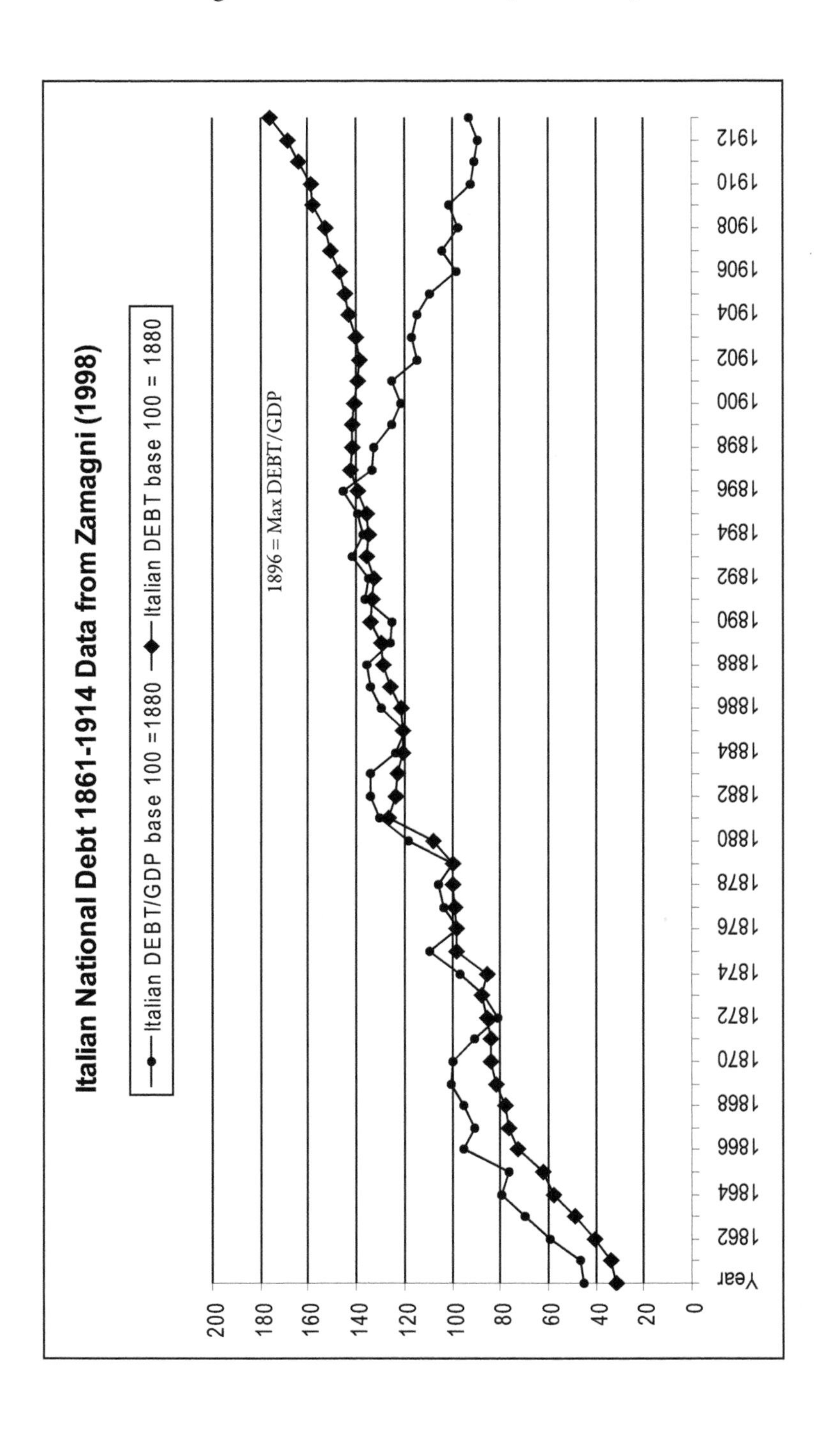

Figure 11.2a Net year-to-year change of the Italian National Debt.

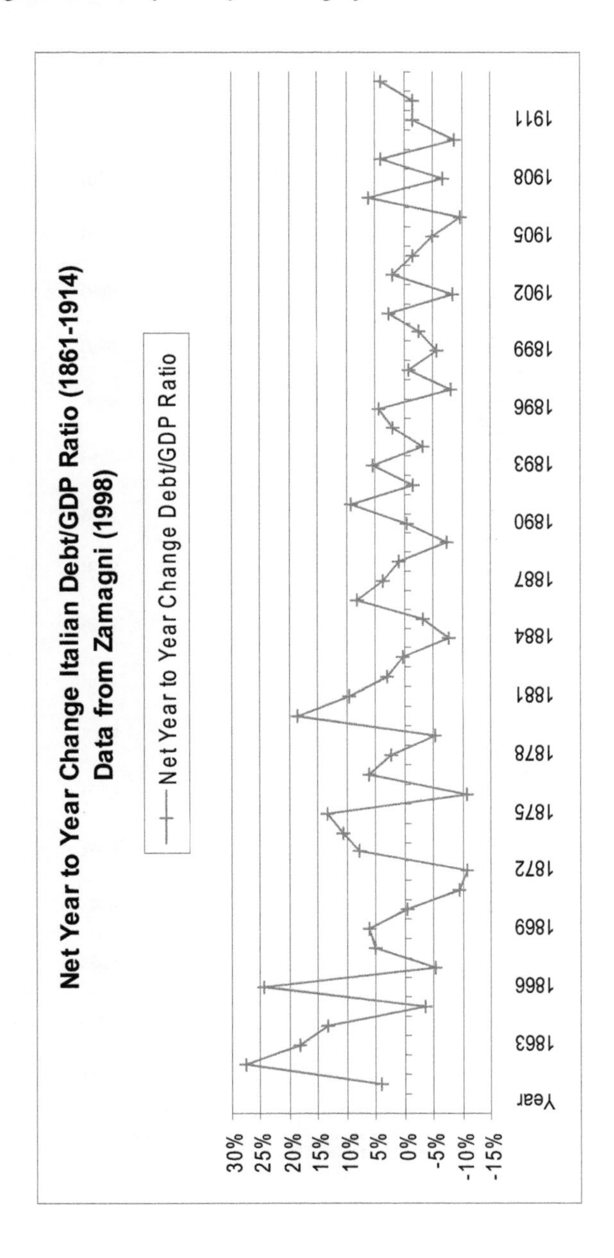

Figure 11.2b Net year-to-year change of DEBT/ GDP Ratio.

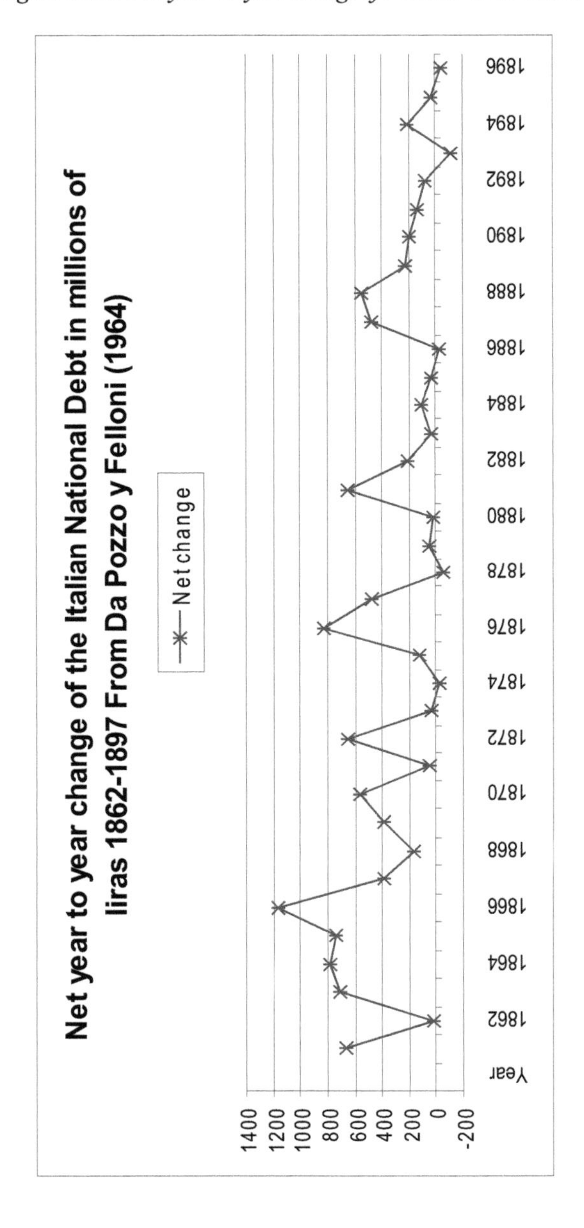

The Early History of the Italian Banking System: a Fragmented Banking System with a Succession of Internal Monetary Regimes

In this section we will first briefly relate the major episodes of the early history of the Italian banking system – before the creation of the Bank of Italy. 1861 celebrated the creation of the unified state of Italy. Italy chose bimetallism (gold and silver) and became in 1865 a member of the Latin Monetary Union together with France, Switzerland, Belgium and later Greece. The newborn state inherited from the five banks of issue that used to operate before the unification in the different kingdoms: Banca Nazionale Sarda (BNS)[6] from Piemonte, Banca Nazionale Toscana (BNT) and Banca Toscana di Credito (BTC) from Tuscany, Banco di Napoli (BN) and Banco di Sicilia (BS).[7] Before the banking law in 1874, the banks of issues' activities were regulated by their own statutes.

The early Italian banking history can be divided in four sub-periods each characterized by a specific monetary regime:

1. 1861–6: Full convertibility and competition in notes issuance but without free entry in the market.
2. 1866–74: Suspension of convertibility exclusively granted to BNI notes.
3. 1874–81: Creation of the consortium and suspension of convertibility exclusively granted to the notes issued by the consortium.
4. 1881–93: Full convertibility resumed and suspension of the inter-bank settlements.

1861–6: the 'Competition' Years

During this period, the business of the five banks of issue – BNS, BNT, BTC, BS, BN – was regulated by their own statutes and their notes were not enjoying legal tender. BN and BS were not even actually issuing notes in bearer form redeemable on demand but issued in the name of the depositors. Those two institutions were issuing notes similar to certificates. Moreover the BS certificates were issued against 100 per cent metallic reserves. Most of the time the amount of notes issued was regulated by the amount of metallic reserves and/or equity held. The five banks were issuing notes redeemable into gold. Their circulation was limited to their local territory except for the BNS notes circulating nationwide. As a matter of fact, before the unification of Italy the only bank represented extensively over the territory was the BNS. It was then possible for BNS note's holders to pay with BNS notes outside of the BNS territory since the note could be redeemed at a BNS branch against other local notes or against gold. *De facto* the players were not of the same size: the BNS was the big player and the other four were of a relatively smaller size. Moreover in 1862 the BNS was granted the monopoly over coinage. Given the fragmentation of the banking system the use of notes for inter-regional payments was low and to the exclusive benefit of the BNS given its extensive network.

1866–74: Suspension of Convertibility into Specie Exclusively Granted to BNI Notes

In 1866, the suspension of the BNS (which will become the BNI in 1867) notes convertibility[8] into metallic currency was declared in exchange of a 250 billion lira loan to the government at a preferred rate of 1.5 per cent. Legal tender was granted to all banks of issues' notes on their respective territory. Moreover the certificates issued by the BN and BS became notes in bearer form. Nonetheless the amount of notes privately issued by the BNI was still regulated by its reserves in specie. The other four banks of issue – and then five in 1870 – had to redeem their notes into metallic currency or into BNI notes. They could hold BNI notes as reserves in an amount not exceeding two thirds of their metallic reserves but they could not be used to further expand their notes circulation. The BNI notes held as reserves by other banks were not counted in the BNI circulation. *De facto* BNI notes became the monetary base of the monetary system enjoying a higher demand compared to the previous period. The BNI became temporarily a legal monopoly bank even though legal tender was restricted. To conclude on this period it is worth noting the discount rate was no longer set by the banks but instead by the Finance Minister.

1874–81: the 'Consortium' Years and Partial Suspension of Convertibility into Specie

In 1874 was enacted the first banking law. Moreover a 'consortium' of the six banks of issue was created exclusively to accommodate the government financial needs by issuing distinct notes not redeemable into specie in the name of the government. The six banks of issue were equal stakeholders in the consortium. These two changes were designed to make the rules under which the six banks of issue were operating fairly. The first banking law regulating the private circulation stated that:[9]

- Issuing private notes could not exceed three times metallic reserves and three times the equity capital;
- Notes issued privately were redeemable into metallic currency or into state notes issued by the 'consortium';
- Interbank settlements were from now on subject to a common regulation.

Notes issued against loans granted to the state were no longer exclusively managed by the BNI but by the 'consortium'. The 'consortium' was seen as the first step before resuming full convertibility of notes into gold. The BNI notes privately issued like any notes issued by the other five banks of issue were redeemable into 'consortium' notes or into specie. The regime under which the BNI was operating was no longer different from the one under which the other banks of issue were operating. They were all enjoying legal tender in their respective territory. Under this new ruling, the BNI position in the market was no longer similar to the legal monopoly case. The notes issued by the consortium became the monetary base of the system.

1881–93: Full Convertibility Resumed and Interbank Settlements Suspended

In 1881, full convertibility was resumed and the 'consortium' was dismantled. Notes issued by the 'consortium' were to be paid back by the government into gold or government bills. Despite the official return to convertibility, interbank settlements had been unofficially suspended. Indeed starting in 1885 the government put pressure on the BNI to suspend clearing settlements. The BNI was asked to spend the notes issued by other banks instead of asking for their redemption into metallic currency. This way the regional banks of issue could maintain their circulation and sustain the local activity and the financing of the government. It is important to recall that in 1887 Italy as a unified state experienced its first major economic crisis. Suspending interbank settlements was seen as a way for the regional banks of issue to support the local business and avoid a major bankruptcy of the system. Eventually it led to the 1893's banking crisis. During this period the BNI accepted to restrict its own notes circulation since interbank settlements were virtually suspended and so contributed to enhance the circulation of its competitors' notes.

Evaluation of the Monetary Creation 1881–93

Italian Macroeconomic Data

There are several studies on the early monetary history of Italy. All these studies (Supino,[10] Di Nardi,[11] Fratianni and Spinelli)[12] show that the period is characterized by a rapid growth of the money supply. We can summarize the monetary creation by analysing the change in the M2[13] series. M2 had been multiplied by five between 1862 and1887, that is by two between 1862 and 1868 and by three between 1862 and 1874. Between 1874 and 1887, the M2 increase was regular, except between 1881–2. The small decrease at this time was due to the return to the Gold Standard.

Figure 11.3. Main Italian Macroeconomics Indicators.

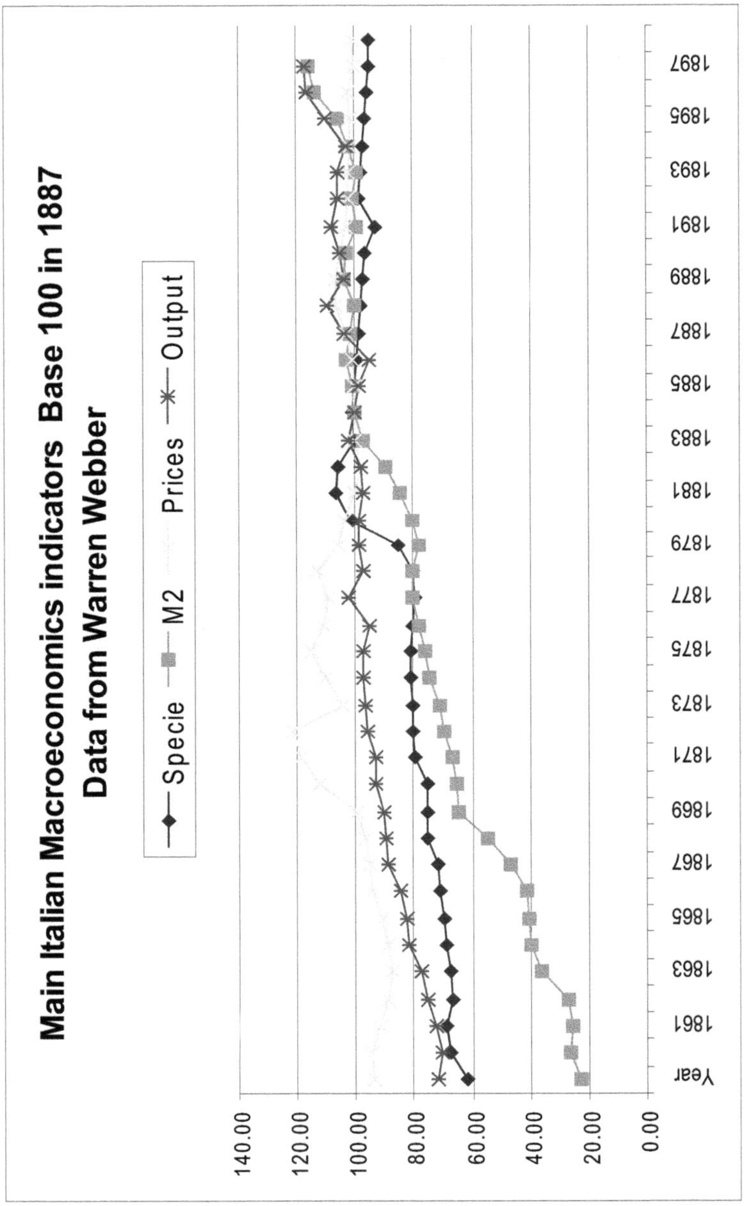

Changes in M2 are given by Figure 11.3. This statistic confirms two main facts. The return to the GS had not enduring impact upon the monetization policy of the Italian Government. The output statistic shows that the Italian economy went through a period of rapid growth until 1883 and after 1894. But this growth, as a side effect, contributed to hiding the effects of monetary creation on consumer prices. Without an increase of national wealth, price inflation would have been even higher. By twentieth-century standards, it seems that there was price stability except for the 1870–3 period which may be a side effect of the Prussian–French crisis. By nineteenth-century standards, the economic growth should have led to price deflation. The Italian economy was more inflationist than the French or British economies. The inflation differential is confirmed by the spread between Italian Bonds and UK Consols (See Figure 11.4). This spread shows the inflation gap between Italian and British economies, and the difficulties for the Italian government in borrowing. It also meant that the Italian bonds market was illiquid, and the banks could not rely on it to sell bonds in order to find liquidity. Nevertheless, the consumer price inflation discussion is not the main problem. The key issue of monetary creation is the distortion in the structure of relative prices, not the ultimate effect on consumer prices. Money creation led to two different assets price inflation: a bubble on the stock market (1866–73) and a bubble on the housing market (1885–93).

Evaluation of the Money Creation by the Liquidity Mismatch

The analysis of the liquidity mismatch is a usual method to evaluate the financial trajectory for a bank or a banking system. This simple indicator gives some crucial information on the way the bank is financed and especially on the relative part of credit financed by monetary creation. The liquidity mismatch measures the gap between liquidity (in this case mainly gold) held by the bank and funds that the bank has to redeem on demand (notes and demand deposits). The main signification of this indicator is not given by its absolute level,[15] but rather by its dynamic change. If the liquidity gap widens, it means that the bank has financed its credit expansion by monetary creation.

Each sub period (1866–73; 1874–81; 1882–93) presents a widening liquidity gap followed by a sudden freefall. The monetization of the national debt was done by the banks of issue. Figure 11.5 shows that the period 1866–73 and the period 1882–93 had a very high increase in liquidity mismatch. But there are some differences between the origins of the monetary creation. During the first period, the BNS was the only bank responsible for the increase of the liquidity gap. For the other periods, the responsibility for the increase of the liquidity mismatch was shared by all the banks of issue except the BTC.

The analysis of the liquidity mismatch confirms the other facts on monetary creation.

Figure 11.4. Spread between UK Consols / Italian Bonds (1880–96) Source: Batley and Ferguson, 'Event Risk' (data from Investor's Monthly Manual).[14]

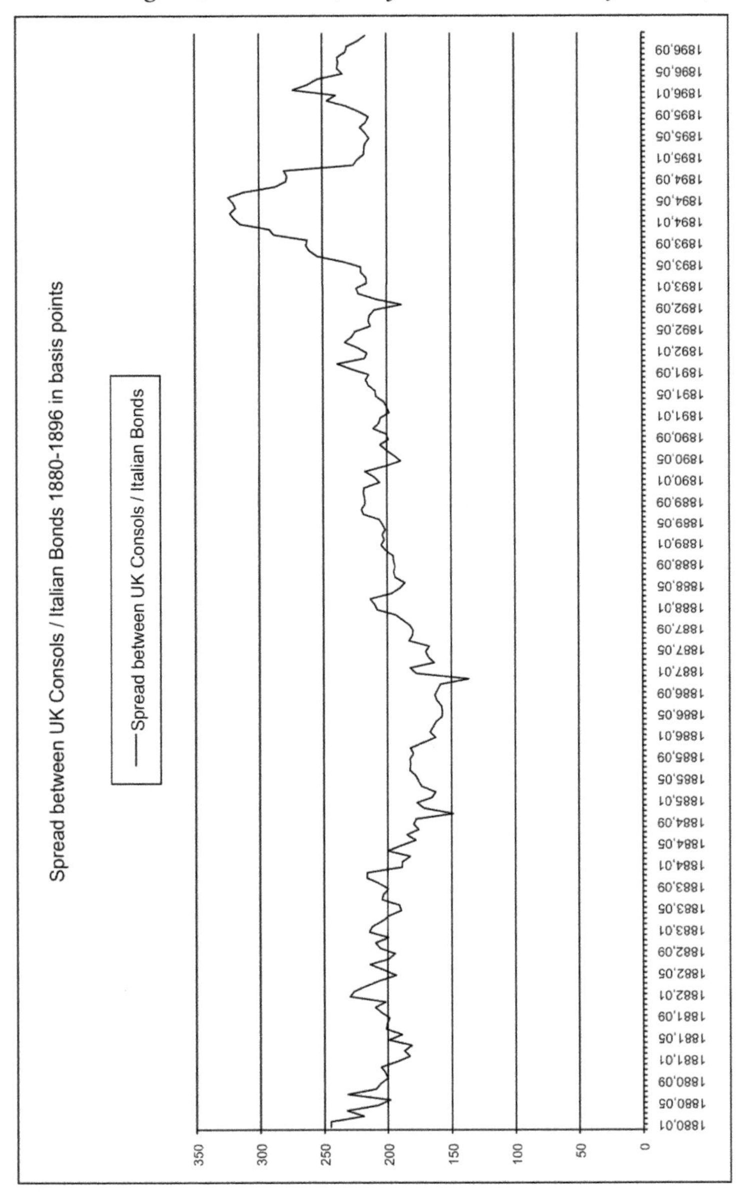

Figure 11.5. Systemic monetary creation.

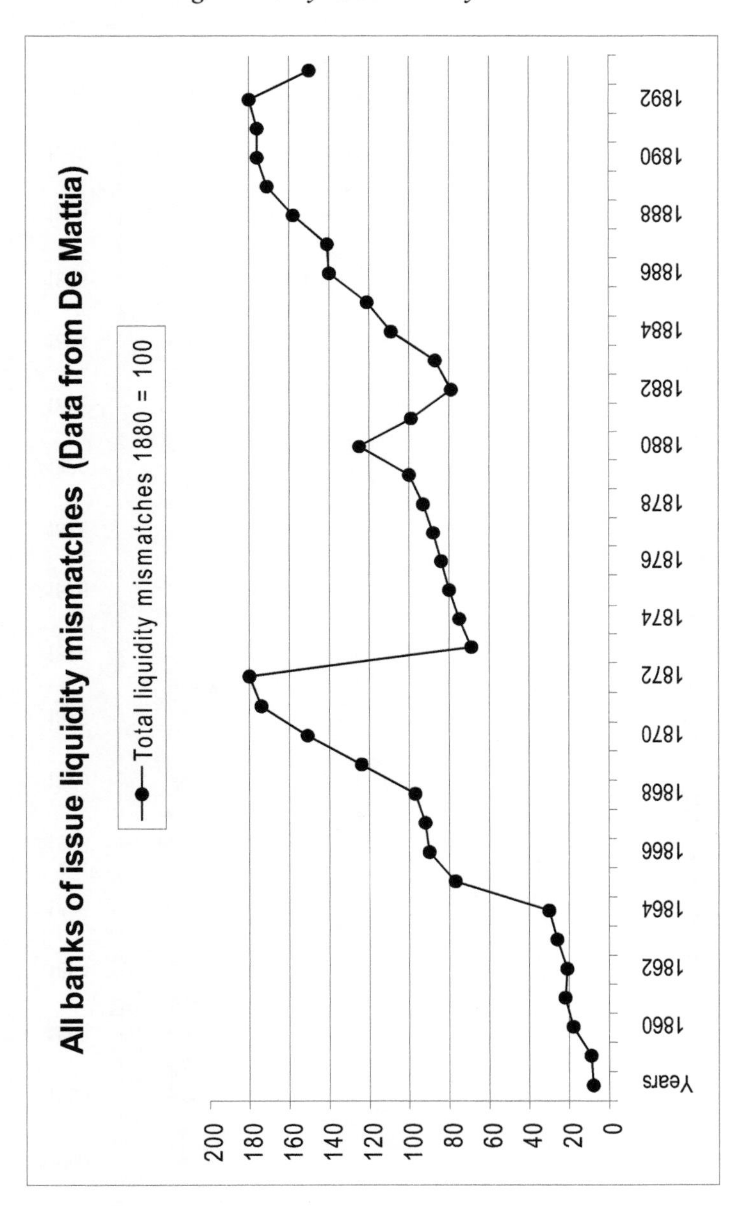

Figure 11.6. Monetary creation by banks of issue.

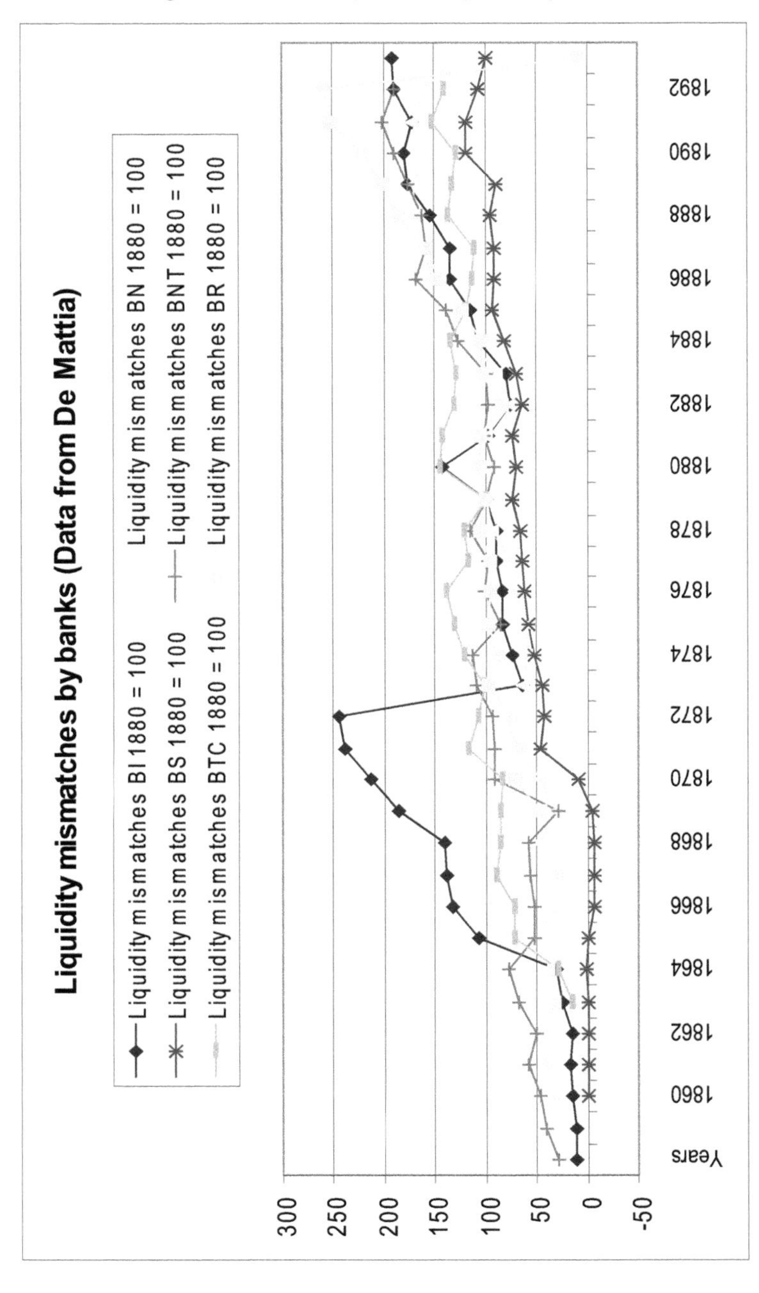

Evaluation of the Banks Solvability

Liquidity mismatch shows that a large part of the credit was financed by monetary creation. Nevertheless, the distress of the Italian banks of issue during the 1893 crisis can also be explained by an analysis of their solvency. The classical ratio [(Net Equity Capital)[16] / Total Credit] usually gives a good indication, but for these banks this ratio is not enough accurate to show why the banking system is in structural insolvency. In fact, the equity capital of the bank was used to finance public credit (especially by holding state bonds). The consequence of the immobilization of the equity capital in state bonds, is that the private credit was backed only by demanding funds (notes and private deposit). So we have calculated a more realistic solvency ratio [(Net Equity Capital–Net Fixed Assets in Public Bonds)[17] / Total Credit]. This ratio shows a structural insolvency of the banking system, and it means that when the banks started to have losses[18] they were on the verge of the bankruptcy. These ratios give the percentage of the equity capital financing the credit. The real issue is why banks couldn't sell their public bonds to compensate for losses. There were two main reasons: because at those moments bonds loose a huge chunk of their value (See Figure 11.4 the spread between UK Consols and Italian Bonds increased at the same time) and also they couldn't sell the bonds in order to preserve what remained of confidence about state solvency. As a result, a large part of the banks' equity capital couldn't guarantee the losses on the private credit activities. Moreover, the default rate on private credit activities was very high during the period (See below, Tables 11.4 and 11.5). The holding of illiquid public bonds increased the insolvency risk of the Italian Banking system.

Table 11.1 Apparent Solvability Ratio.

Apparent Solvability Ratio Net Equity Capital / Total Credit						
Years	BNI	BN	BS	BNT	BTC	BR
1880	27.9 per cent	21.7 per cent	14.9 per cent	39.6 per cent	42.3 per cent	28.7 per cent
1881	21.8 per cent	22.9 per cent	17.1 per cent	42.1 per cent	33.8 per cent	27.9 per cent
1882	30.9 per cent	23.2 per cent	17.2 per cent	38.9 per cent	33.6 per cent	28.7 per cent
1883	38.3 per cent	30.2 per cent	23.7 per cent	40.0 per cent	36.1 per cent	33.7 per cent
1884	35.6 per cent	31.2 per cent	26.3 per cent	39.4 per cent	36.6 per cent	30.8 per cent
1885	27.8 per cent	25.9 per cent	20.0 per cent	34.2 per cent	35.3 per cent	31.8 per cent
1886	26.1 per cent	22.1 per cent	19.6 per cent	31.8 per cent	38.7 per cent	28.0 per cent
1887	23.1 per cent	19.2 per cent	18.9 per cent	26.7 per cent	39.0 per cent	25.3 per cent
1888	22.4 per cent	18.6 per cent	18.6 per cent	28.2 per cent	40.0 per cent	24.0 per cent
1889	19.2 per cent	20.1 per cent	20.5 per cent	28.6 per cent	42.8 per cent	20.2 per cent
1890	19.0 per cent	20.0 per cent	19.2 per cent	28.3 per cent	36.1 per cent	18.5 per cent
1891	17.9 per cent	22.2 per cent	17.4 per cent	26.4 per cent	49.2 per cent	16.0 per cent
1892	18.4 per cent	23.5 per cent	20.9 per cent	25.5 per cent	50.6 per cent	13.9 per cent
1893	17.3 per cent	21.6 per cent	20.8 per cent	26.4 per cent	59.2 per cent	-60.7 per cent
1894	22.9 per cent	24.0 per cent	21.4 per cent			-70.3 per cent
1895	26.1 per cent	25.1 per cent	15.3 per cent			-68.6 per cent

Table 11.2. Realistic Solvability Ratio.

Realistic Solvability Ratio (Net Equity Capital – Net Fixed Assets in Public Bonds) / Total credit						
Years	BNI	BN	BS	BNT	BTC	BR
1880	-5.1 per cent	1.7 per cent	4.6 per cent	9.4 per cent	38.4 per cent	15.3 per cent
1881	-5.8 per cent	0.1 per cent	11.3 per cent	13.0 per cent	27.3 per cent	14.3 per cent
1882	-2.8 per cent	-3.6 per cent	0.1 per cent	9.8 per cent	27.2 per cent	16.1 per cent
1883	-0.5 per cent	11.5 per cent	13.8 per cent	12.9 per cent	26.3 per cent	23.2 per cent
1884	4.4 per cent	18.0 per cent	13.2 per cent	9.8 per cent	32.7 per cent	17.9 per cent
1885	9.9 per cent	12.3 per cent	9.5 per cent	15.8 per cent	23.3 per cent	25.1 per cent
1886	12.5 per cent	12.6 per cent	14.7 per cent	15.4 per cent	25.5 per cent	25.4 per cent
1887	15.3 per cent	8.7 per cent	9.3 per cent	14.3 per cent	29.0 per cent	22.2 per cent
1888	11.9 per cent	5.4 per cent	6.0 per cent	12.8 per cent	29.8 per cent	19.3 per cent
1889	12.0 per cent	9.1 per cent	6.2 per cent	17.0 per cent	28.9 per cent	20.4 per cent
1890	8.6 per cent	8.1 per cent	1.4 per cent	11.5 per cent	25.3 per cent	14.1 per cent
1891	6.4 per cent	2.1 per cent	-2.7 per cent	2.1 per cent	30.2 per cent	11.0 per cent
1892	5.0 per cent	3.1 per cent	-3.8 per cent	5.2 per cent	19.5 per cent	11.3 per cent
1893	4.5 per cent	1.0 per cent	-0.9 per cent	7.3 per cent	15.6 per cent	-61.6 per cent
1894	8.8 per cent	9.7 per cent	2.2 per cent			-71.0 per cent
1895	17.0 per cent	17.9 per cent	-10.8 per cent			-71.4 per cent

Table 11.2 shows that Italian banks of issue operated with nearly no equity capital to guarantee their credit operations. The private credit was financed by monetary creation. It is the other side of the liquidity mismatch. The holding of illiquid public bonds increased the default risk of the banks. The banks had not the same fate during the crisis, but we find the same ranking between them. The BTC, which had never participated in the credit expansion, presented the best ratios in all case. On the other side, the BR had the poorest results. Table 11.2 reveals the weakness of the BNI, BN and BS during the entire period. But the comparison between the BNT and the BTC is very interesting. These two Tuscan banks seem to have similar results in Table 11.1, but Table 11.2 shows a real divergence between them. The holding of illiquid public bonds was a factor that exacerbated the banking crisis.

The Return to GS: between Old Bad Habits and New Problems

The return to the GS did not change the Italian fiscal policy. The same 'solution' was used to cover governmental deficits. The return to the GS without the will to respect the GS rules led the Italian economy into new difficulties.

First, by joining the GS, Italy returned to fixed exchange-rate system. But the monetization of public deficits had led to an increase of domestic prices. Inflation in the fixed exchange-rate system meant that Italian products lost their international competitiveness.[19] Local producers encountered increasing difficulties in selling on the domestic market (imports were cheaper) and exporting. The tariff of 1887 was motivated by private interests but it was also an escape ahead for Italian producers. This remedy contributed to a long slowdown of the Italian economy from 1888 to 1895 and increased poverty of the population.[20] Moreover the causes of the problem were not treated.

Second, the governmental intervention to hamper bank settlements in order to prevent a gold flow from Italy, had opened the gate to opportunistic behaviour from the smaller banks of issue. Because the clearing mechanism had stopped, these banks had the opportunity to finance more credit by monetary creation. This was at the root of the banking crisis of 1893, as detailed in the next section.

Third, the change in the relative price structure induced by inflation modified the incentives for entrepreneurs. For entrepreneurs, investing in industries protected from foreign competition (for example, housing construction) appeared more profitable than other activities. Entrepreneurs had incentives to enter in these industries and they also benefited from cheap credit, helping explain the housing boom of the end of the 1880 decade.[21]

The Stock Exchange and the Banking Crisis

The 1893 crisis was mainly a banking crisis. The banks faced a large value-decrease of their assets. The banks had accumulated suspended bills since 1887. This crisis struck an economy crippled by protectionism but the disaster revealed by the parliamentary inquiry had been anticipated by the stock market. In fact, banks of issue could not pay dividends to shareholders since 1887. The banking sector suffered more during this crisis than other sectors.

The 1893 Crisis

Table 11.3 shows the stock market evaluation of the banking sector health. Between 1882 and 1887 there is a small increase of the stock value (from 89.3 to 98.1) except for railway stocks, which nearly doubled their value (from 56.5 to 97.1). The banks' stocks fluctuated between 93.2 and 99.9. From 1888 to 1896 the stock market capitalization shrunk by half (from 98.1 to 44.4), bank capitalization was divided more than by three (from 99.9 to 28.7), railways and other stocks capitalization diminished by 15 per cent. The fall of the stock market between 1888 and 1893 was due to the financial distress of the banking system. The banks' dividend policy illustrated this distress. Since 1887, banks of issue could not distribute dividends (or very small). Therefore, the market value of the banks' stock fell for two main reasons. The banks presented an increasing risk and there was no extra revenue to cover the risk.

Table 11.3. Index yearly average on Genoa stock exchange 1882–96 (Da Pozzo and Felloni 1964).

Year	Gov. Bonds (Rente 5 Per Cent)	Index Stocks	Index Banks	Index Railways	Index Others
01/1882	92,9	89,3	95,9	56,5	
01/1883	92,6	88,2	93,2	58,6	
01/1884	97,4	90,1	93,5	75,1	
01/1885	98,5	95,8	96,8	85	108,2
01/1886	102	97,2	99,8	92,8	93,2
01/1887	100,5	98,1	99,9	97,1	91,3
01/1888	99,6	96,9	95,5	100,3	98,8
01/1889	98,1	89,5	83,4	98,1	103,2
01/1890	97,8	79,5	72,6	94,3	90,4
01/1891	95,4	66,6	56,9	85,7	86,5
01/1892	96,6	66,8	56	86,7	90,1
01/1893	97	62,8	50,7	87,2	90,8
01/1894	94,2	44,8	31,7	79,9	76
01/1895	103,4	44,9	30,6	86,4	79,6
01/1896	103,4	44,4	28,7	86,1	87,5

The stock-market evaluation had anticipated the scandal created by the parliamentary inquiry of 1893. In 1892, the market value of the banks had already shrunk by half.

Table 11.4. Di Nardi evaluation on suspended bill[22] 10th January 1893, thousands of liras.

Institutions	Bill of exchange	Suspended Bill	Total	Total in per cent of equity capital
BNI	28473	20995.5	49468	26.1
BN	29629	19680.8	49309.8	69
BNT		4600	4600	19.7
BTC				
BR	2897.5	13050.7	16038.2	80
BS	10364.6	3609.5	13974.1	77.3
Total	71454.1	61936.5	133390.6	40.6

Table 11.4 shows the complete bankruptcy of the Italian banking system. Except the Banca Toscana di Credito all banks of issue were in financial distress. The Banca Romana failed in 1893. The new Banca d'Italia came from the merger between BNI, BTC, BNT and BR.[23] The Italian North had a unique bank of issue in 1893. Despite their poor financial performance in 1893, the BS and the BN were saved, and stayed in business until 1926.

Table 11.4 shows the results of the governmental intervention in hampering bank settlements. The banking system had no information on monetary demand, because the clearinghouse mechanism was suspended. Normally, a clearinghouse mechanism gives banks a crucial information on their liquidity risk. And such information would prevent a bank from increasing its credit supply by monetary creation because monetary creation increases its liquidity risk. If the Government prevents banks from using clearinghouse mechanisms, there is an open gate to bad loans accumulation in banks balance sheets. The longer the clearing mechanism[24] is suspended the worse the effects, and this policy had lasted nearly for six years.

The limited clearinghouse mechanism thus allowed a riskier credit policy. It let the banks lend more without worrying about redeeming their debts. This situation gave banks very bad incentives and they took riskier bets with monetary creation. Table 11.5 shows two main facts. First, the percentage of suspended bills over total credit was very high even according to contemporary standards. Second, these defaults of credit were common all along the period, with a dramatic increase at the end. No bank could possibly survive such ratios. The BS, BN and BR played a special role. They used the limited clearing mechanism to finance their expansion. The BNI seemed to be less expansionist but it was the main financial backer of the other three banks. Financing bad credit was not a problem as long as the banks did not have to pay back their debts. That is the reason why the limited clearing mechanism allowed for six years of worsening credits extensions. At the end of the process, the banking system was on the verge of complete bankruptcy, with the BR having more losses than the other banks. The main reason was that the BR was more linked to political powers, which led it to lend even more to non-profitable projects.[25] The BTC was not involved but it was forced to merge to create the BNI. The crisis was also worsened by a real estate crisis, especially on the housing market following a housing boom in Italy documented by several studies.[26]

Table 11.5. Rates of suspended bills (from de Mattia 1967).

Years	per cent of suspended bills over total credit BNI	per cent of suspended bills over total credit BN	per cent of suspended bills over total credit BS	per cent of suspended bills over total credit BR	per cent of suspended bills over total credit Total
1880	1.69 per cent	3.43 per cent	8.26 per cent	5.20 per cent	2.67 per cent
1881	1.71 per cent	3.67 per cent	8.00 per cent	5.12 per cent	2.78 per cent
1882	1.68 per cent	3.79 per cent	8.46 per cent	6.10 per cent	2.81 per cent
1883	1.93 per cent	4.90 per cent	5.20 per cent	7.04 per cent	3.09 per cent
1884	1.40 per cent	4.27 per cent	4.34 per cent	6.86 per cent	2.50 per cent
1885	0.65 per cent	3.77 per cent	3.42 per cent	4.80 per cent	1.62 per cent
1886	0.80 per cent	3.46 per cent	2.71 per cent	3.74 per cent	1.61 per cent

Years	per cent of suspended bills over total credit BNI	per cent of suspended bills over total credit BN	per cent of suspended bills over total credit BS	per cent of suspended bills over total credit BR	per cent of suspended bills over total credit Total
1887	1.32 per cent	3.24 per cent	3.87 per cent	3.27 per cent	1.90 per cent
1888	2.13 per cent	3.70 per cent	6.01 per cent	3.81 per cent	2.63 per cent
1889	2.32 per cent	4.80 per cent	6.22 per cent	4.08 per cent	2.95 per cent
1890	2.08 per cent	6.55 per cent	8.33 per cent	4.72 per cent	3.23 per cent
1891	2.06 per cent	7.09 per cent	6.86 per cent	4.71 per cent	3.16 per cent
1892	2.66 per cent	8.87 per cent	6.69 per cent	5.24 per cent	3.82 per cent
1893	4.10 per cent	10.52 per cent	12.38 per cent	75.72 per cent	11.90 per cent
1894	3.20 per cent	11.29 per cent	12.08 per cent	85.72 per cent	12.27 per cent
1895	0.00 per cent	0.52 per cent	11.92 per cent	90.75 per cent	7.99 per cent

Years	per cent of suspended bills over total discounted bills BNI	per cent of suspended bills over total discounted bills BN	per cent of suspended bills over total discounted bills BS	per cent of suspended bills over total discounted bills BR	per cent of suspended bills over total discounted bills Total
1880	2.17 per cent	7.31 per cent	15.57 per cent	6.65 per cent	3.95 per cent
1881	2.12 per cent	6.68 per cent	15.32 per cent	6.66 per cent	3.99 per cent
1882	1.97 per cent	7.41 per cent	15.77 per cent	8.02 per cent	3.92 per cent
1883	2.26 per cent	11.03 per cent	8.31 per cent	9.50 per cent	4.42 per cent
1884	1.64 per cent	7.72 per cent	6.82 per cent	9.62 per cent	3.39 per cent
1885	0.84 per cent	6.41 per cent	5.32 per cent	6.44 per cent	2.26 per cent
1886	1.14 per cent	5.89 per cent	3.66 per cent	5.58 per cent	2.38 per cent
1887	2.09 per cent	5.50 per cent	5.57 per cent	5.17 per cent	3.04 per cent
1888	3.65 per cent	6.74 per cent	9.39 per cent	6.48 per cent	4.50 per cent
1889	4.07 per cent	8.66 per cent	11.71 per cent	7.95 per cent	5.14 per cent
1890	4.09 per cent	11.73 per cent	14.79 per cent	9.40 per cent	6.05 per cent
1891	4.36 per cent	12.58 per cent	12.09 per cent	8.56 per cent	6.18 per cent
1892	5.45 per cent	16.85 per cent	11.26 per cent	8.66 per cent	7.26 per cent
1893	8.38 per cent	19.03 per cent	24.05 per cent	344.06 per cent	22.55 per cent
1894	13.65 per cent	23.72 per cent	24.30 per cent	715.00 per cent	44.59 per cent
1895	0.00 per cent	2.10 per cent	28.71 per cent	1408.88 per cent	37.22 per cent

Table 11.5 shows the financial distress of the Italian banking system. A significant part of the credit was lent to people that never had to pay it back. The rate of suspended bills was, even by nowadays' standards, on credit default very high,[27] and a bank cannot survive with this kind of credit default rate. The lack of clearing mechanism allowed banks to go on this credit policy, and postponed the necessary bankruptcy.

Conclusion

The return to the gold standard was not directly responsible for the banking crisis of 1893. Nevertheless, the return to the gold standard had created new constraints that led the Italian government to take new measures in order to satisfy its endless financial needs. All the desperate means used by the Italian government had perverse effects on the economy. Protectionism durably increased the poverty of Italians and the regulation towards banks of issue led to a major banking crisis. Moreover, all these desperate means had no real effect on the cause of the problem. These policies just treated the symptoms and not the main cause of the disease: the monetization of the public deficit through the banks of issue. From this it appears clearly that the GS is not an automatic rule for price stability. It is the political will to implement a sustainable fiscal policy in regard to the GS that could have changed the destiny of the Italian banking system and led to a convergence with other Western European banking and monetary practices.

Acknowledgements

I would like to thank Nathalie Janson, Giuseppina Gianfreda, Patrice Baubeau and the participants of the Frejus seminar CODYSINA for their comments.

Abbreviations

- The BNS Banca Nazionale Degli Stati Sardi became BNI in 1867 Banca Nazionale nel regno d'Italia and BI Banca d'Italia in 1894.
- BN Banca di Napoli
- BS Banca di Sicilia
- BR Banca Romana
- BTC Banca Toscana di Credito
- BNT Banca Nazionale Toscana

12 FINANCING GERMANY: AMSTERDAM'S ROLE AS AN INTERNATIONAL FINANCIAL CENTRE, 1914–31

Jeroen Euwe

After Germany's defeat in 1918 by the Entente, the economic prospects of the country were dire. High inflation, political turmoil, famine, the loss of significant areas of high industrial and agricultural importance, and the prospect of punitive damages to be paid to the victors – the height of which were being discussed at Versailles – weakened the German economy. To the Netherlands, the German economic difficulties threatened to have disastrous consequences. Since the start of industrialization in both countries during the 1860s they had become economically dependent upon one another. The Ruhr area in Germany – near the Rhine, close to the border with the Netherlands – had by the start of the war become Europe's most important industrial region.[1] For the transportation of the raw materials it needed and the products it exported, it relied on shipping along the Rhine and railroad transportation. In the Netherlands, the transport sector – sea shipping, Rhine shipping, railroad traffic, transhipment and related activities in the Dutch ports of Rotterdam and Amsterdam – relied on the Ruhr industry. The densely populated Ruhr also needed to import foodstuffs, and a large portion of Dutch exports were shipped there. The importance of the Netherlands as a supply route and supplier to the Ruhr is illustrated by the fact that Germany decided to respect Dutch neutrality during the Great War. As the German Chief of General Staff, Helmuth von Moltke, put it as early as 1909: 'it will be of great importance to have in the Netherlands a country whose neutrality allows us to import and export. It has to remain our windpipe, allowing us to breathe'.[2]

Dutch–German economic bonds were strong, and a German economic recovery was thus important to the Netherlands. Immediately after the war, influential Dutch bankers such as C. E. ter Meulen of *Hope & Co.* and G. Vissering, president of the Dutch central bank, were internationally active, trying in vain to enable not only Germany, but the entire world to resume international trade by promoting plans for international loans, barter or bilateral clearing.[3] The Dutch government was also acutely aware of the importance of a German economic recovery. It was mainly with this purpose in mind that the Coal and Credit Treaty of 1920 was negotiated.[4] With the treaty Germany was granted a loan of *f* 60 million to buy Dutch foodstuffs, and a revolving – i.e. once repaid, the credit would be available again – credit of *f* 140 million to finance raw materials for German industry. While these loans by themselves were not enough to satisfy Germany's need for funds, it was hoped other countries would follow the example set by the Dutch. Widespread monetary instability in Europe and a worldwide economic crisis starting in 1920 meant that – even if they would be willing – others could not follow. The monetary instability did allow Amsterdam – which during the war had grown into an international financial centre of some importance – to expand and consolidate its newfound role. Its growth was further aided by the exclusion of Germany from the London financial market and an influx of flight capital from Central Europe. Many German banks established themselves in Amsterdam in order to conduct their international business from there, seemingly setting in motion a process of convergence of the Dutch and German financial markets. During the 1920s Amsterdam would be the most important international financial centre of continental Europe. Once the German currency was stabilized, trade expanded and Amsterdam – together with New York and London – became one of Germany's most important creditors. The economies of both countries would once again be entwined. By the end of the decade, Th. Metz – who wrote extensively on economic issues during the interwar years – described the Dutch–German economic ties: 'the Netherlands are today the most important buyer of German products, one of Germany's largest suppliers and with their colonies Germany's largest commercial partner. Germany is its main supplier and buyer. The Netherlands are Germany's largest or second-largest creditor and Germany is its largest debtor'.[5]

Because of the German reliance on foreign creditors to finance its economic recovery, the role of the Amsterdam financial market – one of the former's main creditors – in Dutch–German economic interdependence merits further research. Did a process of convergence of the Dutch and German financial markets take place, that is: did Amsterdam become a primarily German financial centre, where German banks met Germany's international financial needs using German capital? Or was the rise of Amsterdam mostly the result of a structural domestic surplus of capital that was now put to use on the financial market of Amsterdam, instead of London? What was the policy of the *Nederlandsche Bank* – the Dutch central bank – with regards to market developments, and the establishment *en masse* of German banks on Dutch shores?[6] This essay addresses these questions, in order to focus on the central question of whether – and if so, how

– Dutch–German economic interdependence was reflected in the structure of Dutch financial services to its neighbouring country.

The Development of Amsterdam as an International Financial Centre

The 1860s and early 70s saw the emergence of a modern banking system in the Netherlands, as a number of banks were founded which would develop into the major Dutch banks.[7] The connection to Germany, which at that time was turning into an important economic hinterland to the Netherlands,[8] was already firmly established by the founding of the *Rotterdamsche Bank* in 1863 and the *Amsterdamsche Bank* in December 1871. By the turn of the century, both banks were in the top five Dutch banks. 80 Per cent of the shares in the *Amsterdamsche Bank* were originally in German hands, and German capital also participated – although to a far lesser degree – in the *Rotterdamsche Bank*.[9] The *Amsterdamsche Bank* was intended to stimulate trade with Germany, to connect the German and Dutch money markets – the market for short-term loans – and to further the investment of foreign money on the Dutch market. This foreign capital was mostly of German origin, as the German money market was exceptionally liquid as a result of French payments after the Franco–Prussian War of 1870.[10] The Amsterdam capital market – the market for loans for a period of more than a year – was at that time an international capital market of some importance.[11] Partly as a result of a relative lack of domestic securities – Dutch companies preferred other means of financing their needs – Dutch investors were interested in foreign securities.[12] Considerable sums were invested in Europe, North and South America, Asia and Africa.[13] In particular Russian bonds, American mortgage banks, and American railroads were in high demand. Amsterdam was even a key financier of the latter.[14] Dutch investments in foreign securities grew from a total of *f*643 million in 1854–7 to *f*2,204 million in 1879–82, or *f*2,414 million when adjusted for deflation.[15] This was equivalent to 88 per cent of the average Gross Domestic Product at market prices (GDP) during the period 1854–7 and 195 per cent for the period 1879–82.[16] Possession of domestic securities remained fairly constant during the period, increasing from *f* 1,122 million to 1,190 million (1,282 when adjusted), which illustrates how few domestic securities were available at the time.[17] A generally favourable economic climate, starting around 1895 and lasting until the outbreak of the Great War, meant increased activity on the capital market, as not only established industries, but also new capital-intensive companies such as the chemical industry were attracting capital.[18] Domestic issues thus gained in volume at the expense of foreign issues. Nevertheless, on the eve of the Great War foreign securities (excluding Dutch colonial securities) still amounted to 47 per cent of the Amsterdam capital market.[19]

In contrast to the capital market, and despite the German interests in the Dutch banking sector that were mentioned earlier, the money market was almost entirely local.[20] The vast majority of funds were furnished as so-called *prolongatiekrediet*: renewable credit on a monthly basis, using stocks as collateral. Call loans (day-to-day loans), *beleeningen* (three month loans using stocks as collateral) and acceptances (also known as bills of exchange) were of negligible importance. Most Dutch imports and exports were financed through the London money market, with prices and bills of exchange made out in pounds sterling.[21] Much of the money involved in Dutch international trade thus bypassed the Amsterdam money market. As of July 1914, according to an inquiry by the *Nederlandsche Bank*, the volume of outstanding loans on the money market amounted to *f* 325 million.[22]

The First World War would drastically change the outlook of the Dutch money market. The crisis leading up to the outbreak of war on 28 July 1914 caused a disruption of the financial markets that resulted in the closure of the exchanges at Paris, Brussels, Frankfurt, Berlin and Vienna. In Amsterdam lenders – who, like many people, were expecting problems – wanted to be liquid and gave notice on their outstanding loans. Simultaneously, stocks were sold on a large scale and plummeted in value. This caused a similar decrease in value of the collateral on existing renewable credits.[23] The financial market was in crisis. The board of the *Vereeniging voor den Effectenhandel* – the private association regulating the Amsterdam exchange – decided to close the exchange for a single day on 29 July, so that measures might be taken to ensure the functioning of the exchange. However, this effort failed and the exchange remained closed, thereby extending all existing short-term renewable credit for an unknown period. This threatened to have disastrous consequences for Dutch businesses, as these had used short-term loans to manage funds that were temporarily surplus to requirements. With their money tied up in loans that were frozen for an indeterminate period, these companies were facing liquidity problems because the closing of the exchange also meant that new credit could not be obtained. A syndicate of bankers, backed by the *Nederlandsche Bank*, used their *Vereeniging voor den Geldhandel* (Banking association) to grant credit to those businesses that were facing financial difficulties as a result of the credit crisis. The plan could necessitate a growth of the money supply of *f* 200 million, while the situation was further complicated by a – albeit short-lived – run on savings accounts that had started on the 28th.[24] The amount of money in circulation therefore needed to be significantly increased. As the *Nederlandsche Bank* was bound by its legal obligation to keep gold coverage of paper money in circulation at 40 per cent, it could only increase circulation by *f* 100 million. On 31 July the gold standard was suspended. The minimum coverage of the banknotes in gold was decreased to 20 per cent, allowing the *Nederlandsche Bank* to increase the amount in circulation, effectively restoring stability of the Dutch financial institutions. Nonetheless, the exchange would not reopen until 9 February 1915, over a month after the London exchange.[25] Upon its reopening almost all of the formerly blocked renewable credits were repaid before the year was out, as many people made a profit on the sale of their American shares on the New York Stock Exchange and the amount of money available on the market increased rapidly.[26] This significant expansion of the money market was partly a result of the fact that the war severely impeded international trade. This resulted in the gradual selling out of stores by Dutch companies both at home and abroad, and a growing stream of the proceeds going to the Dutch banks. Another important factor was the influx of a growing amount of foreign capital – mostly from the Central Powers – in the form of shares and money. The latter consisted of the proceeds of German exports – many of which were destined for the Dutch colonies[27] – as well as Mark balances and cash.[28] Surprisingly, it would take until August 1916 before the German authorities took measures to stem the flight of capital.[29] Still, in 1923 prof. G. W. J. Bruins, a close friend of G. Vissering, the President of the *Nederlandsche Bank*, and therefore in an excellent position to adequately judge this, estimated the total amount of flight capital that had flowed from Germany to the Netherlands during the war and the subsequent period of inflation at between *f* 500 and *f* 800 million (equivalent to between 9.6 per cent and 15.3 per cent of Dutch GDP in 1923).[30] According to the German ministry of foreign affairs this was just over half of the total capital that had fled Germany during this period.[31]

The flight capital contributed to a marked increase of the gold reserves, as did the growing trade surplus. Although the Netherlands – being neutral – was able to trade with any country, imports were at a fraction of the pre-war level, and the usual trade deficit had become a trade surplus. To limit this influx of gold, and its potentially harmful economic effects, the *Nederlandsche Bank* took on a central role in the granting of credit for foreign trade.[32] It guaranteed the loans, on condition that it was consulted beforehand, and the loans were in the common interest.[33] As collateral, treasury issues and industrial issues in guilders were to be deposited at the Dutch banks. The *Nederlandsche Bank* closely monitored both the nature and adequacy of these issues.[34] As described by Richard Roberts in his paper on the London financial crisis of 1914, the London acceptance market – which had financed most of the international trade – broke down at the beginning of the war. The president of the *Nederlandsche Bank*, G. Vissering, recognized an opportunity to expand the Dutch acceptance market.[35] The acceptance market is a part of the money market where short-term credit (usually for a period of three months) is supplied in the form of acceptances. These acceptances can be divided in two main groups: financial bills and reimbursement credits. Both kinds are less expensive than other forms of short-term credit.

Reimbursement credits are used to finance the import and export of goods, and are self-liquidating as they use the goods they finance as security. It was the use of such reimbursement credits – in guilders – that Vissering promoted. Financial bills on the other hand were regarded as undesirable since these did not serve Dutch trade and were considered less secure. For the Amsterdam money market to be able to consolidate its new international stature, the use of acceptances in guilders was important. The stability shown by the Dutch guilder was a great help in this regard, the British journal *The Economist* stating as early as December 1915 that 'the position of the London exchange market is encroached upon by Amsterdam, so that Dutch currency has for the time being become a standard of value for other currencies'.[36] In spite of progressively decreasing foreign trade, the acceptance market expanded gradually. In 1913, the seven most important Dutch banks had a turnover of *f*62 million. In 1918 these banks reached their highest wartime turnover in acceptances at just over *f*77 million.[37] Given that the total amount of short-term loans due at the end of the war was *f*440 million, other forms of credit were thus still more popular. Most of these loans – *f*195 million and *f*142 million respectively, 44.1 per cent and 32.3 per cent of the sum total – were granted to Germany and Great Britain, which indicates the importance of Dutch trade with these countries. Austria-Hungary was the third most important debtor with *f* 85 million, followed by France (*f*12 million), Luxembourg (*f*4.4 million) and Belgium (*f*1 million).[38]

After the war, it turned out that loans granted to German customers amounted to even more than the *f*195 million recorded by the *Nederlandsche Bank*. A number of Dutch banks had not bothered to consult the central bank, and had granted an additional *f*113 million to German customers, bringing the total outstanding credit granted to Germany to *f*308 million or 55.7 per cent of the total.[39] All combined, the Central Powers accounted for 71 per cent of the loans to the combatants that were due at the end of the war. Whether the loans extended to others, such as the British, were higher as well, is unknown. As of 3 February 1919, the total outstanding loans to the former belligerents amounted to *f*499.3 million. Some of these loans had been granted after the war: as part of the General Agreement with the Allied powers, a credit of *f*123 million had been agreed upon, while *f*7.2 million had been loaned to others.[40]

Because of the uncertainty regarding the conditions of the Treaty of Versailles, which was under negotiation at the time, the German banks sought extensions on their loans. In Switzerland this resulted in a general *sauve qui peut* in banking circles, while payments to the Swedes – who had not demanded collateral on their loans – had stopped altogether.[41] Dutch bankers, however, remained calm, as not only had many loans already been repaid as they came due during the war, this had continued after the armistice.[42] Since the *Nederlandsche Bank* had consistently demanded a high quality of collateral for these loans – which may explain the high amount of unreported credit that some banks had granted to their German relations – most banks could afford to retain their composure. The *Nederlandsche Bank* continued to play a central role between the Dutch creditors and their German debtors, and showed a highly cooperative attitude towards the German debtors. Just a few days after the armistice, Vissering sent a telegram to Franz Urbig – as director of the *Disconto-Gesellschaft* one of the most influential German bankers – suggesting he send a representative to the Netherlands to discuss possible extensions on the German loans, some of which were due two days later.[43] Urbig came in person, and would remain in constant communication with the Dutch creditors throughout 1919.[44] Nevertheless, because of the uncertain political and financial situation in Germany – and despite additional collateral – Dutch banks were not eager to extend existing loans. A number of them instead were asking the *Nederlandsche Bank* for permission to call in their loans, permission they did not formally need and which shows how the *Nederlandsche Bank* wielded power in informal ways as well.[45] In response the *Nederlandsche Bank* called a meeting with the banks, where Vissering argued that they should agree to the German requests for extensions. He was backed by the larger banks, with Van Tienhoven of the *Rotterdamsche Bankvereeniging* stating 'it would be unwise if the Netherlands should be unwilling to respond to the need for credit in its hinterland'.[46] Refusing the extensions would not be in the best interests of the banks, as the result would be that 'the money would be repaid, but the Netherlands would be out of it commercially'.[47] The banks complied and the existing loans were extended, and paid in due time.[48]

While the Germans were seeking extensions on their loans, they were also approaching the Dutch banks for new credits. As most of these were not directly linked to the financing of Dutch–German trade, the *Nederlandsche Bank* was not in favour of this.[49] The policy of the *Nederlandsche Bank* during the war and immediately afterwards can thus be characterized as being geared towards using the Dutch financial market to ensure the continuation of Dutch international trade. Due to circumstances, in practice this meant predominantly the financing of trade with Germany. In the years to come, Dutch–German financial ties would grow stronger, as German companies and local and state governments increasingly turned toward Amsterdam's financial market, and a large number of German banks established themselves there.

Foreign Banks in the Netherlands

Germany needed to revive its international trade, and to do so it needed money to finance its imports and exports. Before the war, this had been mainly done in London, where all the important German banks had established branches. These, however, had been seized and liquidated by the British as enemy property. Furthermore, in the first few years after the war they no longer had access to the London money market.[50] Given post-war circumstances, German banks thus needed a neutral country to conduct their international financial business.[51] The Netherlands was a logical choice, not only because of its geographical location, but also because of the stability of the guilder, the low and stable interest rates, the low commission that was charged, and Dutch banking secrecy. As Norway and Sweden did not allow foreign banks to be set up, Switzerland was the only real competitor. However, Berne discouraged the establishment of foreign banks, had not yet embraced banking secrecy and was also regarded as being too isolated.[52] Already during the war, several German banks planned to establish themselves in the Netherlands,[53] resulting in the founding of the *Bank voor Handel en Scheepvaart* in July 1918 by Vulcaan Rotterdam, a subsidiary of the Thyssen concern that had already invested substantially before the war.[54] In December of the same year it was followed by the *Internationale Wisselbank*, whose German directors had been bankers in Belgium and France prior to the war. By March 1926, the *Nederlandsche Bank* listed no less than 69 financial institutions it regarded as 'foreign'. The number of newly founded institutions was even larger, as some only had a short lifespan. The branch of the *Standard Bank of South-Africa* for instance – which had been the first to establish itself in the Netherlands after the war – was not mentioned on this list.[55] Three of these institutions already existed before the war, while the remainder had been formed between July 1918 and March 1926 (Table 12.1). The overwhelming majority were of German or Austrian origin, and only six had their origins elsewhere: France, Liechtenstein, Sweden, the United States and Poland.[56] Because most of these new banks were of German origin, they were in common parlance referred to as 'German banks'.

Table 12.1. *Foreign financial institutions in the Netherlands, 1918 – March 1926.*

Year	Unknown	Pre-1918	1918	1919	1920	1921	1922	1923	1924	1925	March 1926
Newly established	2	3	2	4	11	10	5	18	11	2	1
Total		3	5	9	20	30	35	53	64	66	69

Source: Archive DNB; 7/831/1; Vestiging van buitenlandse banken in nederland. Overview 'Niet zuiver *Nederlandsche bank*instellingen, 26 Maart 1926' 'Niet zuiver *Nederlandsche bank*instellingen', 26 March 1926..

The majority of the new banks were subsidiary companies, and as such they were legally Dutch banks although their board of directors consisted mostly of Germans. Only the *Deutsche Bank* chose to open a branch.[57] The new banks had German business connections, German customers and German capital.[58] Many German industrial conglomerates, for instance, decided to ferry to Amsterdam the capital used for their foreign transactions. This was not only done to safeguard this capital; the favourable Dutch tax laws were also duly noted.[59] At first, the new banks limited their activities in the Netherlands to foreign exchange dealings and the managing of German funds, by supplying short-term loans to German industry and acquiring Dutch stocks and treasury bills.[60] Already in 1921, however, their activities were widening – much to the dismay of Dutch bankers – as they started to attract Dutch deposits at a to Dutch banks astonishingly high interest of 6–7 per cent. By lending highly rated currency such as dollars, pounds sterling, and guilders to Central European countries – mostly Germany – they were able to realize up to 12 per cent interest on these deposits.[61]

Foreign banks however, were not the only important companies to settle in the Netherlands. Because of the exceptionally favourable tax laws regarding double taxation, many international holding companies opted to locate their headquarters in the Netherlands.[62] Because of the importance of its financial centre, Amsterdam was a favourite location, thereby further expanding its role.[63] The foreign banks contributed to a broadening of the infrastructure of the Amsterdam financial market, while the capital that fled depreciation and taxation in Germany, Austria and the Balkans added to a growing supply of funds in search of short- and long-term investment.[64] The reasons why so many of these funds sought refuge in the Netherlands both during and after the war, are more or less the same as those that convinced the German banks, although in this case the fact that the Dutch banks guaranteed banking secrecy will have been especially important.[65] When the Mark was stabilized in the autumn of 1923, the German flight capital was only partially repatriated, as there was still taxation to be avoided and residual fears of depreciation still existed. Moreover, any decrease was more than offset by the capital, which by then started to pour in from Belgium, France and Italy, as a result of monetary difficulties in those countries.[66]

Nevertheless, although the influx of money from abroad was important, the funds generated by the Dutch economy should not be underestimated. Thanks to the rapidly expanding economy after the crisis of 1920 – between 1922 and 1924 Dutch GDP showed an average growth of 5.2 per cent, and 4.4 per cent during the period 1925–9 – each year considerable sums were in need of investment.[67] Additionally, every year some *f*200 million was paid out as dividends from the Netherlands-Indies, while many fortunes that had been amassed in the Indies were put to work on the Dutch capital and money markets.[68] Both the population and Dutch companies saved increasing amounts of money, starting during the war. Companies had little opportunity to invest their earnings in replenishing stocks, and they – as well as the general public – had turned increasingly towards savings banks and the stock exchange.[69] This would continue after the war, as the savings rate – for which data are available from 1923 on – rose from 4.4 per cent to 14.2 per cent of GDP in 1928. After 1929 it would decline.[70] Part of the reason for this high savings rate was the taxation policy at the time, which had no corporate tax: taxes were only payable on dividends.[71] Because many Dutch firms were family businesses, they would thus refrain from paying dividends, choosing instead to keep the money within the company. Saving thus brought considerable fiscal benefits. The role of flight capital was thus important, but was outweighed by a structural surplus of Dutch capital that was in excess of domestic requirements.

The Capital Market

After the war the capital market initially showed no sign of its prewar international orientation. Foreign issues were rare, while domestic issues showed a flurry of activity as the Dutch economy expanded and the Dutch government sought to finance its debts, which had grown considerably during the war (Table 12.2).[72] The new German banks were very active in this market, being especially interested in Dutch government bonds, and were considered to be responsible for the success of many post-war Dutch issues.[73] As the global economic crisis of 1920 set in, however, activity on the capital market was cut short. Although between 1920 and 1924 there were some foreign emissions, it was only with the end of the economic crisis and the re-adoption of the gold standard in 1925 by a number of countries – among them the Netherlands, Germany and Britain – that the international capital market expanded significantly (Table 12.2). While Amsterdam would remain significantly smaller than London and New York, until 1930 the volume of international emissions in Amsterdam was substantially larger than in Paris or any other continental market.[74] With regards to German bonds – few German shares were issued here – Amsterdam was even an important competitor to London, as during 1926 and 1927 significantly more German bonds were issued in Amsterdam than in London.[75] A growing number of bonds and stocks from other countries were also placed, but German bonds were in the majority. Between 1926 and 1928 – the heyday of Amsterdam as an international financial centre – 39.5 per cent of the foreign issues offered were of German origin, while France (13.6 per cent), Belgium (10 per cent), and the United States (7 per cent) were of far lesser importance.[76] These foreign issues usually offered a better return than the local ones, thus not only attracting foreign capital, but Dutch capital as well. As a result, they were often greatly oversubscribed.[77] According to the economic writer Th. Metz, by 1930 about 75 per cent of German issues remained in Dutch hands.[78] A survey by the *Netherlands Bank* in 1933 confirms this: over 47.500 replies were received, stating the total nominal value of the German bonds in Dutch possession as *f* 430.6 million, plus shares with a total nominal value of *f* 263 million.[79] These bonds were all dated after the German inflation, as the introduction of the new *Reichsmark* had made older bonds worthless. Of the German issues from 1926 up to and including 1928, over 51 per cent were done by industry, with banks (including mortgage banks) a distant second at 28.4 per cent. The bonds issued by the German state, its constituent states and local government comprised 13.7 per cent of all German issues floated in Amsterdam during these years.[80]

Table 12.2. *Bonds and stocks issued in the Netherlands 1918–31.*

	(in millions of guilders)			(in percentages of total emissions)	
Year	Netherlands and colonies	Foreign bonds and stocks	Total	Netherlands and colonies	Foreign bonds and stocks
1918	663.1	–	663.1	100	0
1919	1209.9	–	1209.9	100	0
1920	1213.5	1.7	1215.2	99.9	0.1
1921	500.1	17.5	517.6	96.6	3.4
1922	448.3	21.5	469.9	95.4	4.6
1923	298.9	10.8	309.7	96.5	3.5
1924	394.4	49.1	443.5	88.9	11.1
1925	233.4	155.7	389.1	60.0	40.0
1926	264.2	300.7	565.0	46.8	53.2
1927	210.0	379.6	589.6	35.6	64.4
1928	428.6	377.4	806.0	53.2	46.8
1929	402.0	162.4	564.5	71.2	28.8
1930	439.3	250.7	690.1	63.7	36.3
1931	264.7	42.2	307.0	86.2	13.8

Source: D. C. Renooij, *De Nederlandse emissiemarkt van 1904 tot 1939* (Amsterdam: De Bussy, 1951) p. 100; own calculations.

The capital export that resulted from the extraordinarily high number of foreign emissions – in 1926 and 1927 foreign emissions surpassed domestic emissions (Table 12.2) – was a matter of some concern for the government. Already in November 1925, an 'advisory committee on the admissibility of foreign emissions' was therefore called into being, which delivered its report nineteen months later.[81] Unsurprisingly, the report argued that the free movement of capital was essential for international payments, which – considering the importance of international trade for the Dutch economy – should not be hampered. Nevertheless, in cases where the national interests would be threatened, the government should be able to intervene. The committee questioned the effectiveness of a ban on foreign emissions however, since these could always be acquired abroad.[82] Other ways of establishing a measure of control were ineffective. Neither the *Nederlandsche Bank* nor the *Vereeniging voor Effectenhandel* had any real influence on the issues that were floated on the Amsterdam market, as the latter could only deny an official quotation on the exchange while the former could only refuse issues as collateral for loans. Since issues that were not accepted for quotation on the exchange found a substantial unofficial market in Amsterdam, the effect of such a refusal was limited.[83] While its refusal to ban foreign emissions indicates the importance of foreign trade, only the promotion by the Dutch government of the issues placed in Amsterdam as part of the Dawes plan in 1924 demonstrates clearly that whenever possible the government tried to steer the capital market towards financing German economic recovery.[84] The promotion of these loans was successful: after the United States, Great Britain and France – who for political reasons were forced to take a large share – the Dutch were the largest participants in the Dawes- and the Young loans.[85]

The Money Market

Much more than the capital market, the money market shows the extent of the economic ties between the Netherlands and Germany. When in July 1931 the *Stillhalte* – the agreement between Germany and its foreign creditors for a temporary reduction of interest payments and a temporary stop on repayments – was put into effect, Germany needed to take stock of its short-term financial obligations. Its obligations – detailed in Table 12.3 – show a remarkable correlation between the nature of the Dutch–German economic ties and the structure of Dutch short-term credit to its neighbour. Of all short-term credits granted by the Dutch to Germany, 67 per cent were from Dutch banks and companies to German companies. For the other major creditors, the United States and Great Britain, this was 28 per cent and 40 per cent respectively.[86] After the United States, the Netherlands was Germany's largest short-term creditor. More importantly, while American banks had predominantly furnished loans to German banks, Dutch banks financed German industry, agriculture and trade. In this aspect, the Dutch were by far Germany's most important creditor with 33.2 per cent of all short-term credit (Table 12.3). The same applies to the loans from foreign companies to German companies: with 22.6 per cent of all credit, again the Dutch were by far the most important creditors to Germany.

The structure of Dutch credits reflected the economic relations between the two countries, which were based on trade and transit shipping to and from Germany. By furnishing these loans, Germany could import products from the Netherlands and the Dutch East Indies, while German industry was enabled to import the raw materials it needed, which were mostly shipped through Rotterdam and from there were transported to the Ruhr by Rhine barge or train. Given the importance of acceptances in financing international trade and the fact that the Dutch acceptance market came to be the largest of continental Europe, it is therefore of interest to examine both the developments on the acceptance market, such as the growth of its volume, the role of the German banks, and the policy of the *Nederlandsche Bank*.

Table 12.3. *Germany's short-term debt by most important creditors as of 28 July 1931, in million Reichsmark.*

	Netherlands	U.S.A.	United Kingdom	France	Switzerland
Foreign banks to:					
German industry, agriculture, trade	793	389	506	50	507
German banks	458	1724	1083	279	621
German government bodies	18	116	65	24	63
Reichsbank and *Golddiskontbank*	0	210	21	5	0
Foreign trade and industry to:					
German trade and industry	587	491	318	163	333
German banks	189	201	38	128	325
Other foreign creditors to other German debtors	24	12	23	7	29
Totals:	2069	3143	2054	656	1878

Source: Archive DNB, 2.3/501/1, Duitslands schulden, German report 'Aufteilung der kurzfristigen ausländischen Kredite an Deutschland nach Gläubigern, Schuldern und Ländern (Stand v. 28.Juli 1931)', dated 10 December 1931.

A prerequisite for a flourishing acceptance market is the existence of an active currency market, because unless both buyer and seller are using the same currency, there will have to be a moment when currencies are converted. Before the war, there had been no such market of importance. However, due to the combination of post-war monetary instability in many countries and the volume of the Dutch money market, such a market came into being, as the German Mark was actively traded in Amsterdam. Because of diminishing activity of Dutch trade and industry during the war, account balances at the banks had grown considerably.[87] As these deposits could be requested at any moment, the banks were in dire need of short-term investments. Some of these were found in speculation *á la hausse* in the German Mark, which was steadily decreasing in value (but would not reach hyperinflation for some time) as it was thought over and over again that this time, the German currency really had hit rock bottom, and would start to rise again. Dutch civilians and banks bought large amounts of Marks, which the German banks were only too willing to sell as both they and the German population (which was speculating *á la baisse* on a similar scale) expected the Mark to decrease still further in value.[88] With an estimated daily trading volume of 5 million pounds (*f* 60.5 million at pre-war parity) the Amsterdam currency market was of great importance, but suffered tremendous losses.[89] This trading volume was only partly due to the German banks: several central banks from Central

Europe maintained large balances in Amsterdam to support their exchanges.[90] As the currency market (and the use of currency options to safeguard against the then frequently wildly fluctuating currencies) was exceedingly important for the development of the burgeoning acceptance market, the *Nederlandsche Bank* was also actively involved, using a substantial portfolio of foreign acceptances and currency in order to restrict sudden fluctuations in the exchange rate.[91]

The popularity of acceptances had started to grow during the war, causing the president of the *Nederlandsche Bank* to conclude in June 1917: 'The Dutch florin has assumed a far greater significance on the international money and bill market, and this fact will come into even greater prominence when at the conclusion of peace the international bill market has recovered its freedom of movement on all sides.'[92] He would turn out to be right, even though the 'freedom of movement on all sides' turned out not to apply to Germany. On the contrary, the Dutch acceptance (or bill) market would even gain extra impetus because of the restricted German access to international money and capital markets. During the latter half of the 1920s, acceptances comprised about 30 per cent of the volume of the money market.[93] Most of the acceptance credits were for German debtors: according to the director of the German bank *H. Albert de Bary & Co.* in Amsterdam, by February 1931 they accounted for 75 per cent of the acceptance market.[94] When comparing the statistics of the Netherlands bank (Table 12.5) with the statistics given in reports on the German debts at the time of the *Stillhalte*, this percentage seems credible. Within the Dutch business community, credit on *prolongatie* – a renewable loan using stocks as security – remained the financial instrument of choice, comprising 40–50 per cent of the money market.[95]

The development of the acceptance market was in no small measure the result of the policy of the *Nederlandsche Bank*. This institution not only strived to maintain a low and stable discount rate compared to competing financial centres, it also regulated the growth of the acceptance market.[96] To do so, it had two official instruments: firstly, it decided which banks were allowed to rediscount – i.e. sell – their acceptances to the central bank. Normally, the banks were limited by their own liquidity – the ratio of obligations to pay and their capability to do so – in the amount of acceptance credit they could grant. The option of rediscounting acceptances at the *Nederlandsche Bank* removed this limitation. The added security offered by the central bank transformed these acceptances into beloved instruments for short-term investment by the general public. Banks whose acceptances were eligible for rediscounting were thus able to resell these to the public, freeing money to grant new acceptances. As long as sufficient interest existed in acceptances as investment, this market was able to expand. Those banks whose acceptances were declared eligible for discount – bankable – were limited to a maximum amount payable based on the ratio between acceptances and the banks' own capital. This ratio – the second policy instrument of the

Nederlandsche Bank – was not a given, but depended on the risks involved with a particular portfolio. When the market was perceived to be unstable, or when either individual portfolios or the market as a whole focussed too much on a particular commodity, the bank would adjust the ratio.[97]

From the start, the policy of the *Nederlandsche Bank* was geared towards maximizing the use of the acceptance market to further Dutch economic interests. This is evident both from its promotion of reimbursement credits and from its policy regarding the eligibility for discount of acceptances. When in 1917 the acceptances created by Dutch banks were declared bankable, this was subject to prior consent by the central bank and their benefit to Dutch interests. In April 1922 the first rule was dropped – the paperwork caused delays that harmed trade as well as the growth of the sector – with the exception of larger acceptances and those of a special nature.[98] At that time, the German banks in Amsterdam were increasingly active on the acceptance market. Their acceptances were not bankable, and thus could not be sold in Amsterdam where there was no market for such acceptances. Therefore, these either had to be held in portfolio – limiting their volume of business – or they had to be sold in London or New York, where there was such a market.[99] Naturally, the German banks approached the *Nederlandsche Bank* with the request to declare their acceptances bankable as well. At first, the bank discussed the matter within its Commission of Advice, were the consensus was that there should be no discrimination against the new banks, as long as they were legally Dutch. Nevertheless, it was concluded that it would be prudent to see how these banks developed and whether they were here to stay.[100] When over a year and a half later the bank was again confronted with requests regarding rediscounting, the central bank decided to take soundings in the Dutch banking community. In a meeting of its Advisory Committee (*Commissie van Advies*) on 15 December 1922, and again on 22 December, their response – which was decidedly negative – was discussed.[101] In the judgement of both the Dutch banks and the *Nederlandsche Bank*, to grant the request would at that time not result in an expansion of the acceptance market. As the *Nederlandsche Bank* had no insight into the financial standing and activities of the German banks, the risks were also considered to be too great. In principle though, the majority of the members had no fundamental objections to granting the request at a later date. The following years, the question would arise regularly, every time resulting in a refusal. The reasons for this varied over time, from an assessment that the Dutch banks had more than enough capacity to ensure further growth – i.e. the German banks would only provide unwanted competition – to a belief that the German banks would exclusively use German companies in all aspects related to their acceptances: German shipping companies, insurance, etc. An important and probably decisive argument, which was shared by the *Nederlandsche Bank*, was that the stability of the guilder would suffer because it was feared the German banks would work on too large a scale for the Amsterdam market.[102] In the words of J. P. van Tienhoven of the *Rotterdamsche Bankvereeniging* – one of the most important banks – he was 'delighted when the German banks established themselves here and he would at this time [March 1923] not like to see them leave.'[103] He was, however, of the opinion that 'they only help the Amsterdam market, as long as they are prevented from endangering the guilder, in other words: as long as their acceptances are ineligible for rediscounting'.[104] The possibility that these banks would relocate to another country because of the continued refusal was considered to be negligible, as their acceptances would not be bankable there either.[105]

Early in 1924, a workaround was constructed: the German banks joined forces with Dutch banks, as well as banks from Switzerland, England and Sweden, and founded specialized acceptance institutions. In January and February, the *Internationale Bank*, the *Nederlandsche Accept Maatschappij*, and the *Internationale Crediet Compagnie* were founded. In October that year, the *Wolbank* followed. The latter specialized in the financing of the continental wool trade, which had shifted from Antwerp to Amsterdam after the war.[106] The reimbursement credits of these institutions were immediately declared to be eligible for rediscounting. In March 1925 – probably in anticipation of the return to the gold standard in April that year, and the renewed international competition this would bring – the *Nederlandsche Bank* dropped the requirement that the acceptances eligible for rediscount had to further Dutch interests, thus paving the way for further growth. Now, it merely required that the acceptances would not harm these interests. In November of the same year, the Bank also recognized the need for a more active role for bill brokers in order to assure a more even match between supply and demand on the bill market, which had been decidedly uneven. It enhanced the possibilities of the bill brokers to borrow money on acceptance credits, thereby enabling them to do more business.[107] It was in these circumstances, that W. Redelmeier, director of the German bank *H. Albert de Bary & Co.* in Amsterdam, decided to use the public opinion as a means to get the *Nederlandsche Bank* to declare the acceptances of the German banks eligible for rediscounting. In January of 1926, an article written by Redelmeier about the importance of the German banks in Amsterdam for the Dutch financial market appeared.[108] Redelmeier argued that the German banks should be allowed to rediscount their acceptances at the *Nederlandsche Bank*. This time, the plea did not fall on deaf ears. Firstly, the article started a broad discussion in the Dutch papers. The *Telegraaf* – a popular daily newspaper – for instance, remarked that while the German banks had become an important factor in the Amsterdam financial market, they had done so without undue competition with the Dutch banks. Yet they were still discriminated against, as they could not become a member of the stock exchange and their acceptances were ineligible for rediscounting.[109] Once again, the *Nederlandsche Bank* decided to do a survey of opinion within the banking community.[110] This was followed by a meeting of the board of directors with Redelmeier, who was asked how he envisioned the German banks would be able to promote further growth of the acceptance market.[111] Although the Dutch banks turned out to be still deeply divided on the issue, several influential bankers had changed position and were now in favour, albeit solely regarding self-liquidating reimbursement credits: acceptances used to pay for goods. The latter was a standard condition for the rediscounting of acceptances with the central bank, however, it was suspected that the German banks tried to disguise finance bills as reimbursement credits.[112]

All things considered, the board of the *Nederlandsche Bank* was convinced the measure would indeed promote further growth and on 25 March declared the acceptances of the German banks to be – albeit within certain restrictions – bankable.[113] This was unprecedented, as the German banks in London had never been granted this privilege by the Bank of England. It should however be noted that the German banks in Amsterdam were, with the exception of the branch of the *Deutsche Bank*, formally Dutch banks, whereas in London the German banks mostly had branches. Moreover, because of the volume of the London money market the German banks had never needed this privilege. Interestingly, due to circumstances beyond the control of the central bank, the rate their acceptance credits commanded on the market was still – and would continue to be – slightly above prime rate.[114] Another year would pass, before in May 1927 the constrictions regarding the rediscounting by German banks were lifted. As of that date, those banks wishing to have the ability to rediscount their acceptances with the central bank, only had to report these. Except for the provisions of the arrangement of April 1922, the acceptance market was now free of limiting regulations. However, all participating banks were allocated a maximum sum of acceptances based on their balance – which they had to provide for inspection – and the precise nature of the acceptances was checked as well.[115] The control by the *Nederlandsche Bank* of both the quality and the maximum volume of the bills in circulation was thus still very much intact.

Despite the strict policy of the *Nederlandsche Bank*, it is difficult to say just how much of the success of the Amsterdam acceptance market, which in 1930 – despite the re-emergence of Paris as an international financial centre after the stabilization of the Franc in 1926 – was the largest on the European continent, was due to its policy.[116] The Bank wanted to ensure a steady rather than explosive growth, as it regarded stability on the Amsterdam financial market a prerequisite for the long-term establishment of an international financial centre. That this conservative policy assured stable foundations for the acceptance market should be clear, and was demonstrated in July 1931 as Amsterdam banks remained unshaken when as a result of the *Stillhalte* all acceptances and many other financial claims on Germany were frozen.[117] Just how much its policy actually influenced the growth of the market is another matter. The market for acceptances that were automatically eligible for rediscounting following the stipulations of April 1922 – also known as 'Arrangement 4-22B' – started to expand during 1924, and reached a new plateau at an annual turnover of on average 735 million guilders during the period 1927–30 (Table 12.3). This was not the true turnover of the market as a whole, however. All acceptances used with regards to the financing of seasonal or storage credit, finance bills for companies, or acceptances for large sums had to be approved on a case-by-case basis by the Advisory Committee.[118] During the period of the expansion of the acceptance market, these specially approved acceptances remained fairly constant, albeit at a high level (Table 12.4).

Given the fluid nature of the money employed on the money market, and the acceptance market in particular, the interest rate was of great importance. The discount rate was lowered several times during 1924 and 1925, and from April 1925 until October 1927 Amsterdam was considerably cheaper than its competitors. When eventually the interest rate had to be raised, it was at the same level as London. When the latter raised its discount rate in early February 1929, the *Nederlandsche Bank* was able to refrain from doing so until over six weeks later.[119] A clear cause-and-effect relation cannot be established however, as the period coincided with growing German economic activity due to the end of the hyperinflation in November 1923 and the adoption of the Dawes plan in August 1924, and because the expansion on the Dutch market cannot be compared to developments in other financial centres.

Table 12.4. *Turnover of acceptances, as reported to the Nederlandsche Bank under the stipulations of April 1922 (arrangement 4-22B), 1922–32.*

Financial year	Total, in million guilders	Divided by financier, in percentages			
		Dutch banks	'German' banks	Acceptance banks	Other foreign banks
1922–3	36.2	100	0	-	0.0
1923–4	34.6	100	0	-	0.0
1924–5	59.0	95.1	0	4.9	0.0
1925–6	130.3	87.1	0	10.4	2.5
1926–7	368.8	80.9	0	14.7	4.4
1927–8	709.5	74.7	16.6	4.7	3.9
1928–9	707.5	78.6	15.8	3.3	2.4
1929–30	798.8	75.3	16.3	1.7	6.8
1930–1	723.9	76.7	15.1	6.1	2.1
1931–2	376.3	81.7	12.6	4.4	1.3

Sources: Archive DNB, 2.121.3/0010/1, Arrangement, betreffende discontabiliteit van wissels waaraan goederentransacties met buitenland ten grondslag liggen, arrangement, verstrekte opgaven gedurende een boekjaar. Miscellaneous reports for the period 1922-1933; own calculations.

Table 12.5. Acceptances reported to the Nederlandsche Bank, February 1926–April 1929 (in million guilders).

Year	Month	Arrangement 4-22B	Special arrangement	Total
1926	February*	45*	129*	174
	July	62	125	187
	October	72	84	156
1927	January	103	144	247
	April	125	169	294
	July	186	146	332
	October	182	144	326
1928	January	177	145	322
	April	162	137	299
	July	152	124	276
	October	161	124	285
1929	January	161	142	303
	April	224	141	365

Sources: Archive DNB, 2.121.3/0008/1, kredieten waarbij het buitenland betrokken is, N&E kredieten. Various reports, February 1926-April 1929; own calculations.

* The figures available for February 1926 are divided in unusual categories: 'Arrangement 4-22B', 'Special arrangements', and 'Acceptance banks'. On average, one third of the bills accepted by the special acceptance houses were part of arrangement 4-22B. The remaining two-thirds were granted special dispensation from the *Nederlandsche Bank*. Using this formula, the total for the acceptance houses has been distributed across the two categories. The figures for the other months are the figures as reported to the *Nederlandsche Bank*.

When the specialized acceptance banks were formed in 1924, their acceptances were immediately declared bankable. However, the market share of these new banks was small in proportion to the growth of the market during the same year (Table 12.3). When in March 1926 the German banks were allowed to rediscount their acceptances at the *Nederlandsche Bank*, followed by the decision, a year later, that they would have the same rights as the Dutch banks, these banks started to use the Amsterdam centre for part of the business they formerly conducted in London. The fears of both the Dutch banks and the central bank that the acceptance market would expand too fast because the German banks would conduct business on too large a scale – thereby endangering the stability of the guilder – proved unfounded. Because their acceptances were still above prime rate, the difference in cost between London, New York and Amsterdam was marginal, and they continued to do much of their business elsewhere. Again, the growth of the Dutch acceptance market was significantly larger than the market share of these banks. Considering that the available credit on the market always far exceeded the actual volume of acceptances, and their small market share compared to the expansion of the market, the policy regarding the German banks had a relatively small impact on the development of the market.

Of far greater importance where the general restrictions regarding the rediscounting of acceptances. When in March 1925 the condition that each acceptance credit should further Dutch economic interests was replaced by the condition that they should not harm these interests, the potential for growth was multiplied. That this decision was not made earlier is not surprising, as the Dawes plan had only been accepted six months before. Nevertheless the *Nederlandsche Bank* could have shown its faith in the German economy by revising its restrictions in August 1924. In view of the growth of the German economy that year, it is quite likely that the turnover of the acceptance market would have expanded a few months earlier.

Conclusion

Due to temporary circumstances, Amsterdam was able to expand and consolidate its newly attained position as an international financial centre, and would be the most important international financial centre of continental Europe during the period 1919–31. As a result of increasing monetary instability in Europe both during and immediately after the war, large amounts of flight capital from central European countries found a safe haven in Amsterdam. In its wake, no less than sixty-seven foreign – mostly German – banks were founded in the Netherlands as legally Dutch firms. That these banks should choose to settle in the Netherlands is not surprising. German banks no longer had access to London – which prior to the war had financed most of its international trade – and were therefore in need of a neutral financial centre. The Netherlands was a favoured choice, not only due to its stable monetary system, its favourable tax laws and good location, but also because of the significant economic ties that existed between the Netherlands and Germany. The Netherlands and its colonies were an important trading partner to Germany, and Germany was – together with Great Britain – the most important trading partner to the Dutch. Yet in spite of the influx of German capital and German banks, there was no convergence of the Dutch and German financial markets. Amsterdam never became a primarily German financial centre, were German banks met Germany's international financial needs using German capital. Instead, thanks to a large structural Dutch capital surplus that was now employed in Amsterdam rather than London, and because of the policy of the *Nederlandsche Bank*, Dutch banks had a leading role.

The strong Dutch–German economic ties were apparent in all aspects of the financial market. On the capital market, between 1926 and 1928, 39.5 per cent of all foreign emissions were of German origin, most of which were done by industry. In their efforts to help German economic recovery, the Dutch government not only granted a *f*200 million credit with the Coal and Credit Treaty of 1920, but also actively promoted the Dawes loan and did not ban foreign emissions from the Amsterdam capital market. However, a far more telling illustration of the nature of the economic bonds between both countries can be found in the money market. Of all short-term loans the Dutch granted to German debtors, 67 per cent were from banks and companies to German industry, trade and agriculture. For Germany's other two main creditors - the United States and Great Britain - this was 28 and 40 per cent respectively. Whereas the structure of its financial services clearly demonstrates the nature of Dutch–German economic interdependence, the extent of this interdependence is shown by the sheer scale of the Dutch credits to Germany: the Dutch were by far the most important creditor to German trade, industry and agriculture, far outstripping even the Americans. At the time of the *Stillhalte*, 27.7 per cent of all international credit for German trade and industry was supplied in Amsterdam. The Americans were a distant second with 17.7 per cent of the total.

The acceptance market – a part of the money market that was by its very nature geared to financing trade – was for the most part used to finance German trade. Of all credit granted there, 75 per cent was to German debtors, predominantly by Dutch banks. The development of this market is a good indicator for both the extent of the financial ties between the two countries, and of the policy of the *Nederlandsche Bank*. Although the German banks were welcomed by the Dutch banking sector, the *Nederlandsche Bank* did not grant these new banks the same privileges their Dutch counterparts enjoyed, mainly because the Dutch worried that the Germans would overpower and thereby weaken the Dutch financial market. Only as competition from other centres grew were the German banks gradually granted the same privileges. This increasing competition from other centres also led to a relaxation of the regulations with regards to the acceptance market as a whole, without the ill effects feared by the Dutch central bank. For although the German banks had a significant share of the burgeoning acceptance market, Dutch banks would retain their lead in the market as a whole and in the granting of short-term credit to Germany.

Overall, the policy of the *Nederlandsche Bank* can be characterized as focused on a stable growth of the acceptance market – and the financial market as a whole – while promoting Dutch economic interests as much as possible. Within the goals the *Nederlandsche Bank* had set itself, its policy can therefore be judged to have been successful. Meanwhile its policy regarding the German loans during the war and the extension of these loans after the German defeat shows that – although its main concern always was the stable development of the financial market – the *Netherlands Bank* was aware both of the importance of a German economic recovery and how the Dutch money market could both profit from, as well as help such a recovery.

Given the structure and volume of Dutch credit to Germany and the policies of the Dutch government as well as the *Nederlandsche Bank*, it can therefore be concluded that the Dutch used the Amsterdam financial market to actively promote German economic activity that was of benefit to the Dutch economy. The rise to prominence of Amsterdam as an international financial market and its focus on Germany was thus not part of a convergence of the Dutch and German financial markets, but rather an expression of the intense Dutch–German economic relations.

Acknowledgements

I am indebted to Hein A. M. Klemann, Joost Jonker, Ben Wubs and Drs. Martijn Lak for their helpful comments on an earlier version of this paper, and to the employees of the historical archives of the *Nederlandsche Bank* for their assistance.

NOTES

Baubeau, Introduction: The Convergence of National Financial Systems: Wishful Thinking or Irresistible Trend?

1. M. Friedman and A. J. Schwartz, *A Monetary History of the United States, 1867–1960* (Princeton, NJ: Princeton University Press, 1963). P. Cagan, *Determinants and Effects of Changes in the Stock of Money: 1875–1960* (New York and London: Columbia University Press, 1965).
2. J. Gurley and E. Shaw, *Money in a Theory of Finance* (Washington: Brooking Institutions, 1960).
3. A. Gerschenkron, *Economic backwardness in historical perspective. A book of essays* (Cambridge, MA: The Belknap Press of Harvard University Press, 1966).
4. Gerschenkron, *Economic backwardness,* p. 355.
5. R. W. Goldsmith, *Financial Structure and Development* (New Haven, CT and London: Yale University Press, 1969).
6. M. Amano, 'The Gurley-Shaw Hypothesis, Growth, Regressions and Granger-Caulsality', *Economic Journal of Chiba University,* 19:3 (December 2004), http://mitizane.ll.chiba-u.jp/metadb/up/AN10005358/KJ00003964075.pdf.
7. R. G. King and R. Levine, 'Finance and Growth: Schumpeter Might be Right', *Quarterly Journal of Economics,* 108:3 (1993), pp. 717–37.
8. J. Boyd and B. Smith, 'The Coevolution of the Real and Financial Sectors in the Growth Process', *World Bank Economic Review,* 10:2 (1996), pp. 371–96.
9. R. Sylla, R. Tilly and G. Tortella (eds), *The State, the Financial System and Economic Modernization* (Cambridge: Cambridge University Press, 1999).
10. D. J. Forsyth and D. Verdier (eds), *The Origins of National Financial Systems. Alexander Gerschenkron reconsidered* (London and New York: Routledge, 2003).
11. C Fohlin, *Finance Capitalism and Germany's Rise to Industrial Power* (Cambridge: Cambridge University Press, 2007).
12. M. Amano, 'The Gurley-Shaw Hypothesis'. P. L. Rousseau and P. Wachtel, 'What is happening to the impact of financial deepening on economic growth?', Department of Economics Vanderbilt University, Nashville, Working Paper n° 09–W15 (September 2009) at www.vanderbilt.edu/econ.
13. J. Robinson, 'The Generalization of the General Theory', in J. Robinson, *The Rate of Interest and Other Essays* (London: Macmillan, 1952), pp. 67 sq.
14. P. Verley, 'Convergence and divergence', in A. Iriye and P.-Y. Saunier (eds), *Dictionary of Transnational History* (London: Macmillan, 2009). I am very thankful to Patrick Verley for having provided me with a PDF version of this text.

15. F. Allen and D. Gale, 'Comparative Financial Systems: A Survey', Center for Financial Institutions Working Papers 01–15, Wharton School Center for Financial Institutions, University of Pennsylvania (April 2001).
16. For a discussion of these issues, see A. W. A. Boot and A. V. Thakor, 'Financial System Architecture', *The Review of Financial Studies*, 10:3 (1997), pp. 693–733. R. Levine, 'Bank-Based or Market-Based Financial Systems: Which is Better?', William Davidson Institute Working Paper 442 (February 2002). W. Carlina and C. Mayer, 'Finance, investment and growth', *Journal of Financial Economics*, 69 (2003), pp. 191–226.
17. R. Carney, 'The Political Economy of Financial Systems: why do developed countries have such financing arrangements?', Paper presented at the annual meeting of the American Political Science Association, Boston, Massachusetts (28 August 2002). R. La Porta, F. Lopez-de-Silanes, A. Shleifer and R. W. Vishny, 'Legal Determinants of External Finance', *The Journal of Finance*, 52:3 (July 1997), pp. 1131–50.
18. Gerschenkron, *Economic Backwardness*. Fohlin, *Finance Capitalism and Germany's Rise to Industrial Power.*
19. General introduction in M. Lescure, 'Banking and Finance', in G. Jones and J. Zeitlin (ed.), *The Oxford Handbook of Business History* (Oxford: Oxford University Press, 2008), pp.319–46. See also P. L. Rousseau and R. Sylla, 'Financial Systems, Economic Growth and Globalization', *NBER Working Paper 8323* (June 2001). D. J. Forsyth and D. Verdier (ed.), *The Origins of National Financial Systems.*
20. For example, see the first steps of institutionalized international monetary cooperation with the BIS, built by political will and refrained by political interests, but that was 'a non-negligible step in the long convergence process of monetary practices and doctrines in Europe' ('une étape non négligeable dans le long processus de convergence des pratiques et des doctrines monétaires en Europe'), O. Feiertag, 'Les banques d'émission et la BRI face à la dislocation de l'étalon-or (1931–1933) : l'entrée dans l'âge de la coopération monétaire internationale', *Histoire, Economie et Société*, 18:4 (1999), p. 736.
21. T. Kuhn, *The Structure of Scientific Revolutions* (Chicago, IL: University of Chicago Press, 1962).
22. As A. Smith himself stated long ago.
23. S. Vitols, 'The Origins of Bank-Based and Market Based Financial Systems: Germany, Japan and the United States', in W. Streeck and K. Yamamura (ed.), *The Origins of Non-liberal Capitalism, Germany and Japan in Comparison* (Ithaca, NY: Cornell University Press, 2001), pp. 171–99. This volume has been published in the series Cornell Studies in Political Economy, edited by P. Katzenstein.
24. P. J. Katzenstein, 'From Many One and From One Many: Political Unification, Political Fragmentation and Cultural Cohesion in Europe since 1815', Western Societies Occasional Paper N° 1 (Ithaca, NY: Cornell University, November 1974).
25. M. Harrison, 'The Frequency of Wars', The University of Warwick, Warwick Economic Research Papers n° 879 (2008). See also R. Carney, 'National Security and National Finance: Locating the Origins of Modern Financial Capitalism', European University Institute, EUI Working Paper RSCAS n° 2004/21 (2004).

1 Verley, Organization of National Financial Markets and Convergence of Practices: Institutions and Networks of Parisian Brokers in Nineteenth-Century Parisian Financial Markets

1. French state *rente* were the functional equivalent to consols: they were 3 or 5 per cent interest-bearing annuities tradeable on the Exchange with fiscal and legal privileges attached to them.
2. The *coulisse* (the wings, as in a theatre) was the unofficial part of the Paris financial market, trading securities not yet listed in the official market, a functional equivalent to the New York Curb. Stockbrokers trading in the *coulisse* were labelled *coulissiers*.
3. A. Aupetit, 'Le marché financier de Paris', in A. Aupetit, L. Brocard, J. Armagnac, G. Delamotte, G. Aubert, *Les grands marchés financiers. France (Paris et Province) – The great financial markets, London, Berlin, New York (...) (*Paris: Félix Alcan, 1912). The members of the *coulisse*, see note 2, above.
4. J. Armagnac, 'Le marché financier de Londres', in Aupetit, *Les grands marchés financiers*.
5. Clearly emphasised in P. Marguerat, L. Tissot and Y. Froidevaux (ed.), *Banques et entreprises industrielles en Europe de l'Ouest, XIX-XX siècles : aspects nationaux et régionaux* (Geneva: Droz, 2000).
6. P. Verley, 'Convergence and divergence', in A. Iriye and P.-Y.Saunier (eds), *Dictionary of Transnational History* (London: Macmillan, 2009).
7. According to our calculations.
8. According to our calculations, national income from the data collected by M. Lévy-Leboyer and F. Bourguignon, *L'économie française au XIXe siècle, Analyse macro-économique* (Paris: Economica, 1985).
9. For example S. Robert-Milles, *La grammaire de la Bourse. Traité pratique élémentaire des opérations de Bourse* (Paris: Flammarion, date unknown (successive editions, towards 1900–1910)).
10. As a translation of 'banquiers en valeurs'.
11. C.S., 20/11/1843, p. 338.
12. Forward markets – markets for futures – were first implemented in France during the eighteenth century. They developed again soon in the nineteenth century especially on the French *rente* (consolidated state annuities). The maturity of these futures was usually set at middle or end of month, at which term a general settlement occurred. But is was possible to prolong the future through a 'report' operation, until the next settlement date, which means that the futures could be eschew much later than the first settlement date.
13. Example of placing shares in the 'Houillères de la Grande-Veine' (CS, 21/2/1842).
14. The *remisier* (the remise was his revenue for intermediating between investors and brokers) is a half-commission man.
15. CS, 30/7/1867.
16. The Béjot family, for example, who after having an ancestor who ran the practice from 1819–31, took it over from 1858 and remained at its head until the end of the twentieth century.
17. Voir P. Verley, 'Les opérateurs du marché financier', in P.-C. Hautcoeur (ed.), *Le marché financier français au XIX siècle* (Paris: Publications de la Sorbonne, 2007), pp. 21–86.
18. Minutes of the Union Chamber of Stockbrokers, meetings of 29 October and 10 November 1911.
19. Archives of the Finance Ministry, B 33236.

20. For example J.-F. Jeannotte-Bozerian, *La Bourse, ses opérateurs et ses opérations* (Paris: Dentu, 1859), vol. 1, p. 83. G. Boudon, *La Bourse et ses hôtes* (Paris: G. Pedone-Lauriel, 1896), p. 233, suggested, with certain relevance apparently, a 1:20 ratio between both types of transactions.
21. The De Castro brothers, the Singer brothers, the Bardach brothers, the Pognon brothers, to name but the most famous.
22. For example a pleasant book, N. Lévy, *La Bourse en 1890* (Paris, bureaux de la 'Revue Théâtrale', date unknown), with humorous portraits of sometimes picturesque characters of the Parisian market of the time.
23. The banker Albert Kahn was also interested, between 1898 and 1905, in *Louis Bernard et Cie, Chauve, Lajeunesse et Cie, Albert Legat et Cie, Haramboure et Cie.*
24. Banquiers en valeurs à terme.
25. Banquiers en valeurs au comptant.
26. Chambre de compensation des Rentes françaises.
27. Cote du marché des banquiers en valeurs au comptant.
28. Up to the 1940 Act.
29. Defined as the proportion of existing links relative to the possible links between all the individuals of the group.
30. Bibliographic note: the legal aspects of the organization of the Parisian official market are handled in the voluminous legal literature of the nineteenth century. The people – stockbrokers and bank brokers and their companies have hardly been the subject matter of studies apart from P. Verley, 'Les opérateurs du marché'. The sources are mainly the archives of the SBF and the registries of the deliberations of the Union Chamber of Stockbrokers (designated here as CS).

2 Mastin, The Resistance of the Lille Marketplace to National Convergence: A Regional Financial System between Autonomy and Sclerosis, 1880–1914

1. *Crédit Lyonnais, Société Générale, Crédit Industriel et Commercial* and *Comptoir National d'Escompte de Paris* (*CNEP*) were the four 'big' French banks of the time, the only ones really national in scope and size. Called '*sociétés de credit*' at the time, we shall designate them as the national banks or national branching banks.
2. G. Tassin, *Le rôle du marché financier lillois dans le développement de l'économie du Nord-Pas-de-Calais, de 1882 à 1914*, doctoral thesis under the direction of Albert Broder (Créteil, Université Paris 12, 2000), vol. 1, p. 132.
3. J.-P. Hirsch, *Les deux rêves du commerce. Entreprise et institution dans la région lilloise (1780–1860)* (Paris: EHESS, 1991).
4. One of the first shareholders of the Mines de Lens, Charles Crespel-Tilloy, remained chairman of the board of administration of the Crédit du Nord from 1866 until he died in 1897 and also became chairman of the board of administration of the Etablissements Kuhlmann when their founder passed away in 1881.
5. The Lyon Stock Exchange counted thirty stockbrokers, those of Marseilles 16 (Bordeaux 18, Nantes 10, Toulouse 7).
6. J. Lambert-Dansette, 'Une institution financière au service du développement régional : la Compagnie des agents de change de Lille depuis sa création jusqu'au premier conflit mondial, 1801–1914', *Revue du Nord*, 170 (April–June 1961), p. 175.

7. During the wool crisis at the end of 1900, which impacted all securities, certain 'complicities around the ring' might account for the abnormal prolongation of the drop in prices which enabled 'a large number of important bankers in the region' to repurchase securities at ridiculously low prices and thereby to keep control over *collieries* in Lille.
8. Such as Emile Doucet, in Roubaix, mentioned by H. Bonin, *Histoire de la Société Générale, 1864–1890* (Geneva: Droz, 2006), p. 265.
9. Inspection report of the branch of the Banque de France (R.I.BdF) in Roubaix, November 1879.
10. R.I.BdF. Lille and Roubaix.
11. M. Lescure, A. Plessis (dir.), *Banques locales et banques régionales en France au XIXè siècle* (Paris : Albin Michel, 1999), pp. 330–1.
12. Crédit Lyonnais, 1893 balance sheets.
13. For two main reasons: the regional banks, thanks to more and more abundant deposits available, could 'feed' their paper longer; the competition of the national branching banks with their agency networks and more strongly of the 'outside Banque' market. A. Plessis, 'Les concours de la Banque de France à l'économie (1842–1914)', *États, fiscalités, économies. Actes du Vè Congrès de l'AFHE, juin 1983* (Paris: Publications de la Sorbonne, 1985), pp. 169–80.
14. By reason of the drop in its lending but especially in the discount rate between 1871 and 1897.
15. i.e. drawn and payable in the same town. The figures of local bills approximate very well those of finance bills.
16. M. Lescure, 'La formation d'un système de crédit en France et le rôle de la banque d'émission (1850–1914) : approche comparée', in O. Feiertag and M. Margairaz (ed.), *Politiques et pratiques des banques d'émission en Europe (XVII–XX siècle). Le bicentenaire de la Banque de France dans la perspective de l'identité monétaire européenne* (Paris: Albin Michel, 2003), p. 145.
17. Indeed, there was no point in seeking to accumulate volume by multiplying small transactions as in credit establishments, since the point to make profits at least sufficient to compensate for the increasing overheads resulting from the creation of branches and of auxiliary bureaus.
18. In April 1907: Charles Tiberghien & fils; Tiberghien frères; Motte-Bossut fils; Paul Desurmont & fils. In May 1911: the last three, plus the (Eugène) Motte group and the François Masurel Frères firm, a wool-spinning company in Tourcoing.
19. 0.2 million FF (MFF) in December 1905; 0.4 MFF in June 1906; 1.25 MFF in April 1907; 1.35 MFF in October 1908; 1.7 MFF from 1909 to 1911. 'Family paper' consists of non-commercial bills drawn on or endorsed by members of the family of the drawer.
20. By rediscounting, in the 1860s, the financial paper issued by the local banks to represent the overdrafts granted to their clients.
21. G. Tassin, *op. cit.*, p. 154 ; A. Straus, 'Les marchés régionaux de valeurs mobilières--: une approche comparative', *Banque et investissements en Méditerranée à l'époque contemporaine, Actes du colloque de Marseille*, 4–5 February 1982 (Marseille: Chambre de commerce et d'industrie de Marseille, 1985), pp. 131–51.
22. 67 in 1892, 150 in 1913.
23. In average annual gross flows: 4.6 M.F (1883–1893); 14.2 M.F (1894–1900); 20.1 M.F (1901–1908); 57.4 M.F (1909–1914).

24. G. Tassin, *Le rôle du marché financier lillois*: Average number of quotations calculated from the total of the quotations in the second semester: 9 in 1895; 24 in 1900; 36 in 1905; 40 in 1910; 52 in 1914 (first semester).
25. Created essentially since 1911, in Gallicia and Romania, by the industrialists and the merchants in Lille, Roubaix, Tourcoing.
26. Société anonyme.
27. La Czenstochovienne (S.A. created in 1900) and the Manufacture de jute d'Odessa (created in 1909). These investments in jute and in the Russian Empire represented a double risk for a group centred on wool and cotton.
28. G. Tassin, *Le rôle du marché financier lillois*. J. Lambert-Dansette, 'Une institution financière au service du développement régional', pp. 159–99.
29. P.-C. Hautcœur, 'Le marché financier entre 1870 et 1900', in Y. Breton, A. Broder, M. Lutfalla, *La longue stagnation en France: l'autre grande dépression, 1873–1897* (Paris : Economica, 1997), pp. 235–65.
30. A. Straus, 'Les marchés régionaux de valeurs mobilières. P. Cornut, *Répartition de la fortune privée en France par département et nature de biens au cours de la première moitié du XX siècle (*Paris: A. Colin, 1963).
31. P.-C. Hautcoeur, 'Le marché financier entre 1870 et 1900'.
32. J. Lambert-Dansette, 'Une institution financière au service du développement régional', pp. 177–9.
33. According to agreements executed between both companies, the Parisian stockbrokers granted the Lille stockbrokers a 40 per cent discount for forward market business and a 15 per cent discount for amounts carried forward, J. Lambert-Dansette, 'Une institution financière au service du développement régional', p. 177–9).
34. In a *Confidential note to the Colliery companies of the Nord and of the Pas-de-Calais*, signed by the Compagnie of the Lille stockbrokers, printed in January 1901, one can read about collieries' stock values a confessed conflict of interest: 'In our region these stock values are so highly rated and available in such quantities in local portfolios that they probably account for over one hundred million Francs just with the relatives or allied of the Lille stockbrokers, which cannot but increase and stimulate the interest and the popularity they have always shown for large Colliery companies.' (Archives du Monde du Travail, Roubaix, 1994 055 099: archives of the Mines de Lens).
35. *Confidential note to the Colliery companies of the Nord and of the Pas-de-Calais*, January 1901 (Archives du Monde du Travail, Roubaix, 1994 055 099: archives of the Mines de Lens).
36. P. Pouchain, *Ébauche d'une histoire du Crédit du Nord de la fondation à 1939*, mémoire de DES (Lille, 1969).
37. J. Laloux, *Le rôle des banques locales et régionales du Nord de la France dans le développement industriel et commercial* (Paris : Giard, 1924), p. 136.
38. CIC was the Paris bank of the Union of Provincial Banks, providing market access, funds, technicality and so on to provincial banking partners.
39. G. Tassin, *Le rôle du marché financier lillois*.

3 Oosterlinck and Riva Competition among the French Stock Exchanges during the Second World War

1. S. B. Ramos, 'Competition between exchanges: A survey', *FAME Research paper n°77* (2003), p. 35.
2. W. O. Brown, J.H. Mulherin and M. D. Weidenmier, 'Competing with the NYSE', *NBER Working Paper* 12 343 (2006), p. 59.
3. R. Girault, *Emprunts russes et investissements français en Russie 1887–1914* (Paris: Armand Colin, 1973).
4. P.-C. Hautcoeur and A. Riva, 'The Paris Financial Market in the 19th Century: an efficient multi-polar organisation?', paper presented at the Conference of the European Historical Economics Society 2007 in Lund (Sweden) (June 2007).
5. W. O. Brown, J. H. Mulherin and M. D. Weidenmier, 'Competing with the NYSE'.
6. E. White, 'Competition among the exchanges before the SEC: Was the NYSE a natural hegemon?', Rutgers University, Mimeo (2007).
7. R. Dubost, *La Bourse de Lyon* (Lyon: Bosc frères M. & L. Riou, 1938), pp. 174–5.
8. Dubost, *La Bourse de Lyon*.
9. K. Oosterlinck, 'The Bond Market and the Legitimacy of Vichy France', *Explorations in Economic History*, 40:3 (2003), pp. 327–45; F. Occhino, K. Oosterlinck and E. White, 'How much can a victor force the vanquished to pay?', *Journal of Economic History*, 68:1 (2008), pp. 1–45; P. Lagneau-Ymonet and A. Riva, 'L'épuration à la Bourse de Paris', in D. Barjot, P. Fridenson, H. Joly and M. Margairaz (eds.), *L'épuration économique en France à la libération* (Rennes: Presses Universitaires de Rennes, 2008); K. Oosterlinck, 'French Stock Exchanges and Regulation during World War II', *Financial History Review* (2010), forthcoming.
10. R. Guillorit, *La réglementation des bourses de valeurs en France depuis juin 1940 : Transition ou parenthèse?* (Paris: Librairie Générale de Droit et de Jurisprudence, 1946); K. Oosterlinck, 'French Stock Exchanges and Regulation during World War II'.
11. Archives nationales (AN) AJ 40 vol. 832.
12. R. Guillorit, *La réglementation des bourses de valeurs en France*, p. 42.
13. The Paris bourse was reopened for a week (30 July 1940–7 August 1940) before being closed by the German occupation forces.
14. J. Koebe, 'Das Französische Börsenwesen', *La revue économique franco-allemande, organe du centre en France des organisations économiques allemandes*, 39 (1944), pp. 3–8.
15. AN AJ 40 vol. 832.
16. Archives de la Compagnie des agents de change de Lyon (ACACL), 24 December 1940.
17. W. O. Brown, J.H. Mulherin and M. D. Weidenmier, 'Competing with the NYSE'.
18. 500 000 FF/day. Assumptions consider 52 weeks of 5 days (holidays are not taken into account but Saturdays are also omitted).
19. Between 70 and 80 millions/day.
20. Between 100 and 120 millions/day.
21. Between 60 and 70 Million FF/day for the first quarter of 1944. AN AJ40 vol. 832, Reisevermerk, 4 July 1944.
22. Not taking into account the other exchanges and the coulisse.
23. AN AJ40 vol. 832 'Bericht der Lille Börse', 30 June–7 July 1941.
24. See Le Bris, in this volume.
25. AN AJ 40 vol. 832. Report dated 12 April 1943.

26. Free translation: Professional Organization Committee for Banks and Financial Institutions.
27. Archives de la Compagnie des Agents de Change de Paris (ACACP), Reports of the meeting, 22 December 1941.
28. Stock Exchange Committee.
29. R. Guillorit, *La réglementation des bourses de valeurs en France*, p. 112.
30. The French state-controlled central bank.
31. J. Koebe, 'Das Französische Börsenwesen', p. 5.
32. R. Guillorit, *La réglementation des bourses de valeurs en France*, pp. 112–13.
33. See P. Verley, in this volume.
34. According to a German report dated 3 September, 1940 (AN AJ 40 vol. 832).
35. R. Guillorit, *La réglementation des bourses de valeurs en France*. A German report dated from 3 September 1940, states that out of 89 curb brokers, 43 were 'non-Aryan', AN AJ 40 vol. 832.
36. J.-M. Dreyfus, *Pillages sur ordonnance. Aryanisation et restitution des banques en France 1940–1953* (Paris: Fayard, 2003); P. Lagneau-Ymonet and A. Riva, 'L'épuration à la Bourse de Paris'.
37. ACACP, Reports of the meeting, 16 December 1940.
38. Securities Brokers.
39. R. Guillorit, *La réglementation des bourses de valeurs en France*, p. 110.
40. In 1943, Lievin and Hydro-Energie would follow this path.
41. ACACL, Reports of the meeting, 22 December 1942.
42. R. Guillorit, *La réglementation des bourses de valeurs en France*, p. 197.
43. The 1940 increase is underestimated in the *timbres* (stamps) statistics because they are paid only on officially listed securities transactions. The official listing of national securities took place in Lyon from 1941 on.
44. 'Une occasion inespérée de profiter d'une période de prospérité exceptionnelle et de donner à notre marché une activité susceptible de persister après la suppression des zones', ACACL, Reports of the meeting 24 December 1940.
45. 'une vie nouvelle allait commencer pour la bourse de Lyon' ACACL, Reports of the meeting, 24 December 1940.
46. Within the framework of the circuit, the government tried to render shares less interesting than public bonds.
47. ACACL, Reports of the meeting, 23 December 1941. In March–April 1941 a new law would reduce the maximum legal price increase to 3 and 1.5 per cent.
48. A French public state-sponsored financial body, it was one of the main bond issuers in France at the time.
49. The Caisse Centrale des Dépôts et Virements de Titres was a clearing and delivery system created to manage the registration of all traded securities for supervision and fiscal purposes, following the law passed on 28 February 1941.
50. By comparison, these increases are not so impressive however since the Paris Bourse employed in 1942 close to 800 employees.
51. Value in real terms of the figures, allowing for retail or industrial prices and overall increase in quotation values.
52. 'en temps normal, tout titre coté à Paris est pour nous perdu' ACACL.
53. 'Ces courtages nous auraient semblé exceptionnels avant 1940', ACACL.

54. 'L'avenir de notre marché dépend aussi de décisions d'ordre général ... Avant 1940, Paris seul existait. Maintenant, nous n'avons pas la première place, mais avons une situation prépondérante à Paris', ACACL.
55. 'Nous devons prévoir le pire', ACACL.
56. Reports of the meetings, Archives de la Compagnie des Agents de Change de Marseille (ACACM), 17 December 1940.
57. 'il est juste et nécessaire que notre Compagnie maintienne et développe son activité et par là même son rôle dans l'économie générale du Pays'. ACACM, Report of the meetings, 15 December 1942.
58. ACACM, Report of the meetings, 13 February 1943.
59. This rate has been increased from 25 up to 35 per cent in the aftermath of the 1930 crisis for attracting new orders in Marseille.
60. It is worth noting that the Parisian brokers accepted the proposal from the Marseille Committee only after they offered their common solidarity on this kind of operations.

4 Le Bris, Shocks Impact on Long Term Market Correlations. Portfolio Diversification and Market Integration between France and the United States

1. J. Siegel, *Stocks for the Long Run* (Burr Ridge, IL: Irwin Professional Publishing, 1994).
2. P. T. Spiller and, C. J. Huang, 'On the extent of the market: wholesale gasoline in the Northern United States', *Journal of Industrial Economics*, 35:1 (1986), pp. 131–45.
3. K. H. O'Rourke and J. G. Williamson, *Globalization and History: The Evolution of a Nineteenth Century Atlantic Economy* (Cambridge: MIT Press, 1999).
4. K. H. O'Rourke and J. G. Williamson, 'Late 19th century Anglo-American factor price convergence: were Heckscher and Ohlin right?' *Journal of Economic History*, 54 (1994), pp. 892–916.
5. R. Findlay and K. H. O'Rourke, 'Power and Plenty: Trade, War and the World Economy in the Second Millennium (Preface)', *Trinity Economics Papers*, 0107 (2007).
6. C. Hoag, 'The Atlantic Telegraph Cable and Capital Market Information Flows', *Journal of Economic History*, 66:2 (2006), pp. 342–53.
7. Y. Kaukiainen, 'Shrinking the world: Improvements in the speed of information transmission, 1820—1870', *European Review of Economic History,* 5:1 (2001), pp. 1–28.
8. M. Feldstein and C. Horioka, 'Domestic Saving and International Capital Flows', *Economic Journal,* 90 (1980), pp. 314–29.
9. M. Obstfeld and A. M. Taylor, 'Globalization and Capital Markets', *NBER Working Paper,* 8846 (2002).
10. D. Le Bris and P. C. Hautcoeur, 'Challenge to the Triumphant Optimists. A Blue Chips Index for the Paris Stock Market, 1854–2006', *Financial History Review*, forthcoming (2010).
11. R. Rajan and L. Zingales, 'The Great Reversals: The Politics of Financial Development in the 20th Century', *NBER Working Paper*, 8178 (2001).
12. M. Obstfeld and A. Taylor, 'The Great Depression as a Watershed: International Capital Mobility over the Long-Run' in M. Bordo, C. Goldin and E. White (eds), *The Defining Moment: The Great Depression and the American Economy in the Twentieth Century* (Chicago, IL: University of Chicago Press, 1998).

13. M. Flandreau and F. Zumer, *The Making of Global Finance. 1880–1913* (Paris: OECD, 2004).
14. P. Mauro, N. Sussman and Y. Yafeh, 'Emerging Market Spreads: Then Versus Now', *Quarterly Journal of Economics,* 117:2 (2002), pp. 695–733.
15. N. Ferguson and M. Schularick, 'The Empire Effect: The Determinants of Country Risk in the First Age of Globalization, 1880–1913', *Journal of Economic History,* 66:2 (2006), pp. 283–312.
16. M. Edelstein, *Overseas Investment in the Age of High Imperialism: the United Kingdom* (New York: Columbia University Press, 1982).
17. Edelstein, *Overseas Investment in the Age of High Imperialism.*
18. M. A. Clemens and J. G. Williamson, 'Wealth Bias in the First Global Capital Market Boom, 1870–1913', *Economic Journal,* 114:495 (2004), pp. 304–37.
19. W. Goetzmann and A. Ukhov, 'British Overseas Investment 1870–1913: A Modern Portfolio Theory Approach', *Review of Finance,* 10:2 (2006), pp. 261–300.
20. From Edelstein, *Overseas Investment in the Age of High Imperialism.*
21. C. A. Michalet, *Les placements des épargnants français de 1815 à nos jours* (Paris: PUF, 1968).
22. A. Parent and C. Rault, 'The Influences affecting French Assets abroad Prior to 1914', *The Journal of Economic history,* 64:2 (2004), pp. 328–62.
23. D. Le Bris, 'Why did French Savers Buy Foreign Assets before 1914? The Decomposition of the Diversification Benefit', *Discussion Paper* presented at the Eurhistock Madrid (2008).
24. Siegel, *Stocks for the Long Run.*
25. W. Goetzmann, Ibbotson R. and L. Peng, 'A New Historical Database for the NYSE 1815 to 1925: Performance and Predictability', *The Journal of Financial Markets,* 4:1 (2000), pp. 1–32.
26. Cowles (1871–1924) and S&P according to Shiller's data online.
27. Discount rate of the Bank of France, the French central bank, funded 1800.
28. Currency rate were almost stable during this period, except between 1862–1877. The US dollar had been on the gold standard since 1879.
29. The p-value of equal average (T-test) is 91,42 per cent. This result needs to be viewed very carefully since a valid T-test needs three conditions not met in this kind of series: a Gaussian distribution, independence and a similar size for the series variances. A shorter period analysis (1854–1904) indicates only a 3 per cent probability of equal mean for the Sharpe ratio. A rolling window T-test shows a probability of equal Sharpe ratio decreasing during the First World War to a minimum of 36 per cent on April 1922 followed by a huge increase to 99 per cent in July 1924. A vertical fall leads the t-test to 0 per cent in October 1927.
30. F. Black, M. C. Jensen and M. Scholes, 'The Capital Asset Pricing Model: some Empirical Tests', in M. C. Jensen (ed.), *Studies in the Theory of Capital Markets* (New-York: Praeger, 1972).
31. French stocks and Rente 3 per cent are measured by author; discount rate of the Bank of France comes from INSEE's Statistical Yearbooks ; US Bonds and Bills and UK Bonds and bills, come from S. Homer and R. Sylla, *A History of interest rates* (New Brunswick, NJ: Rutgers University Press, 1998).
32. Goetzmann and Ukhov, 'British Overseas Investment 1870–1913'.

33. H. Markowitz, *Portfolio selection: Efficient diversification of Investments* (New York: John Wiley, 1959).
34. Michalet, *Les placements des épargnants français*, p. 147.
35. B. Solnik, 'Why not diversify internationally rather than domestically?', *Financial Analyst Journal*, 30 (1974) pp. 48–54.
36. These portfolios and the calculations on their risks and returns are built on the hypothesis that their returns derive only from the variations in quoted prices and dividends, but not of strategies such as short sales and option operations. While restrictive given the extent of futures operations on the French and US markets before WW1 (see Riva and Oosterlink, this volume), this hypothesis helps calculating the underlying return and risk profiles on the two markets, which is our main goal in this paper. Allowing short sales does not change the optimal combination indicated in Figure 4.3.
37. S. Kandel, R. McCulloch and R. F. Stambaugh, 'Bayesian inference and portfolio efficiency', *Review of Financial Studies,* 8 (1995), pp. 1–53.
38. Michalet, *Les placements des épargnants français*, p. 147.
39. Goetzmann and Ukhov, 'British Overseas Investment 1870–1913'.
40. Using data from eight emerging markets over 1977–2000 period, F. Carrieri, V. Errunza and K. Hogan, 'Characterizing World Market Integration through Time', *Journal of Financial and Quantitative Analysis*, 42:4 (2007), pp. 915–40, provide evidence on the impropriety of directly used correlation of market-wide index returns as a measure of financial integration.
41. F. Longin and B. Solnik, 'Is the Correlation in International Equity Returns Constant: 1960 – 1990?' *Journal of International Money and Finance,* 14:1 (1995), pp. 3–26.
42. Mauro, Sussman and Yafeh, 'Emerging Market Spreads'.
43. W. Goetzmann, L. Lingfeld and G. Rouwenhorst, 'Long-Term Global Market Correlations', *Journal of Business*, 78:1 (2005), pp. 1–38.
44. Obstfeld and Taylor, 'Globalization and Capital Markets'.
45. Goeztman, Lingfeld and Rouwenhorst, 'Long-Term Global Market Correlations' or Obstfeld and Taylor, 'Globalization and Capital Markets'.
46. B. Dumas, C. Harvey and P. Ruiz, 'Are Correlation of Stock Returns Justified by Subsequent Changes in National Output?', *Journal of International Money and Finance*, 22:6 (2003), pp. 777–811.
47. M. Levy-Leboyer and F. Bourguignon, *L'Économie Française au XIXème siècle, analyse macroéconomique* (Paris: Économica, 1985) and INSEE for France and Stats-USA for the United States.
48. K. F. Forbes and R. Rigobon, 'No Contagion, Only Interdependence: Measuring Stock Market Co-movements', *The Journal of Finance*, 57:5 (2002), pp. 2223–61.
49. Le Bris and Hautcoeur, *'Challenge to the Triumphant Optimists'.*

5 Brambilla, Assessing Convergence in European Investment Banking Patterns until 1914

1. D. Landes, 'Vieille banque et banque nouvelle: la révolution financière du XIXe siècle', *Revue d'histoire moderne et contemporaine,* 3 (1956), pp. 204–22; R. Cameron, *France and the Economic Development of Europe, 1800–1914; Conquest of Peace and Seeds of War* (Princeton, NJ: Princeton University Press, 1961).
2. Cameron, *France.*

3. Starting from the 1860s, laws on joint stock companies underwent a process of progressive liberalization in Europe, see C. P. Kindleberger, *A Financial History of Western Europe* (London: Allen & Unwin, 1984).
4. Landes, 'Vieille banque et banque nouvelle'; B. Gille, 'La fondation de la Société Générale', *Histoire des entreprises*, 1961, pp. 5–64.
5. R. Cameron, 'Founding the Bank of Darmstadt', *Explorations in Entrepreneurial History*, 8:3 (1956), pp. 113–30; Cameron, *France*; R. Tilly, *Financial institutions and industrialization in the German Rhineland, 1815–1870* (Madison, WI: University of Wisconsin Press, 1966); R. Tilly, 'Germany, 1815–1870', in R. Cameron et al. (eds.), *Banking in the early stages of industrialization* (New York: Oxford University Press, 1967), pp. 151–82.
6. See for instance, among others, Gille, 'La fondation de la Société Générale'; E. Bussière, *Paribas 1872–1992, L'Europe et le Monde* (Antwerp: Fonds Mercator, 1992); J. Riesser, *The German great banks and their connection with the economic development of Germany*, 1st edn 1911 (New York: Arno Press, 1977); K. E. Born, *International banking in the 19th and 20th centuries* (Leamington Spa: Berg Publishers Ltd, 1983); A. M. Galli, 'Sviluppo e crisi della Banca generale', in E. Decleva (ed.), *Antonio Allievi, dalle scienze civili alla pratica del credito* (Milan-Bari: Cariplo-Laterza, 1997), pp. 561–651.
7. Owing to their failure in 1893–4 and the almost complete loss of their archives, we have but little information about Credito Mobiliare Italiano and Banca Generale. The former was founded under the aegis of Pereire brothers' Crédit Mobilier, with the participation of outstanding Italian bankers, such as Bastogi and Balduino; while the latter was constituted in Milan by a group of Italian and Centre-European bankers, among whom were Bischoffsheim and Goldschmidt. See M. Pantaleoni, *La caduta della Società generale di credito mobiliare italiano [1895]* (Turin: Utet, 1998); G. Luzzatto, *L'economia italiana dal 1861 al 1894* (Turin: Einaudi, 1993); A. Polsi, *Alle origini del capitalismo italiano. Stato banche e banchieri dopo l'Unità* (Turin: Einaudi, 1993); Galli, 'Sviluppo e crisi'.
8. On their origins and groups of control see A. Confalonieri, *Banca e industria in Italia, 1894–1906* (Bologna: Il Mulino, 1981), vol. 2 and P. Hertner, *Il capitale tedesco in Italia dall'Unità alla prima guerra mondiale: banche miste e sviluppo economico italiano* (Bologna: Il Mulino, 1984); as for their character of German-style banks see, among others, J. S. Cohen, 'Financing industrialization in Italy, 1894–1914: The Partial Transformation of a Latecomer', *Journal of Economic History*, 27 (1967), pp. 363–82; G. Mori, 'L'economia italiana dagli anni Ottanta alla prima guerra mondiale', in *Storia dell'industria elettrica in Italia*, vol. 1, *Le origini 1882–1914* (Bari: Laterza, 1992), pp. 1–106; C. Fohlin, 'Capital Mobilisation and Utilisation in Latecomer Economies: Germany and Italy Compared', *European Review of Economic History*, 2 (1999), pp. 139–74.
9. Confalonieri, *Banca e industria in Italia 1894–1906;* Id., *Banca e industria in Italia dalla crisi del 1907 all'agosto del 1914* (Milan: Banca commerciale italiana, 1982); G. Toniolo, *An economic history of liberal Italy, 1850–1918* (London and New York: Routledge, 1990); G. Federico and G. Toniolo, 'Italy', in R. Sylla and G. Toniolo (eds.), *Patterns of European industrialization: the nineteenth century* (London and New York: Routledge, 1991), pp. 197–217; G. Conti, 'Le banche e il finanziamento industriale', in F. Amatori et al. (eds.), *Storia d'Italia, Annali*, 15, *L'industria* (Turin: Einaudi, 1999), pp. 441–504.
10. J. Bouvier, *Le krach de l'Union Générale 1878–1885* (Paris: Presses Universitaires de France, 1960); J. Bouvier, *Le Crédit Lyonnais de 1863 a 1882: les années de formation d'une banque de dépôts*, 1 edn 1961 (Paris: EHESS, 1999); H. Bonin, *Histoire del la Société Générale 1864–1890* (Geneva: Droz, 2006).

11. J. Bouvier, 'Les monnaies et les banques', in P. Leon (ed.), *Histoire économiques et sociale du Monde* (Paris: Colin, 1978), IV, pp. 225–97; M. Lévy-Leboyer, 'Le crédit et la monnaie', in F. Braudel and E. Labrousse (eds), *Histoire économique et sociale de la France* (Paris: Presses universitaires de France, 1976), I, 3, pp. 347–471; M. Lévy-Leboyer and M. Lescure, 'France', in Sylla and Toniolo, *Patterns of European Industrialization*, pp. 153–74. See also M. Lescure, 'La banque et le financement de l'économie', in B. Dejardins et. al. (eds.), *Le Crédit Lyonnais 1863–1986* (Geneva: Droz, 2003), pp. 363–6.
12. As it is well known, the Crédit Mobilier is not the first continental big joint stock investment bank, this primacy belongs to the Société Générale de Belgique, but it has been a paradigm to which all other 'new banks' in Europe and in particular in the three countries, refer.
13. The Crédit Lyonnais for instance had three different profits and losses accounts, one for the general manager and his staff, one for the board of directors and one for shareholders; see Bouvier, *Le Crédit Lyonnais*, p. 164.
14. Clustering was computed using the statistical package R. The single linkage method presents the advantage of being independent from the particular shape of the cluster to be found and thus of showing the natural distribution of objects in groups or categories; see J. A. Hartigan, *Clustering algorithms* (New York: Wiley, 1975); A. Rizzi, *Analisi dei dati. Applicazioni dell'informatica alla statistica* (Rome: Nuova Italia Scientifica, 1985). See C. Brambilla, *Affari di banche. Banche universali in Italia in prospettiva comparata, 1860–1914* (forthcoming 2010), ch. 2, for wider discussion on sources and clustering.
15. Data concerning the Crédit Mobilier refer to the previous decade because the bank had already failed by the late 1860s.
16. Aimed at giving a common administrative and legal framework to the new country, it was a sort of emendation of the Piedmontese code of 1842, in its turn derived from the *code Napoléon*. See Camera dei Deputati, *Ricerca sulle società commerciali. Linee evolutive della legislazione italiana e ordinamenti stranieri* (Rome: 1968).
17. G. Conti, 'Finanza d'impresa e capitale di rischio in Italia, 1870–1939, *Rivista di storia economica*, n.s., 10:3 (1993), pp. 307–32.
18. Even the shortlived experience of the *Sindacato governativo* (a sort of controlling Commission on joint stock companies depending on the ministry of Agriculture, Industry and Commerce) did not improve the situation, characterized by high degrees of opacity in financial and economic information on companies. On this body see F. Belli and A. Scialoja, 'Vocazioni interventiste, miti ed ideologie del liberismo all'indomani dell'unificazione nazionale; il controllo delle società commerciali e degli istituti di credito nell'esperienze del Sindacato governativo (1866–1869)', in C. De Cesare, *Il Sindacato governativo, le società commerciali nel Regno d'Italia* (Bologna: Forni, 1979), pp. 1–44.
19. In 1867, for instance, Banca Nazionale refinanced Credito Mobiliare with 10 million lire (Bouvier, *Le Crédit Lyonnais*).
20. Confalonieri, *Banca e industria in Italia 1894–1906.*
21. See Pantaleoni, *Credito Mobiliare*; Luzzatto, *L'economia Italiana*; Confalonieri, *Banca e industria in Italia 1894–1906.*
22. A. Errera, *Il nuovo codice di commercio del Regno d'Italia* (Florence: Pellas, 1883); Conti, 'Finanza d'impresa'; R. Teti, 'Imprese, imprenditori e diritto', in F. Amatori et al., *L'industria*, pp. 1211–303.
23. L. Cellérier, *Etudes sur les sociétés en France et dans les pays voisins* (Paris: L. Larose et L. Tenin, 1905); G. Zappa, *Le valutazioni di bilancio con particolare riguardo ai bilanci delle società per azioni* (Milan: Società editrice libraria, 1910); for a wider discussion on these

issues see also C. Brambilla and G. Conti, 'Informazione e regole contabili nei rapporti tra banca e industria', in G. Conti, *Creare il credito e arginare i rischi. Il sistema finanziario tra nobiltà e miserie del capitalismo italiano* (Bologna: Il Mulino, 2007), pp. 247–92.

24. Conti, 'Finanza d'impresa'; A. K. Kuhn, *A comparative study of the law of corporations with particular reference to the protection of creditors and shareholders* (New York: Columbia University, 1912); C. Vivante, 'Per la riforma delle società anonime', *Rivista del diritto commerciale e del diritto generale delle obbligazioni*, 2 (1913), n. 2.
25. Banca d'Italia arose from the ashes of Banca Nazionale and of two regional issuing banks, having moreover taken charge of the liquidation of Banca Romana's frozen assets and displayed a more thrifty behaviour in offering refinancing facilities to the banking system. See F. Bonelli, 'Introduzione', in Idem (ed.), *La Banca d'Italia dal 1894 al 1913. Momenti della formazione di una banca centrale* (Rome and Bari: Laterza, 1991), pp. 3–114.
26. Kuhn, *A Comparative Study*, pp. 69–85; Vivante, 'Per la riforma'; W. Rathenau, 'Le società per azioni. Riflessioni suggerite dall'esperienza degli affari', *Rivista delle società*, 5 (1960), pp. 912–47; C. Fohlin, *Finance capitalism and Germany's rise to industrial power* (Cambridge: Cambridge University Press, 2007).
27. Brambilla and Conti, 'Informazione e regole contabili', G. Siciliano, *Cento anni di borsa in Italia* (Bologna: Il Mulino, 2001); S. Baia Curioni, *Regolazione e competizione. Storia del mercato azionario in Italia (1808–1938)* (Bologna: Il Mulino, 1995).
28. Indeed, interlocking directorates were a practice Comit and Credit widely used. See F. Pino, 'Sui fiduciari della Comit nelle società per azioni, 1898–1918', *Rivista di storia economica*, n.s, 8 (1991), n. unico, pp. 115–48; C. Fohlin, '*Fiduciari* and firm liquidity constraints: the Italian experience with German-style universal banking, *Explorations in economic history*, 35:1 (1998), pp. 83–107; M. Vasta and A. Baccini, 'Banks and Industry in Italy, 1911–36. New Evidence using the Interlocking Directorates Technique', *Financial History Review*, 4:2 (1997), pp. 139–59.
29. In some years they even exceeded total assets (Brambilla, *Affari di banche*, Appendix, tables 1–15).
30. *Ibidem*.
31. F. Bonelli, *La crisi del 1907 una tappa dello sviluppo industriale in Italia* (Turin: Fondazione Einaudi, 1971); Siciliano, *Cento anni di borsa*; Confalonieri, *Banca e industria in Italia 1907–14*.
32. Conti, 'Le banche e il finanziamento industriale; G. Piluso, 'Mercati settoriali e squilibri regionali nella formazione di un sistema bancario in Italia (1860–1936)', in G. Sapelli (ed.), *Capitalismi a confronto: Italia e Spagna. Atti del secondo seminario internazionale di storia d'impresa* (Soveria Mannelli: Rubbettino, 1998), pp. 83–157.
33. A. Confalonieri, *Banche miste e grande industria in Italia, 1914–1933* (Milan: Banca commerciale italiana, 1994), vol. 1; P. Ciocca and G. Toniolo, 'Industry and finance in Italy, 1918–1940', *Journal of European Economic History*, 13:2 (1984), pp. 113–36; S. Battilossi, 'Banche miste, gruppi di imprese e società finanziarie (1914–1933)', in G. Conti and S. La Francesca (eds.), *Banche e reti di banche nell'Italia postunitaria*, vol. 1 (Bologna: Il Mulino, 2000), pp. 307–52.
34. G. Toniolo (ed.), *Industria e banca nella grande crisi 1929–1934* (Milan: Etas, 1978).

6 Dreschel, Swiss Banking Crises During the Gold Standards, 1906–71

1. D. Aigner, C. Lovell and P. Schmidt, 'Formulation and Estimation of Stochastic Frontier Production Function Models', *Journal of Econometrics*, 6 (1977), pp. 21–37.
2. W. Meeusen and J. Van Den Broeck, 'Efficiency Estimation from Cobb-Douglas Production Functions with Composed Error', *International Economic Review*, 18 (1977), pp. 435–44.
3. T. Coelli and G. Battese, 'A Model for Technical Inefficiency Effects in a Stochastic Frontier Production Function for Panel Data', *Empirical Economics*, 20:2 (1995), pp. 325–32.
4. See L. R. Christensen, D. W. Jorgenson and L. J. Lau, 'Transcendental Logarithmic Production Frontiers', Review of Economics and Statistics, 55:1 (1973), p. 28–45. A Fourier-flexible specification is not considered, as Berger and Mester showed that the results differ not significantly from a translog function; A. Berger and L. Mester, *Inside the Black Box: What Explains Differences in the Efficiencies of Financial Institutions* (Washington DC: Federal Reserve Board, 1997).
5. The parameters are simultaneously estimated by applying the maximum likelihood method implemented in the computer program Frontier 4.1; T. Coelli, 'A Guide to FRONTIER Version 4.1: A Computer Program for Stochastic Frontier Production and Cost Function Estimation', CEPA Working Paper No. 7/96 (1996).
6. B. Rime and K. Stiroh, 'The Performance of Universal Banks: Evidence from Switzerland', *Journal of Banking and Finance*, 27:11 (2003), p. 2121–50.
7. Basel Committee on Banking Supervision, *Basel II: International Convergence of Capital Measurement and Capital Standards: A Revised Framework* (Basel: Bank for International Settlements, 2004).
8. Data on salaries becomes available only from 1935 onward. For 1930–34 it has been extrapolated by using the constant share of salaries to administration costs of 78 per cent in the period from the mid-1930s to the mid-1940s. Data on total administration costs (salaries and office expenses) are available for 1930–1934. Omitting the years 1930–1934 in a robustness check did not change the results markedly.
9. D. Drechsel and T. Straumann, 'Historical Perspective of Swiss Banking Crises', University of Zurich Working Paper, 2010.
10. H. Bauer, *Schweizerischer Bankverein 1872–1972* (Basel: Schweizerischer Bankverein, 1972).
11. E. Wetter, *Bankkrisen und Bankkatastrophen der Letzten Jahre in der Schweiz* (Zürich: Orell Fuessli, 1918).
12. Schweizerische Bankiervereinigung, *VIII. Jahresbericht* (Basel: Schweizerische Bankiervereinigung, 1919/1920).
13. Bauer, *Schweizerischer Bankverein 1872–1972*.
14. P. Ehrsam, 'Die Bankenkrise der 30er Jahre in der Schweiz', in U. Zulauf (Ed.), *50 Jahre Eidgenossische Bankenaufsicht* (Zürich: Schulthess Polygraphischer Verlag, 1985), pp. 83–118.
15. M. Ikle, *Die Schweiz Als Internationaler Bank- und Finanzplatz* (Zürich: Orell Füssli, 1970).
16. P. Ehrsam, 'Die Bankenkrise der 30er Jahre in der Schweiz'.
17. M. Zurlinden, 'Goldstandard, Deflation und Depression: Die Schweizerische Volkswirtschaft in der Weltwirtschaftskrise', *SNB Quartalsheft*, 2003, 2, pp. 86–115.
18. Zurlinden, 'Goldstandard, Deflation und Depression'.

7 Baubeau and Ögren, Determinants of National Financial Systems: The role of historical events

1. See the Introduction of the present volume.
2. C. P. Kindleberger, *Manias, Panics and Crises. A History of Financial Crisis* (Hoboken: John Wiley & Sons, 5th edn, 2005), pp. 1–2.
3. P. Baubeau, 'Militarization: a Political Clue to Financial Structures?', Paper presented at the EABH conference *The Critical Function of History in Banking and Finance*, Cyprus – May 15 and 16 2009. Available on demand.
4. A. Demirguc-Kunt and R. Levine, 'Bank-Based and Market-Based Financial Systems: Cross-Country Comparisons', *World Bank Working Paper n°2143* (2000), pp. 42–3. R. Levine, 'Bank-Based or Market-Based Financial Systems: Which is Better?', *William Davidson Working Paper Number 442* (February 2002).
5. C. Calomiris, 'Financial History and the Long Reach of the Second 30 Years War', in T. Guinnane, W. A. Sundstrom and W. C. Whatley, *History Matters: Essays on Economic Growth, Technology and Demographic Change* (Stanford, CA: Stanford University Press, 2004), pp. 115–41.
6. L. Scialom, *Economie bancaire* (Paris: La Découverte, 2007), pp. 15–22.
7. P. Arbulu, 'Le marché parisien des actions au XIX siècle', in G. Gallais-Hamonno (ed.), *Le marché financier français au XIX siècle. Volume 2. Aspects quantitatifs des acteurs et des instruments à la Bourse de Paris* (Paris: Publications de la Sorbonne, 2007), pp. 366–458.
8. J. Franks, C. Mayer and H. Miyajima, 'Equity Markets and Institutions: The Case of Japan', RIETI Discussion Paper Series 09–E -039 (27 July 2009).
9. R. Rajan and L. Zingales, The great reversals: The politics of financial development in the twentieth century, Working Paper, July 2002 Draft (Published in *The Journal of Financial Economics*, 69:1 (July 2003), pp. 5–50).
10. R. La Porta, F. Lopez-de-Silanes, A. Shleifer and R. W. Vishny, 'Legal Determinants of External Finance', *The Journal of Finance*, 52:3 (July 1997), pp. 1131–50. R. La Porta, F. Lopez-de-Silanes, A. Shleifer and R. Vishny, 'Law and Finance', *Journal of Political Economy*, 106:6 (December 1998), pp. 1113–55.
11. A. Demirguc-Kunt and R. Levine, 'Bank-Based and Market-Based Financial Systems', pp. 36–7.
12. P. Dunn and F. Coulomb, 'Peace, War and International Security: Economic Theories', University of the West of England, Department of Economics, Developing Quantitative Marxism Working Paper Series, N° 0801 (November 2008), p. 3.
13. J. Brewer, *The Sinews of Power. War, Money and the English State, 1688–1783* (Cambridge, MA: Harvard University Press, 1990 (1st edn 1988)), p. 21.
14. A. Demirguc-Kunt and R. Levine, 'Bank-Based and Market-Based Financial Systems, p. 36.
15. A. Gerschenkron, *Economic backwardness in historical perspective. A book of essays* (Cambridge, Mass.: The Belknap Press of Harvard University Press, 1966) p. 355. See this volume's Introduction.
16. P. L. Rousseau and R. Sylla, 'Financial Systems, Economic Growth and Globalization', *NBER Working Paper 8323* (June 2001). D. J. Forsyth and D. Verdier (ed.), *The Origins of National Financial Systems, Alexander Gerschenkron reconsidered* (London: Routledge, 2003). M. Lescure, 'Banking and Finance', in G. Jones and J. Zeitlin (ed.), *The Oxford Handbook of Business History* (Oxford: Oxford University Press, 2008), pp. 319–46.

17. C. Fohlin, *Finance Capitalism and Germany's Rise to Industrial Power* (Cambridge, Mass.: Cambridge University Press, 2007).
18. Y. Cassis, *Les capitales du capital. Histoire des places financières internationales, 1780–2005* (Paris: Honoré Champion, 2008).
19. G. Gallais-Hamonno and P.-C. Hautcœur (ed.), *Le marché financier français au XIX siècle*, 2 vols (Paris: Publications de la Sorbonne, 2007).
20. D. Verdier, *Moving Money, Banking and Finance in the Industrialized World* (Cambridge: Cambridge University Press, 2002).
21. R. Sylla and G. Toniolo (eds), *Patterns of European Industializatuon. The Nineteenth Century* (London and New York: Routledge, 1991) and R. Sylla, R. Tilly and G. Tortella (eds.), *The State, The Financial System And Economic Modernization* (Cambridge, Cambridge University Press, 2007).
22. R. Carney, 'The Political Economy of Financial Systems: why do developed countries have such financing arrangements?', Paper presented at the annual meeting of the American Political Science Association, Boston, Massachusetts (28 August 2002).
23. Rajan and Zingales, 'The Great Reversals: The Politics of Financial Development in the Twentieth Century'.
24. H. Spencer, *The Man versus the State* (1884) in H. Spencer, *The Man versus the State: with Four Essays on Politics and Society* (Harmondsworth: Penguin, 1969).
25. Original quotation in French – translated passage in italic: 'Tandis que tous les peuples et tous les gouvernements veulent la paix, malgré tous les congrès de la philanthropie internationale, *la guerre peut naître toujours d'un hasard toujours possible... Toujours votre société violente et chaotique, même quand elle veut la paix, même quand est à l'état d'apparent repos, porte en elle la guerre, comme une nuée dormante porte l'orage*. (Très bien ! très bien ! à l'extrême gauche.)' Jean Jaurès, 7 March 1895, in J. Jaurès, *Textes choisis* (Paris: Editions Sociales, 1959), p. 88.
26. Original quotation in French : 'Pour l'historien, rien n'est 'exogène'', in M. Margairaz, 'Les politiques économiques sous et de Vichy', *Histoire@Politique*, 9, September–December 2009. www.histoire-politique.fr, p. 6.
27. A. Demirguc-Kunt and R. Levine, 'Bank-based and market-based financial systems: cross-country comparisons'.
28. Y. Cassis states accordingly that 'International Financial centres thrive in times of peace, not in times of war' (translated from the French 'Les places financières internationales prospèrent en temps de paix, pas en temps de guerre', in Cassis, *Les capitals du capital*, p. 205.
29. Our table was set by using general books about First and Second World War (S. Pope and E.-A. Wheal, *The Dictionary of the First World War* (New York: Saint Martin's Press, 1995); J.-J. Becker, *La première guerre mondiale* (Paris: MA Editions, 1985); S. C. Tucker (ed.), *World War I Encyclopedia*, 5 vols. (Santa Barbara: ABC-Clio, 2005), the two books from M. Harrison (S. Broadberry, and M. Harrison, *The Economics of World War I* (Cambridge: Cambridge University Press, 2005); M. Harrison, (ed.), *The Economics of World War II: Six Great Powers in International Comparison* (Cambridge: Cambridge University Press, 1998)) and completed with *Encyclopaedia Britannica* and *Encycloaedia Universalis*, plus all relevant books at hand (direct access) in the French National Library history section concerning the different countries and the two World Wars. The gathering of information was mainly based on indexes.

30. D. North and B. Weingast, 'Constitutions and Commitment: The Evolution of Institutions Governing Public Choice in Seventeenth-Century England', *The Journal of Economic History*, 49:4 (December, 1989), pp. 803–32.
31. 'Europe has a set of primary interests which to us have none; or a very remote relation. Hence she must be engaged in frequent controversies, the causes of which are essentially foreign to our concerns. Hence, therefore, it must be unwise in us to implicate ourselves by artificial ties in the ordinary vicissitudes of her politics, or the ordinary combinations and collisions of her friendships or enmities', 1996 The Avalon Project, The Avalon Project: 'Washington's Farewell Address 1796', downloaded 09/21/2008 at http://www.yale.edu/lawweb/avalon/washing.htm.
32. A. Demirguc-Kunt and R. Levine, 'Bank-Based and Market-Based Financial Systems: Cross-Country Comparisons'.
33. The OLS regressions are stable with normally distributed residuals.
34. For a discussion of the Japan case, M. Amano, 'The Gurley-Shaw Hypothesis, Growth, Regressions and Granger-Caulsality', *Economic Journal of Chiba University*, 19:3 (Dec. 2004), http://mitizane.ll.chiba-u.jp/metadb/up/AN10005358/KJ00003964075.pdf.
35. On infra-national variations in financial structures and associated political, social or business strategies, see in this volume the essays by Dirk Drechsel; Pablo Martín-Aceña, Elena Martinez Ruiz and María A. Pons; Jean-Luc Mastin; Angelo Riva and Kim Oosterlink; Patrick Verley.
36. For example, Sigurt Vitols, while enquiring on the factors that led to bank-based or market-based system, fails to address the question of wars proper, which is treated on the same footing as industrial policy. S. Vitols, 'The Origins of Bank-Based and Market Based Financial Systems: Germany, Japan and the United States', in W. Streeck and K. Yamamura (eds), *The Origins of Nonliberal Capitalism, Germany and Japan in Comparison* (Ithaca, NY: Cornell University Press, 2001), pp. 171–99.

8 Martín-Aceña, Martínez Ruiz and Pons, The Financing Of The Spanish Civil War, 1936–9

1. Among many previous works (see below) the latest and most comprehensive contribution M. A. Pons, 'La Hacienda pública y la financiación de la guerra', in P. Martín Aceña and E. Martínez Ruiz (eds.) *La economía de la Guerra Civil* (Madrid: Marcial Pons, 2006), pp. 357–91.
2. A recent publication edited by E. Malefakis (ed.), *La Guerra Civil Española* (Madrid: Taurus, 2006) includes papers dealing with all aspects of the civil war. The economy of the civil war has been studied extensively in Martín Aceña and Martínez Ruiz (eds), *La economía de la Guerra Civil.*
3. Pons, 'La Hacienda pública y la financiación de la guerra'.
4. Pons 'La Hacienda pública y la financiación de la guerra', pp. 359–62. F. Comín and S. López, 'La Hacienda del gobierno de la República española (1936–1939)' in E. Fuentes Quintana (ed.), *Economía y Economistas españoles en la Guerra Civil* (Barcelona: Galaxia-Guteberg, 2008), pp. 867–899.
5. Comín and López, 'La Hacienda del gobierno de la República española', p. 870.
6. Archivo Juan Negrín, Legajo 136.
7. Generalitat de Cataluña, *La Política Financiera de la Generalitat durante la revolución y la Guerra*, vol. 1 (Barcelona, 1937), p. 35.

8. A. de Miguel, 'Fundamentos técnicos para la construcción de una escala de desbloqueo. El tránsito de la peseta roja a la peseta nacional' in Moneda y Crédito (December 1977 (1944)), pp. 9–24.
9. A. Viñas, J. Viñuela, F. Eguidazu, C. F. Pulgar and S. Florensa, *Política comercial exterior en España (1931–1975)* (Madrid: Banco Exterior, 1979), p. 175 and G. Sánchez Recio, *La República contra los rebeldes y los desafectos. La represión económica durante la guerra civil* (Alicante: Universidad de Alicante, 1991), ch. 2.
10. J. M. Bricall, *Politica econòmica de la Generalitat (1936–1939). Vol. 1. Evolució i formes de la produció industrial* (Barcelona: Edicions 62, 1970), p. 48.
11. Despite their efforts, revenues from taxes in Catalonia underwent a sizeable fall.
12. The Catalonian government also adopted other exceptional financing measures. In particular, they approved the issue of 20 million pesetas (although in 1938 the Catalonian authorities agreed the withdrawal of this issue).
13. J. Arias Velasco, *La Hacienda de la Generalitat, 1931–1938* (Barcelona: Ariel, 1977), p. 248.
14. P. Martín Aceña, *El Oro de Moscú y el Oro de Berlín* (Madrid: Taurus, 2001).
15. G. Howson, *Arms for Spain: the untold story of the Spanish Civil War* (London: J. Murray, 1998).
16. This analysis is based on Velarde Fuertes, J., 'La economía de guerra', Historia de España. España Actual. La Guerra Civil (Madrid: Editorial Gredos, 1989), Pons, 'La Hacienda pública y la financiación de la guerra' and M. Martorell and F. Comín, 'La Hacienda de guerra franquista' in Fuentes Quintana, E. (dir) *Economía y Economistas españoles en la Guerra Civil* (Barcelona: Galaxia-Gutenberg, 2008), pp. 901–37.
17. Martorell and Comín, 'La Hacienda de guerra franquista'.
18. Pons, 'La Hacienda pública y la financiación de la guerra'.
19. Velarde, 'La economía de guerra'.
20. C. E. Harvey, *The Rio Tinto Company: An Economic History of a leading international mining concern, 1873–1954* (Penzance, Cornwall: Alison Hodge, 1981). A. Gómez Mendoza, *El 'Gibraltar económico': Franco y Riotinto, 1936–1954* (Madrid: Biblioteca Civitas economía y empresa, 1994).
21. C. Albiñana and E. Fuentes Quintana, *Sistema fiscal español y comparado* (Madrid: Facultad de Económicas, 1967).
22. Data in F. Comín and D. Díaz, 'Sector público administrativo y estado del bienestar' in A. Carreras and X. Tafunell (coords.) *Estadísticas históricas de España. Siglos XIX y XX* (Madrid: Fundación BBVA, 2005), p. 947.
23. A. Viñas prefers the higher figure of 8,668 million lire (A. Viñas, *Guerra, dinero, dictadura, ayuda fascista y autarquía en la España de Franco* (Barcelona: Crítica, 1984), p. 193), which V. Giura reduces to 8,500 million lire (V. Giura, *Tra política ed economia. L'Italia e la guerra civile spagnola* (Roma-Napoli: Edizioni Scientifiche Italiane, 2002), p.93).
24. See Viñas, *Guerra, dinero, dictadura*, pp. 196–7; R. García Pérez, *Franquismo y Tercer Reich* (Madrid: Centro de Estudios Constitucionales, 1994), pp. 81–2 and C. Leitz, *Economic Relations between Nazi Germany and Franco's Spain 1936–1945* (Oxford: Oxford University Press, 1996), pp. 93–4.
25. See García Pérez, *Franquismo y Tercer Reich*, pp. 129–30 and pp. 135–45 and E. Martínez Ruiz, *Guerra civil, comercio y capital extranjero. El sector exterior de la economía española (1936–1939)* (Madrid: Banco de España, Madrid, 2006).

26. See A. Viñas, *El oro español en la Guerra Civil* (Madrid: Instituto de Estudios Fiscales, 1976) and Viñas, *Guerra, dinero, dictadura*.
27. These methods exhaust the means by which the government financed the war, but they do not exhaust the means by which the government acquired resources. Nor do they represent the total cost of the war that should include at least both the loss of human capital and physical destruction.
28. M. Harrison (ed.), *The Economics of World War II: Six Great Powers in International Comparison* (Cambridge: Cambridge University Press, 1998); S. Broadberry and M. Harrison, *The Economics of World War I* (Cambridge: Cambridge University Press, 2005).
29. R. L. Ransom, 'The Economics of the Civil War", *EH Net Encyclopedia*, ed. by R. Whaples (24 August 2001), URL http://eh.net/encyclopedia/article/ransom.civil.war.us.
30. A. Gómez-Galvarriato and A. Musacchio, 'Un nuevo índice de precios para México, 1886–1929' in *El Trimestre Económico*, 67:1 (2000), pp. 47–91.
31. P. Gatrell, 'The First World War and War Communism, 1914–1920' in R. W. Davies, M. Harrison and S. G. Wheatcroft (eds), *The Economic Transformation of the Soviet Union, 1913–1945* (Cambridge: Cambridge University Press, 1994).

9 Roberts, The London Financial Crisis of 1914

1. R. Roberts, 'The Economics of Cities of Finance', in H. Diederiks and D. Reeder (eds), *Cities of Finance* (Amsterdam: North Holland, 1996), pp. 7–20.
2. H. Withers, *War and Lombard Street* (London: Smith, Elder & Co, 1915), p. 1.
3. 'The Great Crisis', *Bankers Magazine*, September 1914, p. 320; Bank of England Archive (BEA), 'The Bank of England 1914–1921' (1928) vol. 1, p. 61.
4. B. Brown, *Monetary Chaos in Europe: the End of an Era* (London: Croom Helm, 1988), pp. 2–3; N. Ferguson, 'Political Risk and the International Bond Market between the 1848 Revolution and the Outbreak of the First World War', *Economic History Review*, 59:1 (2006), p. 99; Rothschild Archive London (RAL), XI/130A/8, 14 July 1914.
5. 'The Great Crisis', *Bankers' Magazine*, September 1914, p. 321.
6. BEA. 'Bank of England, 1914–1921', vol. 1, p. 62.
7. R. C. Michie, 'The City of London as a Global Financial Centre, 1880–1939: Finance, Foreign Exchange and the First World War', in P. L. Cottrell, E. Lange and U. Olsson (eds), *Centres and Peripheries in Banking* (Ashgate: Aldershot, 2007), pp. 66–8.
8. S. E. Thomas, *The Principles and Arithmetic of Foreign Exchange* (London: Macdonald and Evans, 1929), p. 168.
9. J. Atkin, *The Foreign Exchange Market of London: Development since 1900* (London: Routledge, 2005), pp. 11–13.
10. R. G. Hawtrey, *A Century of Bank Rate* (London: Longmans, 1938), p. 123.
11. The Times, *History of the War, vol. 1* (London: The Times, 1914), p. 170.
12. 'The Financial Situation at Home and Abroad', *The Economist*, 1 August 1914, p. 219.
13. BEA. 'Bank of England, 1914–1921', vol. 1, p.63; Times, *History of the War*, p. 169.
14. Times, *History of the War*, p. 170.
15. Times, *History of the War*, p. 168.
16. R. Roberts, 'What's in a name? Merchants, Merchant Bankers, Accepting Houses, Issuing Houses, Industrial Bankers and Investment Bankers', *Business History*, 35:3 (July 1993), pp. 22–38; S. Chapman, *The Rise of Merchant Banking* (London: George Allen & Unwin, 1984) p. 107.

17. The National Archives, Kew (TNA). T172/134, Conference between the Chancellor of the Exchequer, Members of the Cabinet and Representatives of Accepting Houses, 12 August 1914, p. 13.
18. R. Roberts, *Schroders: Merchants & Bankers* (London: Macmillan, 1992), p. 130–2.
19. Hawtrey, *Century of Bank Rate*, p. 123.
20. BEA. 'Bank of England, 1914–1921', vol. 1, p. 63; W. A. Brown, *The International Gold Standard Reinterpreted, 1914–1934* (New York: National Bureau of Economic Research, 1940), p. 12.
21. E. V. Morgan, *Studies in British Financial Policy, 1914–25* (London: Macmillan, 1952), p. 8.
22. London School of Economics Archive (LSEA). Sir George Paish, 'My Memoirs' (*c.* 1950), p. 59.
23. 'The Great Crisis', *Bankers' Magazine*, December 1914, p. 701; 'The Loan Positions of the Stock Exchange', *Economist*, 17 October 1914, p. 634.
24. E. Sykes, 'Some Effects of the War on the London Money Market', *Bankers' Magazine*, February 1915, p. 76.
25. 'The Great Crisis', *Bankers' Magazine*, September 1914, p. 322.
26. Hawtrey, *Century of Bank Rate*, p.124; Times, *History of the War*, p. 179.
27. 'The Financial Crisis of 1914', *The Economist*, 24 October 1914, p. 685.
28. 'The Stock Exchange Crisis Day by Day', *The Economist*, 1 August 1914, p. 221. J. M. Keynes, 'War and the Financial System, August 1914', *Economic Journal*, 24 (September 1914), pp. 462–3. Guildhall Library Archive (GLA). London Stock Exchange, Committee of General Purposes, 24 March 1915. Published crisis diary of Chairman Sir R. W. Inglis; 'The Financial Situation at Home and Abroad', *The Economist*, 1 August 1914, p. 219.
29. W. L. Silber, *When Washington Shut Down Wall Street: The Great Financial Crisis of 1914 and the Origins of America's Monetary Supremacy* (Princeton NJ: Princeton University Press, 2007), pp. 1–13.
30. TNA. T170/55, Conference between Chancellor of the Exchequer and Representative Bankers and Traders, 4 August 1914. Sir Edward Holden, p. 4.
31. T. Seabourne, 'The Summer of 1914', in F. Capie and G. E. Wood (eds), *Financial Crises and the World Banking System* (London: Macmillan, 1986), pp. 79–82.
32. TNA. T170/14, 'Joint Stock Proposal to Deposit Gold & Security for Notes', 31 July 1914; Memorandum by John Bradbury, Treasury, to Mr Bonham Carter, Prime Minister's Office (no date); R. S. Sayers, *The Bank of England 1891–1944* (Cambridge: Cambridge University Press, 1976), pp. 72–3.
33. Sayers, *Bank of England 1891–1944*, p. 73.
34. Lombard Street Research.
35. BEA. 'Bank of England, 1914–1921', vol. 3, p.7.
36. LSEA. Paish, 'My Memoirs', p. 59.
37. *The Times*, 2 August 1914.
38. E. Johnson (ed), *Collected Writings of John Maynard Keynes: Volume XVI, Activities 1914–1919* (London: Macmillan, 1971), p. 3.
39. Johnson (ed), *Collected Writings of John Maynard Keynes*, p. 20; J. M. Keynes, 'War and the Financial System, August 1914', *Economic Journal*, xxiv (September 1914) pp. 460–86; J. M. Keynes, 'The City of London and the Bank of England, August 1914', *Quarterly Journal of Economics*, 29:1 (Nov 1914) pp. 48–71; J. M. Keynes, 'The Prospects of Money, November 1914', *Economic Journal*, vol.xxiv (December 1914) pp. 610–34;

Keynes also wrote commentaries on the crisis headed 'From A Correspondent' for the *Morning Post*.

40. Keynes, 'War and the Financial System, August 1914', pp. 472.
41. D. Kynaston, *The City of London: Golden Years, 1890–1914 vol. 2* (London: Chatto & Windus, 1999), p. 608.
42. BEA. 'Bank of England, 1914–1921', vol. 1, p. 65.
43. 'Correspondence between the Treasury and the Bank of England', House of Commons Papers, 1914–16, no. 37; J. Clapham, 'Sir John Clapham's Account of the Financial Crisis in August 1914', Appendix 3, R. S. Sayers, *The Bank of England, 1891–1944* (Cambridge: Cambridge University Press, 1976), p. 35.
44. D. Lloyd George, *War Memoirs of David Lloyd George* (London: Ivor Nicolson & Watson, 1933), vol. 1., p. 62.
45. Withers, *War and Lombard Street*, p. 11.
46. Keynes, 'War and the Financial System, August 1914', p. 481.
47. Withers, *War and Lombard Street*, p. 12.
48. BEA. 'Bank of England, 1914–1921', vol. 1, p. 79.
49. LSEA. Paish, 'My Memoirs', p. 19; 'Sir George Paish', *The Statist*, 15 August 1914, p. 427.
50. Sayers, *Bank of England 1891–1944*, p. 68; Lloyd George, *War Memoirs*, p. 112; W. R. Matthews, *Memories and Meanings* (London; Hodder & Stoughton, 1969) p. 80.
51. Johnson (ed.), *Collected Writings of John Maynard Keynes*, p. 15; R. Skidelsky, *John Maynard Keynes: Volume One: Hopes Betrayed 1883–1920* (London: Macmillan, 1983), p. 289.
52. LSEA. Paish, 'My Memoirs', p. 19; R. Skidelsky, *John Maynard Keynes*, p. 299.
53. BEA. 'Bank of England, 1914–1921', vol. 1, p. 90.
54. RAL. T65/59, Memorandum on the Gold Market, 1937; R. Ally, 'War and Gold – The Bank of England, the London Gold Market and South Africa's Gold, 1914–19', *Journal of Southern African Studies*, 17:2 (June 1991), p. 225; G. Hardach, *The First World War 1914–1918* (London: Allen Lane, 1977), p. 140.
55. Clapham, 'Account of the Financial Crisis in August 1914', p. 39.
56. J. Peters, 'British Government and the City - Industry Divide: the Case of the 1914 Financial Crisis', *Twentieth Century British History*, 4 (1993), pp.141–7.
57. TNA. T170/28, 'The Conduct of the Banks 1914.' Letter from Austen Chamberlain to the Chancellor of the Exchequer, 11 August 1914.
58. Clapham, 'Account of the Financial Crisis in August 1914', p. 35.
59. TNA. T172/134, Conference, 12 August 1914. Sir George Anderson, Bank of Scotland, p. 28.
60. Clapham, 'Account of the Financial Crisis in August 1914', p. 35; T170/35, Correspondence with Messrs. De La Rue, 1914.
61. TNA. T170/57, Adjourned Conference between the Chancellor of the Exchequer, Members of the Cabinet, Representatives of the Bankers, 6 August 1914, p. 21.
62. D. K. Sheppard, *The Growth and Role of UK Financial Institutions 1880–1962* (London: Methuen, 1971), Table (A) 3.2, pp. 180–1.
63. TNA. T170/26, Memorandum by Sir John Bradbury for the Prime Minister, 'The Financial Situation Arising Out of the War', 7 November 1914; Sayers, *Bank of England 1891–1944*, p. 76.
64. BEA. 'Bank of England, 1914–1921', vol. 1, p. 85; Hawtrey, *Century of Bank Rate*, p. 129.

65. H. G. Wells, *Mr Britling Sees It Through* (London: Cassell, 1916), p. 208.
66. Hawtrey, *Century of Bank Rate*, p. 128.
67. BEA. 'Bank of England, 1914–1921', vol. 2, pp. 247–9. Morgan, *Studies in British Financial Policy, 1914–25*, p. 22.
68. Ally, 'War and Gold – The Bank of England, the London Gold Market and South Africa's Gold, 1914–19,' pp. 221–38; BEA. *Bank of England 1914–1921*, vol. 1, pp. 9–11.
69. BEA. 'Bank of England, 1914–1921', vol. 2, pp. 248.
70. TNA. T172/183, Memorandum by Sir George Paish, 6 August 1914.
71. BEA. 'Bank of England, 1914–1921', p. 86.
72. 'The Financial Situation', *The Statist*, 15 August 1914, p.4 17.
73. 'The Great Crisis', *Bankers' Magazine*, September 1914, p. 334.
74. TNA. T172/134, Conference between the Chancellor of the Exchequer, Members of the Cabinet and Representatives of Accepting Houses, 12 August 1914, p. 2; S. Nishimura, *The Decline of Inland Bills of Exchange in the London Money Market 1855–1913* (Cambridge: Cambridge University Press, 1971) p. 66; F. B. Makin, 'Treasury Bills', *Bankers' Magazine*, 157 (July–December 1939), p. 400; Chapman, *The Rise of Merchant Banking*, pp. 106–7; Sir Robert Kindersley, evidence to the *Committee on Finance and Industry*, British Parliamentary Papers, 1931, I, p. 76.
75. TNA. T170/28, Edwin Montagu, 'Treasury Assistance to Banks and Discount Houses, Continuance of Moratorium and nature of Banking Facilities Available', 27 August 1914.
76. B. Mitchell and P. Deane, *Abstract of British Historical Statistics* (Cambridge: Cambridge University Press, 1962), p. 398.
77. 'The Great Crisis', *Bankers' Magazine*, September 1914, p. 334; 'The Financial Situation', *The Statist*, 15 August 1914, p. 428.
78. D. Kynaston, *The City of London: Illusions of Gold, 1914–1945 vol. 3* (London: Chatto & Windus, 2000), p. 6.
79. TNA. T172/134, Conference between the Chancellor of the Exchequer, Members of the Cabinet and Representatives of the Traders, 12 August 1914, p. 62.
80. 'The Financial Situation. Process of Adjustment', *The Statist*, 22 August 1914, p. 427.
81. TNA. T170/28 Edwin Montagu, Treasury Secretary, to David Lloyd George, Chancellor of the Exchequer, reporting a conversation with Sir George Paish, 15 August 1914.
82. 'Money', *The Statist*, 22 August 1914, p. 448.
83. Hansard. House of Commons debate, 26 August 1914. Mr Lloyd George, c 71.
84. 'Money', *The Statist*, 22 August 1914, p. 448.
85. 'The Great Crisis', *Bankers' Magazine*, September 1914, p. 336.
86. TNA. T172/162, Reports on the Advisability of Continuing the Moratorium; Hansard. House of Commons Debate, 26 August 1914. Mr Lloyd George, cc 67–76.
87. 'The Financial Outlook', *The Statist*, 5 September 1914, p. 531.
88. Peters, 'British Government and the City', p. 147.
89. TNA. T170/28, Edwin Montagu, Treasury Secretary, to David Lloyd George, Chancellor of the Exchequer, 15 August 1914.
90. 'Restoring Credit', *The Statist*, 12 September 1914, p. 563.
91. TNA. T172/158, Adjourned conference between the Cabinet Committee and the Accepting Houses, 4 September 1914; Roberts, *Schroders*, pp. 153–4; 'The Great Crisis', *Bankers' Magazine*, October 1914, p. 445.
92. BEA. 'Bank of England, 1914–1921', vol. 1, p. 364.
93. Hansard. House of Commons debate, 27 November 1914. Mr Lloyd George, c 1545.

94. Hansard. House of Commons debate, 21 February 1916. Statement by the Prime Minister, c 448.
95. BEA. 'Bank of England, 1914–1921', vol. 1, p. 373.
96. Morgan, *Studies in British Financial Policy, 1914–25*, pp. 31–2.
97. 'Treasury Bills and the Discount Market', *The Economist*, 19 September 1914, p. 492.
98. 'The Joint Stock Banks', *The Economist*, 24 1914, p. 687.
99. W. M. Scammell, *The London Discount Market* (London: Elek, 1968), p. 196.
100. *The Economist*, 3 October 1914.
101. BEA. 'Bank of England, 1914–1921', p. 89.
102. Morgan, *Studies in British Financial Policy, 1914–25*, p.23; 'The Great Crisis', *Bankers' Magazine*, November 1914, p. 580.
103. R. Michie, *The London Stock Exchange: a History* (Oxford: Oxford University Press, 1999), p.147; E. V. Morgan and W. A. Thomas, *The Stock Exchange: Its History and Functions* (London, Elek, 1962), p. 218.
104. BEA. 'Bank of England, 1914–1921', vol. 1, p. 95.
105. Lloyd George, *War Memoirs*, vol. 1, chapter 4: 'The Financial Crisis: I. How We Saved the City', pp. 100–16.
106. Michie, *London Stock Exchange*, p. 146.
107. Makin, 'Treasury Bills', p. 400.
108. Hansard. House of Commons debate, 27 November 1914. Mr Lloyd George, c 1553; Morgan, *Studies*, p. 106.
109. 'The War Loan', *The Statist*, 28 November 1914, p. 479.
110. 'The Financial Crisis of 1914', *The Economist*, 24 October 1914, p. 686.
111. Morgan, *Studies in British Financial Policy, 1914–25*, p. 29.
112. C. H. Feinstein, *Statistical Tables of National Income, Expenditure and Output of the UK 1855–1965* (Cambridge: Cambridge University Press, 1972), Table 65, p. T140; Scammell, *London Discount Market*, p 197; 'Bankers' Gazette', *The Economist*, 8 August 1914; 'Bankers' Gazette', 23 November 1918.
113. Morgan, *Studies in British Financial Policy, 1914–25*, p. 32.
114. TNA. T172/183, Memorandum to the Chancellor by Sir George Paish, 6 August 1914.
115. Hansard, House of Commons Debate, 27 November 1914. Mr Lloyd George, c 1546.
116. 'The War, Trade and Finance', *The Economist*, 22 August 1914, p. 338.
117. Hansard. House of Commons Debate, 21 February 1916, Statement by the Prime Minister.
118. 'Pre-Moratorium Bills', *Bankers' Magazine*, 1921 p. 310.
119. BEA. 'Bank of England, 1914–1921', p. 364.
120. BEA. C92/110, 'Advances O/A Pre-Moratorium Advances'.
121. TNA. T160/998, Letter from Sir Otto Niemeyer, Treasury, to Arthur Kiddy, City Editor, *Morning Post*, 28 December 1926.
122. J. Euwe, 'Financing Germany: Amsterdam's Role as an International Financial Centre, 1914–1931', in this collection; M. F. Joliffe, *The United States as a Financial Centre 1919–1933* (Cardiff: University of Wales Press, 1935).
123. Silber, *When Washington Shut Down Wall Street*.
124. F. C. Costigliola, 'Anglo-American Financial Rivalry in the 1920s', *Journal of Economic History*, 37:4 (December 1977), pp. 911–34.

10 Dimitrova and Fantacci, The Establishment of the Gold Standard in Southeast Europe: Convergence to a New System or Divergence from an Old One?

1. E. Helleiner, *The Making of National Money. Territorial Currencies in Historical Perspective* (Ithaca, NY: Cornell University Press, 2003).
2. N. Kiosseva, *Istoria na parichnite krizi v Bulgaria: 1879–1912 (History of the monetary crisis in Bulgaria: 1879–1912)* (Sofia: Economic university press, 2000), p. 47.
3. R. Avramov, 'The Bulgarian National Bank in a Historical Perspective: Shaping an Institution, Searching for a Monetary Standard', in R. Avramov and Ş. Pamuk (eds), *Monetary and fiscal policies in Southeast Europe. Historical and comparative perspective* (Sofia: Bulgarian National Bank, 2006), pp. 98–9.
4. J. K. Galbraith, *Money. Whence it came and where it went* (Boston, MA: Houghton Mifflin, 1975), p. 178.
5. A. Kuroda, 'What is the complementarity among monies? An introductory note', *Financial History Review*, 15:1 (2008), pp. 7–15.
6. A. Redish, *Bimetallism: an Economic and Historical Analysis* (Cambridge: Cambridge University Press, 2000).
7. To be sure, in the country that invented it, namely Britain, the gold standard lasted two full centuries: and the value of the pound in terms of gold was fixed throughout the whole period from its inception, in 1717, till its ultimate cessation in 1932. Nonetheless, even remaining on a purely factual ground, it is evident that monetary regimes, in which metal coins had a variable value in terms of the unit of account, have had a greater diffusion and a longer duration than those in which that value was fixed.
8. L. Einaudi, 'The Theory of Imaginary Money from Charlemagne to the French Revolution', in L. Einaudi, R. Faucci and R. Marchionatti (eds. *Luigi Einaudi. Selected Economic Essays* (London: Palgrave Macmillan, 2006), pp. 153–81.
9. L. Fantacci, 'Complementary Currencies: a Prospect on Money from a Retrospect on Premodern Practices', *Financial History Review*, 12:1 (2005), pp. 43–61.
10. Of course, this is not to deny, but rather to acknowledge even more explicitly, the possibility that autonomy could be abused and oriented towards less noble goals by irresponsible rulers.
11. The Ottoman Empire had adhered to bimetallism, with a gold/silver ratio of 15:09, in 1844 (Ş. Pamuk, *A Monetary History of the Ottoman Empire* (Cambridge: Cambridge University Press, 2000). Hence, as part of the Empire, Bulgaria had already been under a bimetallic standard for over a generation. However, as we shall have a chance to mention below, the Ottoman version of bimetallism shared and continued to share even after 1878, many of the peculiarities that affected Bulgaria in the same period.
12. J. Petkof, *Prix, circulation et change en Bulgarie de 1890 à 1924* (Paris: Jouve & Co., 1926), p. 18.
13. See text of law in appendix to K. Nedelchev, *Parichnoto delo v Bulgaria: 1879–1940 (Monetary affairs in Bulgaria: 1879–1940)* (Sofia: Knipegraf Printing House, 1940), pp. 101–8.
14. P. Trifonoff, *La banque nationale de Bulgarie et l'histoire de sa politique monétaire* (Lyon: Bosc Frères: 1930), p. 30.
15. L. Fantacci, 'The dual currency system of Renaissance Europe', *Financial History Review*, 15:1 (2008), pp. 55–72.

16. Pamuk, *A Monetary History of the Ottoman Empire,* pp. 219–20.
17. Bulgarian National Bank, *Jubileen sbornik po sluchai 50–godishninata na BNB (Jubilee collection on 50 Anniversary of the BNB)* (Sofia: State Print, 1929), p. 56.
18. R. Avramov, *120 years Bulgarian National Bank: 1879–1999* (Sofia: Bulgarian National Bank, 1999), pp. 28–9.
19. According to Joseph Petkof, foreign silver coins continued circulating in Bulgaria until 1888 (Petkof, *Prix, circulation et change en Bulgarie de 1890 à 1924,* pp. 17–18).
20. D. Gnjatovic, 'Introduction of limping gold standard in the principality of Serbia' in R. Avramov and Ş. Pamuk (eds), *Monetary and fiscal policies in Southeast Europe. Historical and comparative perspective* (Sofia: Bulgarian National Bank, 2006), pp. 46–7.
21. Pamuk, *A Monetary History of the Ottoman Empire,* pp. 219–20.
22. Petkof, *Prix, circulation et change en Bulgarie de 1890 à 1924,* p 23.
23. M. Sojic and L. Djurdjevic, 'National Bank of Serbia 1884–2006. Establishment and beginning of operation', in R. Avramov and Ş. Pamuk (eds), *Monetary and fiscal policies in Southeast Europe. Historical and comparative perspective* (Sofia: Bulgarian National Bank, 2006), p. 150.
24. M. Friedman, 'The Crime of 1873', *The Journal of Political Economy*, 98:6 (1990), pp. 1159–94.
25. Pamuk, *A Monetary History of the Ottoman Empire,* pp. 218–19.
26. For a detailed motivation and analysis of the possible factors of the agio in Bulgaria see L. Fantacci, *Autonomy vs. stability: the relationship between internal and external money in Bulgaria*, BNB Discussion Paper No.73 (Sofia: Bulgarian National Bank, 2009).
27. The existence of a link between BNB holdings and actual circulation of silver and gold coins is assumed, albeit without specific arguments, also by Avramov, *120 years Bulgarian National Bank: 1879–1999*, p. 36.
28. Reconstruction of the nominal and real effective exchange rate of the Bulgarian lev for the period under study is provided by K. Dimitrova, M. Ivanov and R. Simeonova-Ganeva, *Effective Exchange Rates of the Bulgarian Lev 1879–1939*, ICER Working Paper no. 4 (Torino: International Centre for Economic Research, 2009.
29. Trifonoff, *La banque nationale de Bulgarie et l'histoire de sa politique monétaire*, pp. 53–4.
30. Petkof, *Prix, circulation et change en Bulgarie de 1890 à 1924*, p. 9.
31. Trifonoff, *La banque nationale de Bulgarie et l'histoire de sa politique monétaire*, pp. 22–4.
32. BNB was put under state ownership by the Karavelov government, to rebuff Russian attempts to control Bulgarian banks and railways (R. Crampton, *A Concise History of Bulgaria*, 2nd edn (Cambridge: Cambridge University Press: 2005), p. 94.
33. The reform was inspired mainly by the statute of the Bank of Greece (Trifonoff, *La banque nationale de Bulgarie et l'histoire de sa politique monétaire*, p. 32).
34. Petkof, *Prix, circulation et change en Bulgarie de 1890 à 1924*, p. 21.
35. The first Ottoman banknotes, called *kaime*, were issued in 1840. Their quantity was kept under control and their value was maintained stable until 1852. It was the financing of the Crimean War that induced massive amounts to be issued, well above the requirements of circulation, causing the banknotes to depreciate by 75 per cent with respect to gold. After this failed attempt on the part of the Turkish government, the Imperial Ottoman Bank had been created, with the purpose of issuing gold-backed banknotes (Pamuk, *A Monetary History of the Ottoman Empire,* pp. 209–11).

36. Bulgarian National Bank, *Jubileen sbornik po sluchai 50-godishninata na BNB (Jubilee collection on 50 Anniversary of the BNB)*, p. 63.
37. Avramov, *120 years Bulgarian National Bank: 1879–1999,* p. 39.
38. M. Bloch, *Esquisse d'une histoire monétaire de l'Europe* (Paris: A. Colin, 1954), p. 77.
39. At this date, convertibility was suspended only de facto and it was not suspended de jure until 3 January 1919 (K. Dimitrova and M. Ivanov, 'Bulgaria', in P. Mooslechner and E. Gnan (eds), *The Experience of Exchange Rate Regimes in Southeastern Europe in a Historical and Comparative Perspective*, Workshop proceedings No.13 (Vienna: Oesterreichische Nationalbank, 2008), p. 419.
40. N. Nenovsky, *Improving monetary theory in post-communist countries. Looking back to Cantillon*, BNB Discussion Paper 28 (Sofia: BNB, 2002), pp. 21–2.
41. Gnjatovic, 'Introduction of limping gold standard in the principality of Serbia', pp. 45–66; B. Radovanovic, *110 Years of the National Bank. Establishment and Beginning of Operation of the Privileged National Bank of the Kingdom of Serbia* (Belgrade: Institute for Manufacturing Banknotes and Coins, 1998).
42. S. Lazaretou, 'The Drachma, Foreign Creditors and the International Monetary System: Tales of a Currency during the 19th and the early 20th centuries', *Explorations in Economic History*, 42:2 (2005), pp. 202–36.
43. Pamuk, *A Monetary History of the Ottoman Empire.*
44. A. Christoforoff, *Kurs po Bulgarsko bankovo delo. Chast I: Istorichesko razvitie (Course on Bulgarian Banking. Part I: Historical development)* (Sofia: n.a., 1946), p. 65.

11 Gentier, Money Creation under the Gold Standard: The Origins of the Italian Banking Crisis of 1893

1. I would like to thank Nathalie Janson, Giuseppina Gianfreda, Patrice Baubeau and the participants of the Frejus seminar CODYSINA for their comments.
2. M. Fratianni and F. Spinelli, *A Monetary History of Italy* (Cambridge: Cambridge University Press, 1997).
3. Fratianni and Spinelli, *A Monetary History of Italy*, p. 23 tab. 1.4.
4. See Figure 11.1a.
5. M. Da Pozzo and G. Felloni., *La Borsa Valori Di Genova Nel Secolo XIX* (Torino: Industria Libraria Tipografica Editrice, 1964), p. 65 and V. Zamagni, 'Il Debito Pubblico Italiano 1861–1946: Ricostruzione Della Serie Storica' *Rivista Di Storia Economica*, 14:3 (December 1998), pp. 207–42.
6. The BNS Banca Nazionale Degli Stati Sardi became BNI in 1867 Banca Nazionale nel regno d'Italia and BI Banca d'Italia in 1894.
7. The Banco di Napoli and Banco di Sicilia had been both created by the local kingdoms. They were not privately owned.
8. See Fratianni and Spinelli, *A Monetary History of Italy,* pp. 75–7, the suspension decree took place on 1 May 1866.
9. Detailed accounts of this period in: G. Gianfreda and N. Janson, 'Le Banche Di Emissione In Italia Tra Il 1861 E Il 1893: Un Caso Di Concorrenza?', *Rivista Di Politica Economica* (January 2001), pp. 15–73; G. Di Nardi, *Le Banche Di Emissione In Italia Nel Secolo XIX* (Torino: Unione Tipografico – Editrice Torinese, 1953); C. Supino, *Storia della Circolazione Cartacea in Italia dal 1860 al 1928,* 2nd edn (Milano: Società Editrice Libraria, 1929).

10. Supino, *Storia della Circolazione Cartacea in Italia.*
11. Di Nardi, *Le Banche Di Emissione In Italia Nel Secolo XIX.*
12. Fratianni and Spinelli, *A Monetary History of Italy.*
13. In M2 there are coins, notes, demand deposits and some liquid saving deposits. The prices are consumer prices.
14. We are very grateful to David Le Bris for these data.
15. Of course, a system with a larger liquidity mismatch has more liquidity risk than a system with a smaller one.
16. Net from credit losses.
17. Net Fixed Assets in Public Bonds = Public Credit – Public Deposits
18. See section 4.
19. There was a stability in Italian consumer prices and deflation (induced by growth) in other countries
20. V. Pareto, *Le Marché Financier Italien (1891–1899)*, in G. Busino (ed) (Geneva: Droz, 1965), see the introduction.
21. We have no much room to expose this real estate aspect of the crisis. Nevertheless several works confirm the housing and construction boom in the second mid of the 1880s. See for instance C. Ciccarelli, S. Fenoaltea and T. Proietti, 'The Comovements of Construction in Italy's Regions, 1861–1913', *MPRA Paper 8870* (Munich: University Library of Munich, 2008); C. Ciccarelli and S. Fenoaltea, 'Construction in Italy's Regions, 1861–1913', *MPRA Paper 9714* (Munich: University Library of Munich, 2008); C. Ciccarelli and S. Fenoaltea, 'Business Fluctuations in Italy, 1861–1913: The New Evidence', *Explorations in Economic History*, 44:3 (July 2007), pp. 432–51; S. Fenoaltea, 'The growth of the Italian economy, 1861 1913: Preliminary second-generation estimates,' *European Review of Economic History*, 9:3 (December 2005) pp. 273–312.
22. Di Nardi, *Le Banche Di Emissione In Italia Nel Secolo XIX*, p. 417.
23. Fratianni and Spinelli, *A Monetary History of Italy*, p. 62.
24. Sometimes, during a liquidity crisis it could be useful to delay banks settlement. But it cannot be a long-term policy.
25. Pareto, *Le Marché Financier Italien* had described how Italian people quit their current jobs to start business in housing market with any equity capital. The housing boom attracted new incomers.
26. Ciccarelli, Fenoaltea and Proietti 'The Comovements of Construction in Italy's Regions, 1861–1913'; Ciccarelli and Fenoaltea, 'Business Fluctuations in Italy, 1861–1913'; Ciccarelli and Fenoaltea, 'Construction in Italy's Regions, 1861–1913'.
27. J. Bessis, *Risk Management Banking* (Chichester: John Willey & Sons Ltd, 2002) uses standard default rates around 1 per cent.

12 Euwe, Financing Germany. Amsterdam's Role as an International Financial Centre, 1914–31

1. H. A. M. Klemann, *Waarom bestaat Nederland eigenlijk nog? Nederland-Duitsland: economische integratie en politieke consequenties 1860–2000* (Rotterdam: Erasmus Universiteit Rotterdam, 2006), p. 22.
2. Cited in: Klemann, *Waarom bestaat Nederland eigenlijk nog?* p. 46. The original quote reads: '... *wird es für uns von größer Bedeutung sein, in Holland ein Land zu haben, dessen*

Neutralität uns Ein- und Zufuhren gestattet. Es muß unsere Luftröhre bleiben, damit wir atmen können.'

3. Archive DNB, 2.1/332/1, Kredietverlening aan het buitenland, plan Ter Meulen. Various statutes, reports, meetings; Archive DNB, 7/300/1, Barterinstituut (vereeniging voor den goederenruil) vergaderingen en besprekingen betr de oprichting in Nederland van de vereeniging voor den goederenruil. Correspondence, reports and minutes from meetings, February–June 1920.
4. 'Het Crediet van 200 millioen aan Duitschland' in: *Handelingen Tweede Kamer*, 1008 (1920); Idem, 1094 (1920).
5. Th. Metz, *Die Niederlande als Käufer, Hersteller, Vermittler und Kreditgeber: grundsätzliches zum deutsch-niederländischen Warenaustausch* (Leipzig; s.n., 1930), pp. 16, 20–1. The original text reads: '*die Niederlande sind heute der beste Käufer deutscher Waren, einer der größten Lieferanten und mit ihren überseeischen Gebieten der größte deutsche Handelskontrahent überhaupt. Deutschland ist Hollands bester Lieferant und bester Käufer. Holland ist Deutschlands größter oder zweitgrößter Kreditgeber und Deutschland ist Hollands größter Schuldner.*'
6. The *Nederlandsche Bank* is a private institution, which has received by law a so-called patent or charter for the issue of banknotes. The bank is restricted by a number of regulations. However, the government has no direct influence on its policy.
7. W. J. Hartmann, 'Amsterdam als financieel centrum: een beschrijvende critische en vergelijkende studie' (PhD dissertation, Universiteit Gent, 1937), p. 19.
8. Klemann, *Waarom bestaat Nederland eigenlijk nog*, pp. 15–28.
9. H. Riemens, *De financiële ontwikkeling van Nederland* (Amsterdam: N.V. Noord-Hollandsche Uitgevers Maatschappij, 1949), p. 66; G. M. Verrijn Stuart, *Bankpolitiek* (Wassenaar; s.n., 1935 (3rd revised printing)), p. 125; K. Strasser, *Die deutschen Banken im Ausland. Entwicklungsgeschichte und Wirtschaftliche bedeutung* (Münich: Ernst Reinhardt, 1924), p. 87. Its main founding partners were the German *Darmstädter Bank*, the *A. Schaafhausen'scher Bankverein* and the *Österreichische Creditanstalt für Handel und Gewerbe*, with smaller contributions made by a number of Dutch banks.
10. P. C. Harthoorn, *Hoofdlijnen uit de ontwikkeling van het moderne bankwezen in Nederland vóór de concentratie* (Rotterdam: De Wester Boekhandel, 1928), p. 64.
11. W. J. Hartmann, *Amsterdam als financieel centrum*, 20; F. H. Repelius, 'Niederlande, Geld- und Kapitalmarkt', in M. Palyi and P. Quittner (eds), *Handwörterbuch des Bankwesens* (Berlin: Springer, 1933), pp. 383–87; H. M. Hirschfeld, 'Amsterdam comme centre financier international', *Revue Économique Internationale* (July 1924), pp. 7–24, there p. 9; 'Amsterdam als internationaal financieel centrum. I.', *Nieuwe Rotterdamsche Courant*, 19 Sept. 1925; 'Amsterdam als internationaal financieel centrum. II.', *Nieuwe Rotterdamsche Courant*, 20 September 1925.
12. A. J. Veenendaal, *Slow Train to Paradise. How Dutch Investment Helped Build American Railroads* (Stanford, CA: Stanford University Press, 1996), p. 5, p. 33; J. Barendregt, 'Op weg naar nationale bekendheid, het handelsbankwezen tussen 1870 en 1914', in Joh. de Vries, W. Vroom and T. de Graaf (eds), *Wereldwijd bankieren. ABN Amro 1824–1999* (Amsterdam: ABN AMRO Bank, 1999), pp. 127–84, there p. 173.
13. Hartmann, *Amsterdam als financieel centrum*, p. 19; K. D. Bosch, *De Nederlandse beleggingen in de Verenigde Staten* (Amsterdam: Elsevier, 1948), p. 74.
14. F. de Roos and W. J. Wieringa, *Een halve eeuw rente in Nederland* (Schiedam: Levensverzekering-maatschappij HAV Bank, 1953), p. 8, p. 38; Hartmann, *Amsterdam als financieel centrum*, p. 19; Veenendaal, *Slow Train to Paradise*, p. 174.

15. C. A. Verrijn Stuart, *Inleiding tot de beoefening der statistiek* (Haarlem: Erven Bohn, 1917), p. 355.
16. R. J. van der Bie and J. P. H. Smits, *Tweehonderd jaar statistiek in tijdreeksen, 1800–1999* (Amsterdam: Stichting Beheer IISG, 2001); own calculations.
17. C. A. Verrijn Stuart, *Inleiding tot de beoefening der statistiek*, p. 355.
18. Idem, pp. 31–2
19. E. Hellauer, *Internationale Finanzplätze. Ihr Wesen und ihre Enstehung unter besonderer Berücksichtigung Amsterdams* (Berlin: Junker & Dünnhaupt, 1936), p. 135.
20. P. J. C. Tetrode, 'Het Buitenlandsch Kapitaal in Nederland', *Economisch Statistische Berichten*, 31 January 1923, pp. 86–8, there p. 88. Tetrode was a member of the board of directors of the *Nederlandsche Bank*.
21. W. J. Schmitz, *Der Amsterdamer Geldmarkt mit besonderer Berücksichtigung der Zinsschwankungen* (Cologne: Kölner Görreshaus, 1931), p. 31, p. 37; A. Houwink, *Acceptcrediet. Economische en bankpolitieke beschouwingen over den in het bankaccept belichaamden credietvorm* (Amsterdam: Van der Maerck, 1929), p. 35.
22. C. D. Jongman, *De Nederlandse geldmarkt* (Leiden: Stenfert Kroese, 1960), p. 156. *f* 325 Million equals 13.5 per cent of Dutch GDP for 1913. See: J.P. Smits, E. Horlings and J.L. van Zanden, *Dutch GNP and its components, 1800–1913* (Groningen Growth and Development Centre Monograph Nr. 5): http://www.ggdc.net/publications/monoabstract.htm?id=5; own calculations.
23. Jongman, *Geldmarkt*, p. 158.
24. Nationaal Archief, Den Haag, Nederlandsche Spaarbankbond, 1906–2000, nummer toegang 2.18.29, inventarisnummer 15, Minutes of the general meeting July 2, 1920. Point 3, Annual report by the secretary; Hartmann, *Amsterdam als financieel centrum*, p. 21; Jongman, *Geldmarkt*, pp. 159–60.
25. Hartmann, *Amsterdam als financieel centrum*, p. 22; Jongman, *Geldmarkt*, pp. 158–60.
26. Jongman, *Geldmarkt*, p. 164; De Roos and Wieringa, *Rente*, p. 86.
27. Archive DNB, 8/1501/1, Duitsland, conferenties met Duitsers, valorisatie, tarievenkwestie markenportefeuille dnb van voor 1914, H. Fabri, *Holland als doorvoerland en de huidige stand van het vraagstuk der Duitsche spoorwegtarieven van en naar Holland.* Attachment to a letter by Fabri to Vissering, 26 January 1926.
28. Hartmann, *Amsterdam als financieel centrum*, p. 23, p. 32; G. Vissering, *Crediet-verleenen in Nederland* (Den Haag: Stockum, 1917) p. 13; Tetrode, 'Het Buitenlandsch Kapitaal in Nederland', pp. 86–8.
29. F. Benfey, *Die neuere Entwicklung des deutschen Auslandsbankwesens 1914–1925 (unter Mitberücksichtigung der ausländischen Bankstützpunkte in Deutschland)* (Berlin: Spaeth & Linde, 1925), p. 35.
30. J. Houwink ten Cate, *De Mannen van de Daad' en Duitsland, 1919–1939. Het Hollandse zakenleven en de vooroorlogse politiek* (Den Haag: Sdu Uitgevers, 1995) p. 87; Idem, 'Amsterdam als Finanzplatz Deutschlands', in: G. D. Feldman (ed.), *Konsequenzen der Inflation* (Berlin: Colloquium Verlag, 1989), pp. 149–79, there p. 156; CBS, *Macro-economische ontwikkelingen, 1921–1939 en 1969–1985. Een vergelijking op basis van herziene gegevens voor het interbellum* (The Hague: Staatsuitgeverij/CBS-publikaties, 1987), p. 55; own calculations.
31. Houwink ten Cate, *Mannen van de Daad*, p. 87.
32. Joh. de Vries, *Geschiedenis van de Nederlandsche Bank. Vijde deel: De Nederlandsche Bank van 1914 tot 1948. Visserings tijdvak 1914–1931* (Amsterdam: Nederlandsche Bank, 1989), pp. 78–80.

33. Vissering, *Crediet-verleenen*, pp. 15–16.
34. Archive DNB, 2.121/153/1, Duits krediet, onderpand Duitse industrie en schatkistwissels. Dossier No.44, Valuta-regeling; Archive DNB, 2.121/154/1, Duits krediet door Lippmann Rosenthal & co Rotterdamsche Bankvereeniging en Amsterdamsche Bank (onderpand duitse effecten). Various letters between Dutch banks and the *Nederlandsche Bank* regarding German loans, extensions on German loans, quality of collateral for these loans.
35. Vissering, *Crediet-verleenen*, p. 12.
36. *The Economist*, December 18, 1915, 'Supplement', p. 9.
37. Rotterdamsche Bankvereeniging, 'Development of Dutch Banking Business', in: *Monthly Review* (October 1920), pp. 25–9, there p. 29.
38. Archive DNB; 2.1/332/1, Kredietverlening aan het buitenland; own calculations.
39. Archive DNB, 2.132/151/1, Regeringskredieten 1914–1918, verlenging kredieten na de oorlog, verlenging duitse kredieten. Visit by Urbig to the secretary of the *Nederlandsche Bank*, 8 January 1919.
40. Archive DNB, 2.1/332/1, Note by Vissering to Ant. van Gijn dated February 3, 1919.
41. Archive DNB, 2.132/151/1, Visit by Wertheim and Hartogh to the secretary of the *Nederlandsche Bank*, 3 December 1918; Archive DNB, 2.132/151/2, Visit by Paul May to Vissering and Tetrode, 10 April 1919, 11.30 am.
42. Idem, Report of a meeting between J. Wertheim and Mr. Hartogh (both with the firm Wertheim & Gompertz) and the president of the *Nederlandsche Bank*, Friday 6 December 1918, 12:15.
43. Archive DNB, 2.132/151/1, Telegram by Vissering to the board of the Disconto Gesellschaft in Berlin, 13 November 1918, 24:00.
44. Idem, Minutes of various meetings of Urbig with officials of DNB and representatives of Dutch banks.
45. Idem, Various reports of meetings with representatives of Dutch banks.
46. Archive DNB, 2.132/151/2, Statement by Van Tienhoven of the Rotterdamsche Bankvereeniging during a meeting of Dutch bankers and the board of the *Nederlandsche Bank* concerning the extension of German loans, 20 March 1919, 11:30. The original statement reads: 'Het is toch niet aan te bevelen dat Nederland zich gesloten zou houden voor de credietbehoeften van zijn achterland.'
47. Idem, Statement by Van Tienhoven of the Rotterdamsche Bankvereeniging during a meeting of Dutch bankers and the board of the *Nederlandsche Bank* concerning the extension of German loans, 20 March 1919, 11:30. The original text reads: '...dan komt [...] het geld weliswaar terug, maar Holland ligt er commercieel uit.'
48. Archive DNB; 2.132/151/1, Various reports of meetings with representatives of Dutch banks.
49. Archive DNB, 2.132/151/2, Report of a telephone conversation between director P. J. C. Tetrode and G. H. Hintzen of the bank *R. Mees & Zoonen*, Thursday 15 May 1919, 9:45.
50. J. T. Madden and M. Nadler, *The International Money Markets* (London: Pitman, 1935), p. 466.
51. Archive DNB; 2.1/18/1, Bevorderen betalingsverkeer met het buitenland vestigingen van buitenlandse banken in Amsterdam; discontofaciliteiten. Visit by Redelmeier to the board of the *Nederlandsche Bank*, 19 February 1926.
52. W. J. Schmitz, *Der Amsterdamer Geldmarkt*, p. 13; E. Hellauer, *Internationale Finanzplätze*, pp. 103–4; J. L. de Jager, 'De harde leerschool, 1914–1950', in J. de Vries, W.

Vroom and T. de Graaf (eds), *Wereldwijd bankieren. ABN Amro 1824–1999* (Amsterdam: ABN AMRO Bank, 1999), pp. 241–98, there p. 275; Archive DNB, 7/0831/1, Vestiging van buitenlandse banken in Nederland. Statements by Mr Dr Van Tienhoven, director of the Rotterdamsche Bank, regarding foreign plans to establish banks in the Netherlands, 1 March 1918 and 2 March 1918.

53. Idem; Archive DNB, 2.1/18/1, Report of a telephone conversation between the secretary of the *Nederlandsche Bank* with Mr Dr J. P. van Tienhoven, director of the *Rotterdamsche Bankvereeniging*, 8 October 1918.
54. Archive DNB, 7/831/1, Vestiging van buitenlandse banken in Nederland. Overview 'Niet zuiver Nederlandsche bankinstellingen, 26 March 1926, item no.12; *Bank voor Handel en Scheepvaart* translates as 'Bank for Trade and Shipping'.
55. Archive DNB, 2.1/18/1, Bevorderen betalingsverkeer met het buitenland, vestigingen van buitenlandse banken in Amsterdam; discontofaciliteiten. Report on a visit by the directors of the Amsterdam branch of the *Deutsche Bank*, 25 August 1921.
56. Archive DNB, 7/831/1, Vestiging van buitenlandse banken in nederland. Overview 'Niet zuiver Nederlandsche bankinstellingen, 26 March 1926.
57. Archive DNB, 1.121/245/1, Corr. met G Vissering, allerhande onderwerpen: bib, reichsbank, kredieten oost-europa. Letter by Bruins adressed to Vissering, 24 December 1925.
58. Hartmann, *Amsterdam als financieel centrum*, p. 24.
59. Schmitz, *Der Amsterdamer Geldmarkt*, p. 37.
60. Hartmann, *Amsterdam als financieel centrum*, p. 24; 'Effecten- en Geldmarkt. Wekelijks overzicht', *Bijvoegsel Algemeen Handelsblad* (27 February 1926) p. 6.
61. Archive DNB, 8.2/2060/1, Duitsland, Duitse rijksbank. Report of a meeting of Ornstein with the president, the secretary and director De Beaufort of the *Nederlandsche Bank*, 5 July 1921; Archive DNB, 2.111.3/121/1, Schaarste aan zilverbons, grote aantallen bevinden zich in Duitsland. Letter by DNB to the minister of Finance, 27 August 1923; Archive DNB, 2.1/18/1, Meeting of Vissering, Van Vollenhoven, Defoer and the secretary of the *Nederlandsche Bank* with Paul May (*Lippmann, Rosenthal & Co.*), J.P. van Tienhoven and D. Ornstein (*Rotterdamsche Bankvereeniging*), P. Hofstede de Groot (*Amsterdamsche Bank*) and J. M. Telders (*Twentsche Bank*), 21 March 1923.
62. Schmitz, *Der Amsterdamer Geldmarkt*, p. 37.
63. Idem.
64. Archive DNB, 2.3/2079/1, Invloed wegtrekken buitenlandsche saldi op positie Nederlandsche gulden. Report with the same title, 5 December 1922.
65. Hartmann, *Amsterdam als financieel centrum*, p. 24–5; Madden and Nadler, *International Money Markets*, p. 426. In February 1923 the president of the *Nederlandsche Bank* had to appear in court to furnish information on a client. He declined to give specific information, which the court accepted. Nationaal Archief, Den Haag, Archief van De Nederlandsche Bank NV (1643) 1814–1980 (1995), nummer toegang 2.25.08, inventarisnummer 3319. DNB Commissie van Advies, 9 February 1923.
66. Hartmann, *Amsterdam als financieel centrum*, pp. 24–5; Madden and Nadler, *International Money Markets*, pp. 465–6; G. M. Verrijn Stuart, *Bankpolitiek*, p. 83.
67. CBS, *Macro-economische ontwikkelingen*, p. 28.
68. Idem, p. 37 (table 3.6), p.55 (table 1); own calculations; Metz, *Die Niederlande als Käufer*, pp. 18–19. Metz states an average inflow of dividends of *f* 250 million, calculations based on revised data by the Dutch central bureau for statistics (CBS) suggest *f* 200 million.

69. D. C. Renooij, *De Nederlandse emissiemarkt van 1904 tot 1939* (Amsterdam: De Bussy, 1951), p. 61; Hartmann, *Amsterdam als financieel centrum*, p. 23; NL-HaNA, Nederlandsche Spaarbankbond, 2.18.29, inv.nr. 15. Minutes of the general meeting 2 July 1920, point 7: speech by J.H. Lugt on the influence of the war on savings.
70. J. G. Post, *Besparingen in Nederland, 1923–1970: omvang en verdeling* (Amsterdam: s.n., 1972), p. 38, Table 3: 'Nationale spaarquote en deelspaarquoten voor de periode 1923–1939 in procenten van het nationaal inkomen.' The savings rate is given by Post as the relation between net national savings and net national income at market prices. Using data on savings from his source (J. C. Wijnmaalen, 'De besparingen van de Nederlandse Volkshuishouding voor en na de oorlog', in: *Prae-adviezen van de vereniging voor de staathuishoudkunde* (The Hague: Martinus Nijhoff 1953), pp. 109–13), and national income (CBS, *Het nationale inkomen van Nederland 1921–1939* (Utrecht: W. de Haan 1948) p. 46), this has been recalculated by the author using data for GDP (CBS, *Macro-economische ontwikkelingen*, p. 55).
71. Idem, p. 43.
72. Archive DNB, 2.3/544/1, Kapitaalmarkt/emissies te Amsterdam. Report 'The Dutch Capital Market 1925–1928', dated 9 January 1929; Renooij, *De Nederlandse emissiemarkt*, pp. 108–9.
73. Tetrode, 'Het Buitenlandsch Kapitaal in Nederland', p. 86.
74. Hartmann, *Amsterdam als financieel centrum*, p. 174. Until 1928 France had a law forbidding the export of capital. After this law was repealed, some foreign issues were floated in Paris, but still considerably less than in Amsterdam.
75. Hartmann, *Amsterdam als financieel centrum*, p. 26.
76. Rotterdamsche Bankvereeniging, *Monatsbericht No.2* (February 1928), pp. 40–1; idem (February 1929), pp. 37–8; own calculations.
77. Schmitz, *Der Amsterdamer Geldmarkt*, p. 44.
78. Metz, *Die Niederlande als Käufer*, p. 18.
79. De Nederlandsche Bank N.V., *Verslag van de Nederlandsche Bank N.V. over het boekjaar 1933–1934, uitgebracht in de algemeene vergadering van aandeelhouders op 12 juni 1934* (Amsterdam: Blikman & Sartorius, 1934), p. 21.
80. Rotterdamsche Bankvereeniging, *Monthly Review* (February 1928), pp. 40–1 and (February 1929), pp. 37–8; own calculations.
81. In Dutch: 'Commissie van advies inzake de toelating van buitenlandsche emissies'.
82. Rapport der commissie van advies inzake de toelating van buitenlandsche emissies, p. 8, p. 18, pp. 42–3. Considerable German emissions that were placed in New York found their way to Dutch investors. See also, p. 34.
83. Hartmann, *Amsterdam als financieel centrum*, p. 86.
84. 'Pleidooi voor opname Duitsche emissies in notering prijscourant Ver.v.Effectenhandel', supplement *Algemeen Handelsblad*, 26 September 1925.
85. Hartmann, *Amsterdam als financieel centrum*, pp. 26–7.
86. Archive DNB, 2.3/501/1, Duitslands schulden. German report 'Aufteilung der kurzfristigen ausländischen Kredite an Deutschland nach Gläubigern, Schuldern und Ländern (Stand v. 28.Juli 1931)', dated 10 December 1931; own calculations.
87. 'Onze groote banken in 1918 en de voorafgaande 5 jaren', *In- en Uitvoer. Handels-economisch maandblad voor Nederland en zijne kolonien* (23 July 1919); Rotterdamsche Bankvereeniging, 'Development of Dutch Banking Business, part II', *Monthly Review* (October 1920), pp. 25–9; Hartmann, *Amsterdam als financieel centrum*, p. 23.

88. A. Frankfurther, *In klinkende munt. Herinneringen van een bankier* (Amsterdam: De Brug-Djambatan N.V., 1961) p. 50; 'De Markenkoers', *H.D. de Vos' Wekelijksch Uitlotingsblad* (1 Sept. 1921); 'De dalende mark. Hoog-conjunctuur en beurswinst', *De Telegraaf* (4 October 1921); 'De groote uitverkoop', *Handelsblad* (Avondblad 19 November 1921).
89. Christoph Kreutzmüller, *Händler und Handlungsgehilfen. Der Finanzplatz Amsterdam und die deutschen Grossbanken (1918–1945)* (Stuttgart: Steiner, 2005), p. 38.
90. Madden and Nadler, *International Money Markets*, p. 466; Hartmann, *Amsterdam als financieel centrum*, p. 24.
91. Archive DNB, 2.3/63/1, De Amsterdamse wisselmarkt. Report with the same title by G. van Buttigha Wichers of the Nederlandsche Bank on the Amsterdam foreign exchange market, June 1928; Hartmann, *Amsterdam als financieel centrum*, pp. 60–2, pp. 112–3.
92. G. Vissering, 'The Netherlands Bank and the War', *The Economic Journal*, 27:106 (June 1917), pp. 159–86, p. 186.
93. Schmitz, *Der Amsterdamer Geldmarkt*, p. 7; Hartmann, *Amsterdam als financieel centrum*, pp. 47–9.
94. Houwink ten Cate, 'Amsterdam als Finanzplatz Deutschlands', p. 178.
95. Schmitz, *Der Amsterdamer Geldmarkt*, p. 7, p. 22.
96. G. W. J. Bruins, 'The Netherlands Bank, 1926–7', *The Economic Journal*, 37:148 (December 1927) pp. 672–6, there pp. 675–6.
97. Hartmann, *Amsterdam als financieel centrum*, p. 102.
98. Archive DNB, 2.3/681/1, Discontering. Declaration by the *Nederlandsche Bank*, 7 February; Idem, Standard confirmation to the replies by the individual banks, 7 April 1922.
99. Schmitz, *Der Amsterdamer Geldmarkt*, p. 106; A. Houwink, *Acceptcrediet*, p. 90.
100. NL-HaNA, DNB, 2.25.08, inv.nr. 3317. Commissie van Advies, 11 March 1921.
101. Idem, inv.nr. 3319. Commissie van Advies, 15 December 1922 and 22 December 1922.
102. Archive DNB, 2.1/18/1, Meeting of the board of the *Nederlandsche Bank* with representatives of the major Dutch banks, 21 March 1923; NL-HaNA, DNB, 2.25.08, inv. nr. 3319, Commissie van Advies, 2 March 1923; Idem, 23 March 1923.
103. Archive DNB, 2.1/18/1, Meeting of the board of the *Nederlandsche Bank* with representatives of the major Dutch banks, 21 March 1923. The original text reads: 'De heer Tienhoven zegt, dat hij zich heeft verheugd toen de Duitsche banken zich hier vestigden en dat hij thans ook niet gaarne zou zien, dat zij weder vertrokken.'
104. Idem. The original text reads: 'Spreker meent dat zij hier niet anders dan goed doen aan de Amsterdamsche markt zoolang men hen maar belet, aan de gulden te komen, d.w.z. zoolang hun accept maar niet discontabel is.'
105. Archive DNB, 2.1/18/1, Meeting of the board of the *Nederlandsche Bank* with representatives of the major Dutch banks, 21 March 1923.
106. Madden and Nadler, *International Money Markets*, p. 467; Jongman, *Geldmarkt*, p. 225; NL-HaNA, DNB, 2.25.08, inv. nr. 3319. Commissie van Advies, 30 October 1922.
107. Archive DNB, 2.12/282/1, Geldmarktbeleid, discontopolitiek faciliteiten aan wisselmakelaars, speciale belenings en discontofaciliteit. 24 Nov. 1925 and 2 December 1925. Meetings of representatives of Dutch bill brokers with members of the board of the *Nederlandsche Bank*.
108. W. Redelmeier, 'Die Deutschen Banken in Amsterdam' in: *Jubileumnummer In- en Uitvoer* (January 1926) pp. 18–29.
109. *De Telegraaf*, 27 February 1926.

110. Archive DNB, 2.1/18/1, Reports of meetings of representatives of leading Dutch banks, 5–25 February 1926.
111. Idem, Meeting of W. Redelmeier with the board of directors of the *Nederlandsche Bank*, 19 February 1926.
112. Idem, Meeting of C.E. ter Meulen with the board of the *Nederlandsche Bank*, 5 February 1926; Idem, Meeting of A.J. van Hengel with the board of the *Nederlandsche Bank*, 4 February 1926.
113. Idem, Declaration by the *Nederlandsche Bank*, 25 March 1926.
114. 'Continental Discount Markets. I. – Amsterdam', *The Economist* (4 October 1930).
115. Archive DNB, 2.121.3/10/1, Arrangement, betreffende discontabiliteit van wissels waaraan goederentransacties met buitenland ten grondslag liggen. Reports on total acceptances allowed versus actual acceptances in portfolio and on the nature and quality of the material; Archive DNB, 2.3/681/1, Declaration by the *Nederlandsche Bank*, 7 Februari; Idem, Standard confirmation to the replies by the individual banks, 7 April 1922.
116. 'Continental Discount Markets. I. - Amsterdam' in: *The Economist* (4 October 1930).
117. Hartmann, *Amsterdam als financieel centrum*, p. 102.
118. NL-HaNA, DNB, 2.25.08, inv. nr. 3316–3328. Minutes of meetings of the *Commissie van Advies*, 1919–33.
119. Hartmann, *Amsterdam als financieel centrum*, pp. 34–6.

WORKS CITED

Archives and Primary Sources

The Avalon Project: Washington's Farewell Address 1796 at http://www.yale.edu/lawweb/avalon/washing.htm

France

ACACL: Archives de la Compagnie des Agents de Change de Lyon (1939–1945), Procès verbaux, Archives départementales du Rhône, Lyon.

ACACM : Archives de la Compagnie des Agents de Change de Marseille (1939–1945), Procès verbaux, Euronext, Paris.

ACACP : Archives de la Compagnie des Agents de Change de Paris (1939–1945), Procès verbaux, Euronext, Paris.

AN, Archives Nationales (1939–1945), Fonds AJ40, vol. 832, Archives Nationales, Paris.

Netherlands

Historical archive of the *Nederlandsche Bank*

- 1.121/245/1, Correspondentie met G Vissering, allerhande onderwerpen: bib, reichsbank, kredieten oost-europa.
- 2.1/18/1, Bevorderen betalingsverkeer met het buitenland vestigingen van buitenlandse banken in amsterdam, discontofaciliteiten.
- 2.1/332/1, Kredietverlening aan het buitenland, duitsland, verenigd koninkrijk, verenigde staten van amerika, plan ter meulen.
- 2.111.3/121/1, Schaarste aan zilverbons, grote aantallen bevinden zich in Duitsland.
- 2.12/282/1, Geldmarktbeleid, discontopolitiek faciliteiten aan wisselmakelaars, speciale belenings en discontofaciliteit.
- 2.121/153/1, Duits krediet, onderpand Duitse industrie en schatkistwissels.
- 2.121/154/1, Duits krediet door lippmann rosenthal & co rotterdamsche bankvereeniging en amsterdamsche bank (onderpand duitse effecten)

- 2.121.3/8/1, Kredieten waarbij het buitenland betrokken is, N&E kredieten.
- 2.121.3/10/1, Arrangement, betreffende discontabiliteit van wissels waaraan goederentransacties met buitenland ten grondslag liggen.
- 2.132/151/1, Regeringskredieten 1914–1918, verlenging kredieten na de oorlog, verlenging duitse kredieten.
- 2.132/151/2, Regeringskredieten 1914–1918, verlenging kredieten na de oorlog, verlenging Duitse kredieten.
- 2.3/63/1, De Amsterdamse wisselmarkt.
- 2.3/501/1, Duitslands schulden.
- 2.3/544/1, Kapitaalmarkt/emissies te Amsterdam.
- 2.3/681/1, Discontering.
- 2.3/2079/1, Invloed wegtrekken buitenlandsche saldi op positie Nederlandsche gulden.
- 7/300/1, Barterinstituut (vereeniging voor den goederenruil) vergaderingen en besprekingen betreffende de oprichting in nederland van de vereeniging voor den goederenruil.
- 7/831/1, Vestiging van buitenlandse banken in nederland.
- 8/1501/1, Duitsland, conferenties met Duitsers, valorisatie, tarievenkwestie markenportefeuille dnb van voor 1914
- 8.2/2060/1, Duitsland, Duitse rijksbank.

National Archives

- 2.18.29, Nederlandsche Spaarbankbond, 1906–2000.
- 2.25.08, Archief van De Nederlandsche Bank NV (1643) 1814 - 1980 (1995)

Spain

Ministerio de Hacienda, *Resumen provisional sobre la evolución de la Hacienda desde el 18 de julio de 1936 hasta el presente* (Madrid: 1940).

Switzerland

Schweiz, Bundesamt für Statistik, *Statistisches Jahrbuch der Schweiz* (Zürich: Orell Fueslli, 1930-2008).

Schweizerische Bankiervereinigung, *VIII. Jahresbericht,* Basel, Schweizerische Bankiervereinigung, 1919/1920.

Schweizerische Nationalbank, *Die Banken in der Schweiz; Das Schweizerische Bankwesen,* Zürich, Orell Fuessli, 1907–2008.

Basel Committee on Banking Supervision, *Basel II: International Convergence of Capital Measurement and Capital Standards: A Revised Framework* (Basel, Bank for International Settlements: 2004).

United Kingdom

Bank of England Archive (BEA):

- 'The Bank of England 1914–1921' (1928) vol. I to III.
- C92/110, 'Advances O/A Pre-Moratorium Advances'.

Sir Robert Kindersley, *Evidence to the Committee on Finance and Industry*, British Parliamentary Papers, 1931, I.

'Correspondence between the Treasury and the Bank of England', *House of Commons Papers*, 1914–16, no.37.

Guildhall Library Archive (GLA). London Stock Exchange, Committee of General Purposes, 24 March 1915. Published crisis diary of Chairman Sir R. W. Inglis.

Hansard:

- House of Commons Debate, 26 August 1914. Mr Lloyd George.
- House of Commons debate, 27 November 1914. Mr Lloyd George.
- House of Commons debate, 21 February 1916. Statement by the Prime Minister.
- House of Commons debate, 27 November 1914. Mr Lloyd George.
- House of Commons Debate, 21 February 1916, Statement by the Prime Minister.

London School of Economics Archive (LSEA). Sir George Paish, 'My Memoirs' (*c.* 1950).

Rothschild Archive London (RAL):

- XI/130A/8, 14 July 1914.
- T65/59, Memorandum on the Gold Market, 1937.

The National Archives, Kew (TNA):

- T160/998, Letter from Sir Otto Niemeyer, Treasury, to Arthur Kiddy, City Editor, The Morning Post, 28 December 1926.
- T170/14, 'Joint Stock Proposal to Deposit Gold & Security for Notes', 31 July 1914; Memorandum by John Bradbury, Treasury, to Mr Bonham Carter, Prime Minister's Office (no date)
- T170/26, Memorandum by Sir John Bradbury for the Prime Minister, 'The Financial Situation Arising Out of the War', 7 November 1914.
- T170/28, 'The Conduct of the Banks 1914.' Letter from Austen Chamberlain to the Chancellor of the Exchequer, 11 August 1914.
- T170/28 Edwin Montagu, Treasury Secretary, to David Lloyd George, Chancellor of the Exchequer, reporting a conversation with Sir George Paish, 15 August 1914.

- T170/28, Edwin Montagu, 'Treasury Assistance to Banks and Discount Houses, Continuance of Moratorium and nature of Banking Facilities Available', 27 August 1914.
- T170/35, Correspondence with Messrs. De La Rue, 1914.
- T170/55, Conference between Chancellor of the Exchequer and Representative Bankers and Traders, 4 August 1914.
- T170/57, Adjourned Conference between the Chancellor of the Exchequer, Members of the Cabinet, Representatives of the Bankers, 6 August 1914.
- T172/134, Conference, 12 August 1914. Sir George Anderson, Bank of Scotland.
- T172/134, Conference between the Chancellor of the Exchequer, Members of the Cabinet and Representatives of Accepting Houses, 12 August 1914.
- T172/158, Adjourned conference between the Cabinet Committee and the Accepting Houses, 4 September 1914.
- T172/162, Reports on the Advisability of Continuing the Moratorium.
- T172/183, Memorandum to the Chancellor by Sir George Paish, 6 August 1914.

Bankers Magazine:

- 'The Great Crisis', *Bankers Magazine*, September 1914.
- E. Sykes, 'Some effects of the war on the London money market', *Bankers' Magazine*, February 1915.
- 'Pre-Moratorium Bills', *Bankers' Magazine*, 1921.

The Economist:

- 'The Financial Situation at Home and Abroad', *The Economist*, 1 August 1914.
- 'The Stock Exchange Crisis Day by Day', *The Economist*, 1 August 1914.
- 'Bankers' Gazette', *The Economist*, 8 August 1914.
- 'The War, Trade and Finance', *The Economist*, 22 August 1914.
- 'Treasury Bills and the Discount Market', *The Economist*, 19 September 1914.
- *The Economist*, 3 October 1914.
- 'The Loan Positions of the Stock Exchange', The *Economist*, 17 October 1914.
- 'The Joint Stock Banks', *The Economist*, 24 1914.
- 'The Financial Crisis of 1914', *The Economist*, 24 October 1914, p.686.
- 'Bankers' Gazette', *The Economist*, 23 November 1918.

The Statist:

- 'Sir George Paish', *The Statist*, 15 August 1914.
- 'The Financial Situation', *The Statist*, 15 August 1914.
- 'The Financial Situation. Process of Adjustment', *The Statist*, 22 August 1914.
- 'Money', *The Statist*, 22 August 1914.
- 'The Financial Outlook', *The Statist*, 5 September 1914.

- 'Restoring Credit', *The Statist*, 12 September 1914.
- 'The War Loan', *The Statist*, 28 November 1914.

The Times:

- The Times, *History of the War*, vol. I (London: The Times, 1914).

Bibliography

Aigner, D., C. Lovell, and P. Schmidt, 'Formulation and Estimation of Stochastic Frontier Production Function Models', *Journal of Econometrics*, 6 (1977), pp. 21–37.

Albiñana, C., and E. Fuentes Quintana, *Sistema fiscal español y comparado* (Madrid: Facultad de Económicas, 1967).

Allen, F., and D. Gale, 'Comparative Financial Systems: A Survey', Center for Financial Institutions Working Papers 01–15, Wharton School Center for Financial Institutions, University of Pennsylvania (April 2001).

Ally, R., 'War and Gold – The Bank of England, the London Gold Market and South Africa's Gold, 1914–19', *Journal of Southern African Studies*, 17:2 (June 1991), pp. 221–38.

Amano, M., 'The Gurley-Shaw Hypothesis, Growth, Regressions and Granger-Caulsality', *Economic Journal of Chiba University*, 19:3 (Dec. 2004), at http://mitizane.ll.chiba-u.jp/metadb/up/AN10005358/KJ00003964075.pdf.

Arbulu, P., 'Le marché parisien des actions au XIXe siècle', in G. Gallais-Hamonno (ed.), *Le marché financier français au XIXe siècle. Volume 2. Aspects quantitatifs des acteurs et des instruments à la Bourse de Paris* (Paris: Publications de la Sorbonne, 2007).

Arias Velasco, J., *La Hacienda de la Generalitat, 1931–1938* (Barcelona: Ariel, 1977).

Armagnac, J., 'Le marché financier de Londres', in A. Aupetit, L. Brocard, J. Armagnac, G. Delamotte, G. Aubert, *Les grands marchés financiers. France (Paris et Province) – The great financial markets, London, Berlin, New York ...* (Paris: Félix Alcan, 1912).

Atkin, J., *The Foreign Exchange Market of London: Development since 1900* (London: Routledge, 2005).

Aupetit, A., 'Le marché financier de Paris', in A. Aupetit, L. Brocard, J. Armagnac, G. Delamotte, G. Aubert, *Les grands marchés financiers. France (Paris et Province) – The great financial markets, London, Berlin, New York ...* (Paris: Félix Alcan, 1912).

Aupetit, A., L. Brocard, J. Armagnac, G. Delamotte, G. Aubert, *Les grands marchés financiers. France (Paris et Province) – The great financial markets, London, Berlin, New York (...)* (Paris: Félix Alcan, 1912).

Avramov, R., 'The Bulgarian National Bank in a Historical Perspective: Shaping an Institution, Searching for a Monetary Standard', in R. Avramov, and Ş. Pamuk (eds.), *Monetary and fiscal policies in Southeast Europe. Historical and comparative perspective* (Sofia: Bulgarian National Bank, 2006), pp. 93–108.

Avramov, R., *120 years Bulgarian National Bank: 1879–1999* (Sofia: Bulgarian National Bank, 1999).

Baia Curioni, S., *Regolazione e competizione. Storia del mercato azionario in Italia (1808–1938)* (Bologna: Il Mulino, 1995).

Barendregt, J., 'Op weg naar nationale bekendheid, het handelsbankwezen tussen 1870 en 1914', in J. Vries, W. Vroom, and T. de Graaf (ed.), *Wereldwijd bankieren. ABN Amro 1824–1999* (Amsterdam: De Bussy Ellermans Harms bv, 1999), pp. 127–84.

Battilossi, S., 'Banche miste, gruppi di imprese e società finanziarie (1914–1933)', in G. Conti, and S. La Francesca (eds), *Banche e reti di banche nell'Italia postunitaria,* vol. 1 (Bologna, Il Mulino: 2000), pp. 307–52.

Baubeau, P., 'Militarization: a Political Clue to Financial Structures?', Paper presented at the EABH conference The Critical Function of History in Banking and Finance, Cyprus (May 2009).

Bauer, H., *Schweizerischer Bankverein 1872–1972* (Basel: Schweizerischer Bankverein, 1972).

Becker, J.-J., *La première guerre mondiale* (Paris: MA Editions, 1985).

Belli, F., and A. Scialoja., 'Vocazioni interventiste, miti ed ideologie del liberismo all'indomani dell'unificazione nazionale; il controllo delle società commerciali e degli istituti di credito nell'esperienze del Sindacato governativo (1866–1869)', in C. De Cesare, *Il Sindacato governativo, le società commerciali nel Regno d'Italia* (Bologna: Forni, 1979), pp. 1–44.

Benfey, F., *Die neuere Entwicklung des deutschen Auslandsbankwesens 1914–1925 (unter Mitberücksichtigung der ausländischen Bankstützpunkte in Deutschland)* (Berlin: Spaeth & Linde, 1925).

Berger, A., and L. Mester, *Inside the Black Box: What Explains Differences in the Efficiencies of Financial Institutions* (Washington DC: Federal Reserve Board, 1997).

Bessis, J., *Risk Management Banking* (Chichester: John Willey & Sons Ltd, 2002).

Bie, R. J. van der, and J. P. H. Smits, *Tweehonderd jaar statistiek in tijdreeksen, 1800-1999* (Amsterdam: Stichting Beheer IISG, 2001).

Black, F., M. C. Jensen, and M. Scholes, 'The Capital Asset Pricing Model: some Empirical Tests', in M.C. Jensen (ed.), *Studies in the Theory of Capital Markets* (New-York: Praeger, 1972).

Bloch, M., *Esquisse d'une histoire monétaire de l'Europe* (Paris: A. Colin, 1954).

Bonelli, F., 'Introduzione', in Idem (ed.), *La Banca d'Italia dal 1894 al 1913. Momenti della formazione di una banca centrale* (Rome and Bari: Laterza, 1991), pp. 3–114.

Bonelli, F., *La crisi del 1907 una tappa dello sviluppo industriale in Italia* (Turin: Fondazione Einaudi, 1971).

Bonin, H., *Histoire de la Société Générale 1864–1890* (Geneva: Droz, 2006).

Boot, A. W. A., and A. V. Thakor, 'Financial System Architecture', *The Review of Financial Studies,* 10:3 (1997), pp. 693–733.

Born, K. E., *International Banking in the 19th and 20th Centuries* (Leamington Spa: Berg Publishers Ltd, 1983).

Bosch, K. D., *De Nederlandse beleggingen in de Verenigde Staten* (Amsterdam: Elsevier, 1948).

Boudon, G., *La Bourse et ses hôtes* (Paris: G. Pedone-Lauriel, 1896).

Bouvier, J., 'Les monnaies et les banques', in P. Léon (ed.), *Histoire économique et sociale du Monde* (Paris: Colin, 1978), vol. IV, pp. 225–97.

Bouvier, J., *Le Crédit Lyonnais de 1863 à 1882: les années de formation d'une banque de dépôts* (Paris: Editions de l'EHESS, 1999).

Bouvier, J., *Le krach de l'Union Générale 1878–1885* (Paris: Presses Universitaires de France, 1960).

Boyd, J., and B. Smith, 'The Coevolution of the Real and Financial Sectors in the Growth Process', *World Bank Economic Review*, 10:2 (1996), pp. 371–96.

Brambilla, C., and G. Conti, 'Informazione e regole contabili nei rapporti tra banca e industria', in G. Conti, *Creare il credito e arginare i rischi. Il sistema finanziario tra nobiltà e miserie del capitalismo italiano* (Bologna: Il Mulino, 2007), pp. 247–92.

Brambilla, C., *Banche di investimento in Europa. Tipologie e strutture operative prima del 1914* (Pisa: Il Campano, 2008).

Brewer, J., *The Sinews of Power. War, Money and the English State, 1688–1783* (Cambridge, Mass.: Harvard University Press, 1990).

Bricall, J. M., *Politica econòmica de la Generalitat (1936–1939).* Vol. I. *Evolució i formes de la produció industrial.* Vol II. *El sistema financier* (Barcelona: Edicions 62, 1970–8).

Broadberry, S., and M. Harrison, *The Economics of World War I* (Cambridge: Cambridge University Press, 2005).

Brown, B., *Monetary Chaos in Europe: the end of an era* (London: Croom Helm, 1988).

Brown, W. A., *The International Gold Standard Reinterpreted, 1914–1934* (New York: National Bureau of Economic Research, 1940).

Brown, W. O., J. H. Mulherin, and M. D. Weidenmier, 'Competing with the NYSE', *NBER Working Paper* n° 12 343 (2006).

Bruins, G. W. J., 'The Netherlands Bank, 1926–7', *The Economic Journal*, 37:148 (1927) pp. 672–76.

Bulgarian National Bank, *Jubileen sbornik po sluchai 50-godishninata na BNB (Jubilee collection on 50 Anniversary of the BNB)* (Sofia: State Print, 1929).

Bussière, E., *Paribas 1872–1992. L'Europe et le Monde* (Antwerpen: Fonds Mercator, 1992).

Cagan, P., *Determinants and Effects of Changes in the Stock of Money: 1875–1960* (New York and London: Columbia University Press, 1965).

Calomiris, C., 'Financial History and the Long reach of the Second 30 Years War', in T. Guinnane, W. Andrew Sundstrom, and W. C. Whatley, *History Matters: Essays on Economic Growth, Technology, and Demographic Change* (Stanford, CA: Stanford University Press, 2004).

Camera dei Deputati, *Ricerca sulle società commerciali. Linee evolutive della legislazione italiana e ordinamenti stranieri* (Rome: Stabilimenti tipografici C. Colombo, 1968).

Cameron, R., 'Founding the Bank of Darmstadt', *Explorations in Entrepreneurial History*, 8 (February 1956), pp. 113–30.

Cameron, R., *France and the economic development of Europe, 1800-1914. Conquest of peace and seeds of war* (Princeton, NJ: Princeton University Press, 1961).

Carlina, W., and C. Mayer, 'Finance, investment, and growth', *Journal of Financial Economics*, 69 (2003), pp. 191–226.

Carney, R., 'National Security and National Finance: Locating the Origins of Modern Financial Capitalism', European University Institute, EUI Working Paper RSCAS n° 2004/21 (2004).

Carney, R., 'The Political Economy of Financial Systems: why do developed countries have such financing arrangements?', Paper presented at the annual meeting of the American Political Science Association, Boston, MA (28 August 2002).

Carrieri, F., V. Errunza, and K. Hogan, 'Characterizing World Market Integration through Time', *Journal of Financial and Quantitative Analysis*, 42:4 (2007), pp. 915–40.

Cassis, Y., *Les capitales du capital. Histoire des places financières internationales, 1780-2005* (Paris: Honoré Champion, 2008).

CBS, *Macro-economische ontwikkelingen 1921–1939 en 1969–1985. Een vergelijking op basis van herziene gegevens voor het interbellum* (The Hague: Staatsuitgeverij/CBS-publikaties, 1987).

Cellérier, L., *Etude sur les sociétés anonymes en France et dans les pays voisins* (Paris: L. Larose et L. Tenin, 1905).

Chapman, S., *The Rise of Merchant Banking* (London: George Allen & Unwin, 1984).

Christensen, L. R., D. W. Jorgenson, and L. J. Lau, 'Transcendental Logarithmic Production Frontiers', *Review of Economics and Statistics*, 55:1 (1973), p. 28–45.

Christoforoff, A., *Kurs po Bulgarsko bankovo delo. Chast I: Istorichesko razvitie (Course on Bulgarian Banking. Part I: Historical development)* (Sofia: n.a., 1946).

Ciccarelli, C., and S. Fenoaltea, 'Business Fluctuations in Italy, 1861–1913: The New Evidence', *Explorations in Economic History*, 44:3 (July 2007), pp. 432–51.

Ciccarelli, C., and S. Fenoaltea, 'Construction in Italy's Regions, 1861–1913', MPRA Paper 9714 (Munich: University Library of Munich, 2008).

Ciccarelli, C., S. Fenoaltea, and T. Proietti, 'The Comovements of Construction in Italy's Regions, 1861–1913', MPRA Paper 8870 (Munich: University Library of Munich, 2008).

Ciocca, P., and G. Toniolo, 'Industry and finance in Italy, 1918–1940', *Journal of European Economic History*, 13 (1984), pp. 113–36.

Clapham, J., 'Sir John Clapham's Account of the Financial Crisis in August 1914', Appendix 3, in R. S. Sayers, *The Bank of England, 1891–1944* (Cambridge: Cambridge University Press, 1976).

Clemens, M. A., and J. G. Williamson, 'Wealth Bias in the First Global Capital Market Boom, 1870-1913', *Economic Journal*, 114:495 (2004), pp. 304–337.

Coelli, T., 'A Guide to FRONTIER Version 4.1: A Computer Program for Stochastic Frontier Production and Cost Function Estimation', CEPA Working Paper No. 7/96 (1996).

Coelli, T., and G. Battese, 'A Model for Technical Inefficiency Effects in a Stochastic Frontier Production Function for Panel Data', *Empirical Economics*, 20:2 (1995), pp. 325–332.

Cohen, J. S., 'Financing industrialization in Italy, 1894–1914: The partial transformation of a late comer', *Journal of Economic History*, 27:3 (1967), pp. 363–82.

Comín, F., and D. Díaz, 'Sector público administrativo y estado del bienestar' in A. Carreras, and X. Tafunell (coords.) *Estadísticas históricas de España. Siglos XIX y XX* (Madrid: Fundación BBVA, 2005), pp. 873–965.

Comín, F., and S. López, 'La Hacienda del gobierno de la República española (1936–1939)' in E. Fuentes Quintana (dir) *Economía y Economistas españoles en la Guerra Civil* (Barcelona: Galaxia-Guteberg 2008), pp. 851–99.

Confalonieri, A., *Banca e industria in Italia dalla crisi del 1907 all'agosto del 1914* (Milan: Banca commerciale italiana, 1982).

Confalonieri, A., *Banca e industria in Italia, 1894–1906* (Bologna: Il Mulino, 1981).

Confalonieri, A., *Banche miste e grande industria in Italia, 1914–1933* (Milan: Banca commerciale italiana, 1994).

Conti, G., 'Finanza d'impresa e capitale di rischio in Italia, 1870-1939', *Rivista di storia economica*, n.s., 10:3 (1993), pp. 307–32.

Conti, G., 'Le banche e il finanziamento industriale', in F. Amatori, D. Bigazzii, R. Giannetti, and L. Segreto, *Storia d'Italia, t. XV: L'industria* (Turin: Einaudi, 1999) pp. 441–504.

Cornut, P., *Répartition de la fortune privée en France par département et nature de biens au cours de la première moitié du XXe siècle* (Paris: A. Colin, 1963).

Costigliola, F. C., 'Anglo-American Financial Rivalry in the 1920s', *Journal of Economic History*, 37:4 (Dec. 1977) pp. 911–34.

Crampton, R., *A Concise History of Bulgaria,* 2nd edn (Cambridge: Cambridge University Press: 2005).

Da Pozzo, M., and G. Felloni, *La Borsa Valori Di Genova Nel Secolo XIX* (Torino: Industria Libraria Tipografica Editrice, 1964).

De Cecco, M., *The International Gold Standard: Money and Empire* (London: Blackwell, 1974).

De Mattia, R. (ed.), *I Bilanci Degli Istituti Di Emissione Italiani – 1845–1936* (Rome: Banca d'Italia, 1967).

De Mattia, R., 'I Bilanci Delle Banche Di Emissione Italiane Dal 1861 Al 1874', *Rivista Di Politica Economica*, XLVII:III (November–December 1957), Fasc. 11–12.

Demirguc-Kunt, A., and R. Levine, 'Bank-Based and Market-Based Financial Systems: Cross-Country Comparisons', World Bank Working Paper n° 2143 (2000).

Di Nardi, G., *Le Banche Di Emissione In Italia Nel Secolo XIX* (Torino: Unione Tipografico - Editrice Torinese, 1953).

Dimitrova, K., and M. Ivanov, 'Bulgaria', in P. Mooslechner, and E. Gnan (eds.), *The Experience of Exchange Rate Regimes in Southeastern Europe in a Historical and Comparative Perspective*, Workshop proceedings n°13 (Vienna: Oesterreichische Nationalbank, 2008), pp. 419–23.

Dimitrova, K., M. Ivanov, and R. Simeonova-Ganeva, *Effective Exchange Rates of the Bulgarian Lev 1879–1939*, ICER Working Paper n°4 (Torino: International Centre for Economic Research, 2009).

Douglass, N., and B. Weingast, 'Constitutions and Commitment: The Evolution of Institutions Governing Public Choice in Seventeenth-Century England', *The Journal of Economic History*, 49:4 (Dec. 1989), pp. 803–32.

Drechsel, D., and T. Straumann, 'Historical Perspective of Swiss Banking Crises', University of Zurich Working Paper (2010).

Dreyfus, J.-M., *Pillages sur ordonnance. Aryanisation et restitution des banques en France 1940–1953* (Paris: Fayard, 2003).

Dubost, R., *La Bourse de Lyon* (Lyon: Bosc frères M. & L. Riou, 1938).

Dumas, B., C. Harvey, and P. Ruiz, 'Are Correlation of Stock Returns Justified by Subsequent Changes in National Output?', *Journal of International Money and Finance*, 22:6 (2003), 777–811.

Dunn, P., and F. Coulomb, 'Peace, War and International Security: Economic Theories', University of the West of England, Department of Economics, Developing Quantitative Marxism Working Paper Series n° 0801 (Nov. 2008).

Edelstein, M., *Overseas investment in the age of high imperialism: the United Kingdom* (New York: Columbia University Press, 1982).

Ehrsam, P., 'Die Bankenkrise der 30er Jahre in der Schweiz', in U. Zulauf (ed.), *50 Jahre Eidgenossische Bankenaufsicht* (Zürich: Schulthess Polygraphischer Verlag, 1985), pp. 83–118.

Einaudi, L., 'The Theory of Imaginary Money from Charlemagne to the French Revolution', in L. Einaudi, R. Faucci, and R. Marchionatti (eds.) *Luigi Einaudi. Selected economic essays* (London: Palgrave Macmillan, 2006), pp. 153–181.

Errera, A., *Il nuovo codice di commercio del Regno d'Italia* (Florence: Pellas, 1883).

F. Amatori, D. Bigazzii, R. Giannetti, and L. Segreto, *Storia d'Italia, t. XV: L'industria* (Turin: Einaudi, 1999).

Fantacci, L., 'Complementary Currencies: a Prospect on Money from a Retrospect on Premodern Practices', *Financial History Review*, 12:1 (2005), pp. 43–61.

Fantacci, L., 'The dual currency system of Renaissance Europe', *Financial History Review* 15:1 (2008), pp. 55–72.

Fantacci, L., *Autonomy vs. stability: the relationship between internal and external money in Bulgaria*, BNB Discussion Paper n°73 (Sofia: Bulgarian National Bank, 2009).

Federico, G., and G. Toniolo, 'Italy', in R. Sylla, and G. Toniolo (eds.), *Patterns of European Industrialization. The Nineteenth Century* (London and New York: Routledge, 1992), pp. 197–217.

Feiertag, O., 'Les banques d'émission et la BRI face à la dislocation de l'étalon-or (1931–1933) : l'entrée dans l'âge de la coopération monétaire internationale', *Histoire, Economie et Société*, 18:4 (1999), pp. 715–36.

Feinstein, C. H., *Statistical Tables of National Income, Expenditure and Output of the UK 1855–1965* (Cambridge: Cambridge University Press, 1972).

Feldstein, M., and C. Horioka, 'Domestic Saving and International Capital Flows', *Economic Journal*, 90 (1980), pp. 314–29.

Fenoaltea, S., 'The Growth of the Italian Economy, 1861–1913: Preliminary Second-Generation Estimates,' *European Review of Economic History*, 9:3 (December 2005) pp. 273–312.

Ferguson, N., 'Political Risk and the International Bond Market between the 1848 Revolution and the Outbreak of the First World War', *Economic History Review*, 59:1 (2006), pp. 70-112.

Ferguson, N., and M. Schularick, 'The Empire Effect: The Determinants of Country Risk in the First Age of Globalization, 1880-1913', *Journal of Economic History*, 66:2 (2006), pp. 283–312.

Ferguson, N., and R. Batley, *Event Risk and the International Bond Market in the Era of the Classical Gold Standard* (Oxford:Unpublished Manuscript, Oxford University, 2001).

Ferrara, F., 'Il Corso Forzato De Biglietti Di Banca In Italia', in G. Bottai, and C. Arena (eds), *Nuova Collana Di Economisti, vol. 2, Economisti Italiani Del Risorgimento* (Torino: Unione Tipografico-Editrice Torinese, 1933).

Ferrara, F., 'L'abolizione del corso forzato', in G. Bottai, and C. Arena (eds), *Nuova Collana di Economisti, vol. 2, Economisti Italiani del Risorgimento* (Torino: Unione Tipografico-Editrice Torinese, 1933).

Findlay, R., and K. H. O'Rourke, 'Power and Plenty: Trade, War and the World Economy in the Second Millennium (Preface)', Trinity Economics Papers, 0107 (2007).

Flandreau, M., and F. Zumer, *The Making of Global Finance. 1880-1913* (Paris: OECD, 2004).

Fohlin, C., 'Capital Mobilisation and Utilisation in Latecomer Economies: Germany and Italy Compared', *European Review of Economic History*, 3:2 (1999), pp. 139–74.

Fohlin, C., '*Fiduciari* and Firm Liquidity Constraints: the Italian Experience with German-style Universal Banking, *Explorations in economic history*, 35:1 (1998), pp. 83–107.

Fohlin, C., *Finance Capitalism and Germany's Rise to Industrial Power* (Cambridge: Cambridge University Press, 2007).

Forbes, K. F., and R. Rigobon, 'No Contagion, Only Interdependence: Measuring Stock Market Co-movements', *The Journal of Finance*, 57:5 (2002), pp. 2223–61.

Forsyth, D. J., and D. Verdier (ed.), *The Origins of National Financial Systems, Alexander Gerschenkron reconsidered* (London and New York: Routledge, 2003).

Francois-Marsal, F., *Encyclopédie de Banque et de Bourse* (Paris: Crété, 1931).

Frankfurther, A., *In klinkende munt. Herinneringen van een bankier* (Amsterdam: De Brug-Djambatan N.V., 1961).

Franks, J., C. Mayer, and H. Miyajima, 'Equity Markets and Institutions: The Case of Japan', RIETI Discussion Paper Series 09–E -039 (July 2009).

Fratianni, M., and F. Spinelli, *A Monetary History of Italy* (Cambridge: Cambridge University Press, 1997).

Fratianni, M., and F. Spinelli, *Storia Monetaria d'Italia. L'Evoluzione Del Sistema Monetario E Bancario* (Milano: Arnoldo Mondadori, 1991).

Friedman, M., 'The Crime of 1873', *Journal of Political Economy*, 98:6 (1990), pp. 1159–94.

Friedman, M., and A. J. Schwartz, *A Monetary History of the United States, 1867–1960* (Princeton, NJ: Princeton University Press, 1963).

Galbraith, J. K., *Money. Whence it came and where it went* (Boston, MA: Houghton Mifflin, 1975).

Gallais-Hamonno, G., and P.-C. Hautcœur (ed.), *Le marché financier français au XIXe siècle*, 2 volumes (Paris: Publications de la Sorbonne, 2007).

Galli, A. M., 'Sviluppo e crisi della Banca generale', in E. Decleva (ed.), *Antonio Allievi, dalle scienze civili alla pratica del credito* (Milan-Bari: Cariplo-Laterza, 1997), pp. 561–651.

García Pérez, R., *Franquismo y Tercer Reich* (Madrid: Centro de Estudios Constitucionales, 1994).

Gatrell, P., 'The First World War and War Communism, 1914–1920' in R. W. Davies, M. Harrison, and S. G. Wheatcroft (eds), *The economic transformation of the Soviet Union, 1913–1945* (Cambridge: Cambridge University Press, 1994).

Generalitat de Cataluña, *La Política Financiera de la Generalitat durante la revolución y la Guerra*, Vol. I (Barcelona, 1937).

Gerschenkron, A., *Economic backwardness in historical perspective. A book of essays* (Cambridge, Mass.: The Belknap Press of Harvard University Press, 1966).

Gianfreda, G., and N. Janson, 'Le Banche Di Emissione In Italia Tra Il 1861 E Il 1893: Un Caso Di Concorrenza?', *Rivista Di Politica Economica* (January 2001), pp. 15–73.

Gianfreda, G., *Institutions Monétaires et Stabilité de la Monnaie* (PhD dissertation, Paris Dauphine University, 2004).

Gille, B., 'La fondation de la Société Générale', *Histoire des entreprises*, 1961, pp. 5–64.

Girault, R., *Emprunts russes et investissements français en Russie 1887–1914* (Paris: Armand Colin, 1973).

Giura, V., *Tra política ed economia. L'Italia e la guerra civile spagnola* (Roma-Napoli: Edizioni Scientifiche Italiane, 2002).

Gnjatovic, D., 'Introduction of limping gold standard in the principality of Serbia' in R. Avramov, and Ş. Pamuk (eds), *Monetary and fiscal policies in Southeast Europe. Historical and comparative perspective* (Sofia: Bulgarian National Bank, 2006), pp. 45–66.

Goetzmann, W., and A. Ukhov, 'British Overseas Investment 1870-1913: A Modern Portfolio Theory Approach', *Review of Finance*, 10:2 (2006), pp. 261–300.

Goetzmann, W., L. Lingfeld, and G. Rouwenhorst, 'Long-Term Global Market Correlations', *Journal of Business*, 78:1 (2005), pp. 1–38.

Goetzmann, W., R. Ibbotson, and L. Peng, 'A New Historical Database for the NYSE 1815 to 1925: Performance and Predictability', *Journal of Financial Markets*, 4:1 (2001), pp. 1–32.

Goldsmith, R. W., *Financial Structure and Development* (New Haven and London: Yale University Press, 1969).

Gómez Mendoza, A., *El 'Gibraltar económico': Franco y Riotinto, 1936–1954* (Madrid: Biblioteca Civitas economía y empresa, 1994).

Gómez-Galvarriato, A., and A. Musacchio, 'Un nuevo índice de precios para México, 1886–1929' in *El Trimestre Económico*, 67:1 (2000), pp. 47–91.

Goodhart, C., *The Evolution of Central Banks* (London and Cambridge Massachusetts: MIT Press, 1988).

Guillorit R., *La réglementation des bourses de valeurs en France depuis juin 1940 : Transition ou parenthèse ?* (Paris: Librairie Générale de Droit et de Jurisprudence, 1946).

Gurley, J., and E. Shaw, *Money in a Theory of Finance* (Washington, DC: Brooking Institution, 1960).

Hirschfeld, H. M., 'Amsterdam comme centre financier international', *Revue Économique Internationale* (July 1924), pp. 7–24.

Hardach, G., *The First World War 1914–1918* (London: Allen Lane, 1977).

Harrison, M. (ed.), The Economics of World War II: Six Great Powers in International Comparison (Cambridge: Cambridge University Press, 1998).

Harrison, M., 'The Frequency of Wars', The University of Warwick, Warwick Economic Research Papers n° 879 (2008).

Harthoorn, P. C., *Hoofdlijnen uit de ontwikkeling van het moderne bankwezen in Nederland vóór de concentratie* (Rotterdam: De Wester Boekhandel, 1928).

Hartigan, J. A., *Clustering algorithms* (New York: Wiley, 1975).

Hartmann, W. J., *Amsterdam als financieel centrum: een beschijvende, critische en vergelijkende studie* (Hilversum: s.n., 1937).

Harvey, C. E., *The Rio Tinto Company: An Economic History of a leading international mining concern, 1873 – 1954* (Penzance, Cornwall: Alison Hodge, 1981).

Hautcœur, P.-C., 'Le marché financier entre 1870 et 1900', in Y. Breton, A. Broder, M. Lutfalla, *La longue stagnation en France : l'autre grande dépression, 1873–1897* (Paris: Economica, 1997).

Hautcoeur, P.-C., and A. Riva, 'The Paris Financial Market in the 19th Century: an efficient multi-polar organisation?', paper presented at the Conference of the European Historical Economics Society 2007 in Lund (Sweden) (June 2007).

Hawtrey, R. G., *A Century of Bank Rate* (London: Longmans, 1938).

Hellauer, E., *Internationale Finanzplätze. Ihr Wesen und ihre Enstehung unter besonderer Berücksichtigung Amsterdams* (Berlin: Junker & Dünnhaupt, 1936).

Helleiner, E., *The Making of National Money. Territorial Currencies in Historical Perspective* (Ithaca New York: Cornell University Press, 2003).

Hertner, P., *Il capitale tedesco in Italia dall'Unità alla prima guerra mondiale: banche miste e sviluppo economico italiano* (Bologna: Il Mulino, 1984).

Hirsch, J.-P., *Les deux rêves du commerce. Entreprise et institution dans la région lilloise (1780-1860)* (Paris: EHESS, 1991).

Hoag, C., 'The Atlantic telegraph cable and capital Market Information Flows', *Journal of Economic History*, 66:2 (2006), pp. 342–53.

Homer, S., and R. Sylla, *A History of interest rates* (New Brunswick, NJ: Rutgers University Press, 1998).

Houwink, A., *Acceptcrediet. Economische en bankpolitieke beschouwingen over den in het bankaccept belichaamden credietvorm* (Amsterdam: Van der Marck, 1929).

Houwink ten Cate, J., 'Amsterdam als Finanzplatz Deutschlands', in G. D. Feldman (ed.), *Konsequenzen der Inflation* (Berlin: Colloquium Verlag, 1989) pp. 149–79.

Houwink ten Cate, J., *'De Mannen van de Daad' en Duitsland, 1919–1939. Het Hollandse zakenleven en de vooroorlogse politiek* (The Hague: Sdu Uitgevers, 1995).

Howson, G., Arms for Spain: the untold story of the Spanish Civil War (London: J. Murray, 1998).

Hubbard, J. R. , 'How Franco Financed His War', *Journal of Modern History*, 25:4 (1953), pp. 390-406.

Ikle, M., *Die Schweiz Als Internationaler Bank- und Finanzplatz* (Zürich: Orell Füssli, 1970).

Jager, J. L. de, 'De harde leerschool, 1914–1950', in Joh. de Vries, W. Vroom, and T. de Graaf (eds), *Wereldwijd bankieren. ABN Amro 1824–1999* (Amsterdam: ABN AMRO, 1999) pp. 241–298.

Jaurès, J., *Textes choisis* (Paris: Editions Sociales, 1959).

Jeannotte-Bozerian, J.-F., *La Bourse, ses opérateurs et ses operations (...)* (Paris: Dentu, 1859), Vol. I, p. 83.

Johnson, E. (ed), *Collected Writings of John Maynard Keynes: Volume XVI, Activities 1914–1919* (London: Macmillan, 1971).

Joliffe, M. F., *The United States as a Financial Centre 1919–1933* (Cardiff: University of Wales Press, 1935).

Jongman, C. D., *De Nederlandse geldmarkt* (Leiden: Stenfert Kroese, 1960).

Kandel, S., R. McCulloch, and R. F. Stambaugh, 'Bayesian inference and portfolio efficiency', *Review of Financial Studies*, 8 (1995), pp. 1–53.

Katzenstein, P. J., 'From Many One and From One Many: Political Unification, Political Fragmentation and Cultural Cohesion in Europe since 1815', Western Societies Occasional Paper N° 1 (Ithaca, NY: Cornell University, November 1974).

Kaukiainen, Y., 'Shrinking the world: Improvements in the speed of information transmission, 1820—1870', *European Review of Economic History*, 5:1 (2001), pp. 1–28.

Keynes, J. M., 'The City of London and the Bank of England, August 1914', *Quarterly Journal of Economics*, 29:1 (November 1914) pp. 48–71.

—, 'The Prospects of Money, November 1914', *Economic Journal*, 24 (December 1914), pp. 610–34.

—, 'War and the Financial System, August 1914', *Economic Journal*, 24 (September 1914), pp. 460–86.

Kindleberger, C. P., *A Financial History of Western Europe* (London: Allen & Unwin, 1984).

Kindleberger, C. P., *Histoire Mondiale de la Spéculation Financière* (Hendaye: Valor edition, 2004).

Kindleberger, C. P., *Manias, Panics and Crises. A History of Financial Crisis* (Hoboken, NJ: John Wiley & Sons, 5th edn, 2005).

King, R. G., and R. Levine, 'Finance and Growth: Schumpeter Might be Right', *Quarterly Journal of Economics*, 108:3 (1993), pp. 717–37.

Kiosseva, N., *Istoria na parichnite krizi v Bulgaria: 1879–1912* (*History of the monetary crisis in Bulgaria: 1879–1912) (*Sofia: Economic University Press, 2000).

Klemann, H. A. M., *Waarom bestaat Nederland eigenlijk nog? Nederland-Duitsland: economische integratie en politieke consequenties 1860–2000* (Rotterdam: Erasmus Universiteit Rotterdam, 2006).

Koebe, J., 'Das Französische Börsenwesen', *La revue économique franco-allemande, organe du centre en France des organisations économiques allemandes*, 39 (1944), pp. 3–8.

Kreutzmüller, C., *Händler und Handlungsgehilfen. Der Finanzplatz Amsterdam und die deutschen Grossbanken (1918–1945)* (Stuttgart: Steiner, 2005).

Kuhn, A. K., *A comparative study of the law of corporations with particular reference to the protection of creditors and shareholders* (New York: Columbia University, 1912).

Kuhn, Th., *The Structure of Scientific Revolutions* (Chicago, IL: University of Chicago Press, 1962).

Kuroda, A., 'What is the Complementarity Among Monies? An Introductory Note', *Financial History Review*, 15:1 (2008), pp. 7–15.

Kynaston, D., *The City of London: Golden Years, 1890-1914 vol. II* (London: Chatto & Windus, 1999).

—, *The City of London: Illusions of Gold, 1914–1945* vol. III (London: Chatto & Windus, 2000).

La Porta, R., Lopez-de-Silanes, F., Shleifer, A., and R. W. Vishny, 'Legal Determinants of External Finance', *The Journal of Finance*, LII:3 (July 1997), pp. 1131–50.

—, and R. W. Vishny, 'Law and Finance', *Journal of Political Economy*, 106:6 (December 1998), pp. 1113–55.

Lagneau-Ymonet, P., and A. Riva, 'L'épuration à la Bourse de Paris', in D. Barjot, P. Fridenson, H. Joly, and M. Margairaz (eds.), *L'épuration économique en France à la libération* (Rennes: Presses Universitaires de Rennes, 2008).

Laloux, J., *Le rôle des banques locales et régionales du Nord de la France dans le développement industriel et commercial* (Paris: Giard, 1924).

Lambert-Dansette, J., 'Une institution financière au service du développement régional : la Compagnie des agents de change de Lille depuis sa création jusqu'au premier conflit mondial, 1801–1914', *Revue du Nord*, 170 (avril-juin 1961), pp. 159–99.

Landes, D., 'Vieille banque et banque nouvelle: la révolution financière du XIXe siècle', *Revue d'histoire moderne et contemporaine*, 3 (1956), pp. 204–22.

Lazaretou, S., 'The Drachma, Foreign Creditors, and the International Monetary System: Tales of a Currency during the 19th and the early 20th centuries', *Explorations in Economic History*, 42:2 (2005), pp. 202–36.

Le Bris, D., 'Why did French Savers Buy Foreign Asset Before 1914? Decomposition of the Diversification Benefit' (April 2009). Available at SSRN: http://ssrn.com/abstract=1366172.

Le Bris, D., and P.-C. Hautcoeur, 'Challenge to the Triumphant Optimists. A Blue Chips Index for the Paris Stock Market, 1854–2006', *Financial History Review*, forthcoming (2010).

Leitz, C., *Economic Relations between Nazi Germany and Franco's Spain 1936–1945* (Oxford: Oxford University Press, 1996).

Lescure, M., 'Banking and Finance', in G. Jones, and J. Zeitlin (ed.), *The Oxford Handbook of Business History* (Oxford University Press: Oxford, 2008), pp. 319–46.

Lescure, M., 'La banque et le financement de l'économie', in B. Dejardins et alii (eds.), *Le Crédit Lyonnais 1863–1986* (Geneva: Droz, 2003), pp. 363–66.

Lescure, M., 'La formation d'un système de crédit en France et le rôle de la banque d'émission (1850-1914): approche comparée', in O. Feiertag, and M. Margairaz (ed.), *Politiques et pratiques des banques d'émission en Europe (XVIIe-XXe siècle). Le bicentenaire de la Banque de France dans la perspective de l'identité monétaire européenne* (Paris: Albin Michel, 2003), pp. 131–48.

—, and A. Plessis (dir.), *Banques locales et banques régionales en France au XIXe siècle* (Paris: Albin Michel, 1999).

Levine, R., 'Bank-Based or Market-Based Financial Systems: Which is Better?', William Davidson Institute Working Paper 442 (February 2002).

Lévy-Leboyer, M., 'Le crédit et la monnaie', in F. Braudel, and E. Labrousse (eds.), *Histoire économique et sociale de la France* (Paris: Presses Universitaires de France, 1976), vol. I.3, pp. 347–471.

Lévy-Leboyer, M., and F. Bourguignon, *L'économie française au XIXe siècle, Analyse macroéconomique* (Paris: Economica, 1985).

Lévy-Leboyer, M., and M. Lescure, 'France', in R. Sylla, and G. Toniolo (eds.), *Patterns of European Industrialization. The Nineteenth Century* (London and New York: Routledge, 1992), pp. 153–74.

Lévy, N., *La Bourse en 1890* (Paris: bureaux de la 'Revue Théâtrale', date unknown).

Lloyd George, D., *War Memoirs of David Lloyd George* (London: Ivor Nicolson & Watson, 1933), vol. I.

Longin, F., and B. Solnik, 'Is the Correlation in International Equity Returns Constant: 1960 – 1990?' *Journal of International Money and Finance*, 14:1 (1995), pp. 3–26.

Lucas, A., 'Banques étrangères' in Y. Guyot, and A. Raffalovitch (eds), *Dictionnaire du Commerce de l'Industrie et de la Banque* (Paris: Guillaumin, 1901), pp. 438–40.

Luzzatto, G., *L'economia italiana dal 1861 al 1894* (Turin: Einaudi, 1993).

Madden, J. T., and M. Nadler, *The International Money Markets* (London: Pitman, 1935).

Makin, F. B., 'Treasury Bills', *Bankers' Magazine*, 147 (July–December 1939).

Malefakis, E. (dir.), *La Guerra Civil Española* (Madrid: Taurus, 2006).

Margairaz, M., 'Les politiques économiques sous et de Vichy', *Histoire@Politique*, 9 (September–December 2009) at www.histoire-politique.fr.

Marguerat, P., L. Tissot, and Y. Froidevaux (éd.), *Banques et entreprises industrielles en Europe de l'Ouest, XIXe-XXe siècles : aspects nationaux et régionaux* (Geneva: Droz, 2000).

Markowitz, H., *Portfolio selection: Efficient diversification of Investments* (New-York: John Wiley, 1959)

Martín Aceña, P., 'La economía española de los años treinta' in Juliá, Santos (coord.) *Republica y Guerra Civil. Historia de España dirigida por Menéndez Pidal* (Madrid: Espasa Calpe, 2004), vol. 40.

Martín Aceña, P., and E. Martínez Ruiz (eds), *La economía de la Guerra Civil* (Madrid: Marcial Pons, 2006).

Martín Aceña, P., *El Oro de Moscú y el Oro de Berlín* (Madrid: Taurus, 2001).

Martínez Ruiz, E., 'El campo en guerra: organización y producción agraria', in Martín Aceña y Martínez Ruiz (eds.) *La economía de la Guerra Civil* (Madrid: Marcial Pons, 2006).

Martínez Ruiz, E., *Guerra civil, comercio y capital extranjero. El sector exterior de la economía española* (1936–1939) (Madrid: Banco de España, Madrid, 2006).

Martorell, M., and F. Comín, 'La Hacienda de guerra franquista' in Fuentes Quintana, E. (dir) *Economía y Economistas españoles en la Guerra Civil* (Barcelona: Galaxia-Gutenberg, 2008), pp. 901–37.

Matthews, W. R., *Memories and Meanings* (London: Hodder & Stoughton, 1969).

Mauro, P., N. Sussman, and Y. Yafeh, 'Emerging Market Spreads: Then Versus Now', *Quarterly Journal of Economics*, 17:2 (2002), pp. 695–733.

Meeusen, W., and J. Van Den Broeck, 'Efficiency Estimation from Cobb-Douglas Production Functions with Composed Error', *International Economic Review*, 18 (1977), pp. 435–44.

Metz, T., *Die Niederlande als Käufer, Hersteller, Vermittler und Kreditgeber: grundsätzliches zum deutsch-niederländischen Warenaustausch* (Leipzig: s.n., 1930).

Michalet, C.-A., *Les placements des épargnants français de 1815 à nos jours* (Paris: PUF, 1968).

Michie, R. C., 'The City of London as a Global Financial Centre, 1880-1939: Finance, Foreign Exchange, and the First World War', in P. L. Cottrell, E. Lange, and U. Olsson (eds), *Centres and Peripheries in Banking* (Ashgate: Aldershot, 2007).

Michie, R., *The London Stock Exchange: a history* (Oxford: Oxford University Press, 1999).

Miguel, A. de, 'Fundamentos técnicos para la construcción de una escala de desbloqueo. El tránsito de la peseta roja a la peseta nacional' in *Moneda y Crédito* (December 1977), pp. 9–24.

Mitchell, B., and P. Deane, *Abstract of British Historical Statistics* (Cambridge: Cambridge University Press, 1962).

Morgan, E. V., and W. A. Thomas, *The Stock Exchange: Its History and Functions* (London, Elek, 1962).

Morgan, E. V., *Studies in British Financial Policy, 1914–25* (London: Macmillan, 1952).

Mori, G., 'L'economia italiana dagli anni Ottanta alla prima guerra mondiale', in *Storia dell'industria elettrica in Italia*, vol. 1, *Le origini 1882–1914* (Bari: Laterza, 1992), pp. 1–106.

Nedelchev, K., *Parichnoto delo v Bulgaria: 1879–1940 (Monetary affairs in Bulgaria: 1879–1940* (Sofia: Knipegraf Printing House, 1940).

Nenovsky, N., *Improving monetary theory in post-communist countries. Looking back to Cantillon*, BNB Discussion Paper 28 (Sofia: BNB, 2002).

Nishimura, S., *The Decline of Inland Bills of Exchange in the London Money Market 1855–1913* (Cambridge: Cambridge University Press, 1971).

O'Rourke, K. H., and J. G Williamson, 'Late 19th century Anglo-American factor price convergence: were Heckscher and Ohlin right?' *Journal of Economic History*, 54 (1994), pp. 892–916.

O'Rourke, K. H., and J. G. Williamson, *Globalization and history. The evolution of a nineteenth Century Atlantic Economy* (Cambridge: MIT Press, 1999).

Obstfeld, M., and A. M. Taylor, 'Globalization and Capital Markets', NBER Working Paper, 8846 (2002).

Obstfeld, M., and A. Taylor, 'The Great Depression as a Watershed: International Capital Mobility over the Long-Run' in M. Bordo, C. Goldin, and E. White (eds.), *The Defining Moment: The Great Depression and the American Economy in the Twentieth Century* (Chicago, IL: University of Chicago Press, 1998).

Occhino F., K. Oosterlinck, and E. White, 'How much can a victor force the vanquished to pay?', *Journal of Economic History*, 68:1 (2008), pp. 1–45.

Oosterlinck, K., 'French Stock Exchanges and Regulation during World War II', *Financial History Review* (2010), forthcoming.

Oosterlinck, K., 'The Bond Market and the Legitimacy of Vichy France', *Explorations in Economic History*, 40:3 (2003), pp. 327–345.

Pamuk, S., *A Monetary History of the Ottoman Empire* (Cambridge: Cambridge University Press, 2000).

Pantaleoni, M., *La caduta della Società generale di credito mobiliare italiano [1895]* (Turin: Utet, 1998).

Pardes, P., *La Bourse de Bordeaux* (Paris: Domat-Montchrestien, 1933).

Parent, A., and C. Rault, 'The Influences affecting French Assets abroad Prior to 1914', *The Journal of Economic History*, 64:2 (2004), pp. 328–62.

Pareto, V., 'L'Intervention de l'Etat dans les Banques d'Emission en Italie', *Journal des Economistes* (April 1893), pp. 3–28.

Pareto, V., *Le Marché Financier Italien (1891–1899),* in G. Busino (ed.) (Geneva: Droz, 1965).

Peters, J., 'British Government and the City – Industry Divide: the Case of the 1914 Financial Crisis', *Twentieth Century British History*, 4 (1993), pp. 126–48.

Petkof, J., *Prix, circulation et change en Bulgarie de 1890 à 1924 (*Paris: Jouve & C., 1926).

Piluso, G., 'Mercati settoriali e squilibri regionali nella formazione di un sistema bancario in Italia (1860-1936)', in G. Sapelli (ed.), *Capitalismi a confronto: Italia e Spagna. Atti del secondo seminario internazionale di storia d'impresa* (Soveria Mannelli, Rubbettino, 1998), pp. 83–157.

Pino, F., 'Sui fiduciari della Comit nelle società per azioni, 1898–1918', *Rivista di storia economica*, n.s, 8 (1991), n. unico, pp. 115–48.

Plessis, A., 'Les concours de la Banque de France à l'économie (1842–1914)', in *États, fiscalités, économies. Actes du Ve Congrès de l'AFHE*, juin 1983 (Paris: Publications de la Sorbonne, 1985), pp. 169–80.

Polsi, A., *Alle origini del capitalismo italiano. Stato banche e banchieri dopo l'Unità* (Turin: Einaudi, 1993).

Pons, M. A., 'La Hacienda pública y la financiación de la guerra' in P. Martín Aceña, and E. Martínez Ruiz (eds.) *La economía de la Guerra Civil* (Madrid: Marcial Pons, 2006), pp. 357–91.

Pope, S. and E.-A. Wheal, *The Dictionary of the First World War* (New York: Saint Martin's Press, 1995).

Popoff, K., *La Bulgarie économique* (Sofia: Imprimerie de la Cour, 1920).

Post, J. G., *Besparingen in Nederland, 1923–1970: omvang en verdeling* (Amsterdam: s.n., 1972).

Pouchain, P., *Ébauche d'une histoire du Crédit du Nord de la fondation à 1939*, mémoire de DES (Lille, 1969).

Radovanovic, B., *110 Years of the National Bank. Establishment and Beginning of Operationof the Privileged National Bank of the Kingdom of Serbia* (Belgrade: Institute for Manufacturing Banknotes and Coins, 1998).

Rajan, R. G., and L. Zingales, 'The great reversals: The politics of financial development in the twentieth century', *The Journal of Financial Economics*, 69:1 (2003), pp. 5–50.

Ramos, S. B., 'Competition between exchanges: A survey', *FAME Research paper n°77* (2003), 35 p.

Ransom, R. L., 'The Economics of the Civil War", *EH Net Encyclopedia*, edited by R. Whaples (24 August 2001), URL http://eh.net/encyclopedia/article/ransom.civil.war.us.

Rathenau, W., 'Le società per azioni. Riflessioni suggerite dall'esperienza degli affari', *Rivista delle società*, 5 (1960), pp. 912–47.

Realfonzo, R., and C. Ricci, 'Il Dibattito Sulla "Questione Bancaria". Unicità Versus Pluralità Degli Istituti Di Emissione (1886–1893)', *Il Pensiero Economico Italiano*, III:2 (1995), pp. 97–132.

Redelmeier, W., 'Die Deutschen Banken in Amsterdam' in: *Jubileumnummer In- en Uitvoer* (Januari 1926), pp.18–29.

Redish, A., *Bimetallism: an Economic and Historical Analysis* (Cambridge: Cambridge University Press, 2000).

Renooij, D. C., *De Nederlandse emissiemarkt van 1904 tot 1939* (Amsterdam: De Bussy, 1951).

Repelius, F. H., 'Niederlande, Geld- und Kapitalmarkt', in M. Palyi, and P. Quittner (eds), *Handwörterbuch des Bankwesens* (Berlin: Springer, 1933).

Riemens, H., *De financiële ontwikkeling van Nederland* (Amsterdam: N.V. Noord-Hollandsche Uitgevers Maatschappij, 1949)

Riesser, J., *The German great banks and their connection with the economic development of Germany [1911]* (New York: Arno Press, 1977).

Rime, B., and K. Stiroh, 'The Performance of Universal Banks: Evidence from Switzerland', *Journal of Banking and Finance*, 27:11 (2003), p. 2121–50.

Ripa Di Meana, A., and M. Sarcinelli, 'Unione Monetaria, Competizione Valutaria E Controllo Della Moneta: È D'aiuto La Storia Italiana?', in M. De Cecco (ed), *Monete In Concorrenza. Prospettive Per L'integrazione Monetaria Europea* (Bologna: Il Mulino 1992), pp. 81–138.

Rizzi, A., *Analisi dei dati. Applicazioni dell'informatica alla statistica* (Rome: Nuova Italia Scientifica, 1985).

Robert-Milles, S., *La grammaire de la Bourse. Traité pratique élémentaire des opérations de Bourse* (Paris: Flammarion, successive editions, towards 1900-1910).

Roberts, R., 'The Economics of Cities of Finance', in H. Diederiks, and D. Reeder (eds) *Cities of Finance* (Amsterdam: North Holland, 1996).

Roberts, R., 'What's in a name? Merchants, Merchant Bankers, Accepting Houses, Issuing Houses, Industrial Bankers and Investment Bankers', *Business History*, 35:3 (July 1993), pp. 22–38.

Roberts, R., *Schroders: Merchants & Bankers* (London: Macmillan, 1992).

Robinson, J., 'The Generalization of the General Theory', in J. Robinson, *The Rate of Interest and Other Essays* (London: Macmillan, 1952).

Roos, F. de, and W. J. Wieringa, *Een halve eeuw rente in Nederland* (Schiedam: Levensverzekering-maatschappij HAV Bank, 1953).

Rousseau, P. L., and P. Wachtel, 'What is happening to the impact of financial deepening on economic growth?', Department Of Economics Vanderbilt University, Nashville, Working Paper n° 09–W15 (September 2009) at www.vanderbilt.edu/econ.

Rousseau, P. L., and R. Sylla, 'Financial Systems, Economic Growth, and Globalization' NBER Working Paper 8323 (June 2001).

Sánchez Asiaín, J. A., *Economía y finanzas en la guerra civil española (1936–1939)* (Madrid: Real Academia de la Historia, 1999).

Sánchez Recio, G., *La República contra los rebeldes y los desafectos. La represión económica durante la guerra civil* (Alicante: Universidad de Alicante, 1991).

Sannucci, V., 'The Establishment of a Central Bank: Italy in the 19th Century', in M. De Cecco, and A. Giovannini (eds), *A European Central Bank? Perspectives on Monetary Unification after Ten Years of the EMS* (New York: Cambridge University Press, 1989).

Sardá, J., 'El Banco de España, 1931–1962', in VV. AA., *El Banco de España. Una historia económica* (Madrid: Banco de España, 1970), pp. 421–79.

Sayers, R. S., *The Bank of England 1891–1944* (Cambridge: Cambridge University Press, 1976).

Scammell, W. M., *The London Discount Market* (London: Elek, 1968).

Schmitz, W. J., *Der Amsterdamer Geldmarkt mit besonderer Berücksichtigung der Zinsschwankungen* (Cologne: Kölner Görreshaus, 1931).

Scialom, L., *Economie bancaire* (Paris: La Découverte, 2007).

Seabourne, T., 'The Summer of 1914', in F. Capie, and G. E. Wood (eds), *Financial Crises and the World Banking System* (London: Macmillan, 1986).

Sheppard, D. K., *The Growth and Role of UK Financial Institutions 1880-1962* (London: Methuen, 1971).

Siciliano, G., *Cento anni di borsa in Italia* (Bologna: Il Mulino, 2001).

Siegel, J., *Stocks for the Long Run* (Burr Ridge, Ill.: Irwin Professional Publishing, 1994).

Silber, W. L., *When Washington Shut Down Wall Street: The Great Financial Crisis of 1914 and the Origins of America's Monetary Supremacy* (Princeton NJ: Princeton University Press, 2007).

Skidelsky, R., *John Maynard Keynes: Volume One: Hopes Betrayed 1883–1920* (London: Macmillan, 1983).

Smith, L., 'Banque', in L. Say, and J. Chailley (eds), *Nouveau Dictionnaire de l'Economie Politique* (Paris: Guillaumin, 1900), pp. 141–2.

Smith, V., *The Rationale of Central Banking*, 2nd edn (Indianapolis, IN: Liberty press, [1936] 1990).

Sojic, M., and L. Djurdjevic, 'National Bank of Serbia 1884–2006. Establishment and beginning of operation', in R. Avramov, and Ş. Pamuk (eds), *Monetary and fiscal policies in Southeast Europe. Historical and comparative perspective* (Sofia: Bulgarian National Bank, 2006), pp. 141–56.

Solnik, B., 'Why not diversify internationally rather than domestically?', *Financial Analyst Journal*, 30 (1974) pp. 48–54.

Spencer, H., *The Man versus the State* (1884) in Herbert Spencer, *The Man versus the State: with four essays on politics and society* (Harmondsworth: Penguin, 1969).

Spiller, P.T., and C. J. Huang, 'On the extent of the market: wholesale gasoline in the Northern United States', *Journal of Industrial Economics*, 35:1 (1986), pp. 131–45.

Strasser, K., *Die deutschen Banken im Ausland. Entwicklungsgeschichte und wirtschaftliche Bedeutung* (Munich: Ernst Reinhardt, 1924).

Straus, A., 'Les marchés régionaux de valeurs mobilières : une approche comparative', in *Banque et investissements en Méditerranée à l'époque contemporaine, Actes du colloque de*

Marseille, 4–5 février 1982 (Marseille: Chambre de commerce et d'industrie de Marseille, 1985),), pp. 131–151.

Supino, C., *Storia della Circolazione Cartacea in Italia dal 1860 al 1928*, 2nd edn (Milano: Società Editrice Libraria, 1929).

Sylla, R., and G. Toniolo (eds), *Patterns of European Industrialization. The Nineteenth Century* (London and New York: Routledge, 1991).

Sylla, R., R. Tilly, and G. Tortella (eds), *The State, The Financial System and Economic Modernization* (Cambridge, Mass.: Cambridge University Press, 2007 (1st ed. 1999)).

Tassin, G., *Le rôle du marché financier lillois dans le développement de l'économie du Nord-Pas-de-Calais, de 1882 à 1914*, doctoral thesis under the direction of A. Broder (Créteil, Université Paris 12, 2000).

Teti, R., 'Imprese, imprenditori e diritto', in F. Amatori, D. Bigazzii, R. Giannetti, and L. Segreto, *Storia d'Italia, t. XV: L'industria* (Turin: Einaudi, 1999), pp. 1211–303.

Tetrode, P. J. C., 'Het buitenlandsch kapitaal in Nederland', *Economisch Statistische Berichten* (31 January 1923) pp. 86–8.

Thomas, S. E., *The Principles and Arithmetic of Foreign Exchange* (London: Macdonald and Evans, 1929).

Tilly, R., 'Germany, 1815–1870', in R. Cameron with the collaboration of O. Crisp, H. T. Patrick, and R. Tilly (eds.), *Banking in the Early Stages of Industrialization: A Study in Comparative Economic History* (New York: Oxford University Press, 1967), pp. 151–82.

Tilly, R., *Financial institutions and industrialization in the German Rhineland, 1815–1870* (Madison: University of Wisconsin Press, 1966).

Toniolo, G. (ed.), *Industria e banca nella grande crisi 1929–1934* (Milan: Etas, 1978).

Toniolo, G., *An economic history of liberal Italy, 1850–1918* (London and New York: Routledge, 1990).

Trifonoff, P., *La banque nationale de Bulgarie et l'histoire de sa politique monétaire* (Lyon: Bosc Frères, 1930).

Tucker, S. C. (ed.), *World War I Encyclopedia*, 5 vols (Santa Barbara: ABC-Clio, 2005).

Vasta, M., and A. Baccini, 'Banks and industry in Italy, 1911–1936. New evidence using the interlocking directorates technique', *Financial History Review*, 4:2 (1997), pp. 139–59.

Veenendaal, A. J., *Slow Train to Paradise. How Dutch Investment Helped Build American Railroads* (Stanford, CA: Stanford University Press, 1996).

Velarde Fuertes, J., 'La economía de guerra', *Historia de España. España Actual. La Guerra Civil* (Madrid: Editorial Gredos, 1989).

Verdier, D., *Moving Money, Banking and Finance in the Industrialized World* (Cambridge, Mass.: Cambridge University Press, 2002).

Verley, P., 'Convergence and divergence', in A. Iriye, and P.-Y. Saunier (eds), *Dictionary of Transnational History*, London, Macmillan, 2009.

—, 'Les opérateurs du marché financier', in G. Gallais-Hamonno (ed.), *Le marché financier français au XIXe siècle* (Paris: Publications de la Sorbonne, 2007), pp. 21–86.

Verrijn Stuart, C. A., *Inleiding tot de beoefening der statistiek* (Haarlem: Erven Bohn, 1917).

Verrijn Stuart, G. M., *Bankpolitiek* (Wassenaar: s.n., 1935 (3rd revised printing)).

Viñas, A., *El oro español en la Guerra Civil* (Madrid: Instituto de Estudios Fiscales, 1976).

Viñas, A., *Guerra, dinero, dictadura, ayuda fascista y autarquía en la España de Franco* (Barcelona: Crítica, 1984).

Viñas, A., J. Viñuela, F. Eguidazu, C. F. Pulgar, and S. Florensa, *Política comercial exterior en España (1931–1975)* (Madrid: Banco Exterior, 1979).

Viñas, A., *La Alemania nazi y el 18 de Julio* (Madrid: Alianza, 1977).

Vissering, G., 'The Netherlands Bank and the War', *The Economic Journal*, 27:106 (1917) pp. 159–186.

Vissering, G., *Crediet-verleenen in Nederland* (The Hague: Stockum, 1917).

Vitols, S., 'The Origins of Bank-Based and Market Based Financial Systems: Germany, Japan, and the United States', in W. Streeck, and K. Yamamura (eds), *The Origins of Nonliberal Capitalism, Germany and Japan in Comparison* (Ithaca, NY: Cornell University Press, 2001), pp. 171–99.

Vivante, C., 'Per la riforma delle società anonime', *Rivista del diritto commerciale e del diritto generale delle obbligazioni*, 2 (1913).

Vries, J. de, *Geschiedenis van de Nederlandsche Bank. Vijde deel: De Nederlandsche Bank van 1914 tot 1948. Visserings tijdvak 1914–1931* (Amsterdam: Nederlandsche Bank, 1989).

Weber Warren E., Available at http://research.mpls.frb.fed.us/research/economists/wew-proj.html (1999).

Wells, H. G., *Mr Britling Sees It Through* (London: Cassell, 1916).

Wetter, E., *Bankkrisen und Bankkatastrophen der Letzten Jahre in der Schweiz* (Zürich: Orell Fuessli, 1918).

White, E., 'Competition among the exchanges before the SEC: Was the NYSE a natural hegemon?', Rutgers University, Mimeo (2007).

Withers, H., *War and Lombard Street* (London: Smith, Elder & Co, 1915).

Zamagni, V., 'Il Debito Pubblico Italiano 1861–1946: Ricostruzione Della Serie Storica' *Rivista Di Storia Economica*, XIV:3 (December 1998), pp. 207–42.

Zappa, G., *Le valutazioni di bilancio con particolare riguardo ai bilanci delle società per azioni* (Milan: Società editrice libraria, 1910).

Zurlinden, M., 'Goldstandard, Deflation und Depression: Die Schweizerische Volkswirtschaft in der Weltwirtschaftskrise', *SNB Quartalsheft*, 2 (2003), p. 86–115.

INDEX

People

Firms and other Public and Private Bodies

For Product Safety Concerns and Information please contact our EU
representative GPSR@taylorandfrancis.com
Taylor & Francis Verlag GmbH, Kaufingerstraße 24, 80331 München, Germany

www.ingramcontent.com/pod-product-compliance
Ingram Content Group UK Ltd.
Pitfield, Milton Keynes, MK11 3LW, UK
UKHW021620240425
457818UK00018B/665

* 9 7 8 1 1 3 8 6 6 3 3 1 2 *